India: The Ancient Past

India: The Ancient Past provides a clear and systematic introduction to the cultural, political, economic, social and geographical history of ancient India from the time of the pre-Harappan culture 9,000 years ago up until the beginning of the second millennium of the Common Era. Through topics such as the Indus-Saraswati civilisation, Vedic and heterodox religions, the political economy, and social life in the Indian kingdoms, the book engages with methodological and controversial issues.

This fully revised and updated second edition includes:

- three new chapters examining the differences and commonalities between the north and the south of India;
- extended discussion on contested issues, such as the origins of the Aryans and the role of feudalism in ancient India;
- new source excerpts to introduce students to the most significant works in the historiography of India, and questions for discussion;
- study guides, including a list of key issues, suggested readings and a selection of Internet sources for each chapter;
- specially designed maps to illustrate different time periods and geographical regions.

This richly illustrated guide provides a fascinating account of the early development of Indian culture and civilisation that will appeal to all students of Indian history.

Burjor Avari MBE is Honorary Research Fellow in the Department of History at Manchester Metropolitan University. He has taught history at school and university levels for over five decades. His previous publications include *Islamic Civilization in South Asia: A History of Muslim Power and Presence in the Indian Subcontinent* (Routledge, 2013).

D0061187

India: The Ancient Past

A history of the Indian subcontinent from *c.* 7000 BCE to CE 1200

Second edition

Burjor Avari

Routledge
Taylor & Francis Group

LONDON AND NEW YORK

Second edition published 2016
by Routledge
2 Park Square, Milton Park, Abingdon, Oxon OX14 4RN

and by Routledge
711 Third Avenue, New York, NY 10017

Routledge is an imprint of the Taylor & Francis Group, an informa business

First edition published 2007 by Routledge

British Library Cataloguing-in-Publication Data
A catalogue record for this book is available from the British Library

Library of Congress Cataloging-in-Publication Data
Names: Avari, Burjor, author.
Title: India : the ancient past : a history of the Indian subcontinent from
c. 7000 BCE to 1200 CE / Burjor Avari.
Description: Second edition. | New York, NY : Routledge, 2016. | "First
edition published 2007." | Includes bibliographical references and index.
Identifiers: LCCN 2015042418| ISBN 9781138828209 (hardback : alk. paper) |
ISBN 9781138828216 (pbk. : alk. paper) | ISBN 9781315627007 (ebook)
Subjects: LCSH: India – History. | India – History – 1000–1526.
Classification: LCC DS451 .A87 2016 | DDC 934/.01 – dc23
LC record available at http://lccn.loc.gov/2015042418

ISBN: 978-1-138-82820-9 (hbk)
ISBN: 978-1-138-82821-6 (pbk)
ISBN: 978-1-315-62700-7 (ebk)

Typeset in Times New Roman
by Florence Production Ltd, Stoodleigh, Devon, UK

Maps

Illustrations

Figures

Excerpts

Contents

A vision for India

Where the mind is without fear and the head is held high;
Where knowledge is free;
Where the world has not been broken up into fragments by narrow
domestic walls; . . .
Where the clear stream of reason has not lost its way into the dreary
desert sand of dead habit; . . .
Into that heaven of freedom, my Father, let my country awake.

(From Gitanjali, by Rabindranath Tagore,
Nobel Laureate, 1913)

Dedicated to the memory of my dear parents, teachers and good friend David Melling.

Preface to the second edition

The first edition of this book came out in 2007; over the last eight years it has proved useful to students and other readers for the comprehensive manner in which it explains the history of ancient India in accessible language and form. It was therefore with great pleasure that I agreed to a request from Routledge in 2014 to prepare a second edition.

This new edition is the result of a year's further research in ancient Indian history. This has been necessary because of a great increase in the number of publications in the subject. Controversies over certain topics, such as the place of the Aryans or the role of feudalism in ancient India, are ongoing and there is much to read and ponder over. The valuable suggestions of the referees for this edition have also had to be given full consideration. It has therefore been necessary to revise some of the original text, and to provide additional information. Every chapter contains some new material, and some chapters, particularly Chapter 4, have expanded in size. The last three chapters, 9, 10 and 11, have been re-written in order to clarify some of the differences and commonalities between the two halves of India: the north and the south.

One of the features of the first edition, unusual in textbooks of ancient Indian history, was the inclusion of short excerpts, from a variety of interesting works, at the end of each chapter. More new excerpts have been added in this edition and all have been placed within the body of the text. In this way, each excerpt can help the reader to gain immediately a deeper understanding of the general text. The references to sources are also inserted in brackets within each chapter, not as end notes as in the first edition. Every source is listed within the revised bibliography. At the beginning of each chapter (except Chapter 1) a timeline is aimed to provide a useful chronology. At the end of each chapter is a brief list of the most important issues highlighted in the chapter, along with suggested texts for a deeper understanding of such issues. As students all over the world gain information digitally, and since there is so much online material of mixed value, I have provided an Internet selection of a maximum of five articles of particular relevance to each chapter. Finally, the questions at the end of each chapter have been revised for this edition, and it is hoped that they will provide stimulus to small groups of students to come together and discuss them.

I would like to thank the History Commissioning Editor at Routledge, Laura Pilsworth, and her deputy, Catherine Aitken, for taking interest in this new edition and encouraging me at every stage during the last twelve months.

Burjor Avari
Manchester 2015

Preface to the first edition

There has been a profound change in the study of ancient Indian history within the last six or seven decades. Influential cadres of historians, archaeologists, anthropologists and environmentalists have rejuvenated earlier scholarship in this vast area, opening up unfamiliar lines of investigation, and contributing new insights for our deeper understanding of the multi-faceted aspects of ancient India.

This book is a modest attempt at bringing together some of the recent researches of committed scholars such as Professors D.K. Chakrabarti, R. Champakalakshmi, Brijadulal Chattopadhyaya, François Jarrige, R.S. Sharma, Romila Thapar, André Wink and several others. The book's twofold aim is to generate fresh interest in the culture and history of ancient India among undergraduates qualifying in South Asian history in the colleges and universities of the English-speaking world, as well as those who come under the category of serious-minded enquirers – some perhaps with long-held Eurocentric viewpoints. There are also those, globally dispersed, of Indian and South Asian origin, born and educated in the lands of the sub-continent's diaspora, whose knowledge of their *madar vatan* – the Motherland – is often limited to current issues, but who could benefit from an enduring realisation of their wider cultural antecedents.

Ancient India evolved in many stages, and her development is analysed and explained over the eleven chapters presented here. They are chronologically arranged, from the earliest known human settlements and the examination of their societies from 7000 BC, through to the commencement of the Turco-Afghan military forays into northern India in the eleventh and twelfth centuries AD. Wherever pertinent, the chapters contain the essential details concerning rulers and dynasties; but their critical thrust is to highlight the chief lines of politico-economic, socio-cultural and intellectual developments within each distinct period. The chapters are sectioned and sub-sectioned for detailed information, followed by select extracts linked to the text for review and revisiting, raising relevant questions for reappraisal and discussion. Also included are select glossaries of the most frequently met Indic terms and ancient place-names, a classification of ancient Indian texts by subjects, simplified maps with topographical and historico-geographical relevance to the subject matter of the chapters, and several illustrations which, it is hoped, will convey some immediacy to the book's topicality and heighten the reader's appreciation of the greatness that was ancient India.

Here I take the opportunity to express my gratitude to a number of people who have helped me in this project. Some of them have inspired and encouraged me all along. Professor Lord Bhikhu Parekh is one such person whose wisdom and insights have been constantly stimulating and thought-provoking. I am also very thankful to Mr C.B. Patel, the editor of the London-based newspaper *Asian Voice* and a pioneer of ethnic journalism in Britain, who kindly offered me space in his journal to write twenty-three short historical pieces on ancient India, giving me the confidence to embark on producing a book. Among many other friends, Dr Ajit Halder, formerly of Salford University, Mr Mohammed Ibrahim and Drs Mahesh and Shabani Godbole have over many years been my well-wishers. To my wife, Zarin, and daughters Rushna and Anahita, I owe all the comfort and happiness of a rich family life, within which writing became a joyful exercise. To Anahita I also owe special thanks for helping me cope with the pitfalls and hazards of computer technology. All the fine line drawings are the work of a highly creative Manchester-based artist, Mrs Pat Baker, who has spent many hours at this task.

My sincere thanks are also due to seven colleagues who have spent a great deal of their time reading my chapters. Dr Daud Ali, Senior Lecturer and Research Fellow in Ancient Indian History at the School of Oriental and African Studies, University of London, a scholar steeped in knowledge of his field, has rescued me from a huge number of errors and made me aware of ideas and concepts critical to a balanced understanding of the subject. I owe him a great amount of gratitude. Dr George Gheverghese Joseph, an internationally renowned historian of non-European mathematics, and a treasured friend for the last forty-four years, has enriched the book by his perceptive comments on the intellectual history of ancient India. Mr Farrokh Vajifdar, Fellow of the Royal Asiatic Society of Britain, and a specialist in Indo-Iranian studies, has not only given me advice over many controversial issues and ideas in the early history of India but has gone through the drafts with a fine tooth-comb, bringing polish to my grammar and style of writing, without which the book would be less than perfect. Professor Robin Coningham, Professor of Archaeology at Durham University, has made a number of useful suggestions in the field of pre-history and the Harappan archaeology, for which I sincerely thank him. Dr Ram Prasad, of Lancaster University, and a rising star in the philosophical circles of Britain and India, has kindly read the whole draft. Two colleagues – Dr Leela Joseph, a medical specialist, and Professor Ian Steedman, Professor of Economics at Manchester Metropolitan University – provided critical and thought-provoking comments on some of the chapters from a non-historian's point of view, which I have greatly valued.

The book is a result of many years of teaching Indian history and promoting extra-mural Indian studies at Manchester Metropolitan University. I would like to thank the university authorities, and particularly the Department of History and Economic History, for allowing me time and space to carry on with my research and teaching in a relaxed and friendly atmosphere.

Finally, my sincere thanks are due to my publishers, Routledge, and Victoria Peters, the history editor, for reposing confidence in me to write the book and submit it on time.

Burjor Avari
Manchester, 2006

A note on spellings and the use of italics

For the reader's convenience, diacritics and accents have been omitted. The vast majority of Indic names in the text are spelled as widely pronounced today. Indic terms and toponyms no longer in current use, along with the titles of ancient texts, are given in italics.

Acknowledgements

The publishers would like to thank the following for their permission to reproduce copyright material: Birmingham Museum and Art Gallery, Pat Baker, Columbia University Press, E.J. Brill, Dr George Joseph, Manohar Books, Oxford University Press, Palgrave Macmillan, Princeton University Press, Robert Harding Picture Library, Rowman & Littlefield, Scientific American, Inc., Springer Science and British Media, Sue Morris for the estate of Mortimer Wheeler, United Agents LLP on behalf of The Trustees of G.P. Wells, University of California Press, Yale University Press.

Every effort has been made to obtain permission to reproduce copyright material. If any proper acknowledgement has not been made, we would invite copyright holders to inform us of the oversight.

Synopsis

This book attempts to address the issues concerning the origins of Indian culture, the development of Indian civilisation, and the cultural unity and diversity of ancient Indian society. Chapter 1 provides a contextual introduction, while Chapters 2, 3, 4 and 5 trace the foundations of Indian civilisation to historic developments that took place between 7000 and 300 BCE. Although Indians and all other South Asians are descendants of those who first migrated from Africa many thousands of years ago, the beginnings of a particular form of Indic culture can be first noticed around 7000 BCE, when farming began on the flood plains of the River Indus and its many tributaries (Chapter 2). This culture developed into a recognisable urban social system at a number of locations between *c.* 2600 and 1700 BCE (Chapter 3). The Aryan migration, settlement and domination began from 1700 BCE onwards, but the blending of Aryan and non-Aryan created the Indo-Aryan Vedic culture and religion (Chapter 4). Indian ethics and philosophy grew out of the teachings of three Indic faiths: Hinduism, Buddhism and Jainism, and by the middle of the first millennium BCE India possessed a state system that encompassed both the monarchical and the republican models (Chapter 5).

Chapters 6, 7 and 8 cover the period between *c.* 300 BCE and CE 600, when Indian civilisation reached a high level of achievement and distinction, and when India was in close interaction with the rest of the known world. The compassion shown by the Mauryan emperor, Ashoka, provided a unique model of benevolent governance that is admired today (Chapter 6). Post-Mauryan India was at the centre of all traffic in commerce and culture, leading to greater prosperity among the nations of the world (Chapter 7). With a share of 32.9 per cent of the world's GDP at around the time of Christ, India was richer than any other nation or region, including China, and she continued to maintain her economic supremacy for nearly 1,500 years afterwards (Maddison 2003: 261). The Imperial Guptas followed a model of decentralised power, based on the *samanta* principle of tolerant neighbourliness, and under them the Hindu–Buddhist–Jain civilisation reached the heights of elitist excellence in literature, art and science, which created the Classical culture of India. Many of the original Indian ideas of this period later came to be transmitted abroad (Chapter 8).

Chapters 9, 10 and 11 examine the cultural unity and diversity within the sub-continent between CE 600 and 1200. Geography, ecology, language and historical circumstances contributed to differences in the political economies of the north and the south of India. The north, which had been the heartland of imperial structures, became fragmented into smaller feudal and patriarchal kingdoms that were to face aggressive Muslim intrusions, first from the Arabs and then from the Turco-Afghans (Chapter 9). A more secure atmosphere and a relatively progressive outlook pervaded within the domains of the southern kingdoms, where foreigners were favoured rather than feared (Chapter 10). While a certain unity of ideas pervaded across Indian culture as a whole between CE 600 and 1200, there was also much rich variation in such fields as religion, art and literature (Chapter 11).

1 Introduction

Defining terms

Modern India came into existence in 1947 on the eve of the partition of British India. This is the Republic of India, the largest democracy in the world today and an increasingly powerful economic force in the globalised twenty-first century. Before 1947, and well into the ancient period, however, India geographically embraced the entire Indian subcontinent, including the areas of modern Pakistan and Bangladesh. In fact, the earliest roots of Indian civilisation can only be understood through studying what has been recovered from archaeological excavations and field-work, mainly inside Pakistan. Nepal and Sri Lanka, too, have always had close links with the Indian cultural world. And, during varied periods of ancient history, Afghanistan and India have had a lasting symbiotic relationship.

The etymological roots of the term 'India' lie in a Sanskrit word, *sindhu*, meaning river frontier. The earliest sacred text of India, the *Rig-Veda*, speaks of a land called *Sapta-Sindhava*, which can be identified as the province of Punjab, formerly the land of seven rivers. Today, five rivers flow through it – the Indus, Jhelum, Chenab, Ravi and Sutlej/Beas – but some 4,000 years ago there were two other rivers, called the *Sarasvati* and the *Drasadvati*, which have long since dried up. When the Persians began to penetrate Indian lands in the sixth century BCE, they referred to the modern River Indus, the most westerly of the seven rivers, and the peoples living in the region, by the Old Persian term *Hindhu*, the cognate of the Indic *sindhu* (Basham 1954: 1). When the Macedonians, under Alexander the Great, invaded the same region in the fourth century BCE, they used the Greek *Indos* to refer to the river, and *India* to refer to the land around and beyond the river. So 'India' is actually a Greek expression; no native in ancient India would have thought of using this term. They used Sanskritic proper nouns such as *Bharat* (a descendant of the ancient Puru clan), *Madhyadesha* (the Middle Country), *Aryavarta* (the land of the Aryans) and *Jambudvipa* (the shape of a *Jambu* tree, broad at the top and narrowing at its base, like the map of India) to describe the vast terrain with which they became familiar. Even today, the constitution of the Republic of India recognises the official name of the country as 'India that is *Bharat*'.

The term 'ancient' refers to times long past. But how long ago? And at what point does 'ancient' turn to modern or pre-modern? This book begins with our remotest ancestors in the Stone Age period, but places the starting point for ancient Indian culture and civilisation at approximately 7000 BCE with the emergence of the first farming community at Mehrgarh in Baluchistan. The history of farming is perhaps the most objective criterion to determine the antiquity of a civilisation. The date of 7000 BCE has been arrived at through systematic archaeological research (Jarrige and Meadow 1980: 102–10). It is not based on an interpretation drawn from an ancient text or mythology. We end the story at around CE 1200. This book is therefore a broad survey of 8,200 years of ancient Indian history. The choice of CE 1200 as the end point may be legitimately contested, because it can be argued that the ancient period came to an end with the rise of feudalism from CE 600 onwards. The preference in this book for CE 1200 as the terminal date is based on the fact that after it the Indian civilisation came under intense pressure from two other major world civilisations: Islam and Western Europe. Before CE 1200, India had, to be sure, faced attacks by outside forces and absorbed many foreign influences; but – apart from relatively minor Persian and Greek control on the periphery of north-west India for a few centuries, the occasional Central Asian conquerors such as the Kushans or the Hunas, and Arab and Turkish intruders – the Indian rulers, whether imperial or regional, had managed to remain the masters of their own lands. After CE 1200, however, their autonomy and capacity for independent action came to be increasingly compromised, first by the Turco-Afghan and Mogul rulers who, in due course, came to consider India as their only home, and then by the British, for most of whom India existed essentially for enriching Britain's wealth and prestige. Before CE 1200, the Indian civilisation was already a composite civilisation, but one that was deeply anchored in its native soil; after CE 1200, foreign concepts and practices profoundly modified its character. Fortunately, the ultimate fusion – whether Indo-Islamic or Indo-Western – helped to enhance, not diminish, the cultures of the subcontinent. Nevertheless, the date of CE 1200 was a turning point in India's political and cultural fortunes and, in this sense only, the period before that date may be described as 'ancient'.

Originally coined by the Persians to refer to the people who lived beyond the River Indus, the term 'Hindu' actually came into popular usage with the arrival of the Arabs and the Turks (Thapar 2002: 439–40). At first they called all the people of India 'Hindu', but later, with their increased understanding of Indian social structures, they became discerning enough to distinguish the Hindus from the non-Hindu Buddhist or Jain religious groups. It was even later in history that the Hindus called themselves by that name. In ancient India they had used the names of their particular sects or castes for self-description. They were always a highly diverse group, although their caste system, along with certain ritual practices and the teachings of their religious texts, legends and epics, provided them with the resource of an underlying unity. Despite their numerical preponderance, it would be a mistake to regard the ancient period as the 'Hindu period'. There is very little archaeological evidence of Hindu culture during the first 4,000 years of ancient Indian history, from 7000 BCE to 3000 BCE. Some precocious signs of this culture are traceable, in the north-west, through the artefacts of the following thousand years. What is generally known as Vedic Hindu culture began at around 2000 BCE and flourished for some 1,500 years, until about 500 BCE. This culture came to be influenced during the next eight centuries or so by dissenting groups such as the Buddhists and Jains. From about CE 300 onwards, however, we find evidence of a resurgent, and rebranded, Hinduism known as the Puranic and devotional Hinduism, which has endured ever since. The greatest and the finest monuments of India nevertheless testify to the fact that the classical civilisation of India was the result of a partnership of architects, designers, craftsmen, masons and labourers who could have been Hindus, Buddhists, Jains, dissenters or atheists. This also holds true for the intellectual progress of India in the ancient period.

Why study ancient India?

A most unsatisfactory reason for studying ancient India would be for the purpose of glorifying India and proclaiming the quite unproven achievements of ancient Indians. This unfortunate tendency, prevalent among some modern Indians, is a defensive reaction to Western progress during the last two centuries. It has also been encouraged by excessively lavish praises showered on India by some foreign intellectuals and philosophers, as in **Excerpt 1.1** below.

Another dubious reason for studying ancient India is for the purpose of drawing attention to the so-called decline of India after the arrival of Islam in the country and of comparing negatively the course of post-CE 1200 events in India with the

Excerpt 1.1 The use of hyperbole in praise of India

The following extract is an example of exaggerated admiration for India as displayed by Will Durant, the eminent American thinker and historian. Some statements in the extract are historically accurate; others are just the writer's reflections of his love for India.

India was the motherland of our race, and Sanskrit the mother of Europe's languages: she was the mother of our philosophy; mother, through the Arabs, of much of our mathematics; mother, through the Buddha, of the ideals embodied in Christianity; mother through the village community, of self-government and democracy. Mother India is in many ways the mother of us all.

Source: Will Durant, *The Case for India*, New York: Simon & Schuster, 1931, quoted in Vivekananda Kendra Prakashan, *Imprints of Indian Thought and Culture Abroad*, Madras, 1980, 9. Reprinted with the permission of Simon & Schuster, Inc from *The Case for India* by Will Durant. Copyright © 1930 by Will Durant. Copyright renewed 1957 by Will Durant. All rights reserved.

achievements of the pre-CE 1200 period. Third, for a large number of people in the West, it is religion that seems to have mostly excited their interest in ancient India. This is the result of a great deal of study and popularisation of Hindu and Buddhist traditions by Western scholars. Unfortunately, this has also led to the growth of a number of stereotypes, of which the one repeated most often is that the Indians are a highly spiritual people with a fatalistic outlook. This imbalance in the thinking about India can be corrected by attending to other valuable legacies from ancient India.

Three particular legacies – in relation to intellect, art and morality – are worth considering. The intellectual heritage of ancient India is immense. The Indians composed learned texts long before the Europeans, they were the first great grammarians and their epics dealt with issues of eternal significance. They produced great mathematicians and astronomers, whose work eventually passed into mainstream studies. Without the ancient Indians we would not have had our number system, upon which all modern science and technologies are based. Some ancient Indians were also great dissenters, and quite disputatious (Melling 1993: 1–16, Sen 2005: 3–33;). They were accustomed to debating issues in both a passionate and an icily logical style long before such experiments evolved within European civilisation. Another major heritage of ancient India is the artistic and aesthetic. The craftsman has a distinct place in Indian society (Kramrisch 1959: 18–24). From the very first civilisation of India, the Harappan, archaeologists have retrieved beautiful and stylistic women's jewellery and children's toys, indicating its people's sophisticated lifestyle. The bronze and copper works of Indian craftsmen have always been in demand throughout the ages. Ancient Indian textile designs are still avidly sought after by international fashion houses and the temples of ancient India draw tourists in their millions. Indian trade and trading skills show a people as concerned as any other with material goods. The third great heritage from ancient India is that of a vision of a morally ordered society (Basham 1964: 57–71), busy at its work and generally at peace with itself. Of course there was violence and disorder at many junctures of her history; but essentially ancient India evolved gradually – and, compared with many other countries, peacefully – over the long period of 8,200 years. Internationally, India did not engage in rapacious warfare or humiliate foreign peoples, as so many ancient and modern nations did to their neighbours and peoples abroad. Indian warfare was always constrained by clear ethical guidelines (Date 1929: 80–1). From the earliest times the Indians have borne the strong moral responsibility of promoting international amity and goodwill. In modern times, such distinguished Indians as Mahatma Gandhi (1869–1948), Rabindranath Tagore (1861–1941) and Pandit Jawaharlal Nehru (1889–1964) have much emphasised this particularly affirmative and attractive feature of India and her peoples.

It is clear that there are many positive reasons why we should study ancient Indian history. At the same time, we need to be critical and comparative in our approach. In certain aspects of public life, ancient India lagged behind such civilisations as Mesopotamia, Egypt, China, Greece and Rome, and its shortcomings should be recognised. It does not behove modern Indians to boast about ancient

Indian technology, when it is manifest that China was far more advanced in this area than any other nation. The Indians were also slower in developing intelligible scripts than the ancient Egyptians and Mesopotamians were. The early Indians paid scant attention to the precise documentation and systematic recording of events in their country, whereas other ancient civilisations, particularly the Chinese and Romans, were scrupulous with their historiography. The ancient Indians showed abysmal disregard for issues of inequality and poverty that have disfigured the face of India throughout its history (Ramesh 2006: 10–13). Many Indian texts lament the conditions of poverty and inequality, but in none do we find any effusion of outrage or passion. The caste system had much to do with this passivity, and it remains perhaps the greatest moral blot on the record of ancient India.

Time, space and people

Chronological signposts

Although the ancient Indians were great calculators of time, they did not standardise the dates of important events in a uniform manner. This is because ancient India, except for the two relatively brief imperial periods of the Mauryans (321 BCE to 185 BCE) and the Imperial Guptas (CE 320 to 467), was largely both politically and culturally fragmented and regionalised. There were numerous ancient Indian calendars, each with its own commencement year, used by different dynasties or religious communities. The early modern scholars and historians who systematised ancient Indian studies performed a most valuable service in establishing the credibility of certain dates and then synchronising them with the traditional European system of dating events before and after Christ (BC and AD), now updated to BCE and CE (before and during the Common Era). Part of the success of synchronisation is owed to foreign sources or mathematical calculations from ancient India itself, as the following three examples demonstrate. From the Greek sources, for example, we learn that Alexander the Great invaded India in 327 BCE; this, along with the information about the Buddha's dates from Sanskritic and Pali sources, enabled the scholars to work out the accession date of the first Mauryan emperor, Chandragupta Maurya. Again, the famous astronomer Aryabhatta wrote his definitive mathematical work in CE 499, which was the year that, through his astronomical calculations, he claimed to have completed 3,600 years of the *Kali Yuga*, the latest of the time-periods of the main Hindu religious calendar that began in 3101 BCE. This means that, when the third Christian millennium began in CE 2000–01, the Hindus had just completed the first century of their sixth millennium. Finally, Islamic historiography, being more systematic in its approach than the ancient Indian, also developed a more reliable dating system; calculating the dates from the start-year of the Islamic lunar calendar (CE 622) against the modern solar reckoning, we are on firm ground with Islamic chronology. That is why we can be confident of the veracity of such a date as CE 1000, when Mahmud of Ghazni attacked India. The modern European system of dating is inaccurate, because Christ was born at least four years before what we consider to be its start-year of CE 1, supposedly the year of his birth, and there have also been both slippages of days and days added artificially by the Church authorities at different times in European history. Nevertheless, it is now a well-established universal dating system; it has also been modernised to take account of the fact that most people in the world are not Christian, and we now use the term Common Era (CE) rather than the Year of Our Lord (AD). We are using this updated system in the present edition of this book. It is, of course, worth bearing in mind that all dates of ancient Indian history are somewhat fluid, and in the dating of some events one has to accept a certain 'give and take' of a few years.

Physical geography and its impact on history

Geography plays a crucial part in shaping a country's history, and so it was with ancient India. The geographical shape of the subcontinent was referred to by early writers, as illustrated in **Excerpt 1.2** below.

The physical geography of the subcontinent provides four main landscape profiles, each involved in the shaping of ancient India (Map 1.1). First, there is the great chain of northern mountains, stretching from the Sulaiman, Hindu Kush and Chitral valley in the north-west to the Karakorams (Figure 1.1) and the Himalayas in the north-centre. This chain may appear to be impenetrable but, in fact, numerous mountain passes are dotted along its continuity. The most famous passes are those of the Bolan (Figure 1.2), Gomal and Khyber in the north-west. It was through these passes that the earliest humans from eastern Africa and, later, such Indo-European waves as the Aryans and other Central and West Asiatics must have entered the subcontinent over different periods. The passes along the north, through Chitral and Karakoram, established communications with central

---

Excerpt 1.2 The poetic vision of the geography of India

The great dramatist and poet of the fourth century CE, *Kalidasa, understood correctly the geographical configuration of India and expressed his spatial vision in a poetic form in his poem,* Kumarasambhava, *with the following observation.*

> Along the north (of this land) stretches the divine-souled lord of all mountains, which bears the name Himalaya [the abode of snow]; dipping [his two arms] into the eastern and western seas he stands as the measuring rod [as it were] of the earth.
>
> **Source:** *Kumarasambhavam of Kalidasa*, 1.1, translated by R.T.H. Griffith, London, 1879, quoted in Niharranjan Ray, *A Sourcebook of Indian Civilization*, Hyderabad: Orient Longman, 2000, 360.

Asia, and certain remote high passes linked India directly to Tibet. Buddhism spread from India into central Asia along these passes. The mountains of the north-east, however, with far fewer passes, acted as a barrier between India and China.

The great northern mountains are the source of some of the subcontinent's greatest rivers; the melting of the glaciers in spring and summer fills the rivers with plentiful water to bring to the parched plains below. Three great river systems arise from the Tibetan and Indian Himalayas. The Indus, later joined by its tributaries, begins its long course from Tibet, flows towards the north-west and then drops down south, flowing through Kashmir and the Punjab and emptying

Figure 1.1 Karakoram mountains

Figure 1.2 The Bolan Pass

into the Arabian Sea. The Brahmaputra also starts from Tibet; it flows east for hundreds of miles and then turns south-west into India, progressing through the Garo Hills and converging with the Padma, a tributary of the River Ganges, finally ending up in the Bay of Bengal. From the Indian Himalayas spring two parallel rivers, the Ganges and the Yamuna, which first flow to the south-east, meeting at the modern city of Allahabad, and then progress directly east, also finishing in the Bay of Bengal. It is in the vast plains and river valleys of these three great northern river systems – the Indus, the Brahmaputra and the Ganges–Yamuna – that the greatest concentration of the subcontinent's population lived, farmed and built cities in the ancient period. And they still do. Ample water, from the glaciers and the monsoon rains, has been the life-blood of the entire plains terrain. Farming first began in the relatively fertile areas of Baluchistan and the Indus region. The first of the Indian civilisations, the Harappan, also developed there. During the second millennium BCE the Aryans systematically cleared the dense forests of the Ganges–Yamuna plain for farming; it was on this plain that Vedic culture and some of the great cities of the historic period were established.

South of the plains lie the Vindhya mountains, which, in ancient times, acted as great barriers to communication between the north and the south. However, they too were never entirely impenetrable. Passages on the two sides of the Vindhyas, rather than through them, allowed access between the two natural divisions; and it was through these corridors that the *brahman* priests of the north were able to migrate to the south for settlement and missionary work in the promotion of Vedic Hinduism. With the crossing of the Vindhyas, one enters the rather inhospitable plateau of the Deccan or the south, located in the rain shadow of the monsoon winds. This thirsty land suffers from the fact that its main water supply comes from the rains, which are limited to their monsoon season, and that the rivers carry little water in comparison with those of the north. The three rivers with their source in the Vindhyas – the Narmada, the Tapti and the Mahanadi – bring a sparse sufficiency of water to Gujarat and Orissa, but the other five rivers – the Godavari, the Krishna, the Tungabhadra, the Penner and the Kaveri – are poorer in flow than the northern rivers. Four of these latter easterly rivers have their origin in the Western Ghats, which are fairly low mountains running along the western coast of the peninsula. There are no glaciers, and therefore the quantity of water brought down by these rivers is extremely limited. In the dry, scorching summer they become mere trickling streams. On the eastern coast there are the parallel Eastern Ghats, but not a single major river rises from them. The peninsula has a major water problem, which is why the southern peoples have from the earliest times in ancient history practised irrigation. Irrigation and commerce, both trans-Indian and international, gave the Deccan its importance. For many centuries in the ancient world, great regional kingdoms arose and fell in this area: the kingdoms of the Satavahanas, the Chalukyas, the Rashtrakutas and, outside our period, the Hoysalas and the Vijaynagar Empire. Some of the finest rock-cut temples, monuments and palaces, hewn out of the volcanic rock of the Deccan, testify today to the wealth and glory of these polities. Further in the south, below the Deccan and along the Malabar and the Coromandel coasts, there grew up the ancient kingdoms of the Kerala and Tamil people. The lusher terrain, irrigation skills and international trade created the prosperity of these lands from as early as the first millennium CE.

The fourth important feature of the subcontinent's landscape lies along its coastline. Although not greatly indented and, therefore, devoid of the natural harbours and ports of a highly indented coastline, such as that of Britain, the subcontinent's coastline is very extensive, stretching from the Makran coast in the west to the Bangladesh delta. It was to the ports of the western coastline, running from the Indus delta to the southern tip of India, that traders and travellers from countries such as Mesopotamia, Arabia, Persia, Egypt and Ethiopia, and those of the Roman Empire and East Africa, came, traded, exchanged ideas and sometimes settled. Similarly, on the east coast, trade and traffic flowed between India and South East Asia. In the ancient world, India was the hub of the sea routes to everywhere.

Myths and sacred geography

The idea of geographical sacred space has deeply permeated the Hindu religion and mythology. This space, for the vast majority of Hindus, is the subcontinent of India itself. This, to them, is the land sanctified by saints and sages who left their footprints on its soils and sands over many millennia. The politically inspired modern Hindu revivalist organisations sometimes successfully tap into this most emotive of Hindu sentiments, leading to pointless conflict with other religious communities. This does not, however, detract from the fact that India's fascination lies in the continuity of the myths and legends that the Hindu religious authorities treasure, augment and communicate to the masses. The Hindu myths consist of everything encompassed within human, divine and cosmic universes: nature, creation, planets, the earth, gods, animals, birds, the reincarnation of the soul, heroism, morality, lifestyle and countless themes besides. These myths have been transmitted, in India, by word of mouth over four millennia, but the public appetite for them has never waned or been fully sated because the great storehouses of myth and legend, such as the *Ramayana* and *Mahabharata* epics or the ancient texts of the *Puranas*, are interwoven in Indian life through folklore, festivals, literature, music, dance, drama and, now, cinema, TV and the Internet. They are reflections of human experience and aspiration, constantly reworked through thriving media outlets. They occupy an inner sacred space. Geography has its boundaries, but the human 'inscape' is limitless and infinite.

India is a land of pilgrims and saints. Peoples from various religious communities – Hindus, Muslims, Sikhs, Jains, Buddhists, Parsis, Christians and others – are imbued with the idea of pilgrimage, but the most ancient and hallowed of the sites visited by pilgrims are those venerated by the Hindus (Bhardwaj 1973: 1–13). The Hindu pilgrims visit sacred mountains, rivers, lakes and cities in order to perform rituals and ceremonies and heighten their efficacy. The high peaks of the Himalayas are worshipped because they are considered to be the abode of gods and a repository of their heroic deeds. The mythical mountain *Meru*, also somewhere among the Himalayan ranges, is envisioned as the centre of the universe (Patil 2004: 66, 71–6). Most mountains are endowed with strength and life-giving properties. Rivers are also considered sources of life. In early Vedic sources we read about the seven rivers of the Punjab, the *Sapta Sindhu*, but among them the one that is specially revered is the invisible river, *Sarasvati*, associated with the goddess of learning. From Vedic times onwards, the river that has held an unwavering sacred place in the hearts and minds of the Hindus is the Ganges. Bathing in its waters is a requisite for every devout Hindu; for many of them, the filth and pollution of the modern river is no deterrent whatsoever to drinking it, because for them it is water that is holy. The ineffable power of sacred geography in the Hindu psyche can be testified by what even a very secular person such as Nehru wrote in his will, as illustrated in **Excerpt 1.3** below.

As with rivers, lakes too are associated with the deities and therefore have become part of the 'sacred space'. Many city sites are sacred too. The Hindus assign a particular significance to six city sites in north India and three in the south.

Excerpt 1.3 Sacred geography in the Hindu imagination

Pandit Nehru, the first prime minister of independent India, was a thoroughly modern man. He had little time for religious rituals and conventions. Nevertheless, he made clear in his last will and testament that he wanted part of his ashes to be immersed in the waters of the River Ganges. In the following extract his feelings betray a deep sense of appreciation as to why the Indian people stand in awe of the Ganges, a mere river to those without a sense of the history of India.

The Ganga (Ganges) is the river of India, beloved of her people, round which are intertwined her racial memories, her hopes and fears, her songs of triumph, her victories and her defeats. She has been a symbol of India's age-long culture and civilization, ever-changing, ever-flowing, and yet ever the same Ganga . . . Smiling and dancing in the morning sunlight, and dark and gloomy and full of mystery as the evening shadows fall . . . the Ganga has been to me a symbol and a memory of the past of India, running with the present and flowing on to the great ocean of the future. And although I have discarded much of the past tradition and custom . . . I do not wish to cut myself off from that past completely . . . And as witness of this desire of mine and as my last homage to India's cultural inheritance, I am making this request that a handful of my ashes be thrown into the Ganga at Allahabad to be carried to the great ocean that washes India's shore.

Source: Dorothy Norman, *Nehru: The First Sixty Years*, London: Bodley Head, 1965, 574–5.

The northern ones are: Ayodhya, the birthplace of the Hindu god Rama; Mathura, the birthplace of Krishna, the eighth incarnation of the god Vishnu; Hardwar, a city renowned for its great river festival of Kumbh Mela and a staging-post for the Hindu pilgrims who make arduous treks to the Gangotri glacier, the source of the Ganges, which then flows into the plains; *Kashi*, where the embankments of the Ganges are the last stopping points, in this world, for the dying Hindu; *Prayag*, where the rivers Ganges, Yamuna and the invisible *Sarasvati* meet in a mystical threefold confluence, and where also the festival of Kumbh Mela takes place every twelve years; and Dwarka, on the Gujarat coast, where Krishna came from Mathura for his safety. Most of these northern sites are located in *Madhyadesha*, the spiritual heartland of Hindu, Aryan and Brahmanic culture. The three important southern sites are Madurai, Kanchipuram and Rameshwaram. These sites came to be added to the list of sacred cities only after the south conformed to the Vedic/Brahmanic mainstream religion.

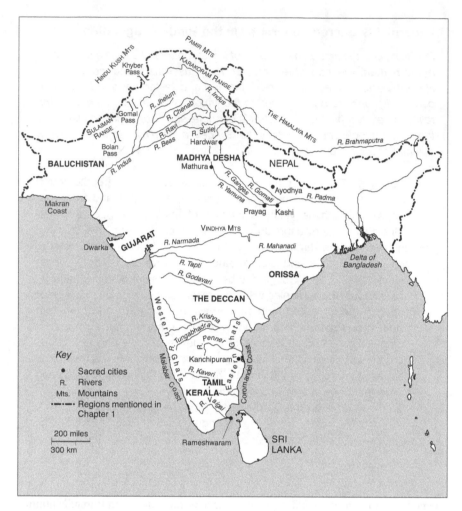

Map 1.1 Physical geography and sacred cities

Social and cultural diversity

Ancient Indians were as diverse as their modern descendants. Older history books, influenced by the nineteenth-century obsession with race and racial classification, adopted such terms as Negrito, Proto-Australoid, Mongoloid, Mediterranean, Alpinoic and Nordic-Aryan to identify the peoples of India, mostly by the pigmentation of their skin (e.g. Rapson 1922: 37–50). This type of racial classification, on the basis of physical features, has now been found to be not only irrelevant but also irresponsibly dangerous. A more meaningful concept than racial classification is that of ethnic diversity. There is but one human race, but history, geography and culture have divided it into ethnic groups. By that criterion, India was, and still is, a nation of many ethnic groups. Some of these groups have lived in India for countless millennia. Sometimes they are called the aborigines or Adivasis. In the Stone Age they were the nomadic hunter-gatherers or forest-dwellers, and constituted the majority of the very small population that existed then in India. In the course of history, different ethnic groups separately developed their particular historical cultures in the diverse geographical terrains, such as mountain regions, river valleys and plains, deserts, coasts or forests. Ethnic groups, such as the Aryans, Iranians, Turco-Afghans, Graeco-Macedonians and Tibeto-Burmans, also came from abroad and were absorbed in the ethnic admixture. Another strand of diversity was occupational. Hunter-gatherers and forest-dwellers dominated the land, except the Indus region, almost until the beginning of the first millennium BCE. After that, major farming activities in the Ganges–Yamuna plains began with the felling of forests and, in the south, with the acquisition of irrigation skills. In time, the farmers and the pastoralists displaced the hunter-gatherers and the forest-dwellers, thereby constituting the majority of the people. Surplus crops enabled farming communities to form the core of the first towns and cities of ancient India; that was how town-dwellers, craftsmen and traders came to fulfil their respective crucial roles (Thapar 2002: 55–62). The bards and priests of ancient India also remind us of the religious diversity of ancient India. Most aborigines were animistic nature-worshippers, but the people of the first civilisation of India, the Harappans, were perhaps beginning to develop some rituals and practices that formally metamorphosed into the more sophisticated religious structure known later as Vedic Hinduism. This new structure was the result of a cultural fusion between the ancient Indians and the incoming Indo-Iranian Aryans. The hierarchical and ritually ordered caste system became a prominent feature of Vedic Hinduism. Although a large number of people adhered to Vedic Hinduism, many remained outside its fold, belonging to either the animistic or the dissenting tradition. Buddhism and Jainism were major challengers to Vedic Hinduism. Ancient India was therefore evolving into a diverse multi-faith society. By CE 1200, at least four non-Indic religions – Judaism, Christianity, Islam and Zoroastrianism – had also become familiar to some of the Indians. Lastly, the linguistic diversity of ancient India should not be forgotten. We have no clear idea of what language the ancient Indians spoke. The language and the scripts of the first Indian civilisation, the Harappan, remain a mystery. We can, however, draw some deductions from the current language map of South Asia. Leaving aside minor languages spoken by the remaining aboriginals or by those living in the peripheral border areas, the two main language families are known as the Indo-Aryan and the Dravidian. It is believed that the Dravidian family is indigenous to India, and that Tamil, the premier Dravidian language, is perhaps the oldest Indian language in use today. Sanskrit, the mother language of the Indo-Aryan family, evolved out of a fusion of Aryan and native Indian tongues. It flourished in ancient India as a classical language of both the north and, later, the south; but the ordinary people in the north came to use the vernacular and non-standard languages known as *Prakrits* and the *Apabrahmashas*, from which the regional languages of the north have developed. For all practical purposes, Sanskrit is moribund today. Tamil, on the other hand, has remained the predominant language of the Dravidian family throughout the ages, although it has been enriched by Sanskrit since ancient times. At least two other Dravidian languages – Telugu and Kannada – also developed during the ancient period.

Sources of study

The contents of this book are drawn from the writings of some of the most eminent historians of ancient India. This means that the evidence presented here is secondary, but the writers themselves drew their evidence from primary sources. In the context of ancient India, there are three valid forms of primary historical evidence: archaeological finds, literary texts and modern multi-disciplinary research findings. Archaeology came to India with the British, and their pioneering work greatly expanded our historical knowledge (Allchin 1961: 241–59). There have been three strands of archaeological work in India. The first, and the earliest, has been that of discovering, recording, restoring, renovating and cataloguing thousands of material remains that stand 'above the ground'. The most important of these remains, for the historian, have been the inscriptions engraved on rocks, stones, pillars, temple walls and wells, and on copper or metallic plates. The inscriptions, written in a variety of Indic scripts, serve different purposes. They consist of declarations of religious piety and worldly advice, such as those of King Ashoka; commemorative inscriptions, such as birth registers, records of deaths or visits of kings and famous people; dedicative inscriptions, recording grants of land by the kings to *brahman* priests, Buddhist and Jainist monks, or to temples and monasteries; and commercial inscriptions issued by guilds of merchants, monarchs or town councils. Many inscriptions also carry lengthy panegyric eulogies, known as *prasastis*, glorifying the kings and proclaiming their administrative prowess. Whatever their weaknesses as reliable sources, it is through the inscriptions that our knowledge of ancient history has both widened and deepened (Ali 2000: 225–9). The care of the buildings and monuments on which inscriptions have been found is the prime responsibility of the Department of Archaeology of the Government of India. By the early twentieth century, many of the structures had fallen into disrepair, but the position was remedied by Lord Curzon, the British viceroy, who provided sufficient funding for repair work and the training of specialists.

A second strand of archaeological work consisted of recovering materials 'under the ground'. The most significant discoveries in this field of work were made in the excavation of prehistoric fossils and tools and, from the 1920s onwards, the uncovering of the Harappan culture and civilisation.

The last of the archaeological strands consists of selected recent diggings at famous religious, urban or commercial sites in order to corroborate some of the available textual and epigraphic evidence.

The literary corpus can be divided into two sections: religious and secular. The religious texts relate to the spiritual heritage of the Hindus, Buddhists and Jains.

These scriptures, composed in Sanskrit, Pali, Tamil or *Prakrit* languages, include such works as the *Vedas* and the related Vedic literature, the *Mahabharata* and the *Ramayana* epics, the great Buddhist works of the *Tripitakas*, the *Nikayas* and the *Dipavamsa*, the *Agam* texts of the Jains, the manuals of religious law such as the *Dharmashastras* and *Dharmasutras*, the devotional texts of the *Puranas*, and the devotional songs and hymns composed by saints who propagated the worship of the gods Vishnu and Shiva. The secular literary texts include a major work of political economy known as the *Arthashastra*, mathematical and astronomical treatises, writings on medicine and surgery, grammatical works and lexicons, volumes on architecture, and works of poetry, music, dance and drama. No systematic historical works by ancient Indians are available, in the way historians such as Herodotus (485–425 BCE), Livy (59 BCE to CE 17), Ssu-Ma Chien (*c.* 145–87 BCE) or the Venerable Bede (*c.* CE 673–735) composed histories of early Greece, Rome, China and England. There are, however, two particular works of value. One is a biography of a famous seventh-century king, Harsha, written by a courtier named Banabhatta, or Bana for short, and the other is a fairly coherent account of the history of Kashmir called *Rajatarangini*, by Kalhana, a scholar and courtier in the Kashmiri kingdom. Among the secular works we include the accounts of India left by Greek, Chinese, Roman and Islamic writers such as Al-Biruni. Despite the paucity of the specifically historical texts written by the ancient Indians themselves, historians have been able to extract a huge amount of material from both the religious and the secular literary texts (Majumdar 1961a: 13–28). Their main challenge is to be able to distinguish the historical from the non-historical evidence.

Apart from archaeology and the literary texts, another form of primary evidence consists of data collated through multi-disciplinary researches. Since the mid-twentieth century, our understanding of the history of ancient India has been greatly facilitated by some exciting developments in areas as varied as anthropology, ethnography, geology, meteorology, genetics, biology and botany. These have provided historians with valuable data and insights. Genetics, for example, gives us clues to the origins of South Asian people, while anthropology guides us towards oral history, which is valuable in piecing together the history of the marginalised subaltern groups of people who exist in large numbers in India.

Reconstructing the history of ancient India

Two important developments took place in India in the middle of the eighteenth century. One was the political ascendancy of the British East India Company, particularly after a victorious battle at Plessey in Bengal. From then on, the British control over India tightened until India eventually became a virtual colony of Britain. The second development concerned the rise of indology, the study of India through European eyes and mindsets (Thapar 2002: 7–15). Until then, most Europeans in India, particularly the British, had been interested primarily in trade; just a few were curious travellers who kept diaries and journals. After the mid-eighteenth century, however, much greater interest in India was aroused by the work of empathetic and committed scholars, administrators and intellectuals, who came to be known as the orientalists. The two developments – British domination and the rise of indology – became inextricably linked but, as we shall see, with varying consequences over the course of time.

There was little achieved by way of a systematic historiography of ancient India until the mid-eighteenth century. This developed only through the rise of indology, but the manner and rate of its progress depended on how scholars responded to the nature and character of British political domination. We can identify four separate phases in this intellectual activity. In the first phase, during the late eighteenth century, there was a uniquely fruitful interaction between power and scholarship. The central political character in this phase was Warren Hastings, the Governor-General of Bengal, who held India and her culture in great esteem. He offered his patronage to a group of empathetic orientalists, such as Sir William Jones (1746–94) and Charles Wilkins (1749–1836). These men sought out suitable Indian tutors for studying Sanskrit, without which they realised they could never access ancient texts concerning early religion, laws and customs. Persisting through many difficulties, they mastered Sanskrit as well as other Indian languages and then translated complex literary works. From the translations came the interpretations and the wider understanding of a society with ancient cultural roots over which the British ruled (Rocher 1993: 215–49). However, a major weakness of the orientalists' approach was that, because they had been tutored mainly by *brahman* Sanskritists, they interpreted the Indian past mostly through the Sanskrit texts, which narrowed their horizons.

During the second phase, the work of the orientalists came to be challenged and threatened. By the end of the eighteenth century, the balance of power between the British and the Indians had shifted dramatically in favour of the former. The rise of such social and economic movements in Britain as utilitarianism, evangelism and free trade also exercised a profound impact in India. The arrogant British men who carried the gospel of these movements to India were imbued with an overweening sense of pride, convinced that they alone had both the superiority and the therapy to cure India of all her ancient maladies. The iconic figure of Indian historiography in this category was James Mill (1773–1836), the father of the famous philosopher John Stuart Mill (1806–73). James Mill's multi-volume book is titled *The History of British India*, but the author ventured far deeper into ancient history as well. He unwisely partitioned Indian history into three periods – Hindu, Muslim and British – and argued that India had been gripped by the terror of oriental despotism during the first two periods, but had a redemptive opportunity to benefit from the wisdom and enlightenment of British rule (Philips 1961: 217–29; Breckenridge and Veer 1993: 263–5). Mill's work provided the justification for colonial rule, as explained by the historian Romila Thapar in **Excerpt 1.4** below.

The early orientalists would not have appreciated Mill's ideas, but their greatest challenge came with the proposal by Lord Macaulay, the government minister in Bengal, that English should be adopted as the medium of instruction in all publicly funded educational institutions. From the 1830s onwards, Mill and Macaulay were to become the icons of imperial historiography in the nineteenth century.

Excerpt 1.4 Colonialism and the perception of India as an ahistorical society

Despite their own shortcomings in the skills of history, many of the contemporary Hindu religious nationalists in India are quick to condemn colonial historians for intentionally undervaluing Indian historical sources. The historian Romila Thapar, on the other hand, has shown in her numerous learned works the diverse ways Indian history can be understood. She has also not been slow to point out the mentality behind colonial thinking.

In the nineteenth century, a different reconstruction of Indian history drew on premises that precluded the need for an historical tradition. It underpinned the requirement of colonial policy in a changing relationship between the colonial power and the colony. A denial of a sense of history was implicit in its major theory – that of Oriental Despotism. (In Mill's view) Indian society was said to be static and, since it did not register change, it had no use for recording the past, one of the functions of the past being to legitimize the present. This stasis could only be broken by British administration legislating change. Mill's history was defining a new idiom for imperial control. Other arguments attributed the absence of a sense of history to a lack of sub-continental political unity, or to the subordination of the human will to the divine, or to obsessive religion and the control of the brahman over intellectual activities.

Source: Romila Thapar, 'Historical Traditions in Early India, *c.* 1000 BC to *c.* AD 600', in Andrew Feldherr and Grant Hardy, *The Oxford History of Historical Writing*, Vol. 1, Oxford: Oxford University Press, 2011, 556–7. By permission of Oxford University Press.

It was only to be a matter of time, however, before the Indians bestirred themselves and reacted against the foreigners' monopoly over the reconstruction of India's ancient past. In this third phase, the Indian response came in two forms. Some highly educated and politicised Hindus, bursting with pride over the evaluations and translations of ancient texts that were increasingly made available in the nineteenth century, adopted a nationalistic fervour with regard to their past (Majumdar 1961b: 416–28). Such writers as B.G. Tilak (1856–1920), Dayanand Saraswati (1824–83), Bankim Chandra Chatterjee (1838–94) and V.D. Savarkar (1883–1966) uncritically examined and glorified Hinduism and the Hindu past. The works of two particular Europeans, Madame Blavatsky (1831–91) and Mrs Annie Besant (1847–1933), also betrayed the same tendency. But there were other Indians, such as R.G. Bhandarkar (1837–1925) and H.C. Raychaudhuri (1892–1957), who adopted a more measured approach in their understanding and interpretation of ancient India by closely studying the historical criteria and refraining from reading too much into the available evidence.

The period since independence from British rule may be described as the fourth phase. There has been a sea change in the attitude of those British and European historians who specialise in India. Gone are some of their predecessors' Victorian assertive declarations. More humble in their approach, they have produced some outstanding works in their specialist fields. Perhaps the most magnificent of these works was *The Wonder that was India*, written by A.L. Basham. Among the Indian historians the name of D.D. Kosambi is worth noting. With his mathematician's logic, ethnologist's acute observation and scholar's incisive interpretation of the Indian texts, Kosambi was the pioneer of a Marxist approach to historiography (Thapar 1993: 89–113). Marx himself was not knowledgeable about India, but the Marxist method of studying the present by asking relevant social and economic questions from the past is one of the soundest ways of studying history. Kosambi took this to heart and introduced new concepts and methodologies in his *An Introduction to the Study of Indian History* (1956) and *The Culture and Civilisation of Ancient India in Historical Outline* (1965). Many scholars have come to appreciate his lines of inquiry, and their works in turn have reflected a new richness and diversity. Perhaps the most prominent and well known among these scholars is the historian Romila Thapar, who has inspired many generations of history students at the Jawaharlal Nehru University in Delhi. Many of the ideas expressed in this book are based upon her formidable research studies in ancient Indian history. Ancient India continues to remain a fertile ground for vast fields of investigative and forensic work from primary sources.

STUDY GUIDE

Key issues

* Reasons for change in the way India has been known and named in history.
* Factors to consider in assessing the achievements of one's ancestors.
* Differences in the understanding of physical geography and sacred geography.
* The immense social and cultural diversity of India.
* Western influence on the historiography of India.

Suggested readings

Doniger 2010: 50–64; Johnson 1996: 13–51; Rawson 1977: 10–24; Thapar 2002: 9–12, 15–22; Thapar 2011: 553–76

INTERNET SELECTION

1) Robert R. Cargill, 'Why Christians should adopt the BCE/CE dating system'. www.bibleinterp.com/opeds/why_3530.shtml

2)   Myths Encyclopedia, 'Hinduism and mythology'. www.mythsencyclopedia.com/
     Go-hi/Hinduism-and-Mythology.html
3)   Gyan Prakash, 'Writing post-Orientalist histories of the third world: perspect-
     ives from Indian historiography'. http://courses.arch.vt.edu/courses/wdun
     away/gia5524/prakash90.pdf
4)   Upinder Singh, 'Changing interpretations of early Indian history'. http://lama
     shree-indianhistory.blogspot.co.uk

QUESTIONS FOR GROUP DISCUSSION

1)   What issues of intellectual significance would the ancient Indians have argued
     about?
2)   What are the main environmental challenges facing Indian farmers today?
3)   What are the benefits and shortcomings of mythological knowledge in
     understanding history?
4)   Attempt to distinguish the characteristics of (a) orientalist, (b) nationalist and
     (c) fundamentalist approaches to the study of Indian history.
5)   To what extent has India benefited from Macaulay's project for the creation
     of a Westernised Indian?

2 From Africa to Mehrgarh:
the early prehistory of India
(before the third millennium BCE)

Timeline/Key Dates

c. 50,000–30,000 BCE	The emergence of Homo Sapiens in South Asia
c. 50,000–26,000 BCE	South Asian Palaeolithic era: Madrasian Culture of Attirampakkam
c. 26,000–10,000 BCE	Mesolithic period
c. 9000 BCE	Beginnings of Indian Neolithic era
c. 7000 BCE	Evidence of first farming in South Asia at Mehrgarh, Baluchistan
c. 7000–4500 BCE	Baluchistan Phase: earliest urbanism at Mehrgarh
c. 4500–3500 BCE	Intermediate Phase
c. 3800 BCE	Evidence of earliest settlements in the *Sarasvati* basin
c. 3500–2600 BCE	The growth of early Harappan/Indus settlements

In the absence of contemporary written records, the skills and methods of archaeology are our principal assistants in the study of the prehistory of any region in the world (Renfrew and Bahn 2000: 49–52, 89–116). The archaeologist can now also call upon the services of specialists in such diverse fields as cultural anthropology (Soundararajan 1981: 3–7), geology (Scarre 2005: 50–1) and climatic (Scarre 2005: 55–7, 177–83) and genetic studies (Wells 2003: iii–xvi) to shed further light on the interpretation of the available data. The cumulative results of archaeological and other researches over the last two centuries have been highly impressive, and, while controversies over the significance of this or that piece of evidence will always continue, we now at least possess a great amount of scientific evidence to probe into questions relating to prehistory. Among such questions that arise while studying the prehistory of India and South Asia, the following are of particular interest: when did the first humans emerge in those regions? What tools did they make? What was their socio-economic lifestyle? At what stage did they take up farming? When do we get the first pointers to urban civilisation in the subcontinent? The answers are frequently unclear because research in this area is still much in progress. On the basis of what is available, however, this chapter attempts to address the questions by examining three settlement phases.

Earliest phases of human settlement and activity

A critical stage in human evolution took place some six million years ago, during the later Miocene, Pliocene and Pleistocene geological time periods, when our remotest ancestors emerged in Africa. Palaeontologists (students of animal and human fossils) and archaeologists refer to them by the term 'hominins'. Their skill of using bipedal locomotion (walking on two feet) gave the hominins an edge over all other primates. Different species of hominins coexisted for the next 3.5 million years, but around 2.5 million years ago we find evidence of the first tool-using members from their lineage in eastern and southern Africa (Scarre 2005: 25). These tool-using hominins continued to evolve inside Africa, and developed into three branches, known as Homo Habilis, Homo Ergaster and Homo Erectus (Toth and Schick 2005: 47–83). The more enterprising members of the last two began to come out of Africa just over one million years ago, reaching as far as Europe, west Asia, east Asia and the Indonesian islands (Klein 2005: 101–3). It would, however, be wrong to conclude that there were no tool-using hominins in places outside Africa before one million years ago; the fossil remains of hominins such as Sivapithecus and Ramapithecus have been discovered in the northern regions of the Indian subcontinent. Further, the recent discovery, in north-west Pakistan, of a chopping tool that is two million years old suggests that the dating of human ancestry is an evolving subject (Coningham 2005: 522); it would be imprudent to be too categorical with the dates.

The culmination of the long period of evolution, adaptation and diffusion by the pre-human species such as the Australopithecines and the three hominin branches was reached when our own species, Homo Sapiens – modern humans biologically similar to us – emerged around 400,000 years ago (Toth and Schick 2005: 62). There are two conflicting hypotheses for the origin of Homo Sapiens. One holds to the multi-regional model of human origin, which asserts that Homo Sapiens arose gradually from the Homo Erectus populations in different regions of the world (Wells 2003: 33; Pettitt 2005: 127–8, 130–1;). This model of human origins held sway among scientists and anthropologists until the 1960s. Racial differences are perhaps more easily explainable under its hypothesis. It was also argued that gene flow, or the introduction of new genes into regional populations, helped to ensure that the evolving regional populations were similar in reproductive and anatomical character and that they all belonged to a single Homo Sapiens type. Central to this hypothesis are fossils from Asia and Australia that have been interpreted as showing evidence for regional continuity in populations. The other model, known as the Out-of-Africa hypothesis, asserts that over thousands of years the African humanity, in the form of Homo Erectus and, later, Homo Sapiens, spread to other parts of the world and dominated all other species (Pettitt 2005: 128, 132–7). Both theories have their champions, but the relative abundance of African fossil remains and sophisticated research into the history of human genes increasingly point to an African origin for modern humans, including South Asians (Fagan 1999: 85–6, 88), as the two quotes in **Excerpt 2.1** below explain.

Most probably, Homo Erectus moved, in significant numbers, from Africa to south Asia via west Asia around 500,000 years ago. Homo Sapiens, on the other hand, arrived much later in the subcontinent from two directions and over two different time sequences. One was by the traditional route through west Asia, around 30,000 years ago, but research in genetics has also indicated that an earlier group might have landed around 50,000 years ago on the shores of south India while on their sea journey towards the Andaman Islands, Indonesia and the Australasian archipelagos (Wells 2003: 182–3; Klein 2005: 102). The entire subject of the first settlements of Homo Sapiens in different parts of the world is wholly fascinating, but new theories, particularly from genetic studies, will undoubtedly help us to obtain further insights. We are, of course, still undecided about the sequence of the peopling of India and south Asia, but there can be no doubt that the South Asian Homo Sapiens has truly flourished and multiplied in the region for at least 30,000 years. The Indian subcontinent holds the largest areal concentrations of humanity in the world today.

By 100,000 years ago, the Homo Sapiens species had shown its dominance throughout the known world, replacing all other *homo* genera. Archaeology comes into its own when, from the later hominins onwards, we see signs of the advancing material culture of stone tools. In time, the artefacts became more complex, as with pottery. In their search and analysis of fossils (human or animal), tools and artefacts, whether of the most primitive kind or of a sophisticated design, archaeologists generally employ three recognised procedures (Renfrew and Bahn 2000: 118–24). One is known as typological classification, by which the similarities and differences among the tools and artefacts are analysed. Another is stratigraphy, by which the layers and strata of the ground are studied. Materials found at deeper levels below the ground, for example, could indicate the remains of an older chronological period, as the levels are covered by the debris of successive generations. Each layer is numbered in relation to a chronological period, and the deepest level, containing the oldest of materials, is treated as Period I. The third important procedure concerns dating, of which there are a variety of methods, such as spectrometric dating of the materials earlier than 10,000 years ago, radio-carbon dating, dendro-chronology and thermoluminescence for dating objects from the last 10,000 years. Archaeological procedures and the researches from other sciences have combined, over the last 150 years, to shed much light on the earliest humans and their activities (Bahn 1996: 222–6; Fagan 1999: 126, 164; Renfrew and Bahn 2000: 133–7, 151–2).

Excerpt 2.1 The African origins of humans

After the pioneering archaeological work carried out by Louis Leakey (1903–72) and Mary Leakey (1913–96) at the Olduvai Gorge in the Serengeti plain of northern Tanzania, researchers became increasingly convinced of the hypothesis of Africa being the geographical cradle of human origins, as the following two passages attempt to clarify.

1) The rise of modern humans is a recent drama that played out against a long and complex backdrop of evolutionary diversification among the hominids, but the fossil record shows that from the earliest times Africa was consistently the centre from which new lineages of hominids sprang. Clearly, interesting evolutionary developments occurred in both Europe and eastern Asia, but they involved populations that were not only derived from but also eventually supplanted by emigrants from Africa. In Africa our lineage was born and, ever since its hominids were first emancipated from the forest edges, that continent has pumped out successive waves of emigrants to all parts of the Old World.

Source: Ian Tattersall, 'Out of Africa Again . . . and Again', *Scientific American*, 276 (April 1997), 60–7. Reproduced with permission. Copyright © (2016) Scientific American, Inc. All rights reserved.

2) . . . all the genetic data shows the greatest number of polymorphisms in Africa; there is simply far more variation in that continent than anywhere else. You are more likely to sample extremely divergent genetic lineages within a single African village than you are in the whole of the rest of the world . . . Why does diversity indicate greater age? [Taking the example of a hypothetical Provençal village, we can ask] why do the bouillabaisse recipes change? Because in each generation, a daughter decides to modify her soup in a minor way. Over time, these small variations add up to an extraordinary amount of diversity in the village's kitchens. And – critically – the longer the village has been accumulating these changes, the more diverse it is. It is like a clock, ticking away in units of rosemary and thyme – the longer it has been ticking, the more differences we see . . . when we see greater genetic diversity in a particular population, we can infer that the population is older – and this makes Africa the oldest of all.

Source: Spencer Wells, *The Journey of Man: A Genetic Odyssey*, New York: Random House, 2003, 39.

The Palaeolithic era

The prehistoric period for all regions of the world is characterised by the gradual increase in the human ability to shape tools from stone, which is why most of the prehistoric period, from the time of the first tool-making hominins 2.5 million years ago, is called the Stone Age. Owing to the difficulties posed in studying such a long period, archaeologists have divided it into three parts: Old (or Palaeolithic), Middle (or Mesolithic) and New (or Neolithic) Stone Ages. The Palaeolithic, being the longest of the three, is itself further sub-divided into three sub-periods, Lower Palaeolithic (the earliest period of the Old Stone Age), Middle Palaeolithic and Upper Palaeolithic (the most recent period of the Old Stone Age). The period divisions do not apply uniformly to all parts of the world because, owing to factors such as time lag, climatic vagaries, great distances or numerous geographical and physical barriers, the peoples in different regions of the world progressed at varying paces. We can affirm that Africa was the first region in the world to display characteristics of the Lower Palaeolithic, but that approximates the limits of our chronology. Even today there are isolated groups of people whose skills lie essentially in working with stone artefacts and who are considered as still living in the Stone Age. The Stone Age, theoretically, comes to an end when human beings start working with metals such as copper, tin and iron.

In the context of Indian and South Asian history, we may be justified in saying that the Stone Age began around 500,000 years ago, assuming that the tool-making members of Homo Erectus had then arrived, and that it lasted until at least the third millennium BCE, at which time we come across copper objects from the Harappan civilisation. A large number of prehistoric sites in south Asia have been unearthed and excavated by archaeologists over the last 150 years. These sites bear testimony to the vast geological and geographical diversity of the subcontinent. Very few human fossils have been discovered, with two notable exceptions: first, the Narmada man, a 250,000-year-old fossil of a Homo Erectus discovered in the valley of the Narmada River in Central India, and, second, a 34,000-year-old fossil of the earliest Homo Sapiens in Sri Lanka (Coningham 2005: 522). The Palaeolithic era of the Stone Age lasted the longest of the Stone Age sub-periods, stretching until about 26,000 BCE. Although we have very little evidence of human remains from most of the Palaeolithic era, the remains of fauna fossils have been recovered in great numbers, giving vital clues to researchers about climatic conditions and their effects on landscapes; we also have a variety of stone implements from all the sub-periods of the Palaeolithic era, unearthed from different sites in south Asia (see Map 2.1). The two predominant utensils of the Lower Palaeolithic era were pebble tools and hand axes. Extensive deposits of pebble tools and choppers were discovered in the Soan river valley in Pakistan, and the hoards found there and at other sites are collectively known as the Soan Culture (Allchin and Allchin 1982: 15–16, 36). A later, more advanced, hoard of the Middle Palaeolithic Era, consisting of flake tools, cores, scrapers and bores, is generally termed the Nevasan Tool Culture, named after the site of Nevasa in the Godavari river valley (Allchin and Allchin 1982: 47–50; Ray *et al.* 2000: 143–7). Further skills of sharpening the cutting edges of tools such as blades and burins were revealed by the artefacts found at the Upper Palaeolithic Era site of Patne in Maharashtra (Kachroo 2000: 73).

The evidence of what is generally known as the Acheulian technology of making sharp, stone hand axes is also found at many south Asian archaeological sites. This technology had at first developed in Africa, where the Homo Ergaster hominins had initiated a tradition of producing flaked stone hand axes with extremely sharp edges around the entire periphery of the stone object. Hand axes and cleavers are part of the Acheulian tradition as a whole, which lasted for nearly a million years in Africa. Owing to the fact that many such hand axes were, much later, also found at St Acheul, a suburb of the town of Amiens in France, all sites where they are now found are generally called Acheulian sites. One site that provides us with particularly strong and comprehensive evidence of the use of Acheulian technology during all the eras of the Palaeolithic Age in south Asia – Lower, Middle and Upper – between 1.5 million and 125,000 years ago, is that of Attirampakkam in Tamil Nadu in south India. The first of the Acheulian style hand axes were discovered there in the early 1860s by Robert Bruce Foote (1834–1912), the father of Indian prehistory. After arriving in India in 1858, Foote spent his whole life working as a geologist and archaeologist, discovering a vast variety of hand axes in different localities in south India. His hand axe assemblage is generally known as the Madrasian Culture, owing to the proximity of the Attirampakkam region to Madras (now Chennai). Continuous archaeological research at Attirampakkam since Foote's time, along with the use of the latest scientific excavating and dating techniques during the last two decades, has now convinced the world's most eminent archaeologists that, even with their small brains and simplest of tools, the earliest of the African Homo Erectus hominins overcame formidable barriers and adapted to the ecological settings of south Asia in remarkable ways. The research at Attirampakkam has revolutionised our understanding of the prehistory of this entire region, as explained in **Excerpt 2.2** below.

The evidence of tools and fossils suggests clearly, however, that the Palaeolithic people remained essentially hunter-gatherers throughout that long period. They hunted and scavenged, collecting berries, roots and fruits of all kinds that grew in the wild. Mostly they lived in nomadic fashion in open spaces, but also used caves for shelter and protection. There is, however, one remote piece of evidence that may help us to reconstruct a picture of their social life in the Upper Palaeolithic Age. This consists of a few of the earliest cave paintings at Bhimbetka, on the bank of the River Narmada in central India, depicting scenes of hunting and fertility symbols (Thapar 2002: 74; Jha 2004: 26). Otherwise, there is nothing except fossils, pebble tools and hand axes.

The Mesolithic era

The transition from the Palaeolithic to the Mesolithic era witnessed the emergence of a new type of stone tool known as the microlith. Although small in size, this was a superior implement. A typical microlith kit would consist of tiny

Excerpt 2.2 India's prehistory pushed back

Over many decades very little attention was paid to the rich prehistoric sites in south India. The pioneering work of Robert Bruce Foote was forgotten; his valuable collections, encased in the museum in Madras (now Chennai), were never properly utilised for the further archaeological or geological education of young people in India. More interest is now being taken, however, as a result of the work of younger specialists who are not only keeping in touch with scientific and technological developments across different parts of the world, but who are also aware of the importance of including archaeological education as part of children's curriculums in schools. A resource base was initially established in Chennai in 1999. Known as the Sharma Centre for Heritage Education, and led by a dynamic archaeologist, Shanti Pappu, its Children's Museum now attracts many young Indians who wish to learn more about the long-forgotten history of their country.

Archaeologists have discovered India's oldest stone-age tools, up to 1.5 million years old, at the prehistoric site of Attirampakkam, near Chennai. The discovery may change existing ideas about the earliest arrival of human ancestors from Africa into India . . . In nearly 12 years of excavation, archaeologists Shanti Pappu and Kumar Akhilesh from the Sharma Centre for Heritage Education, Chennai, have found tools that fall in a class of artefacts called Acheulian that scientists believe were invented by Homo Erectus in Africa about 1.6 million years ago. According to Michael Petraglia, the Oxford-based expert in Asian prehistoric archaeology, this means that soon after early humans invented the Acheulian tools, they crossed formidable geographical barriers to get to southern Asia. Pappu and her colleagues assigned dates to the Attirampakkam tools by analyzing traces of certain elements embedded in them and by correlating the archaeological layers excavated at the site with changes in the earth's magnetic field. In the past, some researchers had attributed the flow of Acheulian tools into southern Asia and Europe to the Homo Heidelbergensis, another ancestor of modern humans but one that appeared long after the Homo Erectus. But the 1.5 million year date assigned to the Attirampakkam tools suggests that groups of Homo Erectus carried the tool-making culture into India. The tools in Attirampakkam suggest that the Homo Erectus carried Acheulian culture into India before the Homo Heidelbergensis carried this tool making culture into Europe, where the earliest sites are about 600,000 years old.

Source: G.S. Mudur, 'Million year old tools found near Chennai – India's prehistory pushed back', in *The Telegraph*, Calcutta, India, 25 March 2011.

micro-blades, triangles, trapezes, crescents and arrowheads, all extremely sharp at their cutting face and truly effective weapons. The earliest evidence of these microliths in south Asia comes from sites in Sri Lanka dating back to 26,000 BCE. The sites on the Indian mainland that have been explored in detail include Bagor in Rajasthan, Langnaj in Gujarat, Sarai Nahar Rai, Mahadaha and Damdama in the Gangetic plains, and Adamgarh, Bhimbetka and Ghagharia in central India (Chakrabarti 1999: 100–10; Coningham 2005: 522–3). The microliths found at all these sites date from a much more recent period than 26,000 BCE. The microlith helps us to interpret life in the Mesolithic as an advance on the Palaeolithic. It was functionally a more useful tool than a large stone pebble because it could be hafted to many other tools, for instance to make knives or scissors. By the use of arrowheads, too, animals could be killed from a distance, reducing the chance

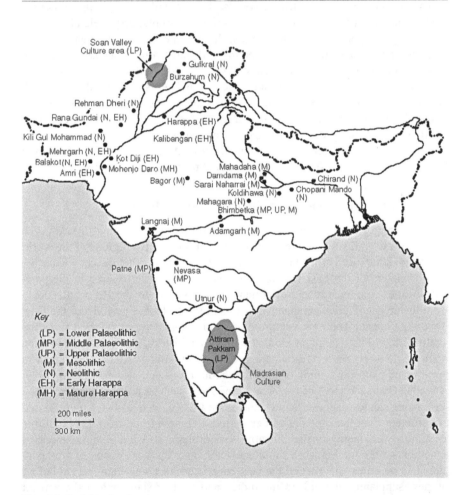

Map 2.1 Prehistoric sites

of their attacking the hunter. The production of microliths depended upon the availability of stones that could be easily flaked, such as quartz, chert or other types of chalcedony (precious stones). As pebble stones became less important, a shift in habitat, from river sites to hills and forests, can be detected. Seasonal mobility has also been noticed in relation to the movement of people between the Gangetic plains and the Vindhya escarpments in central India. Animals generally moved during the winter from the plains to the hills, and the people followed game, taking shelter in hill caves. The reverse movement occurred during the hot season, when people would be able to augment their subsistence with the plant resources of the plains. The discovery of many querns and stone rings at different sites attest to a primitive form of cultivation. Ring stones were probably used as weights on the ends of digging sticks. Animal bones of cows, sheep and goats found in the habitation areas indicate the domestication of animals, but the bones of such other animals as deer, boar and ostrich have also been found among adjacent debris. Within a number of habitation areas are burial sites containing skeletal remains, as well as grave goods such as microliths, shells and even an ivory pendant. This suggests a belief in an afterlife or some form of status consciousness. We cannot be sure. Human remains have been studied, and some of them show signs of osteoarthritis (Thapar 2002: 73). There were, however, some burial sites which were just in middens with rubbish, as in Sri Lanka. Good examples of rock art, accurately depicting animal bodies and human figures, have been discovered across a wide extent of the Indian landscape, at cave sites as far afield as Kerala and Kashmir. There is greater rock-art sophistication at the Bhimbhetka site during the Mesolithic and the Neolithic periods (Chakrabarti 1999: 110–16).

The Neolithic Revolution and the rise of agriculture

Although there was no clear-cut shift from hunting and gathering to farming, a transition was gradually but clearly occurring in four or five regions of the world at around 8000 BCE. This happened after the end of what is known as the Pleistocene era or the Last Ice Age. The retreat of the ice ushered in the post-glacial time – the most recent of climatic eras – known as the Holocene epoch. From the archaeological perspective, it was in the Holocene period that the New Stone Age began. The new venture of farming is sometimes referred to as the Neolithic Revolution, a major landmark in human history, when men and women in Egypt, Mesopotamia, Mesoamerica, China and parts of south Asia began to domesticate plants and animals and learn about crops and seasons (Fagan 1999: 115–53). The stone tools of the New Stone Age, such as polished ground-stone axes, stone sickles, hammer stones and stone blades, were also far more varied and efficient than those of the earlier periods. The evidence from the Neolithic sites, however, suggests that farming, pastoralism and the establishment of settlements did not all emerge simultaneously; developments occurred gradually and, at some times, the old and the new co-existed for a very long period before the new supplanted the old. In the Indian and south Asian context the earliest archaeological evidence of the Neolithic period dates back to almost 11,000 BCE, the end of the Ice Age, but the evidence for the farming and domestication of animals ranges between 7000 BCE and 1000 BCE at different sites. It is, arguably, also believed that the very first farmers of south Asia, in Baluchistan, might have come from Mesopotamia and the Fertile Crescent (Diamond 1998: 101, 181).

Main Neolithic regional concentrations

The Neolithic sites are spread out across the subcontinent, but there are four particular concentrations of sites that help us identify regional similarities and dissimilarities (Coningham 2005: 525–8). The first concentration of Neolithic farming villages is found in Baluchistan, in the vicinity of the Bolan River and its pass, which links the uplands with the plains of the River Indus. The clearest evidence of the development of a farming and pastoral community in this part of the subcontinent is provided by the remains of mud-built structures, chert blades, barley and wheat seeds, and bones of sheep, goats and cattle. The key site is that of the village of Mehrgarh, where, since the 1970s, extensive archaeological excavations have unearthed some of the earliest strata dating back to 7000 BCE (Jarrige and Meadow 1980: 102–10; Jarrige 1982: 79–84). The other linked sites are those of Kili Gul Mohammad and Rana Ghundai. The second concentration of sites is to be found in the Kashmir and Swat valleys of Pakistan. At sites such as Burzahom and Gufkral there is evidence present of Neolithic farming settlements, consisting of the usual Neolithic implements, ceramics and faunal remains. Additionally, there have been discovered peculiar bell-shaped pits, nearly 15 feet in diameter and 13 feet in depth. It has been suggested that these pits served as underground dwellings for humans or as burial hoard sites, and that the people here might have had links with the Central Asian Neolithic communities that dug similar pits. This is still a subject of speculation among the excavators, some of whom think that the pits could have been grain stores or merely gigantic refuse dumps (Bahn 1996: 252; Coningham 2005: 526). The third concentration of sites is located in a very wide area covering the Gangetic basin and stretching into eastern India. Here, some of the Neolithic remains are pre-farming sites, indicating a continuity of the Mesolithic and the Neolithic eras. At certain sites, however, such as Chopani Mando, Mahagara, Koldihawa and Chirand, we have distinct evidence of farming and the domestication of animals taking place around the fourth millennium BCE. The remains of rice grains have been found, but there is continuing debate as to whether rice cultivation was an indigenous development or whether it entered the subcontinent from east and south-east Asia sometime during the second millennium BCE (Allchin and Allchin 1982: 118; Chakrabarti 2004: 18; Coningham 2005: 527). This controversy is alluded to in **Excerpt 2.3** below.

The fourth regional concentration of Neolithic sites is in south India. There, at such a site as Utnur, huge deposited ash mounds have been found. Most probably there were stockades where cattle were seasonally brought and tamed, and the ash mounds could be the result of the burning of successive phases of stockades or pens. In the many open-air settlements of south India, traditional Neolithic tools

Excerpt 2.3 Major crop types: native or foreign?

The controversy among botanists and plant agricultural specialists about whether rice was a native Indian plant or whether it was imported from China is further fuelled by the evidence provided by the great American physiologist and biologist Jared Diamond, who said that all the main cereals consumed by the Indians were first domesticated elsewhere. They include wheat, barley, rice, sorghum and millet. Most probably, apart from rice, these cereals arrived from the Fertile Crescent (Mesopotamia). Diamond agrees that pulses such as hyacinth beans and black and green gram, along with cucumber, cotton and flax, are Indian domesticates. In the case of cotton, Diamond's evidence confirms Jarrige's conclusions about the earliest cotton seeds being found at Mehrgarh. Diamond, however, is quite categorical about the importance of the Fertile Crescent when he writes that:

... even for those crops whose wild ancestor does occur outside of Southwest Asia, we can be confident that the crops of Europe and India were mostly obtained from Southwest Asia and were not local domesticates.

Source: Jared Diamond, *Guns, Germs and Steel:
A Short History of Everybody for the Last 13,000 Years*,
London: Vintage, 1998, 182; see also 126–7, 181–2.

such as polished stone axes and stone blades, along with the remains of pulses, millets and local tubers, provide evidence of a distinct regional farming and pastoral culture (Kachroo 2000: 80; Coningham 2005: 527–8).

The socio-economic consequences of agriculture

Some of the consequences of the rise of agriculture applied universally. One of them was a sharper divergence between the nomadic ways of the hunter-gatherers and the sedentary lifestyle of the cultivators of land. The latter became increasingly dominant in all areas as, compared with the efforts of the hunter-gatherers, they garnered greater rewards for themselves by the more intensive use of a limited amount of land (Diamond 1998: 88; Thapar 2002: 59–60). Technological innovations too, such as irrigation, ploughing and, much later on in India, terracing in hill regions, helped produce sizeable surpluses of food, and this, with the general predictability of food supplies, resulted in the increase of the agricultural population. Yet it would take many millennia after 7000 BCE before the hunter-gatherers became truly marginal figures in the Indian landscape. For a long time, the farmers and hunter-gatherers maintained contact, because the former needed forest produce and honey. As agriculture involved both the cultivation of land and the nurturing of domesticated animals, the cultivators co-laboured seasonally with the settled and semi-nomadic pastoralists. After the harvest the herders brought their cattle, sheep and goats to feed on the stubble, and the animal manure helped to fertilise the land. The barter of essential items normally took place between the cultivators and the pastoralists. Both materially benefited through the exchange of surplus cereals, milk, meat and animal skins. In time, the surplus came to be exchanged with the artefacts and produce of those who were neither peasants nor pastoralists but craftsmen. And eventually the process of exchange came to be increasingly facilitated by another class of people, the traders. While the hunter-gatherers lived a day-to-day existence, the agriculturists could enjoy incremental levels of prosperity. The remains of pots and pans, beads, shells and assorted jewellery that have been discovered in Baluchistan and the Indus basin, the very first areas of farming in South Asia, testify to this diversity from at least the sixth millennium BCE (Chakrabarti 2004: 24). Agriculture helped to establish permanent habitations and settlements that, in turn, became identified with the founding of communities. The concepts of identity, ethnicity and ancestry became meaningful in the context of agricultural communities (Scarre 2005: 190–2). Within such communities, family kinship became a unifying factor among groups bound by marriage ties, and within families there emerged gifted or powerful personalities, on whom the task of leadership devolved. The development of hereditary leadership could also be traced to this stage. The social complexity became more marked with status-seeking by particular families within a community. The remains of grave goods are an indication of this particular trend. A negative element of the social complexity engendered by settled agricultural communities was warfare. The main contentious issue was land. In contrast to the hunter-gatherers, who roamed over vast tracts of land that belonged to no particular clans, the agriculturists had to be protective of their land, or risk losing it to raiding parties of nomadic pastoralists or enemy clans. The remains of defensive enclosures or skeletons of bodies impaled with weapons indicate degrees of violent conflict among both Neolithic and post-Neolithic agricultural people.

Development of proto-urban settlements in the late Neolithic period

While, as we mentioned earlier, Neolithic farming communities and villages have been found in four different regions of the subcontinent, those in the north-western corner hold the key to explaining the next phase in the sequence of South Asian history: early urbanism. The transformation of village communities into proto-urban dwellers took place essentially in the north-west. This process would take us up to the first phase of the Harappan civilisation: the Early Harappan phase, also called the Era of Regionalisation, which was a prelude to its mature phase. The term 'Harappan', referring to the great city-settlement of Harappa in the Punjab, is frequently used to describe collectively the styles and features of monuments and artefacts from the entire Harappan–Indus–Sarasvati civilisation to which the city belonged. Since the antecedents of this civilisation go back to the late

Neolithic times, the development of village settlements into proto-urban forms may be said to be part of the story of the Early Harappan period. It was believed, almost until the mid-twentieth century, that the urban civilisation of the Indus could not have developed indigenously, and that it must have had foreign origins, probably Mesopotamian. The archaeological researches since the 1970s have disproved this thesis (Chakrabarti 2004: 8–9; Coningham 2005: 529). The early archaeologists had paid little attention to the varying ecological and geographical conditions of the many different sites in the entire north-west zone; the focus of their research was very much on the metropolitan cities themselves rather than on the evolution of human occupation before the rise of the cities. Many post-war archaeologists, however, excavated at different and remote sites and, after uncovering layer after layer of habitation levels, have provided us with a unique understanding of the historical sequences of the evolution of human societies before mature urbanism took place. They have shown how, at a number of sites throughout the area, the people of the north-west of the Indian subcontinent ultimately progressed from a Neolithic state of existence to a more sophisticated urban cultural lifestyle of the Copper/Bronze Chalcolithic Age. The roots of the Indus cities lie, therefore, not outside the subcontinent but within.

Within the north-west, the relevant areas for understanding the rural to urban transition are Baluchistan (the key sites being Mehrgarh, Kili Gul Mohammad, Rana Ghundai and Balakot), Sind (the key sites being Amri and Kot Diji), the plains of western Punjab (the key site of Harappa), the Gomal valley (the key site of Rehman Dheri) and the Ghaggar–Hakra valley (the key site of Kalibangan) which runs through the states of Rajasthan and Haryana in modern India. These sites were more than villages, and the clues to their incipient urbanism lie in the relative sizes of their ground plans, the remains of foundations of their houses and streets, household effects, tools and valuable grave goods, and the varied types of pottery manufactures (see Figure 2.1). These sites most often lay on or near agriculturally fertile land and along the trade routes. Chronologically speaking, they vary in antiquity. There is a general consensus among the archaeologists that the Mature Harappan period lasted from about 2600 to 1900 BCE, and that the development phase before 2600 BCE should be designated as Early Harappan, not pre-Harappan, because of the continuity of the tradition (Thapar 2002: 80). On the other hand, it would be too simplistic to call the very early farming phase in the seventh millennium BCE Early Harappan. A compromise could be that the period from *c.* 7000 BCE to 4500 BCE should be called the Baluchistan phase, because of the importance of Mehrgarh, the oldest site documented thus far; that the years from 4500 to 3500 BCE should be considered an age of transition; and that the period between about 3500 and 2600 BCE should be called the Early Harappan phase – or, according to the American historian Jim Shaffer, an Era of Regionalisation (Kochhar 2000: 193; Coningham 2005: 528). Although an increasing amount of data is available from many sites, chosen here are four sites – Mehrgarh, Amri, Kot Diji and Kalibangan – which provide differential evidence of proto-urban features over nearly four and a half millennia (7000 BCE to 2600 BCE) before the Mature period began.

Figure 2.1 Early Harappan pottery fragments

Four proto-urban sites

The most ancient site is that of Mehrgarh in Baluchistan. Owing to the findings of major excavations there in 1974, under Jean-François Jarrige and his Franco-Pakistani team, it provides evidence of links between the Neolithic society and the Mature Harappan culture (Chakrabarti 1999: 120–6; Maisels 2010: 40–4). Nowhere else in the Indian subcontinent does a site exist that offers such an important glimpse into the previous 4,500 years before 2500 BCE when the Harappan metropolis of Mohenjo Daro was at its zenith. The geographical position of Mehrgarh is particularly worth examining. The site lies at the foot of the Bolan Pass on the Bolan River, a tributary of the Indus, at a distance of 250 kilometres north-west of Mohenjo Daro. This means that it belongs to the Indus drainage system, although it is located within the Kachi plain of Baluchistan. The alluvium and floodwaters of the Bolan River and Indus basin made the Mehrgarh site suitable for farming. The seeds of wild and domesticated species of barley, einkorn, emmer and wheat, along with the fruit stones of jujube (zizphus) and date palms, have been found. The presence of einkorn and emmer indicate that domesticated crops might have been introduced by population movement from the west. This is credible if we consider the whole of the Near East, Iran and the Afghan–Baluch region as the 'nuclear zone' for domestication and accept the view that the 'early Holocene peoples across this vast region, from the Mediterranean to the Indus, were engaged in the development of food-producing practices at that time' (Possehl 2002: 28). Also, since the Bolan Pass is, like the Khyber Pass, one of the important access points between India and Afghanistan, Mehrgarh was strategically located on a historical route linking the Indus valley with the Iranian plateau, leading on to central and west Asia (Chakrabarti 2004: 24). It is worth noting that the discovery of some very early bead ware of precious stone, such as lapis lazuli, would indicate that the people of Mehrgarh were trading even during the earliest period of their history (Ray *et al.* 2000: 560–3).

The Mehrgarh site consists of six mounds spread over an area of approximately 500 acres. This was a large site, but as the habitation focus shifted over time each period covered only a small section of that. Archaeologists have named the oldest mound MR3, where they have uncovered evidence of continuous human occupation from about 7000 to 4700 BCE (Kochhar 2000: 60–5). The greater antiquity of Mehrgarh's Period I can be appreciated by comparing it with that of our next site, Amri, where Period I begins only at 3500 BCE. Six other periods followed Period I at Mehrgarh, bringing the chronology down to 2300 BCE. During their seven periods of history, until 2300 BCE, the Mehrgarhians were improving their skills and arts to a level that eventually matched that of the Mature Harappa society. Their pottery, copper ware, figurines and various other ornaments show a people striving towards a state of advancement and perfection by experimenting, innovating and improvising rather than by imitating foreign models. Some of the oldest cotton seeds have been recovered from the mounds of Mehrgarh, again raising the possibility of the first cotton-manufacturing processes having occurred in the Indus zone. A recent report from the Human Biology Department of the University of Rome also credits the people of Mehrgarh with the skills of dentistry (McMahon 2006). The importance of the Mehrgarh discoveries has totally changed our perception of the origin of Harappan culture, as explained in **Excerpt 2.4** below.

If Period I at Mehrgarh dates from 7000 BCE, the equivalent at Amri, on the west bank of the Indus, dates only from 3500 BCE. The earliest phase, covering the first 500 years, is known as the Amri Culture (Khan 1964: 55–9; Allchin and Allchin 1982: 141–3). The remains of this culture include the ruins of very rough, low-level rectangular houses with mud flooring, which were just a few inches higher than the outside level, along with red earthenware jars, black and red hand-moulded pottery and a few scraps of copper, blades, bangles and stone tools. Definite advances in pottery styles and the design of houses are noticeable from Period II (3000 to 2700 BCE). Period III was when Amri was part of the Mature Harappan age, lasting from about 2700 to 2400 BCE, when it reached its highest point of

Excerpt 2.4 Evidence from Mehrgarh

Even as skilled an archaeologist as Sir Mortimer Wheeler refused to acknowledge the usefulness of evidence from Baluchistan in explaining the rise of the Harappa/Indus civilisation. The silent ruins of Mehrgarh would have remained ignored, and our archaeological understanding would have been that much poorer, if J.F. Jarrige had not launched his excavation there.

Based on the presence of ceramic styles similar to types known from Central Asia in southern Turkmenistan, some archaeologists believed that developments in South Asia were the result of external influences. The evidence from Mehrgarh has changed all of that, since the site predates the Central Asian settlements, demonstrating that it was a centre of innovation with a long and extended sequence of development. As J.F. Jarrige has pointed out, we now consider similarities of material culture with those in Central Asia to be the result of cultural interaction not diffusion.

Source: Rita P. Wright, *The Ancient Indus: Urbanism, Economy and Society*, New York: Cambridge University Press, 2010, 77.

urbanism. It was the time when larger houses, constructed from adobe bricks of standardised design, were built, and wheel-turned pottery, with strong individualistic design styles, was popular (Ray *et al.* 2000: 169–71). The rise of Mohenjo Daro, however, was bound to lead to the eclipse of sites like Amri, and in Period IV, or the Late Harappan period, the evidence points to an overall decline. From the four archaeological periods of Amri we can again trace a sequence of styles, skills and developments that document for us the pointers towards Harappan maturity.

The site of Kot Diji in Sind also provides us with unique examples of a culture developing into an urban form. Here first, between about 3200 and 2600 BCE, a major ceramic industry developed, and the Kot Diji ceramic style reached sites as far apart as Rehman Dheri, Amri and Kalibangan. The conspicuous feature of this style was the wheel-thrown globular jar of red ware with decorative motifs such as fish-scales and *pipal* leaves (Khan 1964: 41–4, 49–55). The plain and painted terracotta bangles, cattle figurines, cones, beads of semi-precious stones and many objects of shell and bone testify to a standard of living far advanced of that of the people who inhabited the early Neolithic villages. Kot Diji possessed an important feature of urbanism that both Amri and Mehrgarh lacked: a fortified citadel complex, along with a lower town (Chakrabarti 2004: 26). This pattern of layout in the central area of a settlement was a key pointer to similar planning at the metropolitan sites of Mohenjo Daro and Harappa.

The site of Kalibangan, nearly 300 kilometres north-west of Delhi, lay on the banks of the now dry Ghaggar–Hakra River, which once flowed, parallel to the River Indus, in the east through Rajasthan and Haryana. A number of Indian historians refer to this river by the name of *Sarasvati*. It dried up in around 1000 CE, but within its drainage system have been discovered many of the densest settlement clusters of very early villages, going back to nearly 3800 BCE. The later urban Indus civilisation indeed emerged out of the hard core of these villages. Kalibangan itself is on the northern periphery of the *Sarasvati* basin and its maximum area would have covered approximately 20 hectares, or 50 acres, of land (Coningham 2005: 533). Its antiquity does not match that of Mehrgarh, but its remains indicate a clear line of development from the late Neolithic proto-urban to the Mature Harappan phase. A citadel mound and the lower town anticipate what was found at Mohenjo Daro (Chapter 3); the archaeologists have also uncovered an Early Harappan settlement under the citadel mound that indicates a similar ground plan (Bala 2004: 35–6; Coningham 2005: 531). The fortification wall was made of mass-produced mud bricks of standard size and proportion. Both the inner and the outer faces of this wall were plastered with mud. From the foundation remains of houses it may be surmised that each house had three or four rooms. Many useful household items, such as ovens and storage pits, have been excavated. Some of the antiquities discovered include chalcedony blades, carnelian, faience, gold and silver beads and pottery of various designs. The predominant pottery was red or pink, with black and white painting, and on some of the pottery there was also non-scriptural graffiti that may be seen to anticipate the Mature Harappan script (Bala 2004: 39).

STUDY GUIDE

Key issues

- The Out-of-Africa theory of the migration of the Homo Sapiens.
- Tools and technology of the pre-Neolithic humans.
- Farming in the Neolithic period.
- Stages in the Neolithic evolution of settlements.
- The hierarchy of pre-Harappan settlements.

Suggested readings

Scarre 2005: 46–83, 124–73, 518–51; Wright 2010: 45–78.

INTERNET SELECTION

1) R. Dennell and M. Petraglia, 'The dispersal of Homo Sapiens across southern Asia: how early, how often, how complex?' www.academia.edu/836550/the-dispersal-of-homo-sapiens-across-etc

2)   Shanti Pappu, 'Prehistoric antiquities and personal lives: the untold story of Robert Bruce Foote'. www.academia.edu/8832866/Prehistoric-antiquities-and-persoanl-lives-the-untold-etc

3)   M. Petraglia, 'Out of Africa: new hypothesis and evidence for the dispersal of Homo Sapiens along the Indian Ocean rim'. www.academia.edu/482427/out-of-Africa-new-hypothesis-and-etc

4)   T.S. Subramanian, 'A discovery that changed the antiquity of humankind who lived in the Indian subcontinent'. www.thehindu.com/news/national/a-discovery-that-changed-the-antiquity-etc

QUESTIONS FOR GROUP DISCUSSION

1)   What are the qualities required of a good archaeologist?
2)   How would genetics help to understand the origins of South Asians?
3)   In the context of world history, what is the significance of the 1974 Mehrgarh excavations carried out by Jean-François Jarrige and his team?
4)   In terms of archaeological finds, what differences would an archaeologist notice between Period I and, say, Period V?
5)   Apart from farming, make a list of five major developments during the Neolithic era.

3   The Harappan–Indus–Sarasvati civilisation

(*c.* 2600 to 1700 BCE)

Timeline/Key Dates

c. 2600 BCE	The beginnings of Mature Harappan culture
c. 2500–1900 BCE	Harappan civilisation at its height in Mohenjo Daro and Harappa
c. 1900–1700 BCE	The steady decline of the Harappan culture
c. 1700–1300 BCE	Late Harappan phase
CE 1920–34	Archaeological excavations at Mohenjo Daro and Harappa
CE 1947	Mortimer Wheeler's publication of the incorrect Aryan invasion theory
CE 1960–9	Kalibangan excavated
CE 1974	Mehrgarh archaeological excavations

The Harappan civilisation, which reached its mature phase with the great cities of Harappa and Mohenjo Daro, was the culmination of a long and sustained cultural evolution that took place in the plains, valleys and surrounding regions of a mighty river in the north-west of India: the Indus. This river, with its many tributaries, is still the lifeline of Punjab and Sind – being the basis of their agricultural prosperity – but its importance in world history cannot be overstated. Just as three of the world's oldest civilisations grew along the banks of their great rivers – the Egyptian on the Nile, the Mesopotamian on the Tigris–Euphrates, and the Chinese on the Yangtse – similarly, along the banks of the Indus developed the first major civilisation of the Indian subcontinent. This is the reason why some historians also talk of the Indus civilisation. It may even be said that this term is a more accurate appellation than the term 'Harappan', as it covers a wider span of space and time in reference to both the underlying culture and the resulting urban stage of an entire region. Some scholars also like to use the term '*Sarasvati*' for the name of the civilisation (Maisels 2010: 48–56). They point out that the core culture of the cities of Mohenjo Daro and Harappa, which actually lay on the periphery, developed out of a more dense and substantial cluster of villages and settlements that had existed along the banks of other nearby rivers, the now dried up Ghaggar–Hakra, also called the *Sarasvati*, and the *Drasadvati*. The evidence of these settlements is drawn from the earliest of the Old Indian Vedic literature and from the various modern geological and archaeological surveys (Chakrabarti 2004: 9). Whichever term may be adopted, the fact remains that the area covered by the culture and tradition based on the Indus and other rivers was vast, embracing practically the whole of modern Pakistan and north-west India, along with modern Gujarat (see Map 3.1). The mature urban phase of this civilisation lasted between about 2600 and 1900 BCE but, as noted in Chapter 2, the antecedent of this phase, the Early Harappan, was in the making at least a thousand years before 2600 BCE. Indeed, the very first roots of this civilisation go back even further, through the Baluchistan phase, to 7000 BCE, the earliest date assigned to the findings at Mehrgarh in Baluchistan. Although the great cities of the Indus had markedly declined by 1900 BCE, the cultural influence of this civilisation continued in a modified manner for another few centuries after that date.

From the hindsight of history, one would like to think that the legacy of this civilisation would have been acknowledged, remembered and cherished by at least the thinking and literate section of the Indian population during the subsequent four millennia. Unfortunately, apart from the sparse clues that one may seek in the early Vedic texts, no one seemed to have remembered, or cared to remember, anything about the culture or achievements of the Harappans until the twentieth century. The change came only after the groundbreaking discoveries of the ruins at Mohenjo Daro (see Figure 3.1) and Harappa in the 1920s. Historians then radically revised their interpretation of early Indian history in two stages. During the first stage, in the 1920s and the 1930s, they acknowledged that the history of India was much older than they had expected. The belief, prevalent until that time, that Indian civilisation started with the Aryans sometime around 1500 BCE had to be discarded, and the new consensus was that it went back to at least 3000 BCE. Although historians confirmed the revised chronology, there was nevertheless a certain amount of doubt nurtured concerning the origins of the Harappan civilisation, and some wondered whether it was an imported model from Mesopotamia (Gadd and Smith 1924/1979: 109–10; Dales 1968/1979: 138–44). These doubts were put to rest by research from the 1970s (Jarrige 1982: 79–84). As noted in Chapter 2, this research has clearly indicated that the roots of the Harappan civilisation go back to the Neolithic villages of Baluchistan, as at Mehrgarh, and there is no evidence of the Mesopotamian or any other foreign influence in at least the shaping of the mature phase of this civilisation. This did not, however, imply that the Harappan civilisation was built on Vedic culture – actually the next phase in Indian history – as some modern revisionists are keen to claim, as in **Excerpt 3.1**. These revisionists have a tendency to overstate their case (e.g. Frawley and Rajaram 1995, or Mishra 2004). Although some of the features of the Harappan culture can be slightly detected within Vedic culture (Sastri 1957: 15–24; Sastri 1965: 92–147), there can be little doubt that the former was essentially pre-Vedic and non-Vedic, but indigenous, as the pioneer archaeologist Sir John Marshall affirmed (Kochhar 2000: 198ff., Chakrabarti 2004: 8;). Chapter 4 takes up this discussion further.

Excerpt 3.1 The claim of the Indus civilisation being a Vedic civilisation

This claim is made by some Indian historians essentially on the basis of the Puranas (see Chapter 8) being accepted as a credible source of Indian chronology. The Puranas *provide long lists of ancient dynasties; the so-called Uttanapada dynasty of Manu Swayambhuba of the tenth millennium BCE is considered the first of the dynasties that continue for thousands of years. The* Puranas *are certainly a valuable source of general knowledge for the historians but, as there is no archaeological or any other type of evidence for claiming a continuity of Indian kingship from such an early period, we need to treat what is written in the* Puranas *with a degree of caution. The claim is also based on the false belief that no waves of migrants entered India after the tenth millennium BCE. Despite its intellectual weaknesses, this claim has much resonance among a large number of Hindu religious nationalists imbued with the idea of* Hindutva. *The following passage gives a flavour of this revisionist version of history.*

> The Indus Civilization was essentially a Vedic Civilization . . . That since in India there was a continuity of Kingship from Manu onwards to Candragupta there could have been no 'Aryan' invasion or migration, at least unknown to the closest neighbours, the Persians. Since the majority of the people of this part of the world belonged to the eastern branch of the Mediterranean race from about the 9th or 10th millennium BC, the people of the Indus cities also belonged to the same race, as also the Vedic Indians and, consequently, there can be no question of 'pre-Aryan' or 'non-Aryan' orientation of this civilization. The Indus people belonged to one of the Vedic tribes or 'Janas' and were essentially Indian with Vedic culture. In the circumstances, there could have been no invasion of 'Aryans' or 'Indo-Europeans' into India as professed by occidental orientalists. Hence the Indic Civilization was Rig-Vedic Civilization.
>
> **Source:** A.N. Chandra, *The Rig-Vedic Culture and the Indus Civilisation*, Calcutta: Ratna Prakashan, 1980, 218.

Phases of progress in Harappan archaeology

The story of Harappan archaeology, although perhaps not as romantic or nostalgic as those of Egypt and Mesopotamia, is a remarkable story of scholarly and persevering endeavour in the task of uncovering the forgotten past. A large number of sites, of varying extent, have been excavated in the geographical and cultural zone of the north-west of the subcontinent. The excavations and the

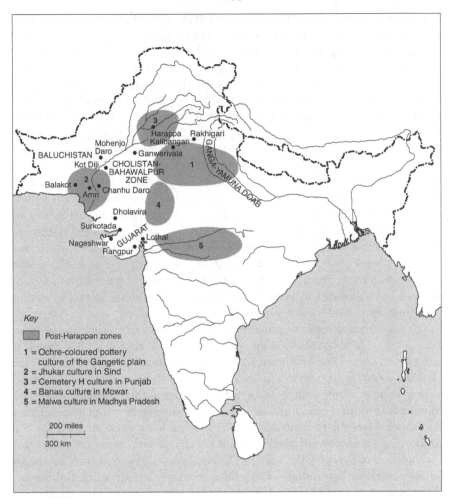

Map 3.1 Mature Harappan sites and post-Harappan zones

unearthing of some astonishing finds have taken place in four major phases, and each phase is distinguished by the remarkable work of one or more archaeologists at one or more specific sites.

The first phase covered the nineteenth century (Pande 1982: 395; Possehl 1982: 406–8). The earliest pioneer was Charles Masson, whose real name was James Lewis. He was actually an English soldier who deserted from the East India Company's army. In his new guise he travelled in the 1820s to the Punjab, where he first encountered the remains of Harappa. He described the site as a 'ruinous brick castle' (Pande 1982: 395; Time-Life Books 1994: 9) with high walls and towers, and noticed a large number of fine and standard-size bricks there. He was followed, some years later, by Lieutenant Alexander Burns who, while making a historic journey up the River Indus, also visited Harappa. Burns described its ruins as extensive and calculated that the site was 3 miles in circumference. He too noted that there were a large number of bricks, but that there was not an entire building standing. Earlier on his journey he had also visited the Indus site of Amri, which was to provide crucial evidence for future archaeologists. When the findings of Masson and Burns came to the attention of Sir Alexander Cunningham, the first director general of the Archaeological Survey of India, he decided to visit Harappa himself. He made three expeditions, two in the 1850s and a third in 1873. During the first two visits he could corroborate the evidence of Masson and Burns, but during the 1873 visit he was much disappointed to witness the depletion of huge quantities of bricks. This was because the British engineers, who were building the railway line between Lahore and Multan, had been using the bricks as ballast under the tracks. Cunningham decided to conduct an archaeological survey of Harappa before all the bricks disappeared. One of the first objects that he discovered was a seal made of unpolished but smooth black stone, on which was deeply engraved a bull, without hump, with two stars under the neck, along with an inscription in six characters. This seal, which is now in the British Museum, is the first of hundreds that are inextricably associated with the Harappan culture (Cunningham 1872–73/1979: 102–4).

The second phase began with the appointment in 1902 of a young and brilliant archaeologist, John Marshall, as the new director general of the Archaeological Survey of India (Time-Life Books 1994: 10–14; Bahn 1996: 170–2, 253–8). Marshall owed his appointment to Lord Curzon, the Viceroy of India, who aimed to keep India in subjugation to the British crown, but who also greatly loved and admired her historical monuments and wished to restore them to their ancient glory. He helped Marshall to make his mark by authorising extra funding for the Archaeological Survey. Marshall's interest in Harappa and other similar sites had been aroused not only by the work of Cunningham but also by that of an Italian scholar, Luigi Pio Tessitori, who had written about another site, called Kalibangan (Dolcini and Freschi 1999: 155–63). Marshall ordered a systematic excavation of Harappa in 1914, but the onset of the First World War delayed it. It was only in 1920 that one of his deputies, Dahya Ram Sahni, embarked on it. His work continued until 1925. The results were not encouraging, as there had been much plundering by the railroad authorities, but Sahni found three more seals with further curious pictographic legends.

The first man to see and write about the other prime site, Mohenjo Daro, was D.R. Bhandakrkar. After his visit there in 1911, he wrote the following words, which he must have long regretted afterwards:

> According to the local tradition, these are the ruins of a town only 200 years old ... This seems to be not incorrect, because the bricks here found ... are of the modern type, and there is a total lack of terra-cottas amidst the whole ruins.

> (Possehl 1982: 405)

Fortunately, his pessimistic assessment of the finds at Mohenjo Daro was not universally accepted, and in 1919 R.D. Banerji began excavating there. He came to the conclusion that the site was very ancient and that it would yield many treasures. To start with, he came across three soapstone seals, similar to those found at Harappa. When both the Harappa and Mohenjo Daro seals and other materials were compared, Marshall and his deputies, Sahni and Banerji, became increasingly certain that the two cities were sites from a common historical civilisation that flourished nearly 4,500 years beforehand. On 20 September 1924, there appeared an article in the *Illustrated London News*, in which Marshall boldly stated his opinion thus:

> Not often has it been given to archaeologists, as it was given to Schliemann at Tiryns and Mycenae, or to Stein in the deserts of Turkestan, to light upon the remains of a long-forgotten civilization. It looks, however, at this moment, as if we were on the threshold of such a discovery in the plains of the Indus.

From 1925 to 1927, Marshall, in collaboration with a team of brilliant Indian deputies, such as M.S. Vats and K.N. Dikshit, worked indefatigably with hundreds of labourers on the Mohenjo Daro site. The results of his efforts were astonishing and stupendous. The interpretations of his findings were to have a monumental impact upon the study of Indian history. It has been said that Marshall 'left India two thousand years older than he found it'.

The third major phase opened in 1944 with the appointment of Mortimer Wheeler as director general of the Archaeological Survey (Time-Life Books 1994: 16; Bahn 1996: 256–7). Wheeler brought new methods of controlled stratigraphic excavation and recording – methods which are still used today. He trained a whole new generation of South Asian archaeologists in his methods and expounded many theories about interpreting Harappan history. Most of them are now rejected by the archaeological community. He believed that the very concept of civilisation came to the Indus from Mesopotamia, the land of the Twin Rivers as he called it (Wheeler 1968: 25), but this has now been disproved by the discoveries at places like Mehrgarh and other earlier proto-urban settlements. With his military background during the Second World War, he was keen to designate many of the ruins with military terms, such as 'bastions' or 'citadels', without truly clear evidence. His theory about the demise of the Harappan cities has also been discredited, as we shall find out in the last section of this chapter. Despite his ideas, later proved to be mistaken, Wheeler was greatly respected for preparing the groundwork for post-independence Indian and Pakistani archaeologists. He was also a larger-than-life character who made his workers disciplined and alert to work, as can be testified from **Excerpt 3.2** below.

All decision-making about the Indus archaeology had remained in the hands of British imperial authority during the three phases described above. The situation dramatically changed after 1947, when Britain partitioned India into two self-governing nations, India and Pakistan, and withdrew from the region. The new

Excerpt 3.2 Mortimer Wheeler's first day at work

Mortimer Wheeler's energy and dedication to work were legendary. As soon as his ship arrived at Bombay in 1944 he took a train to Delhi and then to Simla, where his headquarters were established. The efficiency that he generated among his staff can serve as an example to the many complacent officials and bureaucrats who today man the government departments in India. In the following passage he recalls his first day at work.

On the top floor of the gaunt Railway Board building where the Archaeological Survey was then housed at Simla, I stepped over the recumbent forms of peons, past office windows revealing little clusters of idle clerks and hangers-on, to the office which I had taken over that morning ... As I opened my door I turned and looked back. The sleepers had not stirred, and only a wavering murmur like the distant drone of bees indicated the presence of drowsy human organisms within. I emitted a bull-like roar, and the place leapt to anxious life ... One after another my headquarters staff was ushered in, and within an hour the purge was complete. Bowed shoulders and apprehensive glances showed an office working as it had not worked for many a long day. That evening one of the peons (who later became my most admirable Headquarters Jemadar) said tremulously to my deputy's Irish wife, 'Oh, memsahib, a terrible thing has happened to us this day.'

Source: Sir Mortimer Wheeler, *Still Digging*, New York: E.P. Dutton, 1955, 186.

India continued with the Archaeological Survey, while Pakistan created a new Department of Archaeology. Both Indian and Pakistani archaeologists have broken new ground in the region during this post-1947 fourth phase of Indus explorations. Fresh discoveries are continually being reported from an ever broadening area of land in both countries. A 3,500-year-old stone axe engraved with the Harappan script, recently found in Tamil Nadu, for example, indicates a wider Harappan influence in the subcontinent and a closer historical link between the regions of India (Associated Press 2006). The excavations at the site of Dholavira in Gujarat have yielded remarkable results in terms of differences in the ground plans of buildings and monuments etc. A world-class Museum and Centre of Study for Indus Civilisation has also been established at the University of Vadodara in India. These developments will offer new insights into the various phases of the Harappan culture and civilisation. The most critical excavation of the post-war period took place at Mehrgarh in Baluchistan in 1974–75, under the supervision of Jean-François Jarrige, who led a joint Franco-Pakistani team (Jarrige 1982; Time-Life Books 1994: 32–5). It was the work of this team that demonstrated the thread of archaeological continuity from the earliest foundations of Mehrgarh in the seventh millennium BCE to the great cities of the Indus.

The Indus valley research has now begun to attract the attention of scholars in a variety of fields: archaeobotany, geology, anthropology, sociology, biochemistry, marine biology, climatology, comparative history, etc. They wish to study in detail the various facets of the physical, environmental and social evolution of this region, its interaction with neighbouring regions, and its comparative place in world history. While all this is greatly admirable, a note of caution needs to be sounded here. It concerns the motivations of an over-eager band of highly nationalistic Indians whose varied claims lack substantive evidence. Many of them, in their wish to assert the continuity and originality of Hindu civilisation, interpret the finds of the Indus indiscriminately and carelessly. Thus, for example, they overemphasise the importance of the dried-up River *Sarasvati* (its Vedic Sanskritic name viewed with greater fervour than the Perso-Greek name of Indus) in the making of this rich civilisation. While the *Sarasvati* basin no doubt contained many important village clusters, none of the villages is as ancient as Mehrgarh in Baluchistan.

Understanding the Mature Harappan phase

The mature phase is essentially the high urban phase. The rich material evidence dug out from the ground by dedicated teams of specialists and labourers and systematically studied and interpreted by varied archaeologists helps us to reconstruct this urban civilisation and gain an insight into the lives and customs of the Harappans. The evidence from the mature period covers a time-span of some 700 years, but at any particular site one may discover finds from different epochs. This helps to establish the length and the extent of continuity of cultural evolution of the site. The finds are fascinating in themselves, and each has to be examined in a particular way. Some can speak for themselves, for example, the brick walls or children's toys. There is little argument as to their purpose. Other finds need to be interpreted for their special significance, such as a piece of sculpture, a terracotta seal or a recognisable seal motif. These on their own do not describe themselves, but may provide valuable clues to understanding the art, trade and religion of the Harappans. There are also finds which tell us nothing, such as the Harappan script or the peculiarly shaped figurines and strange animals on seals: it is very difficult to investigate them. The problem of the script is particularly frustrating, because our understanding of the Harappans would be so much more enhanced if it could be deciphered. Despite these difficulties, there is sufficient material evidence for us to discuss the characteristics of the mature urban phase of the Harappan civilisation. We must first examine the pattern of settlements.

A hierarchy of settlements and their interaction

Numerous Harappan settlements have been identified in the regions of Sind, Baluchistan, the Cholistan desert in the Bahawalpur district of Pakistan, Haryana, Rajasthan, Gujarat and the upper areas of the Ganges–Yamuna *doab* – the land between the two rivers. A similar settlement has also been found at Shortughai, near the river Oxus, in north Afghanistan (Chakrabarti 2004: 10). Owing to the variability of their size and importance, a four-tier hierarchy of settlement forms has been proposed (Coningham 2005: 533–5). The first tier consists of five very large sites, at Harappa (west Punjab), Mohenjo Daro (Sind), Dholavira (Gujarat), Rakhigari (Haryana) and Ganveriwala (Bahawalpur). Three of these sites each cover an area of 100 hectares, or 250 acres, while each of the other two is 80 hectares, or 200 acres. The discoveries at Harappa and Mohenjo Daro have been treated as benchmarks against which the relative urbanism of other sites can be judged. The second tier consists of thirty-two sites, each of which has an area of about 20 hectares, or 50 acres. Although smaller in size, they have walled enclosures and other architectural features similar to the first-tier sites. The two prominent sites in this tier are Kalibangan (Haryana) and Lothal (Gujarat). A third tier of settlements, more numerous than those of the second, consists of such sites as Surkotada and Kuntasi (both in Gujarat), which cover on average 3 hectares, or 7.5 acres. Aspects of these sites, such as fortifications and their ceramics, provide evidence of a distinct Mature Harappan style. The fourth and lowest tier consists of nearly 15,000 settlements, each covering about 1 hectare, or 2.5 acres. These were either villages or centres for specialised crafts. Balakot (Sind) and Nageshwar (Gujarat) are typical sites.

The apparent prosperity of the larger first-tier settlements greatly depended ultimately upon the smaller settlements of the fourth tier. Since large numbers of the people who populate urban societies live also outside of the inner core, it follows that there was a mutual dependency between the urban and rural Harappans (Wright 2010: 127–36). A number of urbanites might have had their own small plots for cultivation or for keeping animals, but more numerous craft specialists among them depended upon the products of rural areas to support their families. The fourth-tier settlements were the key interacting places, performing many functions. They were first very convenient places for the exchange of goods. They acted as link places, and those that were strategically located along the tributaries of the River Indus, such as Beas, provided a natural corridor between such large sites as Mohenjo Daro and Harappa. Second, they acted as industrial sites for stone-working, metallurgy and pottery manufacture (as testified by a variety of kiln sites). Third, they were used as camp sites by nomadic pastoral groups with large herds of animals. The smaller settlements therefore were a home to those who pursued agriculture, pastoralism or trade, but it would be wrong to assume that they were merely a support mechanism for the sustenance of the larger sites of the first three tiers. Many rural people living within their boundaries were themselves engaged in inter-regional contacts conceivably independent of their connections with larger centres.

Civic planning and structures

Even before any digging had begun at the two cities of Harappa and Mohenjo Daro, the first archaeologists were already being introduced to the urban splendours of the Indus people through the hundreds and thousands of bricks that they saw stacked or scattered about on the ground. While the brick stocks of Harappa were much depleted owing to railway depredation, those in Mohenjo Daro were massive. There were many mud bricks that belonged to the period before the middle of the third millennium BCE, but the ones that truly fascinated the archaeologists were those from about 2600 BCE onwards. They were bricks baked in kilns fired with charcoal from the wood of the dense forests which, at that time, must have been plentiful throughout the Indus valley. These perfectly shaped baked kiln bricks were all of a standard size, measuring 7 x 14 x 28 cm, with the ratio of thickness to width and to length being 1: 2: 4. After the top layers of debris and overgrowth had been cleared, what emerged at Mohenjo Daro, particularly, was nothing short of spectacular (Marshall 1923–24/1979: 181–6). There appeared, from below, the ruins of an entire city, extremely well planned and divided into sectors or mounds. In the west there was a high citadel mound with strong fortifications, and in the east was the lower city with smaller mounds. On the citadel mound there were the ruins of two or three large public buildings. One is thought to be a granary; another might have been a great hall; the most spectacular and the best known is called the Great Bath. This structure is unique to Mohenjo Daro, and there is nothing like it in the entire ancient world. Its description by Marshall himself is in **Excerpt 3.3** below.

In the lower city, the streets were arranged in grid patterns, with major north–south and east–west streets intersecting each other, while numerous smaller streets and alleyways criss-crossed them. In between them were constructed blocks of houses, none of which opened onto the main streets. A feature of houses, public buildings and streets that fascinates the modern observer or tourist was a system of relatively clean water supply to the inhabitants, along with latrine facilities by which the waste was channelled off without coming into contact with clean water (Kenoyer 1998: 58–62). Each house had its own well, and one authority has calculated that there were nearly 700 wells in the city. A more detailed calculation of water supply comes from the Gujarati settlement of Dholavira, far from Mohenjo Daro. There, for a population of approximately 4,000 people, just over 14 gallons of water per person per day was available (Maisels 2010: 71). Owing to wells, cisterns and reservoirs, the citizens of Mohenjo Daro, Dholavira and other metropolitan settlements had had sufficient water for drinking, cooking, bathing and cleaning. What they enjoyed 4,500 years ago is denied to many millions in India and Pakistan today in the twenty-first century.

What has been discovered at Mohenjo Daro is also noticed at other major sites. With a few exceptions, most of these sites possess a raised citadel sector in the west and a lower town in the east, burnt-brick or mud-brick houses, a drainage system and fairly straight wide streets intersecting narrow lanes. We do, however, notice certain distinct architectural features in other Harappan settlements. Harappa, for example, does not have a citadel mound, but has a unique set of circular brick platforms, supposedly for threshing grain (Time-Life Books 1994: 19). The remains at Lothal reveal an artificial platform with streets and houses along with, arguably, either a unique brick dockyard connected by a channel leading to the Gulf of Cambay, or a bath or a fresh water reservoir (Leshnik 1968/1979: 203–10; Chakrabarti 2004: 15). One of the most interesting sites, Dholavira, contained three

Excerpt 3.3 The Great Bath at Mohenjo Daro

The following extract provides clear evidence of the excellence of the architecture of the Great Bath, and it is also a good example of Marshall's precision in his description of this wondrous treasure of the ancient world.

The Great Bath ... was part of what appears to have been a vast hydropathic establishment and the most imposing of all the remains unearthed at Mohenjo Daro. Its plan is simple: in the centre, an open quadrangle with verandahs on its four sides, and at the back of three of the verandahs various galleries and rooms; on the south, a long gallery with a small chamber in each corner; on the east, a single range of small chambers, including one with a well; on the north, a group of several halls and fair-sized rooms. In the midst of the open quadrangle is a large swimming bath, some 39 feet long by 23 feet broad and sunk about 8 feet below the paving of the court, with a flight of steps at either end, and at the foot of each a low platform for the convenience of bathers, who might otherwise have found the water too deep. The bath was filled from the well in Chamber 16 and possibly from other wells besides, and the waste water was carried off through a covered drain near the S.W. corner, the corbelled roof of which is some 6 ft 6 in. in height ... for careful and massive construction the Great Bath could hardly have been improved upon. From N. to S. its overall measurement is 180 ft, from E. to W. 108 ft. The outer walls were between 7 and 8 ft in thickness at the base, with a batter on the outside of about 6 ft; the inner walls for the most part about half as much ... the actual lining of the tank was made of finely dressed brick laid in gypsum mortar, between 3 and 4 ft in thickness. Backing this was an inch thick damp-proof course of bitumen, which was kept in place and prevented from creeping by another thin wall of burnt brick behind it. Then came a packing of crude brick and behind this again another solid rectangle of burnt brick encompassing the whole, with short cross-walls between it and the verandah foundations in order to counteract any outward pressure ... A more effective method of construction with the materials then available would hardly have been possible, and how well it has stood the test of time is sufficiently apparent from the present state of the tank which, after 5000 years, is still astonishingly well preserved.

Source: Sir John Marshall (ed.), *Mohenjo Daro and the Indus Civilization*, Vol. 1, London: Arthur Probsthain, 1931, 24–5.

Figure 3.1 The Great Bath at Mohenjo Daro

sectors: the castle and bailey sector, the middle sector and the lower town (Chakrabarti 1998: 103–6; Ray *et al.* 2000: 567–9; Chakrabarti 2004: 15–16). It was built of stone, not brick. The citadel there uniquely contained features such as gateways, stairs, corridors, ceremonial routes and guard chambers, none of which has been found at Mohenjo Daro or Harappa. Large reservoirs of water were also integrated into the civic planning at Dholavira (Chakrabarti 1999: 175–6).

Food security, occupations and trading systems

The absence of evidence indicating a unified empire or city-states in the Harappan system does not imply an absence of organisation. The complex civic planning of the settlements of the first three tiers and the standard of living of the people, superior by far to the semi-rural level of the Early Harappan phase, suggest to us a high degree of competency in management and administration by those in authority. The western citadel area was, generally speaking, the headquarters of the elite, although large public buildings have been identified in different parts of the metropolitan cities (Kenoyer 1998: 52). Some major civic affairs were probably organised from there. The paramount concern of those in charge of the large settlements was to ensure a continuous food supply for the inhabitants; this was relatively easy because the larger sites were in proximity to varied geographical zones with rich farming plains, river and coastal fisheries, grazing lands for domestic animals, and dense forests (Kenoyer 1998: 40, 168). Sufficient food was brought into the cities by farmers, who sold it to the state officials overseeing the great granaries. The seeds of wheat, barley, peas, melons, sesame and mustard have all been found, and a number of them have been dated. There is disagreement among the archaeologists as to the identification of the actual granaries, but there can be no doubt that storage depots and food warehouses existed. There is a high probability that there were granaries at both Mohenjo Daro and Harappa, although the two structures were built on different plans. Standardised weights and measures, in graduated sizes and calculated by decimal increments, were used in commercial exchanges between the farmers and the granary officials (Kenoyer 1998: 98–9). There were also stringent trading regulations (Mackay 1948: 103). Animal husbandry was an important aspect of farming, with the faunal bone remains and terracotta animal images indicating the Harappan familiarity with varied types of domesticated and wild animals (Kenoyer 1998: 164–7). We are unsure of the proportion of the meat-consuming classes of people (Mackay 1948: 141–2; Jha 2004: 34).

From the number of artefacts and finds available, we must visualise Mohenjo Daro and other large centres to be very busy settlements. A variety of craftsmen, traders and workmen were occupied everywhere, particularly in the lower city. The most important crafts were in the fields of textiles, ceramic manufacturing, stone carving, household artefacts such as razors, bowls, cups, vases and spindles, and the production of jewellery, statuettes, terracotta figurines depicting men, women and children in varied poses and attires, and children's toys, some of which were mechanical in function. This last category of goods is perhaps the most reliable evidence of the sophistication of this society (Kenoyer 1998: 130–3). The processes employed in the making of these articles demonstrate the best of the Indus valley technology. The Harappans knew how to manufacture bronze by mixing copper and tin, but both metals were difficult to obtain, so, although the Harappans were the first Bronze Age people of Indian history, there are few remains of bronze tools (Jha 2004: 35). Gold and silver were widely used in the manufacture of pendants, armlets, beads and other decorative ornaments (Kenoyer 1998: 75, 138, 146). Brick manufacture and masonry engaged many workers, and a large number of artisans were engaged in the potter's trade (Kenoyer 1998: 151–6). Most Harappan pottery was wheel-turned and produced in large quantities. All traders had their stalls full of consumer goods related to the various crafts; food and drinks were sold by both farmers and city people. Unskilled labourers would have worked in street cleaning, garbage collecting, well-digging, masonry and transporting people in ox-drawn wagons (Jaggi 1969: 81–3; Kenoyer 1998: 89, 127). There were also entertainers, musicians, drummers and jugglers, who would have provided recreation for both the leisured and working classes (Kenoyer 1998: 130, 133).

The most captivating of the smaller material finds from the ruins of Mohenjo Daro and Harappa are the nearly 2,000 inscribed steatite or soapstone seals, which indicate that the making of seals and seal-cutting were extremely important occupations. The imageries on the seals – animals, icons and scripts – suggest to us a high degree of specialisation in their production (Kenoyer 1998: 73–4, 83–9; Chakrabarti 2004: 19). Seals are not unique to the Indus culture; they have been found in Mesopotamia and Iran too. While most of their seals are cylindrical in shape, those of the Indus area are square (Wright 2010: 162–3). They carried a script along the top, an animal in the centre and an icon at the bottom. They could have been used as amulets or talismans, but the general consensus has been that they functioned as 'signatures' or markers of identification. They can be thought of as a means of identifying the signatures of individuals, kin groups or even institutions (Wright 2010: 222–3). As there were many variations in the style of representation of animal or semi-human images, as depicted by faces or necks, archaeologists talk of 'schools' of the production of seals (Wright 2010: 164). From these production centres came a variety of naturalistic representations on seals: of animals such as bulls, buffaloes, rhinoceroses, elephants, tigers, of tree deities, or of a hunter with a ram headdress. The unicorn appears on a majority of seals.

Occasionally there is a tendency to read more into images than is prudent. The existence of the horse has been a subject of controversy. Whether it was native to India or entered India with the Aryans in the post-Harappan phase has been a moot question. It is now generally accepted that the equine's original home was in central Asia and that it entered India during the second millennium BCE. The revisionists have disputed this, and gained some credibility since the eminent Indian archaeologist B.B. Lal entered the debate and pointed to the evidence of the horse's earlier presence in India. However, the recent claim of an image of a horse on a Harappa seal has been met with both scepticism and derision (Witzel and Farmer 2000; Witzel 2005: 487–90). Sealings are impressions made by seals when pressed against a pliable material such as clay. A set of ninety-three clay impressions have been found at the ancient port of Lothal in Gujarat, in which the typical square Indus seal has been impressed on some sort of packages. Most probably, cloth was wrapped around the package or a container before the mud was applied and the package sealed with the sealing (Wright 2010: 222–3). Seals and sealings are important indicators of trade.

The craft and manufacturing activities in the settlements depended for their prosperity on the internal and external trade networks (Chakrabarti 2004: 29–33). Raw materials from across the region were imported by the middlemen who employed craftsmen and skilled workers to manufacture the finished products to satisfy the consumer market. Certain places, particularly ports such as Lothal, acted as *entrepôts* or warehouse depots (Possehl 1976/1979: 212–18). Copper ore was imported from a number of sites for making sharp-edged bronze saws that could efficiently cut through hard shells, collected from a number of coastal sites and passed on to the jewellers who fashioned bracelets and bangles from them. Precious stones were used for making ornaments and utensils. Agate and jasper, the hard stones imported from Kutch and Gujarat, were much valued as they long retained their brightness and polish. The softer varieties, such as turquoise, lapis lazuli or carnelian, were used in the manufacture of assortments of much-prized beads (Kenoyer 1998: 160–62; Jyotsna 2000: 6–7). Raw materials such as stones, marine shells and precious metals were bulk-transported across land by bullocks and buffalo-drawn carts and, on the River Indus and its tributaries and between coastal ports, by boats, sometimes depicted on the Harappan seals.

Figure 3.2 Harappan seals

Although the Indus economic zone is generally self-sufficient, its people have throughout history been enterprising traders who pioneered commercial links with foreign countries. We have evidence of such links made during the Mature Harappan phase. The countries involved were Afghanistan, Turkmenistan, Iran, Mesopotamia and Oman. The only Mature Harappan site outside the subcontinent was at Shortugai in Afghanistan, and it has been argued that its position as a transit point for many routes in that region encouraged a settlement of Indus traders engaged in the exchange of goods. They sought tin and lapis lazuli in return for the Indus products such as textiles, combs, beads, dice, etc. (Francfort 1984: 301–10). Objects from the Indus region have been found in both Turkmenistan and Iran, the latter country providing the main land route to Mesopotamia (Heskel 1984: 333–46; Chakrabarti 2004: 31–2). A flourishing sea trade linked the Indus settlements with Oman and southern Mesopotamia (Oppenheim 1954/1979: 155–63; Lamberg–Karlovsky 1972/1979: 130–7). From Oman came primarily copper and shells, but also dates, honey, incense and salt fish. The exports to Oman included various foodstuffs, boats, livestock and utility artefacts. Beads, bangles, hard woods, pearls, ivory and numerous exotic animals reached Mesopotamia by boat from the Indus region, and the Indus valley seals have also been found there. A Mesopotamian text from the reign of King Sargon of Akkad refers to boats bringing the cargo from a place called *Meluhha*, now identified as the Indus valley; these boats probably sailed from the port of Lothal on the Gujarat–Kathiawar coast (Rao 1968/1979: 174–5; Kenoyer 1998: 98). In the absence of reliable trade figures it is difficult to find out whether the balance of trade worked in favour of the Indus zone or the foreign countries. However, far more Indus valley products have been retrieved in regions outside India than foreign products within the Indus zone (Chakrabarti 2004: 33).

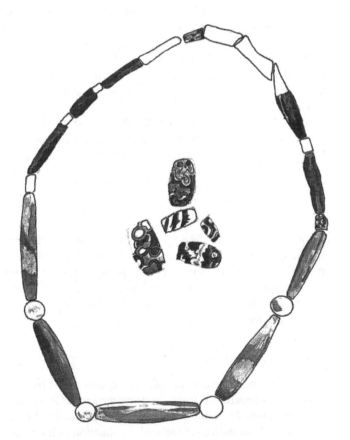

Figure 3.3 A necklace of Harappan beads

Excerpt 3.4 The Indus and an interconnected third-millennium world

In her excellent study of the environmental geography of the Indus valley basin and the socio-economic life of the Harappan people, the American anthropologist Rita P. Wright warns us against preconceptions about ancient peoples. The zest for travel among the Indus people was, for example, as she points out, as strong as may be found among modern Western travellers.

In our modern global society, there is a tendency to think that in earlier times communities were isolated. However the evidence presented here contradicts that notion and leads us to wonder whether our own fascination with distant lands and cultural influences are that unique. Americans travelling in France, for example, will not be surprised to hear rap music in the streets of Paris. At the same time, they will be captivated by the charm of a Parisian café, the essence of which is not easily duplicated outside the French context. But . . . this curiosity about other cultures and even the desire to emulate them is not an innovation of modern Western society. Some Harappans seem to have shown a curiosity and attraction for distant places, most likely based on practical matters and their geographical proximity, but they also rallied around to 'fitting in'. In any event, we should not think of Indus people as totally isolated from their contemporaries.

Source: Rita P. Wright, *The Ancient Indus: Urbanism, Economy and Society*, New York: Cambridge University Press, 2010, 230.

It is clear from the foregoing discussion on trade that the Harappans were themselves an integral part of whatever global system existed in the third millennium BCE. It must have been incredibly hard for people to undertake long overland or sea journeys, yet this was what they did, because human beings always find ways of connecting themselves with others. A modern writer on the subject explains it thus in **Excerpt 3.4** above.

Sculpture, script and mathematics

All the material evidence that we have referred to thus far – the ruins of the great monuments, the standardised bricks and the terracotta seals, along with a great variety of craft goods and tools – adds up to a considerable treasure, but in its overall grandeur and magnificence the entire collection pales in comparison with, say, the treasures of ancient Egypt. This is even more noticeable when we compare the achievement of the two civilisations in the art of sculpture. The Harappan heritage is indeed very undistinguished. A recent scholarly publication has listed just eight major items of true Harappan sculpture (Chakrabarti 2004: 20). One of them, a powerful piece that was retrieved from Mohenjo Daro and is now in the National Museum in Karachi, is that of a personage who has been described as a priest-king (only 17.8 cm high). His gravitas definitely conveys the impression of a person of influence and authority, of which, unfortunately, he is the sole representative. Another well-known item is that of a figurine of the so-called Dancing Girl of Mohenjo Daro, in her graceful and elegant pose, quite nude except for her bangles and a necklace (see Figure 3.4). There is a hint in the sculpture of a woman who has a proud sense of who she is. What is interesting, however, is that there is 'a difference in conceptualisation, form and technique' (Chakrabarti 2004: 20) between the two works. The first one is wonderfully crafted in stone and foreshadows the great stone art of India in the historic period. The Dancing Girl, on the other hand, is a bronze product, made by the lost-wax process, and it too provides a model for the later copper and bronze objects made in the subcontinent. The two examples, along with the fact that a Harappan motif has been identified as the 'inter-circling motif' on the Bodhi stone of Bodh Gaya, at least suggest to us a degree of Harappan precedence to the future sculptural tradition in India.

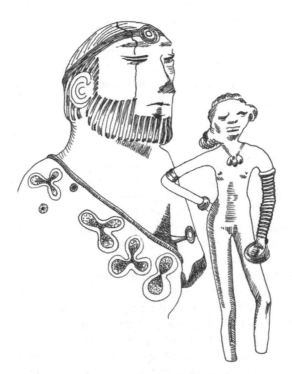

Figure 3.4 Dancing girl and priest-king

The Harappans possessed a script which they used for inscribing on a variety of objects: soapstone or steatite seals, impressible materials such as clay or soft metal, and objects such as stone or copper tablets, bracelets, marble, ivory, shells and bangles. Nearly 4,200 inscribed objects have been recovered, with Mohenjo Daro and Harappa accounting for some 85 per cent (Kochhar 2000: 73; Fischer 2005: 60; Coningham 2005: 532). The script contains 419 signs, of which 113 occur once only, forty-seven twice, fifty-nine fewer than five times and 200 every so often (Kochhar 2000: 73–4). These signs are far too many to constitute an alphabetic or syllabic script; they are mostly logo-syllabic characters. Only eight texts longer than fifteen signs have been found. The average length of an inscription is five signs, although the longest inscription is made up of twenty-six signs. The script was written from right to left, but started from the left when it carried on to the second line (Fischer 2005: 62).[1] Perhaps the most striking Harappan inscription – containing nine signs, each 37 cm high and 25 to 27 cm broad, and each made by joining crystalline pieces and engraved on a wooden board – has been found at Dholavira (Chakrabarti 2004: 19). Were it a signboard, it would indicate a certain degree of literacy among the people. Writing is the key to understanding the mind of a society, and history begins with the written word. We would become more knowledgeable about the Harappans if we were able to read their script or see some clear links between their script and the innumerable scripts used in the subcontinent today. Three great scholars – Professors Mahadevan of the Archaeological Survey of India, Asko Parpola of the University of Helsinki and Walter Fairservis Jr of Vassar College, New York – spent years attempting to understand the mysteries of the script; but they too have been unable to decipher it. Nor are we able to state definitively whether its language belonged to the Indo-Aryan or the Dravidian family of languages. In this sense, the Harappan civilisation must, therefore, be classed as prehistoric. The script remains undeciphered and cannot provide help, despite assertions made to the contrary (Witzel and Farmer 2000; Witzel 2006: 53–4). If, however, a bilingual text containing the Harappan script along with another already understood were to be found on a single seal or some object, then the mystery might unravel, in the same way as the decryption of the Rosetta Stone in Egypt, containing the same text in three languages, solved the puzzle of the hieroglyphs. Most archaeologists, however, seem to be in general agreement that, since the majority of inscriptions are found on seals, and since the seals were an important symbol of authority or an exchange mechanism in trade relations, it is likely that the script must have something useful to say in terms of administration, trade or perhaps spirituality. Up to the present, we can judge the Harappan civilisation only from its material remains.

While mathematical problems were inscribed on the Sumerian and other Mesopotamian clay tablets, there is nothing similar to be found in the Indus region. One should not, however, conclude that the Harappans lacked mathematical insights or knowledge. As with all aspects of this civilisation, the clues to understanding lie in its ruins and artefacts. We have already referred to the standard ratio of 1: 2: 4 in brick technology; and many skills of measuring and computational techniques can be easily discerned from the architectural and town-planning profiles. Weighing scales and instruments for measuring length have also been found. Part of a shell recovered at Mohenjo Daro, measuring 6.62 cm, or 2.6 in, is divided into nine equally spaced parallel lines cut with a fine saw. One of these lines is marked by a circle, and the sixth line from it by a dot. The distance between the circle and the dot has been calculated as 1.32 in, and is known as the Indus inch (Joseph 2010: 318–19). As this Indus inch is equal to two Sumerian equivalent measures called *shushi*, we may rightly assume that perhaps there was some exchange of computational or commercial information between the Harappans and the Mesopotamians (Bose *et al.* 1989: 138). Two other measuring scales, with very finely graduated divisions, have also been discovered at Lothal and Harappa (Mainkar 1984: 146). All three scales indicate a certain uniformity in establishing ratios and in modes of division and measurement. In addition, the Harappans possessed a highly standardised system of cubical stone weights. A red seed, called 'gunja', equivalent to two grains of barley, constituted the base weight, and three different series of stone weight ratios have been calculated. The first series of seven weights doubled in size from 1: 2: 4: 8: 16: 32: 64, while in the second and third series of weights we find a ratio of 160, 320 and 640, and then moving up from 1,600, 3,200 and 6,400 to 12,800. The average 'gunja' seed weighed 0.109 grams; the largest weight found at Mohenjo Daro, weighing 10,865 g, or 25 lbs, is nearly 100,000 times the weight of the 'gunja' seed (Mainkar 1984: 142–3; Kenoyer 1998: 98). From the various weight details gained from such tools as the plumb line balls used by masons, mathematicians have constructed frequency charts that show that the weights were fractions or multiples of a standard weight known as *uncia*. This weight was 27.2 g, and weights on the multiples of 5 *uncia* (136 g) or one-sixteenth *uncia* (1.7 g) have been found, once again suggesting a decimal system of calculation (Mainkar 1984: 145–6; Bose *et al.* 1989: 137). Finally, we must acknowledge that the Harappan farmers, like their Egyptian and Mesopotamian peers, must have relied upon their practical mathematical knowledge and intuition in order to control the flood cycles of their great river with sluices and irrigation channels, and to maximise crop yields by the systematic sequencing of sowing and harvesting of spring wheat and barley and autumn crops such as cotton and sesame (Joseph 2010: 319).

Religion

It is unwise to conjecture about the organised religion of the inhabitants of the Indus cities. We can, however, deduce certain aspects of their religiosity and spirituality from some of the archaeological finds and from the living traditions of India today. Some of them may even be linked to Hinduism itself. The water in the Great Bath on the higher citadel of Mohenjo Daro was, most probably, considered holy and was perhaps reserved for ritual washing by groups of priests (Kenoyer 1998: 64); ritual washing has been one of the immemorial customs of Hindu India. Some interesting symbols of religious art, with close Hindu associations, can be seen on seals and tablets. On some are found images of a male with horned headdress seated in the *Yoga* posture of *padmasana* (Kenoyer 1998: 112).

Yoga is one of the great keys to understanding Hinduism. In contrast to the standard square stamp seals used for commercial purposes, others have many complex images portraying, for example, narrative scenes which may cover stories or myths. Some of the seals have fantastic animals, such as tigers with horns, bulls with three heads, or a mixture of half-human, half-animal figures engaged in physical contests with humans, in curious headdresses, conceived as deities. Tree deities appear frequently on seals. The pipal and the banyan trees, very common trees of India used as symbols of fertility, protection and death in Hindu mythology, are both depicted on seals and ornaments. There are also found a great variety of figurines, the most prominent of which may be representations of fertility god-desses. Comparisons have been drawn between their images and those of Hindu goddesses of popular imagination. Some of the figurines are of women with enlarged buttocks and thighs and with curving pear-shaped bodies nursing babies at their large protruding breasts; they are adorned with textured dresses, distinct hairstyles, garlands of flowers, jewellery and turbans. They perhaps convey to us the Harappans' sense of respect and honour for a woman's fertility and her role as a mother. Whether it means that women were treated fairly or equitably in society at large is a matter of conjecture. We cannot be sure.

In addition to religious and ritual art symbols, there are also found many abstract symbols and geometric designs. The endless-knot, the swastika, the circle, the ring – all have their motifs etched, engraved or carved into seals, pottery, copper and ivory objects. Although these symbolic representations indicate a possible link between whatever religious ideology the Indus people may have possessed and the later development of Hinduism, there is hardly any evidence of the particular sort of religious iconography that is common in Hinduism. It is also worth bearing in mind that the Mesopotamian and Iranian imageries complement those of the Indus, and religious art in all three zones during the third millennium BCE was about the interaction between supernatural and human forces (Wright 2010: 289). Organised ritualism appeared later.

Power and authority

It is clear from the foregoing discussion that those who lived in the cities of the Indus were part of a society that had reached a relatively high level of refine-ment in the way they lived and worked. Historians are right to describe such a society as an early mature civilisation. Many of its manifestations – the layout and landscape of cities, crafts and manufactures, the rich agriculture, the hydraulic works, seals, etc. – are of a standard and originality that we find in those of other ancient civilisations. In one particular aspect, however, the civilisation of the Indus greatly differed from them; that was over the question of who exercised power and authority. We take it for granted that a society or a culture cannot be considered truly civilised until and unless it is governed and regulated by a set of laws imposed by a higher authority. Civilisation and hierarchy seem to go together, and hierarchy is associated with a concentration of power and ultimately a certain amount of tyranny. This was the model of power in the great civilisations of ancient Egypt,

China and Mesopotamia. On the other hand, the Indus valley civilisation provides us with a model of shared or diffused power. Towns and villages were able to work together in an integrative manner because the former were not the ruling centres; they did not oppress the surrounding villages, in the way they do in our modern world. There was no concentration of resources; rather, resources were shared among different groups of people living both in villages and towns. A network of relationships among both urban and rural families and clans ensured the successful working of a prosperous economy for over half a millennium. Competing and collaborating groups were able to work together in the manufacture of arts and crafts, and the uniformity of standards was maintained not through a central regulating agency but through a variety of kinship ties among such groups. It has been suggested that the key to discerning the authority of each clan family or group may lie in the images of animals on soapstone seals. Each animal image could represent a symbol of authority for a particular officer, a dominant lineage or a clan family. Since the unicorn appears on the largest number of seals it might be the power symbol of the most numerous clan. Rich merchants too might have used the seals as their personal or official insignia for goods to be traded (Lamberg-Karlovsky 1972/1979: 132). What is clear is that the integrative mechanisms holding this civilisation lay in the division of labour itself and the interdependency of regions, with family, lineage or clan ownership of the means of production. The primary relation in all this was economic, not political. The key to the origins of the Indian caste system may also be found here.

The Indus civilisation was thus a complex, stateless society of the post-Neolithic era. The absence of the state is testified by the fact that no palaces or royal tombs have been discovered; neither have any systematic dynastic or governmental records been found. State power is normally associated with militarism, but there is very little evidence of such militarism in the Indus cities. A great amount of copper and bronze was used, but mostly in craft manufacture rather than in weaponry. The strong walls in the towns were flood defences rather than military barriers to invading armies. The higher level citadel area of the Indus cities, with impressive public space, should not be considered the seat of power or a military fortification; most probably it was a place where citizens came to relax or worship. Just like the Acropolis of Athens, the Harappan acropolis was a civic or cultic structure, not a castle or a garrison. In the absence of substantial archaeological evidence of a central political authority, it is wise to conclude that the cities and settlements of the Harappan civilisation were loosely integrated by a common material culture, and that there was a great deal of cultural but not political uniformity (Thapar 2002: 83–4).

The demise of the Harappan civilisation

A decline set in at around 1900 BCE in the dynamics of the Harappan system, and there is little doubt that after 1700 BCE little remained of the Harappan civilisation. It did not, however, come to an abrupt end within a particular period of decades or during a particular century. Until quite recently it was believed that the Indus cities were destroyed by the Aryans who entered India from Iran and Afghanistan through north-western passes such as the Bolan and the Khyber. This theory was based on two sets of evidence. One was the reference in the *Rig-Veda*, the premier Vedic text, that the Aryan god Indra destroyed a hostile people called the Dasas or Dasyus who lived in fortified places called *pur* (Wheeler 1947/1979: 289–92; Kochhar 2000: 76–8). The other concerned the discovery of some skeletons of men, women and children from the lower city of Mohenjo Daro, killed during the so-called last massacre (Dales 1964/1979: 293–6). The archaeologist who was most vehement in putting forward this theory of an Aryan onslaught on the Indus cities was Sir Mortimer Wheeler, who, after admittedly considering and rejecting other theories, had no doubt that 'on circumstantial evidence, Indra stands accused' (quoted in Kochhar 2000: 77). Wheeler later admitted the validity of other reasons for the Harappan decline, but nevertheless stuck to his claim about the massacre (Wheeler 1966: 72–83). Most literary scholars and archaeologists today dismiss Wheeler's theory as too simplistic (Dales 1964/1979: 293–6; Raikes 1964/1979: 298–9; Dales 1966/1979: 308; Srivastava 1984: 437–43). For example, the Rig-Vedic *pur* was nothing like an Indus city; it was just a structure of flimsy ramparts and stockades (Kochhar 2000: 78–9). If the *purs* that Indra is supposed to have destroyed were the Indus cities, it is most curious that the first great sacred text of Hinduism, the *Rig-Veda*, does not mention anything about such recognisable features of the Harappan cities as the well-laid-out streets, houses, wells, drains, granaries and seals. Again, the skeletons of some people in the lower city of Mohenjo Daro are considered wholly insufficient evidence of an attack on such a large and complex urban system. This so-called Aryan invasion theory will be discussed further in Chapter 4.

Scholars now consider a combination of natural and socio-economic factors to be the most likely reason for the decline of the Indus cities. Two of the natural factors could be the geological and the climatic (Allchin 1984: 445–54). It is presumed that the Indus region experienced severe tectonic disturbances brought about by earthquakes at the beginning of the second millennium BCE (Agrawal and Sood 1982: 226–9). These upheavals not only affected the normal course of the Indus and its tributaries but also helped to dry up the nearby Ghaggar–Hakra River. This latter river, known to the Hindus as River *Sarasvati*, was the life blood of a vast number of settlements dispersed around it; with its drying up a fatal blow was struck at the heart of the Indus civilisation. Modern satellite imagery confirms the theory that the dramatic shifts in the river courses might have created great floods that could have cut off the food-producing areas from the cities themselves (Kochhar 2000: 123–5). The quantities of silt layers in the upper levels of Mohenjo Daro, which are today many feet above the river course, are also a witness to those floods. Without the surrounding food-producing areas the cities themselves could have been left isolated. And with the frequent uncertainty of regular food supplies, the city populace prudently decided to migrate before starvation overtook them. Research into the history of rainfall patterns brings out the climatic factor of the decline. During the Mature Harappan period, about 2500 BCE, there was a great rise in the amount of rainfall, but by the beginning of the second millennium

BCE it had dropped markedly (Kochhar 2000: 136). This too would have had a damaging effect on food production, further resulting in depopulation of the cities. One of the reasons for the rainfall's unpredictability was the extreme deforestation and loss of trees caused by the burning of charcoal in brick-baking kilns. With the rivers shifting their courses, the rainfall declining and sufficient food failing to arrive from the countryside, we have to recognise a slow but inevitable collapse of the Indus system (Fairservis 1971: 296–306; Allchin 1995: 27–9). This collapse, it should be re-emphasised, cannot be explained by any one particular cause; we must think in terms of a 'combination of factors' (Coningham 2005: 538). The final outcome was catastrophic for the Mature Harappan phase. The Indus cities no longer had surplus produce for trade, and the ensuing loss of revenue would have affected all classes of people. The city authorities became powerless to prevent civil unrest or brigandage, and groups of people were continually leaving the cities for their own safety and survival. As the cities became poorer, their services declined dramatically. The drains and sewers of Mohenjo Daro, kept in good and clean working order for centuries, clogged up with waste and excreta, resulting in disease and pestilence. By about 1700 BCE the desolated Mohenjo Daro had become a ghost town. Thirty-seven centuries would pass before its former grandeur was revealed to a world hitherto ignorant of it.

Civilisations continually rise and fall, but they rarely disappear without trace. It was so with the Harappan civilisation too. The collapse of the Indus system was really a collapse of its urban features (Ghosh 1982: 321–4; Chakrabarti 1998: 138–40). Its culture did not cease to exist wholesale. The sophisticated lifestyle of the Indus people had certainly ended, but their folk culture continued at the village level (Allchin 1982: 329–33). Several of the beliefs and rituals, and the simple crafts and skills for making various utensils and artefacts, along with many rural features, survived and developed into proto-historic cultures in the surrounding regions (Coningham 2005: 539–40). The two important migrations of people, caused particularly by the accelerated drying up of the Ghaggar–Hakra River during the later phase, were in the direction of the Ganges–Yamuna *doab* and Gujarat, leading towards the Deccan (Chakrabarti 2004: 9). It is often claimed that the Dravidian people of south India are descendants of the Harappans. If they are, then it must be during the few centuries after 1700 BCE that they would have migrated. Apart from the two big inter-regional movements, local migrations from the urban settlements into the rural areas similarly occurred. Archaeologically speaking, the cultures that resulted were relatively quite advanced, in the sense that they evolved as part of the Chalcolithic/Bronze Age, and did not regress to the skills level of the Stone Age. Different names have been assigned to these lesser regional cultures, such as the Ochre-Coloured Pottery culture in the Ganges plain (Kochhar 2000: 80–1), the Jhukar culture in Sind (Allchin 1995: 31; Kochhar 2000: 188–90), the Cemetery H culture in the Punjab (Allchin 1995: 33–4; Kochhar 2000: 190–2, 221–2), the Banas culture in Mewar in Rajasthan (Kochhar 2000: 81–2) or the Malwa culture of Madhya Pradesh (Chakrabarti 1998: 148–50). Historians identify these cultures on the basis of their pottery styles, grave goods and burial patterns and the quality of ornaments and tools, particularly those of copper. Some of these cultures survived for many centuries, thus continuing many of the non-urban Harappan traditions. The peoples of these cultures, in the course of time, came into contact with other nomadic foreign groups, such as the Aryans, some of whom began to enter India from 1700 BCE onwards, and a new Indo-Aryan civilisation would come to shape India's history for the next thousand years and more. Even today, however, a historically conscious traveller, making a journey of exploration in Punjab, Sind and Baluchistan, will certainly notice the imprints of the glorious Harappan past.

STUDY GUIDE

Key issues

- Indus or Sarasvati: the significance of dispute over the naming of a civilisation.
- Controversies over the origins of the Harappan civilisation.
- The Harappan characteristics of a civilisation.
- Comparing the authority structures in Mohenjo Daro and Harappa with other ancient civilisations.
- Evidence for post-Harappan clusters and enclaves.

Suggested readings

Chakrabarti 2004: 29–34; Maisels 1999: 186–259; Time-Life Books 1994: 9–43; Wright 2010: 235–69

INTERNET SELECTION

1) Saifullah Khan: 'Sanitation and wastewater technologies in Harappa/Indus valley civilisation'. www.academia.edu/5937322/Chapter_2_Sanitation_and _wastewater_technologies_in_Harappa_Indus_valley_civilization_ca._260019 00_BC
2) Chris J.D. Kostman: 'The Indus valley civilization: In search of those elusive centres and peripheries'. www.adventurecorps.com/archaeo/centper iph.html
3) Iravatham Mahadevan: 'Parpola and the Indus Script'. http://www.thehindu. com/opinion/op-ed/parpola-and-the-indus-script/article462079.ece
4) Vasant Shinde and Rick J. Willis: 'A new type of inscribed copper plate from Indus valley' (Harrapan) civilisation. www.ancient-asia-journal.com/article/ view/aa.12317/97

QUESTIONS FOR GROUP DISCUSSION

1) What is the rationale for describing the Harappan civilisation as the Sarasvati civilisation? To what extent is it a credible rationale?

2) Why did the ancient cities of Mohenjo Daro and Harappa never enter into the Indian consciousness until the early twentieth century?
3) What is the significance of the discovery of the port of Lothal in understanding the dimensions of both the internal and external trade of the Harappans?
4) How valid are some of the reasons given for the demise of the Harappan civilisation?
5) In what ways did the post-Harappans continue the Harappan traditions?

Note

1   In a Boustrophedon fashion: as the ox turns in ploughing (p. 56).

4 Who were the Aryans?

(*c.* 1700 to 600 BCE)

Timeline/Key Dates

c. 2000 BCE	A branch of Indo-Europeans, the Aryans, migrate towards Iran from the European steppe lands
c. 2000–1700 BCE	Aryan bards compose the *Rig-Veda*
c. 1700 BCE	The beginnings of the Aryan migration into north-west India
c. 1400 BCE	The arrival of the Rig-Vedic Aryans in India
c. 1000 BCE	The beginnings of the Iron Age in India
c. 900 BCE	Aryans advance into the Gangetic valley: the Battle of Ten Kings
c. 900–600 BCE	Aryan cultural advance into south India
c. 600 BCE	Completion of early Vedic literature
CE 1786	Sir William Jones postulates the concept of the Indo-European family of languages
CE 19th and early 20th centuries	'Scientific racism' acquires popularity in Europe, and the term 'Aryan' is misused by race-conscious European historians and scholars

The 6,000 or so languages spoken in the world today are classified by scholars into major language family groups. The dominant language family of the northern part of the Indian subcontinent is what is called the Indo-Aryan. This family is also considered to have a sister branch in the Iranian family and both branches are said to belong to a much larger family of families, which is known as the Indo-European family (Mallory 1989, Ch. 1; Gamkrelidze and Ivanov 1990: 82–90; Crystal 1997: 298–305). The longest-established language of this entire family is Sanskrit, and it is from the progressive evolution of Sanskrit, over many millennia, that the other present-day Indo-Aryan languages of India developed.

Apart from being a modern-day label for a family of languages, the term 'Indo-Aryan' can serve to describe the evolution of Indian culture, over more than a thousand years, following the demise of the Harappan civilisation. Groups of nomadic tribal people from eastern and southern Afghanistan started migrating to the Indian subcontinent around 1700 BCE; their movement gained momentum with the arrival, at about 1400 BCE, of a particular sub-group that called itself *Arya*, or noble. We sometimes call them the Rig-Vedic Aryans because they brought with them the earliest portion of a collection of hymns, known as the *Rig-Veda*, which was composed by their bards and seers in a very early form of Sanskrit or Old Indic (Renfrew 1987: 178; Mallory 1989: 35–6). Other tribal groups of that period, who did not call themselves *Arya*, also tend to be included by historians under the generic label of Aryans.[1] In the new society that was born out of the mix of the pre-Aryan and Aryan cultural elements, the Rig-Vedic Aryans increasingly came to occupy a central position. The Indo-Aryan culture that eventually emerged, more commonly known as the Vedic culture, is still with us in India, forming the essential core of Hindu religious, social and cultural life. The word 'Vedic' is the adjective of the noun 'Veda', which refers to the *Rig-Veda* and other collections of sacred hymns and chants.

This chapter examines three different issues regarding the Indo-Aryans: 1) the origins of the Aryans and the controversies surrounding their history; 2) the domination of the Indian subcontinent by the Aryans; and 3) the society and culture of the Indo-Aryans.

Understanding the Aryans

The sign of the swastika is today rightly feared in the Western world for what it stood for during the 1930s and 1940s. It was a Nazi symbol of the superiority of the so-called Aryans of Hitler's imagination. It meant the death and destruction of millions of people. The Nazis misappropriated the term 'Aryan' for a wholly sinister purpose. In Hitler's Germany the populace was segregated on the basis of whether they were Aryans, a race supposedly endowed with extraordinary powers of mind, spirit and beauty, or those considered inferior people, such as the Jews, Gypsies, black people or homosexuals. After the defeat of Hitler and Hitlerism in 1945, Western historians and other scholars wished to marginalise the use of the term 'Aryan'. They did not want to give it any further credence, in order that the remaining band of neo-Nazis might not misuse it for the glorification of Hitler's ideas. This is perfectly understandable in the context of modern European history. In India, however, for countless centuries, the Hindus have considered the swastika a symbol of divinity endowing happiness, peace and prosperity. For them, the Aryans were not genocidal psychopaths but a noble group of ancient Indians. All those who study the history of the subcontinent cannot shy away from using the term 'Aryan', although there is ongoing controversy about the Aryans' origins. In this section, therefore, we shall examine the Aryans from five different angles: scholarship, chronology, comparative religion, racialisation and current Hindu nationalist revisionism.

Sanskrit scholarship and the linguistic context

To understand the term 'Aryan' in the context of Indian history, we must first explore the study of the history of languages. Our starting point has to be with Sanskrit, which can be described as the mother language of almost all the languages of north India. Its wider fame across the world of knowledge owes much to the work of a very eminent eighteenth-century linguist and judge, Sir William Jones (1746–94). After studying it over a number of years, Jones concluded that Sanskrit was also related to some of the most refined languages of Europe; it was even superior to them, in his opinion. His conclusion resonates to this day, and is worth quoting:

> Sanskrit language, whatever be its antiquity, is of a wonderful structure, more perfect than the Greek, more copious than the Latin, and more exquisitely refined than either; yet bearing to both of them a stronger affinity, both in the roots of verbs and in the roots of grammar, than could possibly have been produced by accident; so strong, indeed, that no philologer could examine them all three, without believing them to have sprung from some common source, which, perhaps, no longer exists.
>
> (quoted in Mallory 1989: 12)

Jones certainly held Sanskrit in the highest esteem, placing the profoundness of Sanskrit texts in the same league as the Bible (Kochhar 2000: 89–117). He did not, however, suggest that Sanskrit was the parent of all the Indian and European languages, nor did he think that Sanskrit was the source of all civilisation. His real emphasis was on the linguistic affinities among such well-known languages as Greek, Latin, Persian and Sanskrit; for him 'there was a fundamental unity in human thought, belief and action hidden under the veneer of linguistic differences' (Renfrew 1987: 193). But, above all, there was his view that there was 'some common source' from which these languages had sprung, which strongly influenced the way people perceived the origins of languages. Jones counted among his colleagues distinguished British intellectuals and many men greatly esteemed in public life at that time. The German poet Goethe observed in 1819 that the 'merits of this man (Jones) are universally known and have been emphasized and detailed on numerous occasions' (Kochhar 2000: 104–12).

The most positive aspect of Jones's legacy has been realised, over the last two centuries, in the works of linguists, philologists and grammarians who searched for interconnections linking the world's languages and their structures. Living languages are those that are currently spoken by people, and any attempt to understand the origins and classifications of languages inevitably gives rise to speculation about their past speakers. Despite the several differences within the Indo-European languages, their similarities in grammar, syntax and vocabulary led most nineteenth-century researchers to conclude, like Jones, that in the distant past a group of people might have spoken an original language (*Ursprache*) that was the common ancestor of the modern Indo-European languages. They called this language proto-Indo-European and they earnestly started searching for an ancestral homeland (an *Urheimat*) in which this postulated language had been spoken (Mallory 1989: 143–85). The evidence uncovered thus far suggests that this homeland covered a far smaller area than that in which the spread of modern Indo-European language speakers live, and that it lay in the European steppe lands north and east of the Black Sea and extending towards the Caspian Sea (Renfrew 1987: 9–19; Mallory 1989: 9–23).

We have no hard and fast knowledge of the proto-Indo-European language and we have no direct proof of the existence of proto-Indo-European speakers. What we do know is that, sometime during the third millennium BCE, owing to climatic and environmental changes, differentiated groups of people from the Eurasian steppe lands were migrating to a variety of zones outside their smaller original homeland. We know this partly through archaeology and partly through examination of oral traditions. The people who were migrating had domesticated the horse and developed wheeled vehicles, thereby making their migration process much easier. We should not assume, however, that they came out in one mighty torrent and spread out over Eurasia with force of arms. Migrations in ancient times were always slow, gradual and mostly peaceful. The migrants spoke a variety of dialects and languages. Eventually they came to occupy areas with a natural environment vastly different from their homeland. This meant that their language must also have changed, since many words and expressions peculiar to the requirements of their homeland would not have been useful in their new surroundings. Their original vocabulary would have been augmented and modified by their encounters with settled groups of people who they came to assimilate or displace (Renfrew 1987: 77–86; Mallory 1989: 257–61; Gamkrelidze and Ivanov 1990: 85–6). Among the many models of Indo-European migration, the one considered most plausible is known as the Kurgan hypothesis, originally developed by the eminent Lithuanian scholar Marija Gimbutas (1921–94) from her researches in proto-linguistics and archaeology in the 1950s. It explains the applicability to the various groups of Indo-Europeans of conditions under which a particular culture, the Kurgan, spread outwards (Mallory 1989: 182–5).

Of the many branches of the Indo-European languages of those early migrants, the oldest is called the Indo-Iranian family. It is comprised of two main sub-groups – Indo-Aryan and Iranian – along with two related languages – Romani of the Gypsies and Nuristani of the Hindu Kush region of Afghanistan and Pakistan. A number of undifferentiated Indo-Iranian-speaking groups, mainly pastoralists with their cattle, had migrated southwards on foot from the Eurasian steppe lands at about 2000 BCE and spread over central Asia, Iran and Afghanistan. One branch, speaking a type of Aryan language, possibly a very early form of Sanskrit, might have reached as far as the River Indus as early as 1700 BCE. They would be the first of the Indo-European or Aryan pastoralists speaking some early form of Sanskrit, which would in time fuse with the indigenous languages. The first of the appropriate contexts, therefore, in which the word 'Aryan' may be used is with regard to language families.

The understanding of Indian chronology after the Harappan excavations

Everything that had been discussed and written about Indian historical chronology since the time of Sir William Jones suddenly became obsolete in the year 1924 when the archaeological finds from Mohenjo Daro were revealed to the world. The dating of these finds, and those of Harappa and other Indus valley sites, yielded amazing results which were to create great confusion and disarray among the historians and cultural scholars of India. Traditionally, Indian scholarship had never placed great credence on the time-definitiveness of dates; the great cycles of *yugas* ran into thousands of years, according to astrological calculations. Since the introduction of Western methodologies of studying the past, however, a new generation of trainee historians had been encouraged to view their subject from a secular standpoint, to check all dates by comparative synchronisms and, above all, to disassociate history from mythology as far as possible. From language study and philology, begun by William Jones and continuing all through the nineteenth century, it had been ascertained that the Aryans had come into India in around 1500 BCE. The nineteenth-century Indian history books, based on Western dating methods, began the story of Indian greatness from the supposed time of the invasion of the civilised Aryans in around 1500 BCE. The first volume of the grand *Cambridge History of India*, published in 1922, began with the world of the *Rig-Veda* and the Aryans. The importance of 1500 BCE, however, paled into insignificance when the true dates for Mohenjo Daro and Harappa were revealed. The two cities were at their most glorious between approximately 2600 BCE and 1900 BCE, now referred to as the Mature Harappan phase (discussed in Chapter 3). Long before the advent of the Aryans, the people of the north-west of India were part of an urban civilisation. Two contrasting models of South Asian Indian chronology thus emerge. The simpler chronology, followed by historians until the Indus discoveries, has been replaced by a more accurate periodisation that is currently agreed upon by most historians and archaeologists. It can be presented as follows:

Model followed until the early 20th century

c. 4000 BCE–3000 BCE The era of the proto-Australoids and Aborigines
c. 3000 BCE–1500 BCE The Dravidian Age
c. 1500 BCE–1000 BCE The Aryan Age
c. 1000 BCE–500 BCE The era of the Vedic states

Model agreed now

c. 7000 BCE–4500 BCE Early Neolithic Baluchistan phase
c. 4500 BCE–3500 BCE Later Neolithic phase
c. 3500 BCE–2600 BCE Proto-urban Early Harappan phase
c. 2600 BCE–1900 BCE Mature Harappan phase

c. 1900 BCE–1700 BCE Post-Harappan phase
c. 1700 BCE–600 BCE Indo-Aryan Vedic phase

Although the second of the above two models provides us with a more accurate chronology of the history of the Harappan civilisation within the Indian context, we still need to recognise that there was an India beyond Harappa and Mohenjo Daro. The reference to proto-Australoids, the Aborigines and the Dravidian Age in the first model is therefore very relevant, because they denote forms of culture that existed in other different parts of India. Remote communities of Aborigines, for example, are to be found in India even today; the construction of their history may be a very difficult task, but there can be no doubt that their ancestry goes back far before the time of the Harappans. The Dravidians are often referred to as descendants of the Harappans who might have migrated there after the collapse of the urban system, but the origins of the Dravidian culture also predate the Harappans by many millennia (Narasimhiah 1981: 19–22). India is truly an ancient civilisation.

The Indo-Iranian dimension

Long before the British and European scholars and historians of the eighteenth century evinced interest in the languages, cultures and histories of the Orient, both the Indians and the Persians were familiar with the concept of 'Aryan'. Both recognised and intuitively understood the meaning of such terms as *Arya* (noble): the Indians understood what the space they called *Aryavarta* (the Indo-Gangetic heartland of the Aryans) meant, and the Iranians recognised someone who was an *an-Arya* (non-Aryan). For nearly four millennia, the Indian mind had selectively and subconsciously imbibed the notion of the Aryan as something that was positive, ennobling, and all that was best in India. The *Vedas* and their ancillary literature, along with the later literatures of the *Ramayana*, the *Mahabharata*, the *Puranas* and the varied devotional practices of Puranic Hinduism, had augmented this learning process in a country that lacked a systematic historiographic tradition. In Iran too, ever since the middle of the first millennium BCE, the people have taken pride in calling themselves Aryan or noble: *Iranshahr* meant 'the Aryan land'. It was through Persian that the Europeans first came to understand the significance of the Aryan civilisation in Iran. The French traveller and scholar Anquetil-Duperron translated in 1771 a core religious text of the Zoroastrian religion, the *Zend-Avesta*, which greatly excited the attention of learned people in Western Europe (Kriwaczek 2002: 34–46; Mirza 2002: 164–83). In India, its Sanskrit literature, beginning with the *Vedas*, provided an indispensable key to knowledge of the Aryans.

The revisionists who argue for the exclusively Indian origins of the Aryans tend to forget the crucial role of Iran in the Aryan story. A deeper understanding of the Aryans is gained by juxtaposing both the Iranian and Indian traditions and, additionally, those of Central Asia. Historians employ the word 'Aryan' to describe all the early Indo-Iranian migrants from the Caspian region, and modern Iranians use it in an ethnic and nationalistic context by calling their country, Iran, the land of the Aryans. Strictly speaking, however, the precise self-ascription of the word

'Aryan' applied only to two particular sub-groups, the Avestan and the Rig-Vedic people, who represent the two most important arms of the Indo-Iranian tradition as a whole. They alone, of all the neighbouring and displaced tribes of the original settled peoples, claimed a special status of honour and nobility in the territories they invaded and inhabited (Kochhar 2000: 37). A deeper understanding of this Aryan culture can only be gained by studying the languages, religious customs and traditions of the Avestan and the Rig-Vedic people, who coexisted in eastern Iran and Afghanistan. Common ties of language,[2] culture, mythology and rituals developed among them before they ultimately separated. In their religious beliefs and practices they together worshipped a number of deities. They both shared a tradition of composing lavish hymns in praise of their gods. In both traditions the descriptions of such nature gods as those of wind and sun, for example, are similar in tone and feeling. Some of their earliest prayers also bear similarities. Sanskrit is very close to the language of the *Yashts*, the earliest hymns of the *Avesta*, the sacred text of the present-day Zoroastrians of Iran and India. The Iranian prayers are part of the *Avesta* collection. Some sections of the *Avesta* resemble, not only in language but in content as well, the Rig-Vedic hymns that were composed by the Indian bards (Dange 2002: 185–91). The two groups once shared a common practice of drinking the juice of an originally hallucinogenic plant, called *soma* in the *Rig-Veda*, or *haoma* in the *Avesta*, for strength, virility and wakefulness. The present-day substitute plant has been identified as a species of *ephedra*, and its main habitat is the area around eastern Iran and south Afghanistan (Kochhar 2000: 104–12). The symbolic role of fire in the rituals of worship for both groups should also be noted. In the words of a noted Sanskrit scholar:

> 'taking into account the similarities in mythology, language, religious practice and beliefs, we may safely conclude that the traditions of the *Avesta* and that of the *Rig-Veda* have emerged from a single common source'.
>
> (Dange 2002: 191)

Speaking a form of proto-Sanskrit, the earliest wave of Aryans might have reached India around 1700 BCE, while the Rig-Vedic people followed some 300 years later, around 1400 BCE. The latter brought with them their collection of sacred hymns and chants composed over the centuries during their Iranian and Afghan sojourn. That collection represents the earliest portions of the *Rig-Veda*. The original form of Sanskrit which they utilised would have been more complex and sophisticated than that of their predecessors, but this early Sanskrit too would have had to adjust to the then existing native languages of India. The Rig-Vedic people were, culturally speaking, the most influential of the Aryans, and it is their literary and spiritual opus, the *Rig-Veda*, which provides penetrating insights into the Vedic culture of India. From then on, it was considered to be a purely Indian climactic opus.

The Avestan people continued to follow the old Indo-Iranian religion shared by the Rig-Vedic people, but in around 1000 BCE a visionary philosopher, named Zarathushtra, brought about a momentous religious revolution in the eastern regions of Iran by dethroning most of the Indo-Iranian gods and charting out a new ethic and religious philosophy for his followers (Boyce 2002c: 19–27). The hymns that he composed are known as the *Gathas*. Although the contents of the *Rig-Veda* and the *Gathas* differ in many ways, nevertheless the similarities of the Gathic language and the early Vedic Sanskrit are very striking, as can be seen in **Excerpt 4.1** below (Boyce 1984: 8–11; Hinnells 1985: 30–3). Despite his

---

Excerpt 4.1 Pertinent Sanskrit/Avestan equivalents of some random words

The very close similarity between Vedic Sanskrit and Avestan provides one indication of the common origins of the Aryans of India and Iran.

yo vo apo vasvish yajate asuranish asurasya vashishthabyo hotrabhyo (Sanskrit)

yo vo apo vanguhish yazaite ahuranish ahurahe vahishtabyo zaothrabyo (Avestan)

he who worships you, the good waters, the Ahurian wives of Ahura, with best libations (English)

English	Sanskrit	Avestan
Horse	asva-	aspa-
Cattle	pasu-	pasu-
Pasture	gavyuti-	gaoyaoti-
Cow	go-	gav-
Earth	bhumi-	bumi-
Plough	krs-	karsh-
(To) bind	bandh-	band-
(To) believe	sraddha-	zrazda-
(To) know	vid-	vid-
Man	nar-	Nar
Woman	jani-/nari-	jani-/nairi-
Brother	bhratar-	bratar-
Son	putra-	puthra-
Daughter	duhitar-	Dugedar-
Intelligence	buddhi-	baodha-
Full	purna-	perena-
Part	Bhaga-	Bagha-
Army	sena-	Haena-
Worship	yajna-	Yasna-

Source: from a note communicated to the author by Mr Farrokh Vajifdar, Fellow of the Royal Asiatic Society of Great Britain.

separation from the older Indo-Iranian tradition, Zarathushtra retained fire as the supreme external symbol for the Iranian Aryans. Even today, a common element in the rituals of the Hindus and of the Zoroastrians of Iran and India is this symbolic fire (Jamkhedkar 2002: 193–7).

Racialisation: perceptions of Aryans as a unique race

Sir William Jones, the pioneer of Indo-European studies and the father of the sciences of philology and modern linguistics, had a very high regard for Indian culture and civilisation. The Sanskrit orientalists of his persuasion also felt that the Hindu civilisation had claim to as many achievements as had the classical Greco-Roman. However, the enthusiasm and dedication of these scholars yielded only a modest recognition in the academic and public life of Britain. British power in India became much more secure from the early nineteenth century onwards, and a degree of reluctance, born out of both arrogance and ignorance, pride in their ability to hold down India, or perhaps even shrewd pragmatism, prevented them from wholeheartedly embracing Jonesian vision and idealism. For these reasons, Britain had comparatively few high academic posts in Sanskrit or Indology at her universities. It was much more promising on the continent. Owing to the lack of large-scale meaningful contacts with real Indians on the ground, continental Europeans envisioned India through rose-tinted spectacles. It may be argued that, not having control over India, continental Europeans were less defensive about their culture than the British. Whatever may be the underlying reason, Sanskrit literature and Indian history were in great vogue on the mainland of Europe. In France the Societe Asiatique was founded in 1832. J.L. Burnouf was the great French Sanskritist, while his son Eugene was a specialist in both Pali and Sanskrit; in 1840 Eugene Burnouf translated from Sanskrit the ancient text of *Bhagavata Purana*.

It was in Germany, however, that the major advances in Sanskrit studies and scientific philology took place. In the late eighteenth and early nineteenth centuries, Germany was not yet one nation, but the notion of the Germans as a great people was palpably real (van der Veer 2001: 114–16). A manifestation of this may be noticed in some underlying historical tension between the Germans and the Jews (Poliakov 1974: 246–9). When the news of Jones's literary discoveries reached Germany in the 1790s, a succession of refined and sensitive German writers began to utilise Indian literature in their pursuit of the legends and myths of human origin. These writers collectively come to be known as belonging to the school of German Romanticism (Osborne 2006: 313–15). The great names among them were those of J.G. Herder (1744–1803), Johann Friedrich von Schiller (1759–1805), Friedrich von Schlegel (1772–1829) and the philosopher Arthur Schopenhauer (1788–1860). All of them revered Sanskrit literature, but Schlegel went the furthest, in that he was the first to link Sanskritic excellence with the question of origins. First, he maintained that: 'Everything, absolutely everything, is of Indian origin' (Poliakov 1974: 191). Second, he thought that the ancient Indians, motivated 'by some impulse higher than the spur of necessity', had moved towards the West. Third, he popularised the word 'Aryan', which was then just beginning to circulate in Europe, by linking it to those ancient Indians who had moved westwards, and by connecting the root *ari-* with the German word *Ehre*, or honour (Poliakov 1974: 193). The conclusion that was drawn was that the people of Germany were people of honour – the Aryans. Fourth, the Jews and other Semitic peoples, Schlegel argued, were inferior in achievements to the Aryans, thereby consciously exacerbating the anti-Jewish prejudices of many ordinary Germans.

In time, Schlegel's view of the origins of the world's peoples and their relative status became more contorted by the development of the science of eugenics and what may be called the scientific racism of the nineteenth century. With the increasing industrialisation and modernisation of Europe from the mid-eighteenth century onwards, and the colonisation of the world by the great European powers, European cultural arrogance rapidly festered. Obsessed with a desire to explain the intellectual superiority of the Europeans and their scientific prowess, certain scholars obviously sought answers in some particular roots and origins of the Europeans (de Riencourt 1986: 254–68; Mallory 1989: 266–70; Thapar 2002: 4–5;). Their sought-after answers lay in such concepts as polygenism, geographical determinism, physiognomic measurements and the hierarchy of races (Pieterse 1995: 30–51). Polygenism was the theory of human origination from several independent pairs of ancestors, with the implication that human beings belong to different species. Geographical determinism made place and climate the determining factors in any study of people's attributes. Physiognomic measurements were crude attempts to understand human diversity by measuring ratios and proportions of their skulls, jaws and noses. The hierarchy of races was constructed artificially to provide a specious respectability to the notion that European peoples were superior to all others. To a certain extent, the Darwinian theory of evolution, which proposed a steady process of development from a single-celled creature to Homo Sapiens, along with the so-called Social Darwinism of Herbert Spencer, helped to confirm the contemporary cultural anthropologists in their belief in the hierarchy of races (Poliakov 1974: 215, 233, 282–3, 290ff., 298). In this hierarchy, the superior people were the so-called Caucasians, who included the descendants of the Indo-Europeans and the Aryans; the Caucasians were higher than the Africans and the Chinese. These ideas became common through the works of such writers as Dr Robert Knox (1791–1862), Comte Gobineau (1816–82) and Ernest Renan (1823–92). They promoted the idea of racial purity and attacked the mixing of peoples. Individualistic nationalism within each European nation made the stories of national origin popular among the masses; in the atmosphere of pride and prejudice, they accepted the so-called scientific racism as the truth. It was ironical that, as race science became intertwined with the myths of origin, the term 'Aryan' came to be exclusively appropriated by European racists. For them, it was synonymous with the superiority of Europe's white populations, and the modern descendants of the ancient Aryans living in India and Iran came to occupy only the second rung on the Caucasian ladder.

In Britain, during the second half of the nineteenth century, the most important student of India and her culture was Professor Friedrich Max Muller (1823–1900)

(Chaudhuri 1974; ODNB 2004, Vol. 39: 706–11). A German by birth, he spent most of his life in Britain, teaching at Oxford. A Sanskrit scholar and a student of comparative religion, he held all Indian learning in high regard; he remained a figure of great significance in oriental scholarship. Today his fame rightly rests on the fifty volumes of the *Sacred Books of the East* that he edited in his lifetime. Had he concentrated exclusively on Sanskrit and Eastern religions there would not be any controversy about him over a hundred years after his death (van der Veer 2001: 106–12). He was, however, strongly influenced during the first half of his career by contemporary continental ideas which racialised the Aryan (Trautmann 1997: 172–81). Like all orientalist philologists he had a great admiration for the spiritual and literary heritage of the Aryans contained in the *Vedas* and the *Avesta*, but he also unfortunately went on to propound that the Aryans were a unique race of people. Later in life he retreated from the racialised concepts when he declared that it was 'antiscientific . . . to speak of an Aryan race, Aryan blood or Aryan skulls' (Poliakov 1974: 214). His contrition was in a sense partial. Although he renounced the crude racialised representation of Aryans, he nevertheless viewed them as a superior people who invaded India and eventually civilised its indigenous peoples. When he next argued that the British and the modern Indian descendants of the Aryans were one and the same people by saying that the same blood ran in the veins of English soldiers 'as in the veins of the dark Bengalees' (Poliakov 1974: 209–10), he seemed to imply that the British, as it were, like the latter day Aryans, had come to save their brothers of old who had been under the oriental despotism of the Mughals, and that the British Empire of India was a force for the good of India (Chaudhuri 1974: 311–43). This view, in one sense, might have helped to cement the bonds between British intellectuals and highly Anglophile Hindus, as can be seen in **Excerpt 4.2** below.

The British, at home or in India, did not share Muller's enthusiasm for Aryan brotherliness. Nevertheless, Aryanism subtly influenced British rulers' thinking about India. They came to imbibe the notion of Aryan superiority, and they believed that superiority could be measured scientifically. In their earnest desire to understand the complexity of the peoples of India, the British experimented with newfangled methods and quirky criteria in order to classify and categorise the various social and cultural groups within Indian society (Pinney 1990: 252–63). One particular method, that of anthropometry, was championed and adopted by one of British India's most distinguished civil servants, Sir Herbert Risley (1851–1911), a man who had a thorough grasp of all the tools employed in the service of scientific racism at that time. One of the tools, craniology – the study of skulls – had been much in vogue with the British to determine the level of criminality among lawless bandits etc. (van der Veer 2001: 150–5; ODNB 2004, Vol. 47: 7–8). Now Risley perfected what came to be called the Nasal Index as the scientific indicator of caste differences. Risley argued, from his bizarre experiments, that those Indians who had the most perfectly shaped noses belonged to the higher castes of *brahman* and *kshatriya*, and those with the most ugly and ill-formed noses belonged to the lower castes. Risley believed that the *brahmans* preserved the best of the Aryan genes and indeed were the superior Indians

Excerpt 4.2 Aryanism and Indo-British ties

Aryanism, in a sense, seemed to create a bond between the masters and the subjects. Less than two decades after the great rebellion of 1857–58, an Indian educationist proclaimed in 1876:

What a sublime spectacle is afforded by the present concourse of nations. The Hindu and Englishman are brothers! ... Philosophy has evolved a strange unity out of the hopeless variety of races. Let that unity be the groundwork of future peace and brotherhood.

Source: T. Ballantyne, *Orientalism and Race: Aryanism in the British Empire*, London: Palgrave, 2002, 173. Reproduced with permission of Palgrave Macmillan.

On the foundation stone of the Old Indian Institute at Oxford, built in 1883, there is the following translation of a Sanskrit inscription:

This building, dedicated to Eastern sciences, was founded for the use of Aryans (Indians and Englishmen) by excellent and benevolent men desirous of encouraging knowledge ... By the favour of God may the learning and literature of India be ever held in honour; and may the mutual friendship of India and England constantly increase.

Source: T.R. Trautmann, *Aryans and British India*, Berkeley: University of California Press, 1997, 5.

(Trautmann 1997: 198–204). This was nothing but blatant racism. Combining this with the other general perception that the Aryans were civilising invaders, another negative consequence arose in what may be called the Aryan–Dravidian divide (Inden 1990: 58–66). Linguistically, the Indo-Aryan languages of the north are different from those of the south, but it is simplistic to believe that the Aryans swooped down on the south and civilised the southerners. By continuing to hold on to the theory of Aryan invasion that Max Muller had earlier propagated, British academics and administrators were to open up new fissures in Indian society. Thus, for example, by confirming the elevated status for the *brahmans* within the caste system, they legitimised the *brahman* hegemonic privileges and prerogatives which led in turn to the later large-scale anti-Brahmanic movements (van der Veer 2001: 148–50). Similarly, the issue of Dravidian nationalism was also stirred to life in the twentieth century.

The theme of a superior Aryan civilisation also gripped the imagination of a number of nineteenth-century Indian social thinkers and reformers. Two of them stood out uniquely. Dayananda Sarasvati (1824–83), the founder of the Arya Samaj, was convinced that the decline and degeneracy of the Hindus was due to their straying from the pure and pristine message of the *Vedas* that the Aryan religion encompassed (van der Veer 2001: 49–52; Ballantyne 2002: 176–9). He believed that the Vedic revelation of the ancient Aryans contained all scientific knowledge, and he called upon his fellow Hindus to practise Vedic worship. This particular path of spiritual upliftment of the Hindu society ran parallel to the ideology of Hindu nationalism as expressed by Bal Gangadhar Tilak (1856–1920), another leader suffused with Aryan idealism and vision. Tilak absorbed wholesale all the ideas concerning the Aryans that flowed from European pens, but came to two astonishing conclusions (van der Veer 2001: 123; Ballantyne 2002: 179–81). One was that the home of the Aryans was not originally central Asia or the Caspian region but the far Arctic tundra lands. In his opinion, the retreat of the Ice Age generally at around 10,000 BCE had made the Arctic much more unfavourable for human habitation, thus forcing the Aryans to move with their advanced culture down towards the south and eventually to India. Tilak's other contention was that the Aryans came to India much earlier than the traditional date proposed by Sanskritists such as Max Muller. He used Indian astrology for his evidence and proposed that the *Vedas* dated from 4000 BCE, not Max Muller's date of 1200 BCE. Apart from these assertions, based upon both European and Indian knowledge, Tilak's main forte lay in convincing his readers and listeners of the superiority of the Aryan culture, thereby instilling in them a pride in the Hindu nation. Such ideas of the Aryan were destined to become a weapon in the armory of Hindu nationalists.

(alternate ideas)

A critique of Hindu nationalist versions of revisionism

While our understanding of the Aryans has gone through many changes of interpretation since Jones's time, there is also a measure of consensus on certain key issues among international scholars of linguistics, history and archaeology. These are:

1) There is an Indo-European family of languages; Sanskrit, the mother of Indo-Aryan languages, is related to such other languages as Greek, Latin and Old Persian. There is also the Dravidian language family in the south of India. Over the long time span of Indian history, the Indo-Aryan and Dravidian languages have fruitfully interacted with each other.

2) The Aryans were not an invading race of people. They were nomadic migrants speaking an early form of Old Iranian or proto-Sanskrit. Their original Indo-European homeland was around the Caspian region, and after 2000 BCE they went east and south as part of the concurrent dispersal of peoples. They did not invade India or attack the Harappan civilisation, but did first enter the Swat valley in north-west India through Afghanistan, in two waves at *c*. 1700 BCE and *c*. 1400 BCE. The latter, known as the Rig-Vedic Aryans, possessed an inordinate sense of high self-esteem.

3) The European scholars of the nineteenth century, searching for the roots of their own cultures and nationhoods, appropriated the concept of Aryan and

endowed it with the qualities of a superior race from which had descended their fellow Europeans and, at a lower grade, the northern Indians and the Iranians. The racialisation of the Aryan concept also infected nineteenth-century India.

4) Historians had to completely revise the chronology of Indian history after the discoveries of the Harappan civilisation.

A group of Indian and non-Indian writers has, over the last two or three decades, vehemently challenged some of the above points and reinterpreted them. Their revisionism has sprung out of a combination of certain beliefs and ideas, occasionally backed up by some good research. These include certain underlying beliefs: that European historians have presented the Aryan story in a way that asserts the superiority of Europe over India; that India's ancient history can be understood primarily through the Hindu religious literature and that the evidence from outside of India is of marginal importance (Witzel 2005: 341–404); that the Hindu nation must reassert itself against all foreigners; and that modern Indian secularism is manipulated by groups as disparate as Muslims, Dalits and Marxists. Out of these beliefs have emerged certain Hindu-centric lines of argument, which are briefly examined below.

The first contention is that the Indus valley culture and the Vedic Aryan culture are one and the same, and central to that culture was the River *Sarasvati*, not the Indus. The Indus valley culture, according to the revisionists, was really the *Sarasvati* culture, and the foundations of a number of settlements, discovered along the direction of the now dried-up *Sarasvati*, are cited as proof. An important argument against this view is that the Indus valley culture could not be the same as the Vedic culture because otherwise it would have been celebrated in the extensive Indo-Aryan literature and remembered, in the oral tradition, by posterity. Nowhere in the texts are the cities of the Indus (or *Sarasvati*) mentioned (Thapar 2002: 110), or even remembered with pride and affection. This seems very curious for a people who recited, and passed down the generations, thousands of hymns and verses in the oral tradition. A learned authority has concluded on this matter thus:

> ... the only way that one may retain an Indo-Aryan identity for the Indus Civilization is to assume that, after its collapse about 1800 BC, it receded into the type of world reflected in the Vedic hymns and that these are the product of the degenerate descendants of the Indus Civilization. Given all the other objections, this solution would call for far more special pleading than anyone has reason to credit. All of our earliest evidence for the Indo-Aryans in India, therefore, indicates that they came from elsewhere.
>
> (Mallory 1989: 45)

It should be acknowledged that the Indus valley culture came to light only in the nineteenth century, and it was not recognised in India until then. The *Sarasvati* River certainly flowed either through or near many settlements that provided the life blood of the Indus culture, but the beginnings of that culture are in fact to be traced in Baluchistan. The river was drying up even at the time that the Aryans were first settling in India, and at least one scholar has even suggested that the river glowingly described in the Vedic texts could actually be the River Harahvaiti in Afghanistan (Kochhar 2000: 120–36). By including the name of *Sarasvati* in the title of Chapter 3, the present author has recognised the role that the villages on the banks of that river played in the evolution of Harappan society; there is no need to further exaggerate the river's importance.

The revisionists have also argued that the theory of an Aryan invasion was a nineteenth-century construct of racist writers who strove to justify British rule in India in an oblique way by reminding their reading public about how a glorious civilisation had once come into India from somewhere near Europe. This argument has been well rehearsed, and there is growing agreement that the invasion models were flawed. It was made clear in Chapter 3 that there is no support, for example, for Mortimer Wheeler's assertions of an Aryan invasion of the Harappan cities. Similarly, we no longer accept the nineteenth-century thesis, propounded by people like Schlegel and the early Max Muller, that the Aryans were an invading race. Over three decades ago, the historian Romila Thapar, who has been constantly under attack by the revisionists, clearly stated the following:

> The notion of the Aryan race is alien to the Indian tradition ... Race is not the criterion and obviously could not be, for the concept of race both in the scientific and popular sense is a product of modern Europe.
>
> (Thapar 1975: 2–8; quoted from Gottlob 2003: 221–2)

It is worth remembering that Max Muller himself changed his position because he was open to new evidence and fresh interpretations (Thapar 2002: 12–13).

Another contention has been that the Vedic texts make no mention at all of the foreign lands to the west, in the Afghanistan region, from where the Aryans were supposed to have come. Most linguistic experts, however, are of the opinion that the *Rig-Veda* was first composed in the Afghanistan area; the early parts of the text include references, at least obliquely, to places, rivers, animals, etc. of that land (Witzel 1995: 321–4). Further, the *Rig-Veda* was composed over a long period: by the time of its completion (*c.* 900 BCE), the Rig-Vedic Aryans had been in India for 500 years, while the non-Rig-Vedic Indic speakers had been there for some 800 years. Their integration into Indian society had been so long-established and complete that the composers would have had no need to remember the dim past of their earliest origins (Kochhar 2000: 94).

It is also argued that whatever is composed in the Vedic texts is uniquely Indian. While this has a specious validity, it has been pointed out that three of the oldest written documents containing any reference to Aryan names come not from Iran or India but from Mesopotamia (Mallory 1989: 37–9; Thapar 2002: 107–9). From the documents of the Kassite rulers of Babylon (*c.* 1750 BCE–1170 BCE) we learn of three names: two gods, Suriya (the sun god) and Marutta (the god of war), and a king, Abirattas, or Abhi-ratha ('facing the war chariots'). North-west of Babylon there lay the Mittani kingdom (*c.* 1500 BCE–1300 BCE), from where the cuneiform documents in the Akkadian language list the various princes and noblemen whose names are very strikingly Aryan, for example, Sutarana, Sauksatra, Purusa, Subandhu, Indrota, etc. The final, clinching evidence comes from the cuneiform tablets discovered at Boghazkoi in eastern Turkey. These tablets record the details of a treaty signed in about 1350 BCE between the losers, the Mittani, and their victors, the Hittites. Both sides list their gods, but among the Mittani gods are those who are distinctly Rig-Vedic: Indra, Nasatya, Varuna, Mitra. In the *Rig-Veda* itself these gods are assigned the task of overseeing the treaties between warring peoples. Apart from some of the seal images from the Indus valley culture, no documents about the Aryan gods earlier than these Mesopotamian records have been found in India; it therefore makes sense that some of the earliest of the Rig-Vedic concepts were developed 'in a central area, from where they travelled towards the west as well as the east' (Kochhar 2000: 117). A Belgian revisionist, Koenraad Elst, has nevertheless claimed that the Aryan migration was not towards India but out of India. Their ancestral homeland, their *Urheimat*, was the land of *Sapta-Sindhava* (the Punjab), and from there they expanded outwards towards Afghanistan, Iran, central Asia and, ultimately, towards Europe (Elst 1999: Internet). This Out-of-India theory has not yet gained any acceptance among international scholars, but it deserves careful study in view of the author's substantial knowledge of Indo-European languages and history.

The Aryan expansion

There were two main regions in the Afghanistan area where the Aryans had been settled since 2000 BCE. One was the area around modern Kabul, stretching in the east towards modern Peshawar. The Kabul–Peshawar enclave might have been the initial area from where migration towards the Swat valley began in about 1700 BCE. Another equally important zone was the area around Kandahar, with links to Quetta via the Bolan Pass. It is believed that the Rig-Vedic Aryans moved from there at about 1400 BCE, crossing the various rivers and then proceeding towards either the Swat valley or the Punjab. The entire region, including eastern Afghanistan, the Swat valley, the Punjab and the Indo-Gangetic watershed, is referred to, just once, in the *Rig-Veda* as *Sapta-Sindhava*, the land of the seven rivers. Although the *Rig-Veda* does not dwell at any length on the pre-Indian past of the Aryans, there are some hymns in which the newcomers vaguely remember and reminisce about the Iranian, Afghan and Central Asian localities, tribes and animals.

Among the many sites and regions in the north-west of the subcontinent, scholars and archaeologists have identified the Swat valley of northern Pakistan as possibly the first area of intrusion by the Aryans into the subcontinent (Mallory 1989: 47; Kochhar 2000: 180–5) (see Map 4.1). The valley's extensive layers of settlement from 3000 BCE to 300 BCE have made it possible to examine the continuities in, and interruptions to, the local culture. From the surveys undertaken, it has been found that from 1700 BCE onwards a change occurred in the burial rites of the people. Inside the cemeteries the archaeologists have found both flexed inhumation in a pit and cremation burial in an urn. This dual practice was not common among the contemporary cultures of the same region, but the early Vedic literature indicates that both inhumation and cremation burial were practised among the early Indo-Aryans. Another indication of change is the ceramic style. A new type of grey ware that was handmade and decorated with incisions is much in evidence during this period. On the basis of the change noticed in burial rites and ceramics, the archaeologists call the new culture of the valley the Gandhara Grave culture. Another argument in favour of the Swat valley being the original area of the Aryan reception in the subcontinent is also the fact that the natural features and scenes depicted in the Rig-Vedic hymns match the geographical reality of the valley (Mallory 1989: 47).

The Swat valley was the stepping stone to the Punjab, where the Aryans lived for many centuries. We learn from the *Rig-Veda* that they were confronted by an indigenous people, called by them dasas, dasyus or panis, and by many pejorative names such as blacks, demons or cattle-thieves (Griffith 1920: I 101.5, 104.2; V 29.10), but they were helped by Indra, the war god, to defeat these people. It is important to stress that these defeated people were not the Harappans. Another piece of information concerns the organisation of the Aryans into tribes and clans. It is thought that the term 'fivefold race' of people refers to five clans: Yadu, Turvasa, Anu, Druhyu and Puru (Griffith 1920: I 7.9). Through both inter-tribal fighting and alliance-building the Puru had come to occupy a central position for themselves on one of the seven rivers of the *Sapta-Sindhava*. In due course, one of their branch clans, the Bharata, subdued them and eventually became the dominant group in the Punjab. This was achieved at the famous Battle of Ten Kings, in which Sudas, king of the Bharata, defeated a confederacy of ten Aryan tribes. Various dates, going far back into time, have been proposed for this battle, but most historical opinion has settled on about 900 BCE as its date (Kochhar 2000: 49–53). The third vital piece of information that the *Rig-Veda* provides us about the Aryans in the Punjab concerns their transition from a semi-nomadic life to settled agriculture. After centuries of nomadic life in not very fertile terrain the Aryans found themselves in a land blessed with great rivers and innumerable streams. They had much to learn about the skills of irrigating and harnessing the rivers. In this process too there would be scope for rivalries and inter-clan fighting over land and resources. More importantly, they would come to learn much from the skills of the indigenous people.

From 900 BCE onwards the centre of gravity of the Aryan world shifted to what is called *Madhyadesha*, the Middle Country. This land extended from east of the *Sarasvati* to the Ganges plains. The events of this land form part of the setting of the *Mahabharata*, a post-Vedic epic. New clan formations and amalgamations took place at this time, and two dominant lineages emerged: the Kuru and Panchala. The centre of Kuru power was at Kurukshetra, while the Panchala base was further east. With the steady drying up of the *Sarasvati* and its sister river, the *Drasadvati*, the Kuru had to move their base from Kurukshetra to Hastinapura, and a new centre, called *Indraprashtha*, was founded. This meant a certain amount of tension and warfare with the Panchala. From the post-Rig-Vedic texts and the epics we learn that there were two sets of wars going on: Aryan versus Aryan, and Aryan versus non-Aryan. However, despite constant warfare, the Kuru and Panchala came together at crucial periods, and their hold on power in *Madhyadesha* later inspired many rulers of India to possess this region and make it the centre of their influence (Rapson 1922: 77–108).

From now on, it becomes somewhat simplistic to talk just of the Aryan advance. It was more an Indo-Aryan advance, because the pre-Aryans were as much involved in the building of a new society as the Aryans. We are no longer talking about simple migrant folks from Afghanistan, entering India through the passes in small groups. We now have a new situation, with the Indo-Aryans becoming colonisers. From 900 BCE onwards, the further Aryan expansion, both eastwards and southwards, continued inexorably. The lands of modern Bihar and Bengal were colonised. From the later epic of the *Ramayana* we also learn about the expansion to the south, into modern Madhya Pradesh, Gujarat, Maharashtra and Orissa. A particular clan, called Yadu, might have been forced by the Kuru–Panchala to migrate southwards from their base at Mathura; another Aryan group from Kosala penetrated the Deccan by establishing a kingdom on the River Godavari. The literary sources give us information about the tools and accoutrements that the Indo-Aryans carried with their herds. Chariots and carts, pulled by horses and oxen and laden with weapons made of bronze and iron, bore the Indo-Aryan warriors towards new horizons. The cutting down and the burning of forests were particularly onerous tasks, but they became easier in due course with the use of iron technology. Iron weapons must have had a demoralising effect on the rebellious or uncooperative non-Aryans. The Aryanisation of the entire Gangetic basin was in full swing between 900 BCE and 600 BCE, and powerful warrior-clan settlements became established throughout the area.[3] With the forest clearances came farming; the village no longer meant a band of itinerant warriors and travellers with their wagons but small farmsteads and craftsmen living in huts and simple houses.

The Aryan advance through north India did not result in the elimination of the pre-Aryan people or culture. Both the Aryan and the pre-Aryan learned to co-exist. The Aryan might have become more dominant, but the native Indians' influence and usefulness in the new Indo-Aryan society remained pervasive. For example, in the event of the union of Aryan men and non-Aryan women, the children were greatly influenced by their mothers in matters of custom and attitude. The migrant Aryans also learned from the pre-Aryans a great deal about the Indian landscape and the semi-medical esoteric knowledge concerning herbal drugs and charms. One aspect of the Vedic religion in which both the Aryan and the pre-Aryan rituals were brought together was the ceremony of worship. While the Aryans made their ritual of *homa*, associated with fire-worship, an act of thanks to the gods for favours bestowed by them, the pre-Aryans used a ceremony called the *puja* as a way of invoking the supreme Spirit into an object and then meditating upon that object. In an act of compromise, the Aryan and the pre-Aryan combined the two rituals by introducing the fire-cult into the *puja* ceremony (Marr 1975: 30–7; Daniélou 2003: 11–38).

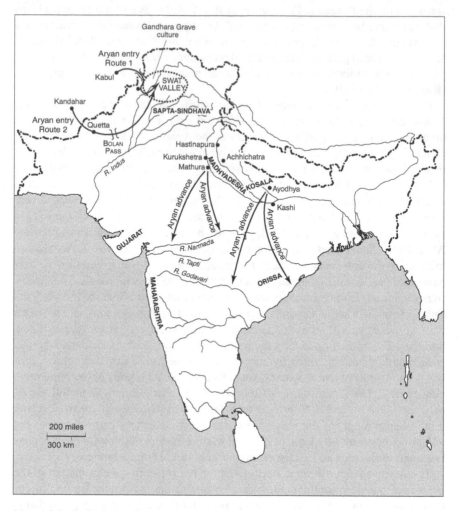

Map 4.1 India in the Vedic age

The Vedic world of the Indo-Aryans

We describe the world of the Indo-Aryans as Vedic, because it is essentially through the Vedic literature that we know so much about them. A significant portion of this extensive literature has been translated into English. The literature that is contemporary with the chronological period of this chapter consists of the four *Vedas*, the three great commentaries of the *Brahmanas*, the *Aranyakas* and the *Upanishads*, and the *Vedanga* and *Upaveda* texts. There is also much literature after 600 BCE, consisting of such great epics as the *Mahabharata* and the *Ramayana*, and they too are useful for learning about this period. We shall explore the epics in Chapter 5. While religious and spiritual themes do dominate much of this literature, there are also many references to a host of other subjects. For a historian, however, this literature has its limitations, because it does not provide a body of systematic historiography from which we can trace and outline a chronological sequence. Also, some of the most abstract as well as abstruse ideas, composed in a highly cryptic form, cannot be easily grasped without the scholarly interpretations of those who are learned in Vedic Sanskrit. The second useful tool in our understanding is archaeology. However, while its indications have been absolutely central to the study of the Indus valley Harappan culture, its role in uncovering the Indo-Aryan world is somewhat limited. Nothing as exciting as the Great Bath or the grid-planned streets of Mohenjo Daro has been discovered elsewhere from the rubble of the Vedic age. What archaeology can do is to corroborate, or confound, textual evidence. Yet another way of studying the Indo-Aryan world is by looking around modern India today and observing the living traditions of the people. The vast ethnic, social and cultural diversity of the Hindu people of India presents a treasure trove of details useful to the anthropologists and sociologists. The traditions followed today are varied and heterogeneous, but some of them go back to Vedic times. Here, in this section, we present six selected aspects of Vedic life (Parpola 2006: 211–15).

Pastoralism, farming and trades

The Aryan migrants were essentially a pastoral people, and for a long time, in India too, their main occupation remained cattle-rearing (Sengupta 1950: 34; Thapar 2002: 112–14). Cattle were the most valued of their possessions, their protection being considered almost a religious duty. As in Iran, cattle raiders and thieves were considered evil people who needed to be destroyed. The Sanskrit term *gavishthi* could mean searching for cows that were stolen or fighting battles with the raiders. In the very early Vedic period cattle might have been owned collectively. Those who herded their cows in the same cowshed belonged to the same *gotra*, a term which later became part of caste terminology, meaning a descent from a common ancestor (Jha 2004: 48). The relative importance of the pastoral economy can be gauged by the fact that the *Rig-Veda* carries more references to pastoralism than to agriculture. Such details as the marking of the ears of cattle for ownership, the accessibility of pasture lands and the daily tasks of the herdsmen are mentioned there. Large quantities of charred bones of cattle and other animals, found at various archaeological sites, also testify to the pre-eminent role the pastoral economy played in the daily life of the early Aryans. From their original Iranian and Afghan backgrounds the early Aryans were familiar with seasons and their role in the promotion of agriculture, but the farming and husbanding of crops was something that they had to learn from the indigenous people. The latter had, after all, been perfecting these skills in Baluchistan and the Indus region since 7000 BCE, and the plough itself was a pre-Harappan tool (Thapar 2002: 116). It was in the lush terrain of the Punjab that the Aryans first appreciated the advantages of farming crops, but it was after the dense forests of the Ganges plain were burnt and felled systematically that agriculture overtook pastoralism as the main daily activity of most people, and rice rather than wheat became the main crop of cultivation. The *Rig-Veda* contains much information about farming in general. There are references to ploughs and plough teams drawn by a number of oxen; to the cutting, bundling and threshing of grain; to irrigation canals and wells; and to such foods as milk, butter, rice cakes, cereals, lentils and vegetables. A copious number of Vedic hymns invoke the blessings of gods for plenty of crops, rains and the welfare of the cattle. While a number of terms describing various types of fields and the practice of measuring land are mentioned, there is no reference to any transaction of land that can be carried out by an individual (Jha 2004: 48–9). Most probably, therefore, there was some form of common ownership of land. In the villages and larger settlements there were people practising a variety of crafts and trades – carpenters, weavers, metal workers, tanners, potters, goldsmiths, bow makers, chariot makers and many others – and a lively trade in their products and a large number of building projects (Sarkar 1928: 1–46) would have created a hub of activity throughout the countryside, particularly in the later Vedic period, from 1000 BCE to 600 BCE.

Pottery and iron: the material base as evinced from archaeology

Over the last six decades or so, extensive archaeological excavations have been carried out in the areas of north India where the Aryans first settled or where they later moved to. The excavations of the Indian archaeologist B.B. Lal at Hastinapura in 1954–55 were the most remarkable, but many other famous sites, such as Ahicchatra and *Indraprashtha*, Mathura and Kausambi, have also been extensively dug and closely inspected (Chakrabarti 1998: 186–8). The archaeologists were particularly keen to find material evidence that would, for example, confirm on the ground poetic descriptions of cities such as Ayodhya in the later epic of the *Ramayana*, but they have been unsuccessful. The most valuable information they have gathered concerns varieties of pottery and the transition, within certain cultures, from the Chalcolithic to the Iron Age.

Pottery provides clues to the quality of life in the ancient world. It was a status symbol of the people in India too. The crudest form of post-Harappan pottery, known as Ochre-Coloured Pottery (OCP), was generally found in the lowest levels of the major sites. It was so called because, on rubbing, it produced a yellow-brown stain on the finger; its worn-out condition was due to poor firing techniques. At all ground levels that contained materials dating before 900 BCE, the most common form of pottery was the OCP (Kochhar 2000: 80–1). This pottery could therefore have belonged to the early Rig-Vedic Aryans. From 900 BCE, with the Aryans branching out from beyond the *Sapta-Sindhava* region to the Ganges basin, a new style of pottery came into fashion. This was the Painted Grey Ware (PGW), the name given to fine, wheel-made, well-fired grey pottery with linear patterns and dots in black. With an imaginative mixture of painted designs, involving various shapes, the PGW was the most excellent form of pottery product available to well-off people of that era. It would, however, be a mistake to believe that the Aryans were particularly involved in the creation of the PGW. Practically all of it would have been produced by the local indigenous pre-Aryans who occupied the bottom rung of the Indo-Aryan social ladder. It is reckoned that PGW formed only between 10 and 15 per cent of the total pottery. From the PGW sites of the period 900 BCE to 600 BCE the materials unearthed include various animal skeletons, several cereal grains, burnt bricks, glass fragments, semi-precious stones, gambling dice and some iron. Of a poorer quality than the PGW but superior to OCP was the vast mass of pottery known as Black-and-Red Ware (BRW). Only after the end of our period, at about 600 BCE, do we see the emergence of the most excellent variety of pottery called Northern Black Polished Ware (NBPW) (Ratnagar 1995: 25–6; Thapar 1995: 89–91; Kochhar 2000: 80–8).

Apart from pottery, another product of importance with which Indo-Aryan archaeology is much concerned is iron. A cheaper and more accessible material than copper, iron came to be used widely by a number of communities within India during the last four centuries of the period covered in this chapter, 1000 BCE to 600 BCE. The earliest Iron Age sites of India were located in three main regions: the Ganges plains, the central regions of Malwa and the Tapti valley, and the megalithic sites in south India. Many of the sites in the Ganges plains are the very ones that are connected to the PGW potteries and the Aryan expansion. From the evidence found, some important conclusions have been arrived at. First, the Iron Age did not succeed the Chalcolithic Age uniformly throughout India at a particular point of time; the progression and transition between the two ages remained extremely uneven in different parts of India. Second, iron technology was not brought by the Aryans; it developed gradually from about 1000 BCE onwards, long after the Aryans had metamorphosed into Indo-Aryans. It is also not particularly useful to start searching for one original site where this technology first developed. Rather, we should think of such a technological advance developing at different places and at different paces. Third, the first iron tools were not axes and ploughshares, but weapons, and so the clearing of forests in the Ganges basin is more likely to have taken place in the later centuries of this period, after 1000 BCE rather than before (Schwartzberg 1992: 155–60; Ratnagar 1995: 20–4; Ray *et al.* 2000: 196–214).

The patriarchal family

Apart from Vedic literature, our sure guide to understanding the family life of the Vedic Aryans is what we can learn of the average Hindu family of our own day. The most Westernised Hindu families in India today may display a number of modern customs and attitudes regarding family relationships, but the vast majority of Hindu families choose to follow what may be called the Vedic model, with certain adaptations. The Vedic family, the *kula*, was highly patriarchal. Extended families of three generations or more were the norm. The senior male, the father or sometimes the grandfather, was the head of the household. Sons lived with their parents for both economic and religious reasons. The sons helped the fathers with the daily chores of farming or any trade and thus increased the general prosperity of the family; both their parents relied upon them when they reached old age; and they also had a valuable role to play in the performance of various ceremonies.

For example, when cremation displaced burial in later Vedic times, the eldest son was made the chief torch-bearer for the funeral pyre of the dead parent. On the other hand, it is more than likely that younger sons were pampered and spoilt by their parents, a phenomenon still noticeable in many Indian homes.

It was a different story with girls. The birth of daughters was generally considered a matter of regret or shame, and the *Atharva Veda* recommends a girl child to be put away, which might mean being married off as soon as possible. Women might be honoured and feted as queens of their households, but basically they were considered to be useful attachments to the males, as wives, daughters, mothers or sisters; they were never to be thought of as independent personalities in their own right (Bose 2010: 58–76). Docility rather than assertiveness was required of them; instead of thinking about their rights in such matters as their share of patrimony or inheritance, they had to concentrate on preparing for marriage, loyalty to their husbands, nurturing children and attending to the family's well-being. The pronouncements and assertions made about the female gender in Vedic literature may occasionally appear complimentary, but their sexist nature cannot be denied. **Excerpt 4.3** below gives a flavour of this attitude.

There were certain positive features of the patriarchy that we must not ignore. The homesteads and households provided comfort and warmth for the whole family. The joint family acted as a support mechanism for the elderly, in particular. In our contemporary world, it is the elderly who suffer so much pain and anguish through loneliness and lack of meaningful social interaction; this would not have happened in a typical Vedic family, where seniority was respected and honoured. The sons considered it their pious duty to carry their infirm parents on pilgrimages to many holy rivers and other auspicious places. Various rituals and ceremonies, both at home and in the public arena, also kept the family bonds tight; and the giving and receiving of gifts (*dana*) would have made individuals feel good about themselves (Prinja 1996: 173–4). The staple diet within the average household included milk, clarified butter, vegetables, fruit, wheat, rice and, on auspicious occasions, meat: a healthy fare for any human being. The very small population of the entire country of India, probably about 20 million at the end of the Vedic age (Thapar 2002: 53), helped to reduce the strains and stresses of living in congested spaces of Indian cities today but, on the other hand, diseases must have been rampant too. The texts give us a diverse picture of the life of the Vedic people. While the poor, the humble and all manner of working people carried on unobtrusively with their daily life, the rich dressed ostentatiously and their women wore much jewellery. A variety of amusements are mentioned in the *Rig-Veda*, such as chariot-racing, horse-racing, dancing and music, but gambling is rightly condemned as an activity leading to ruin (Griffith 1920: X.34). Despite the rigours of the patriarchy, the Vedic family lived in a society that seemed to be at ease with itself.

Political power and social differentiation

While attempts have been made to construct lists of kings and dynastic lines, based mostly on correlating the Vedic texts with accounts from the *Puranas*, the semi-

Excerpt 4.3 Views on women in early Vedic literature

The negative tone of the first three quotes is sufficient testimony to the generally disdainful attitude of the patriarchy towards women. Their intelligence was always doubted. There were, however, women of learning in Vedic times. One was Gargi, whose debating skills and rigorous questioning exhausted the patience of Yajnavalkya, her teacher. Another was Maitreyi, who is mentioned in the last quote. She was one of Yajnavalkya's wives, who understood that the path to immortality lay through intellectual discourse, not wealth. Her wisdom is celebrated, but it made little difference to the general attitude of the male sex towards females. We may, however, add here that 2,000 years ago such an attitude was almost universal among the world's people.

1) Food is life, clothing is protection, gold is beauty, marriage is for men. (One's) wife is a friend, a daughter is misery and a son is the light in the highest heaven. (*Aitareya Brahmana*, 3.33.1).

2) The mind of women brooks no discipline. Her intellect has little weight. (*Rig-Veda*, 8.33.17)

3) A woman, a Sudra (the member of the lowest caste), a dog and a crow are the embodiments of untruth, sin and darkness. (*Satapatha Brahmana*, 14.1.1.31)

4) Yajnavalkya spoke thus to Maitreyi: 'O Maitreyi, I wish to elevate myself (from a householder's life); let me then divide my property between you and Katyayani (his other wife)'. Maitreyi said, 'Reverend One, if this world with all its wealth were mine, would I then become immortal?' Yajnavalkya said, 'Your life would become that of the wealthy but by wealth you will never gain immortality'. Maitreyi said, 'If I did not become immortal by it, of what use would wealth be to me? Tell me, Reverend One, of any (means of obtaining immortality) that you know'. Yajnavalkya said, '(You were) dear to us before, (but what now) you say is dearer. Come, sit down; I will explain to you (the means of earning immortality). Listen with care to understand my explanation. (*Brhadaranyaka Upanishad*, 2.4.1–4).

Source: Mandakranta Bose, *Women in the Hindu Tradition: Rules, Roles and Exceptions*, London: Routledge, 2010, 77, 82, 89–90.

religious texts of the mid-first millennium CE, and the great epics of the *Mahabharata* and *Ramayana*, we need to be more circumspect about this methodology. The *Puranas* contain a good amount of credible history, but it is mixed in with much non-historical or unhistorical material, and the epics are, after all, great works of imagination, not of history as such. It is only from the sixth century BCE onwards, almost at the end of the Vedic period, and with the corroboration of the Buddhist sources, that we can be more certain about the chronology of dynasties and monarchs. This does not, of course, mean that there were no states or monarchs in the Vedic period. There definitely were; we just do not know enough about them. What we do know, however, is that side by side with facts lies a large number of ideas in the Vedic texts, and idealisations of power are but one example (Spellman 1964: 26–42).

As we have mentioned, the basic unit of power lay within the patriarchal family (*kula*); a number of families lived in a village (*grama*), controlled by a headman (*gramani*); groups of villages belonged to the clan (*vis*); and many clans made a community (*jana*). In the early Vedic period there was no real state structure. There were no kings as such, but clan chieftains. Raiding and the extraction of war booty were a way of life and an important way of redistributing wealth. There was also no regularised system of taxation. In the later Vedic period, groups of communities became part of a region or a state (*janapada*). The idea of kingship evolved gradually from clan chieftainship, but there was at first a control exercised on the king (*raja*) by assemblies (*vidatha, parishad, sabha, samiti*). By the end of the Vedic period, the king's authority was beginning to derive less from the support of such assemblies than from his own success in the struggle for power among his warrior-nobles. The hereditary element crept in with the further consolidation of power by the *rajas*, and from that point onwards the role of the courtiers or officers became critical. The main offices within the palace of a *raja* of the late Vedic period would be held by the chief priest (*purohit*), the commander-in-chief (*senapati*), the treasurer (*samagrahitri*), the collector of taxes (*bhagadugha*) and the keeper of the king's household (*kshata*). The legitimisation of the king's power was confirmed by lengthy and elaborate rituals of sacrifice (*yajna*) conducted by the priests, to be examined in the next subsection. The alliance between priest and king, a fundamental feature of Indian polity, became a key element in the maintenance of the hierarchical balance within the caste system.

The legendary caste system of India is the result of social differentiation developing into social stratification. The roots of this system within India lie in the devolutionary emergence of *jatis* (castes) at a time of socio-economic changes following the decline of urban society in Harappa and Mohenjo Daro, when craftsmen and other occupational groups would have locally reinforced their socio-economic bonds by the adoption of specific occupational names, the practice of endogamy and ranking by economic and ritual status (Maisels 2010: 52–4). It is also known that the Iranian Aryans, closely associated with the Rig-Vedic Aryans, practised a threefold division of society, consisting of priests, rulers and producers. What happened in the Indo-Aryan society, however, was something quite novel, extraordinary and most negative in its social impact (Thapar 2002:

122–6). During the Vedic period, the priests (*brahmans*) and the rulers (*kshatriyas*) consolidated their positions. The producers came to be split into two groups. Free peasants and traders became the third group, called *vaishya*, while slaves, labourers and artisans were degraded into the fourth group, the *shudra*. Within a relatively small population, the groups came to be rigidly compartmentalised on the basis of a religiously inculcated system of colour bar, known as *Varnashrama Dharma*. This had little to do with the division between the Aryan and the pre-Aryan. The two higher castes were not necessarily dominated by the Aryans, with the pre-Aryans consigned to the lower rungs. The main reason, however, why many pre-Aryans would have been on the bottom rungs was that they were in the main craftsmen and skilled workers, but those very skills of menial and manual work were derided on grounds of ritual impurity by the learned and the powerful, who could be either Aryan or pre-Aryan. The greatest stigma was attached to pollution of the upper castes by the lower. The Vedic texts not only contain elaborate rationalisations for the fourfold caste system based on colour, or *varna*, but they also describe the specific privileges and disabilities of each group. Many modern Hindus therefore tend to justify the caste system on the basis of the *Vedas*. However, since all Vedic texts were revised by the learned *brahmans*, who were in close alliance with the *kshatriyas*, there is a danger that the inviolate caste system as explained in the texts is a particular form of ideological construct. Apart from the Vedic strictures, there are other ways of understanding the caste system – for example, by studying changes in kinship patterns or the way in which economic resources came to be distributed (Thapar 1995: 101–2). There are also more acceptable social reasons in defence of the caste system than the explanations set out in the scriptures. One's caste can, for example, provide a secure psychological umbrella for someone with no friends or relations settling in a large town (Prinja 1996: 69–72).

The religion of the sacrifice

It is quite likely that the religion of the Indo-Aryans was a mix of ideas from their Indo-European past and what they might have learned from the indigenous pre-Aryans. Essentially, this religion was about a sense of awe and wonder about the forces of nature and the worship of the creator. For the simple and untutored people of that age, the creator took the form of many gods and goddesses, both benign and malign, who had the power of life and death over them. Among the gods, the names of Indra (the warrior god), Agni (fire) and Varuna (supreme judge) are well known. Such goddesses as Usas (dawn), Prthivi (earth), Sarasvati (enlightenment) and Aditi (mother) are thought of as benevolent, while Nirrti (darkness) and Ratri (gloom) represent negative forces. Whatever the nature of gods and goddesses, the way they all had to be kept happy and mollified was through a sacrifice (*yajna*) within the household (Walker 1968: Vol. 2, 316–21). Down through the ages this has been an unchanging phenomenon in a Hindu household. A *brahman* priest would be called upon to perform the ceremony in front of a fire lit in the sacrificial altar, into which were placed various foods such as milk, butter, barley and meat.[4]

As the Aryans had learned from the pre-Aryans the skills of making fire altars with bricks in a particular mystico-geometric formation, different types of altars were made available for specific sacrificial rituals. Square or circular-shaped altars were generally used for household rituals. The priest normally recited the Rig-Vedic hymns for dedication not just to the gods and goddesses but also to sacrificial objects such as the altar or *soma*, the plant of fertility. The chanting of hymns, the placing of foods into the fire, the gifts to the priest, the exchange of gifts among the members of the household, and the consumption of some of the consecrated food were all supposed to bring prosperity and happiness to the family or the clan. This simple ceremony of sacrifice, common in some aspects even today among the Hindus and the Zoroastrians of Iran and India (see Figures 4.1 and 4.2), became a much more spectacular affair in the later Vedic period. The purpose of the sacrifice was gradually transformed from being an offering to the gods to a celebration of the power of the kings (Jha 2004: 60–1). The kings used the sacrifice to confirm their legitimacy. Loyal *brahman* priests were drafted in by the *purohit*, the chief priest, for prayers and chants in front of massive fire altars. Elaborate altars, in the shape of rectangles, triangles and trapeziums, were built to hold the fire. One such altar, particularly impressive in its geometry, was built in the shape of a falcon, as it was believed that the falcon would carry the soul of the supplicant straight to heaven (Joseph 2010: 226) (Figure 4.3). Vast numbers of animals, particularly cattle, were slaughtered, large donations of gifts were made to the *brahmans* by the grateful kings, the people were fed well, and the richer among them gave expensive gifts to the kings. Some kings of the post-Vedic age engaged in even more ostentatious sacrifices, and thereby the original purpose and the modest scale of the sacrifice were both subverted for the glory of men rather than gods. This did not go unchallenged, as can be testified by **Excerpt 4.4** below.

Excerpt 4.4 An early example of dissent against the idea of Vedic sacrifice

. . . The fools who delight in [the] sacrificial ritual as the highest spiritual good go again and again through the cycle of old age and death.

Abiding in the midst of ignorance, wise only according to their own estimate, thinking themselves to be learned, but really obtuse, these fools go round in a circle like blind men led by one who is himself blind.

Regarding sacrifice and merit as most important, the deluded ones do not know of any other higher spiritual good . . .

Source: *Mundaka Upanishad*; quoted in Ainslee Embree (ed.), *Sources of Indian Tradition*, London: Penguin, 1992, 31. Copyright © 2016 Columbia University Press. Reprinted with permission of the publisher.

Figure 4.1 A modern Hindu *yajna* ceremony

Figure 4.2 A modern Zoroastrian fire ceremony

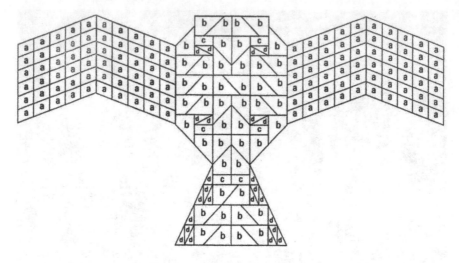

Figure 4.3 A falcon altar

Vedic literature and learning

The crowning glory of the Indo-Aryans lies essentially in their literature. The Vedic texts were composed, and orally transmitted, in Sanskrit for many hundreds of years before they were written down. The earliest parts of the *Rig-Veda*, the oldest of the *Vedas*, may have been composed as early as, or even earlier than, 1700 BCE, but written down only after 500 BCE. For forty generations and more, the Rig-Vedic text was handed down by word of mouth by bards and poets, who chanted the sacred hymns and the ritual prayers. Even today the oral tradition is continued. During the transition from the oral to the written it is natural that both the language and the ideas to be conveyed by the language would have evolved, and linguists have also noted certain differences between what is known as the earlier Vedic Sanskrit from the later Classical Sanskrit.

The *Vedas* constitute the very heart of the Indo-Aryan literature of this period. The word *veda* simply means 'knowledge' – the best of all knowledge in Hindu eyes. There are four main *Vedas* – *Rig-Veda*, *Sama-Veda*, *Yajur-Veda* and *Atharva-Veda* – and each has a core, called *Samhita*, which is a collection of metrical hymns and prayers, spells and exorcisms, mixed in some cases with prose passages. The principal *Veda* is the *Rig-Veda*, which, until the Harappan script is deciphered, must be considered the oldest significant extant Indian literary text. It is also the first major composition in any Indo-European tongue. It has ten books or *mandalas*, with 1,028 hymns and 10,600 verses in all. The books were composed by sages and poets from different priestly families over a period of at least 500 years (1400 to 900 BCE), if not earlier. The sacred hymns were addressed, in the sacrificial ceremonies of nature worship, to the principal Aryan gods, such as Agni and Indra, and to gods such as Varuna and Surya. Occasionally there is also a very high degree of philosophical speculation that can be viewed as highly modern in tone, such as the one below in **Excerpt 4.5**.

In the other three *Vedas* we see the first of the changes affecting the Indo-Aryan religion. The *Sama-Veda* is a rearranged version of some of the hymns of the *Rig-Veda*, but set to music. It is the first Indian treatise on music and chants, so essential in most Hindu worship. The *Yajur-Veda*, which is divided into two versions, known as the Black and White *Yajur*, is the manual of the priest. One of the key duties of a Vedic priest, as we have already mentioned, was to perform a sacrificial ceremony for the glory of the king. As has also been mentioned, this was done around a fire altar, and the geometry involved in the construction of the altars is alluded to in the texts attached to the *Yajur-Veda* and known as *Sulvasutra* (Joseph 2010: 226). In fact, one way of understanding all the *Vedas* is to imagine them as 'a vast and complex instruction manual for the sacrifice ... rather than as sacred books. Sacrifice preceded the *Vedas*, not vice-versa.'[5] The *Atharva-Veda* consists of material of a more popular character and it includes references to plants, herbs and diseases; it may be described as the first Indian treatise on medicine (Bose *et al.* 1989: 216).

Attached to the *Samhitas* of the *Vedas* are the *Brahmanas*, which interpret the rituals. They form a manual of worship and provide explanations of the *Samhitas*. In many ways they Hinduise the Indo-European aspects of the *Vedas* by emphasising the role of the priest in the great sacrifices. Some of the best-known *Brahmanas* are *Aitareya Brahmana*, attached to the *Rig-Veda*, the *Jaiminiya Brahmana*, attached to the *Sama-Veda*, and the *Taittiriya* and *Satapatha Brahmana*, attached to the *Yajur-Veda*. The *Taittiriya* and *Satapatha Brahmana*

Excerpt 4.5 The hymn of creation: *Rig-Veda* Book X, 129.6 and 129.7

The last line from verse seven is an indication of the early Indian thinkers' doubts and uncertainty about creation. This is in marked contrast to the definitive positions on this issue taken up by some contemporary dogmatists and fundamentalists.

(6): Who verily knows and who can here declare it, whence it was born and whence comes this creation?
   The Gods are later than this world's production. Who knows then whence it first came into being?

(7): He, the first origin of this creation, whether he formed it all or did not form it, whose eye controls this world in the highest heaven, he verily knows it, or perhaps he knows not.
   Source: Ralph T.H. Griffith, *The Hymns of the RigVeda*, Vol. 2, Benares: E.J. Lazarus, 1920, 519.

provide information about astronomy and geometry. Both subjects were vital to the work of the priests and the learned interpreters. Astronomical calculations helped with the forecasting of seasons and the construction of calendars for determining auspicious occasions for the great sacrifices. Geometry served a religious function because its noblest use was in the designing of fire altars. It is worth pointing out that the technical results in these subjects can only be elucidated by understanding the meaning of precisely expressed concepts in Sanskrit aphorisms. Hindus consider the *Vedas* and the *Brahmanas* as knowledge born out of *Shruti*, which means inspired revelation, as against the later Classical and traditional knowledge, which they term *Smriti*, or what might simply be called man-made transmitted knowledge. The *Aranyakas*, or the forest-books, are the concluding portions of the *Brahmanas*; they are concerned not with ritual, but with mysticism. A class of texts constituting the last stage or the end of *Veda, Vedanta*, is known as the *Upanishads*. These are normally embedded in the *Aranyakas* or form their supplements. It is in the *Upanishads* that some of the deeper questions of cosmological and personal significance are raised. It has been argued that both the *Aranyakas* and the *Upanishads* represent the thoughts and speculations of intellectually and spiritually advanced thinkers who were less interested in the ritualism of Vedic sacrifices; they foreshadowed the dissenting tradition that emerged after 600 BCE (Walker 1968: Vol. 2, 531).

We can obtain a flavour of what was meant by learning in ancient India by studying the *Upanishads*. There are over a hundred of them, and each *Upanishad* is concerned with the student sitting at the master's feet and receiving instruction. Most of the instruction concerned the main religious concepts of Hinduism, such as the Universal Soul, or *Brahman*, and the Universal Self, or *Atman*, and how ordinary mortals can reach union with the Divine through meditation and *Yoga*. The teaching style was not didactic but discursive and intellectual; the teacher stimulated the student's imagination and thinking by using a variety of pedagogical tools, such as Socratic dialogue, or posing questions in the form of riddles and paradoxes. At the same time, the skills of memorisation were highly esteemed, and students were encouraged to learn by rote the main verses (Roebuck 2000: xix–xxiv). This intense guru–student interaction and relationship is one of ancient India's greatest but largely unacknowledged contributions to the theory of learning. Learning was not just about religion in the abstract. The students had to combine that with the study of the *Sutras*, or traditional learning, concerned with ritual and customary law. Then there were certain texts called the *Vedangas*, which concentrated on such skills as phonetics and pronunciation (*Siksha*); metres (*Chhandas*); grammar (*Vyakrana*); etymology, or understanding roots of words (*Mirukti*); religious practice (*Kalpa*); and astronomy and astrology (*Jyotisha*). Another group of texts, the *Upa-Vedas*, contains information on secular subjects, such as medicine (*Ayur-Veda*), war or, literally, archery (*Dhanur-Veda*), architecture (*Sthapathya-Veda*), and music and arts (*Gandharva-Veda*). These works clearly demonstrate a wide range of interest shown by the Indo-Aryan intellectuals, professionals and practitioners in theoretical and practical studies. They are not dead works of intellect; they are consulted and made use of even today in contemporary India. To take two examples, many modern Indian doctors prescribe to their patients a large number of drugs, therapies and treatments that have been mentioned in the medical corpus of the *Ayur-Veda*, and ancient architectural works are studied for the purpose of building Hindu temples, such as the iconic Swaminarayan temple in Neasden, London, built on ancient architectural concepts. The respect for ancient knowledge in India goes hand in hand with the wish for modern education.

STUDY GUIDE

Key issues

- Understanding terminology: Indo-Europeans, Aryans, Indo-Iranians, Indo-Aryans.
- Stages in Aryan migration into India.
- The continuity of pre-Aryan indigenous traditions.
- Physical and cultural colonisation of India by the Aryans.
- Power and patriarchy in Vedic India.
- The characteristics of Vedic literature of the Indo-Aryans.

Suggested readings

Jha 2004: 42–64; Mallory 1989: 9–65; Stein 1998: 52–8; Trautmann 1997: 8, 172–81, 194–204; Walker 1968, Vol. 1: 69–73, Vol. 2: 530–5, 556–64; Witzel 1995: 307–52.

INTERNET SELECTION

1) Naghme Ghasemi: 'Indo-Iranian relations in pre-Aryan and Aryan periods'. www.academia.edu/5407630/chapter_II_Indo-Iranian_relationship_in_preAr
2) Razib Khan: 'Indo-Aryans, Dravidians, and waves of admixture (migration?)'. http://blogs.discovermagazine.com/gnxp/2013/08/indo-aryans-dravidians-and
3) Stephen Knapp: 'A complete review of Vedic literature and the knowledge within'. www.stephen-knapp.com/complete_review_of_Vedic_literature.htm
4) David Osborn: 'Scientific verification of Vedic knowledge: Archaeology online'. http://archaeologyonline.net/artefacts/scientific_verif_vedas
5) Michael Witzel: 'Autochthonous Aryans? The evidence from old Indian and Iranian texts'. www.people.fas.harvard.edu/-witzel/JVS-7-3.htm

QUESTIONS FOR GROUP DISCUSSION

1) Examine the contexts in which the term 'Arya'/'Aryan' has been used and abused by historians and political leaders in modern times.
2) In what way is racism different from racial prejudice? Why and how did European racism arise?

3)   Where in contemporary India are we likely to find traces of pre-Aryan indigenous cultures?
4)   Examine the sociological, philosophical and psychological reasons why Vedic culture has been so resilient in its survival strategies.
5)   Construct a bird's eye view table of the main works of Vedic literature between c. 1200 BCE and c. CE 500, and write one defining characteristic for each work.

Notes

1   Varied viewpoints on the Aryans can be read in such works as Frawley and Rajaram 1995; Kak (n.d.); Kochhar 2000; Mallory 1989; Renfrew 1987; Thapar 1993; Thapar 2002 (p.65).
2   The indication of a strong concurrence of the Indic and Iranian terms is referred to in Renfrew 1987: 193 (p. 70).
3   For another interesting perspective on the Aryanisation of the Indus culture, see Bhan 2002: 41–55 (p.81).
4   Meat offering stopped in later times, owing to the influences of Buddhism and Jainism (p. 89).
5   From a note to the author from Dr Daud Ali, formerly at the School of Oriental and African Studies, University of London (p. 93).

5 Post-Vedic centuries

(*c.* 600 to 300 BCE)

Timeline/Key Dates

c. 700–550 BCE	The proliferation of kingdoms and clan states
c. 599–527 BCE	Mahavira's life
c. 563–483 BCE	Buddha's life
544 BCE	Bimbisara becomes the first king of *Magadha*
c. 500 BCE	Panini's *Ashtadhyayi* written
377 BCE	Buddhist Council meets at Vaishali
327–326 BCE	Alexander the Great in north-west India
321 BCE	The end of the Nanda dynasty in *Magadha*
c. 300 BCE	The beginnings of the composition of *Mahabharata* and *Ramayana*

It was in north India that two historically important developments took place during what may be called the post-Vedic era, covering three centuries between 600 BCE and *c.* 300 BCE. First, a complex state system encompassing princely kingdoms and clan states emerged out of the petty polities of the Vedic period. This led to a hierarchy of states through warfare, duplicity and alliances, and this in turn resulted in the emergence of a single most powerful state, *Magadha*, which would eventually become the heartland of a great pan-Indian Mauryan empire, the subject of our next chapter. From a very early stage, the newly emerged state system came to be challenged by two foreign intrusions and influences, those of the Achaemenid rulers of Persia and the Macedonians/Greeks, the results of which affected India to a certain extent. Second, the systemic power wielded by the rulers, along with the benefits of iron technology, created huge agricultural surpluses for supporting non-agricultural populations in the new urban centres that developed during this period. This new phase of urbanism engendered much dynamism in the socio-economic life of north India. The urban people, however, were less receptive to the Brahmanic hegemony, and many came to be influenced by various dissenting traditions, particularly Jainism and Buddhism. Despite all the turmoil of change, however, Indian intellectual life remained as vigorous as ever, with new literatures being added to the enormous stock of knowledge compiled by Vedic teachers during the previous thousand years.

The rise of the state system

By 600 BCE, the geography of India was understood by its learned people in terms of five large regions (Schwartzberg 1992: 165). These were: *Madhyadesha*, the Middle Country; *Praticya*, the western lands; *Pracya*, the east; *Uttarapatha*, the northern route; and *Dakshinapatha*, the southern route.

Madhyadesha was the original core land around the Kurukshetra plain, which gradually encompassed the Ganges–Yamuna *doab* and the lands west of *Prayag*. Southwards, it tended to extend towards the Vindhya and Aravalli ranges; in future centuries, the entire area came to be called *Aryavarta*. The western lands of *Praticya* encompassed all the territory from eastern Afghanistan to the Aravalli hills. Two routes were already known then: one through the Bolan Pass and the other along the sea coast. Since the Persians considered the plain of the River Indus their eastern frontier and the Indians regarded eastern Afghanistan as part of their sphere of influence, there was much warfare between the two. The east, *Pracya*, meant all lands between *Prayag* and the Ganges delta. It would be the east that would decide the destiny of India for the next thousand years, because that was where the ascendancy of the Magadhan state was established. *Uttarapatha*, the northern route, led to the north and north-west beyond the Pamirs and the Himalayas and towards central Asia. Here, in this rugged mountainous terrain, lived (and still live) hardy and self-sufficient ethnic and tribal groups who looked both towards Afghanistan and Central Asia on the one hand, and towards the *Madhyadesha* on the other. In contrast to these four regions during this period, there was much less certainty about the boundaries of *Dakshinapatha*. At first, the south began beyond the gates of the Middle Country, but, as the Middle Country itself expanded southwards and pushed towards the Vindhya range, the northern limits of the south came to be revised. The Aryanisation process accompanied the northern expansion, and the first three south-lying regions to be heavily influenced by the colonisers from *Madhyadesha* were Karnataka, Andhra and *Kalinga*.

Clan states and kingdoms

Around the eighth century BCE the *janapadas*, or the territories of the *janas*, the peoples, became more clearly marked (Erdosy 1995b: 115–19). There must have been numerous *janapadas*: in a unique grammatical compendium, the *Ashtadhyayi* of Panini, sixty-nine polities of various sizes are named (Schwartzberg 1992: 167). There were many amalgamations that eventually created sixteen *mahajanapadas*, or the greater states (see Map 5.1). Their geographical spread provides us with a clearer understanding of how human settlement patterns in the northern part of south Asia evolved up to 600 BCE. The focus of settlement in the Harappan era was the Indus basin; in the early Vedic period it was the Punjab; then it moved

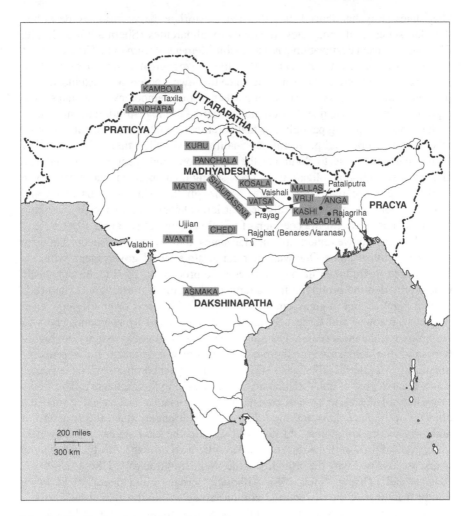

Map 5.1 Regions and states in ancient India

eastwards, and by the end of the Vedic age the entire Gangetic basin consisted of eleven of the sixteen *mahajanapadas* and their capital cities. Central and peninsular India had only three between them, and there were two in the north-west.

As for their political structures, both the *janapadas* and the *mahajanapadas* can be classified into two groups: a smaller one of clan states, and a greater one of numerous kingdoms. The clan states were situated mostly on the periphery of the heartland kingdoms, in the Himalayan foothills, north-west India, the Punjab, Sind, and central and western India. The people of the clan states, hardy and independent-minded hill people, continued with the ancient clan traditions of working together with others whom they regarded as part of a bigger family, which was the clan. Two *mahajanapadas*, *Mallas* and *Vriji*, became the most important clan states (Raychaudhuri 1996: 105–15). Historians have variously described the clan states as democracies, republics or oligarchies (Sharma 1968: 15–80, 85–135), and each designation has a definable element of truth in it. The clan states practised democracy to the extent that there were great assemblies in which people expressed heterodox ideas; but, since the lowest orders were excluded from the consultative process, it was an imperfect sort of democracy. The states were republican in the sense that they did not subscribe to the institution of monarchy, with the accompanying panoply of ritual ceremonies and sacrifices, but a number of clan states produced powerful personalities who called themselves *rajas*, or kings, and who came to dominate the discussions and assembly proceedings. Generally speaking, an oligarchy of a few strong men obtained a dominant voice in the governance of the clan states. Although 'kingship was dissolved and republics were set up, the class divided patriarchal society, bureaucracy, taxation system and an army for the coercion of people remained' (Sharma 1959: 93).

Whichever way we understand the clan states, there were two aspects that were common to all of them. One was their corporate style of government, which is documented in Buddhist literary sources. The procedures of Buddhist monastic orders provided the prototype for patterns of decision in these states. The heads of clan families met in an assembly, or *sangha*, which was ordinarily convened in the main town, and the proceedings were conducted by someone who was recognised as the most senior. The role of the leader was not hereditary but highly honoured, the debates were rigorous, and a vote was taken in the absence of unanimity (Mukherji 1989: 205–13). The second aspect common to the clan states was a great degree of anti-Brahmanic tendency among their citizenry. The Vedic orthodoxy of the caste system based on *varna-ashrama* was rejected, and the alliance of the *brahmans* and the *kshatriya*, which underpinned the structure of authority in the kingdoms, did not hold well in the clan states. The powerful *kshatriya* families in these states accorded little awe or respect to their *brahman* peers, and this was why the orthodox of the Vedic tradition called these *kshatriyas* 'degenerate' (Thapar 2002: 148). Although perhaps coincidental, it is worth noting that most of the dissenting traditions arose within the clan states.

However well run or well organised the clan state oligarchies might have been, they could not expand any further, owing to their decentralised model of decision-making. Even a powerful grouping, such as the one known as the Licchavi confederation, could not in the end resist monarchical states with their greater economic resources. The concept of monarchy became more pronounced and, besides the clan states, the post-Vedic age witnessed the rise of kingdoms, great and small, ruled by monarchs.[1] The monarchical tradition lasted in India for nearly 2,700 years, until the end of British rule in 1947 and the adoption of a republican constitution in 1950. The early history of the *jana* kingship began around the eighth century BCE, during the later Vedic age, when the *rajas* belonging to elite lineages, called *rajanyas*, within the *kshatriya* caste, came to dominate the military–nobility nexus within the Indian context (Raychaudhuri 1996: 139–58). The word *kshatra* means power. The *rajas* derived their authority from two sources. First, the codes of law, known as the *Dharmasutras*, provided the legal basis for their rule. This meant stronger political control, concentrated land ownership, the grant of lands or their revenues to *brahman* priests, regular taxation and a more rigid social stratification, all of which helped to maintain royal power. Second, this authority also depended upon age-old stories of righteous heroism, the examples of which are found in the great epics of the *Mahabharata* and the *Ramayana*, thus bestowing upon the rulers the legitimacy of a sacred right to rule. As what unfolded in the epics has such great resonance within the Hindu psyche, it is to be expected that many Indians even now regard the divine origin of kingship very seriously. There was also a long tradition in India of people trusting their monarchs to do what was right and just. This sense of an unwritten code of conduct was derived from all the religious traditions to which the various monarchs subscribed. They enjoined a monarch to be strong, wise, decisive, kind and a concerned protector of his people; the king's power was to be matched 'by his obligations to his subjects, as is made clear in relation to his right to levy taxes . . . The king who takes his sixth share as tribute and fails to protect his subjects commits a sin' (Brockington 1998: 401). But alas, with a few exceptions, the Indian monarchs turned out to be no less violent and cruel, or vain and stupid, than their many counterparts in various parts of the world in different epochs.

Continuing the late Vedic tradition, the post-Vedic kings used to hold major ceremonies of sacrifice in order to bolster their authority. Among the main ceremonies was the royal sacrifice, called the *rajasuya*. At this annual ceremony, the king honoured his patrons and courtiers with the title of *ratnin*, the jewels, and would make offerings to them, as a way of protecting his patrimony and winning the loyalty of the men closest to him. The king also gave *dana* to the chief priest (the *purohit*) (Sharma 1977: 116–20). There were many royal rituals in ancient India. They involved such activities as cattle raids, games of dice and chariot races, but perhaps the most crucial rite was that of the horse sacrifice, called the *ashvamedha*. In a semi-settled society which was not yet fully agricultural and where territorial boundaries were very fluid, the acquisition of land was a marker of status for any aspiring *raja*. Initially, ambitious *rajas* tested the limits of their rivals' territories by allowing a white stallion to wander at will for a year, monitored by soldiers who, when the horse was challenged, would either fight if they sensed a weaker enemy or prudently withdraw in the face of a stronger one. At the end of the year the *raja* would claim all the territory over which the horse had wandered freely. Then, at a huge sacrificial rite attended by vast crowds, the horse would be consecrated. There then followed a symbolic mating ceremony involving the *raja*'s chief wife and the sacred horse. The horse was then sacrificed by the *brahman* priests. Sex and magic, religion and superstition, were combined in this ceremony, with the aim of symbolically demonstrating the mystical authority of royal power (Jamison 1996: 65–72).

The supremacy of Magadha

The greatest of all the kingdoms was to be *Magadha*. Its location demonstrates an interesting aspect of the historical geography of India. Although the entire

Gangetic basin is generally considered the region where the north Indian civilisation has grown and flourished since 600 BCE, the political heart of that civilisation for the first thousand years, until about the sixth century CE, was in an area south-east of that basin. This area is today covered by the Patna and Gaya districts of Bihar. This is the area where the *mahajanapada* of *Magadha* developed into a great state and then into an empire. Certain key advantages gave it an edge over all its rivals. Even today Bihar is rich in iron ore deposits. Iron was the key resource that gave the Magadhans supremacy in both agricultural and military technology (Raychaudhuri 1996: 577). *Magadha* also controlled the main trade route of the Gangetic basin leading to the Bay of Bengal, which brought in substantial revenues to the state (Thapar 2002: 113). The capital, *Pataliputra*, was a massive fortress-city, impervious to attacks from outside. *Magadha's* supremacy was, at first, challenged by such kingdoms as *Kosala* and *Kashi* and the clan state of *Vriji* (Raychaudhuri 1996: 113), but her kings proved to be brilliant both at strategy and at tactics in warding off their threats.

Three major dynasties guided *Magadha* between the middle of the sixth century BCE and 321 BCE, when the empire of the Mauryas was proclaimed from *Pataliputra*, by then the capital of *Magadha*. The first two kings, Bimbisara (544–493 BCE) and Ajatsatru (492–462 BCE), belonged to the Haryanka dynasty. Under them, the *mahajanapadas* of *Anga*, *Kosala* and *Kashi* were defeated, and the long war with the *Vriji* confederacy was begun. Both kings were men of immense energy and talent. Bimbisara, the first great Indian monarch about whom we have some considerable certainty of knowledge, streamlined his administration by instituting four grades of officer class, known as *mahamatras*. Through them it became easier to collect tax revenues. He allowed a degree of autonomy through a system of sub-kings, or *mandalikarajas*, and yet was able to keep in check the centrifugal tendencies of the system. He was murdered by his own son, Ajatsatru, who proved to be an outstandingly energetic ruler. The latter greatly increased the military capabilities of *Magadha* and built a new capital at *Pataliputra*. The victories over all his enemies were celebrated in great style with horse sacrifices.

Just as he had done, the successors of Ajatsatru all killed their parents to gain the throne. The Haryankas were finally overthrown in 413 BCE by the founders of the dynasty of Shishunaga. The Shishunaga ruled for half a century, from 413 BCE to 364 BCE, and annexed the strategically important *mahajanapada* of *Avanti* in central India, overwhelming its capital, Ujjain. The last of the three dynasties before the Mauryas was that of the Nandas, who ruled between 364 BCE and 321 BCE (Raychaudhuri 1996: 201–10). The dynasty started with a brilliant usurper, Mahapadma, whose mother was a *shudra* and who disliked the *kshatriyas* intensely. With his reign we see the beginnings of non-*kshatriya* involvement in the control of power in different parts of north India (Thapar 2002: 155–6). Mahapadma Nanda was succeeded by his eight sons, one after the other, each ruling only very briefly. Although the nine Nandas ruled altogether for just forty-three years, they are still remembered as the most powerful pre-Mauryan monarchs of India.

Persian and Greek intrusions

The first important foreign intrusion to challenge the emerging state system of India was that of the Persians. They became a power to be reckoned with after the establishment in the sixth century BCE of the Achaemenid dynasty by Cyrus II (550–529 BCE). Although it is not clear how much of the north-west of India he actually controlled, a number of ancient Greek sources have confirmed that his empire included *Gandhara*, i.e. the western Punjab, one of the sixteen *mahajanapadas* (Raychaudhuri 1996: 582–3). From the reign of Darius I (521–486 BCE), the third Achaemenid ruler, we have more substantial evidence from his own inscriptions about the Persian stake in north-west India. The famous Behistun Rock Inscription (520–518 BCE), engraved on a cliff 100 metres off the ground along the road between Hamadan in Iran and Baghdad in Iraq, contains Darius's political testament and autobiographical details; and among the twenty-three lands of the Persian Empire are mentioned *Gandhara*, *Arachosia* (southern Afghanistan) and *Maka* (the Makran coast of Baluchistan) (Chattopadhyaya 1974: 8–24; Cook 1983: 58–9). Two other inscriptions, one in Old Persian block tablets sunk in the wall of the platform at the royal palace of Persepolis (518–515 BCE) and another chiselled around the tomb entrance of Darius at Naqsh-i-Rustam (just after 515 BCE), expressly mention Hi(n)dush – i.e. the Indus basin – as Persian-controlled (Raychaudhuri 1996: 583–6). This could mean that Darius had not fully conquered the Indus area by the time the Behistun Rock Inscription was carved.

Darius's fame rests principally on the efficient ways he ruled the empire and the manner in which he added more territories. He divided it into twenty satrapies (or provincial governments) and judiciously balanced central authority with decentralisation within each territory (Cook 1983: 67–76). His Indian possessions were well integrated into his empire by means of highways. The wealth of his empire was legendary, since resources and tributes flowed into Persia from all directions. The well-known Greek historian Herodotus stated that India (Hi(n)dush or the Indus basin) counted as the twentieth satrapy of the empire, and yet it contributed a third of all the revenues, mostly gold, that came from the Asiatic provinces (i.e. nearly 80 per cent of the empire) (Herodotus 1972: 243–4). *Gandhara*, Sind, the Indus basin, Baluchistan and Afghanistan were the geographical limits of the Persian Empire in the east. The Persians did not enter the Gangetic basin or Rajasthan (Cook 1983: 188–92).

By the middle of the fourth century BCE, a new force came to dominate all the Greek city-states: the kingdom of Macedon. Its ruler, Philip II (382–336 BCE), created a formidable military structure, which was based on phalanxes backed by armoured cavalry and siege trains of catapults. He left this inheritance to his son, Alexander (356–323 BCE), who became king in 336 BCE. Alexander first destroyed the continuing Persian hold over the Greek cities of Asia Minor by his victory over them at the battle of Issus in 333 BCE. Two years later, at Gaugamela, Persian power was decisively broken when the last Achaemenid, Darius III, fled to Bactria, where he was murdered. After burning the capital, Persepolis (330 BCE), Alexander marched through the heart of Iran towards the eastern Persian satrapies of Drangiana, Arachosia, Bactria and Sogdiana. The news of his victories and cruelties preceded him, creating great panic and fear among those who awaited his arrival. In the spring of 327 BCE, he had almost reached the western banks of the River Indus.

The first group of people that Alexander met on South Asian soil were those whom the Greeks called the Assakenois, who lived on the present borders of the North-West Frontier province and Kashmir in Pakistan. They resisted him, in the way that frontier people have done throughout history, but in vain. Alexander proved much too strong for them. Next was the turn of the *Gandhara* satrapy, with its capital of *Pushkalavati* taken. In this case, overwhelming force was unnecessary because of Indian collaboration. The most significant collaboration was offered by the new king of Taxila, Ambhi, whose forces dominated the lands between the rivers Indus and Jhelum. Taxila was an ancient city where Vedic culture had flourished for centuries, and to a certain extent Ambhi's collaboration made sense. His reward came with the confirmation of his kingdom within the Alexandrine world empire. The next stage in Alexander's conquest was the encounter with Porus, the Paurava king, who ruled the lands between the rivers Jhelum and Chenab. Porus has been 'portrayed as a figure of heroic grandeur' and 'a worthy opponent of Alexander' (Bosworth 1996: 8); however, the Porus of history nowhere actually matched Alexander in might and power. He did fight bravely, but his army was massacred and he was decisively beaten. Legend has it that he refused to cringe or be obsequious to Alexander, but the reality was that he became a subaltern to Alexander. The latter awarded him with an extension of territories beyond the Chenab almost to the Ravi, but with the strategic aim of protecting his own larger stake in the Indus basin.

Alexander moved yet further east to the River Beas, which joins up with the Sutlej to become a mighty tributary of the Indus basin. Reaching the Beas was the high point of Alexander's military adventure, but however much further east he wished to go, both he and his men realised that it would be a journey without end in the vast Indian landscape that spread before them. Finally, in July 326 BCE, his pride and ambition gave way before the demands of his armies to turn back. Alexander may have intruded into India but, in a sense, India had conquered him. He turned back up to the River Jhelum and, with great forces and accoutrements, sailed south towards the open sea. On his way he met ferocious resistance from the Mallavas, a hardy and free-spirited people, and from the *brahman* clans who considered it a part of their *dharma*, or religious duty, to fight him. With overwhelming force and some good fortune, he saved himself and his crew (Bosworth 1996: 94–6, 133–46). After sailing through the confluence of the Indus tributaries, he devised a three-pronged exit strategy. One army, under a general called Craterus, was to return through *Arachosia*. Then, at the mouth of the Indus, Alexander ordered his navy, under Nearchus, to proceed through the Arabian Sea towards the Perso-Arabian Gulf, while he himself proceeded to Iran through the scorching desert of Baluchistan. He never reached his Macedonian homeland, dying in Babylon in 323 BCE (see Map 5.2).

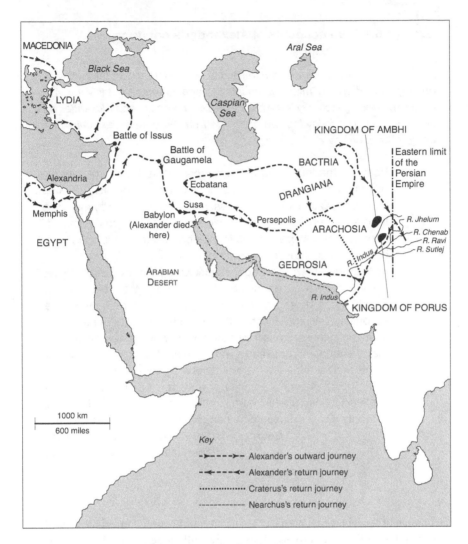

Map 5.2 Marathon march of Alexander the Great

Volumes have been written about the character and personality of Alexander; he was certainly a man of contradictions, as can be seen in **Excerpt 5.1** below.

For the Persian Zoroastrians, Alexander was 'the accursed' (de Jong 2002: 68); for the Indians he was remembered only as a ruthless aggressor who came and went, allegedly leaving no lasting imprint on their imagination; while for most Europeans he still is the 'heroic ideal' (Briant 1996: front title). All three assessments are seemingly correct and yet false. In the context of India, Alexander's intrusion was only a minuscule event: 'India was not Hellenised . . . and soon forgot

**Excerpt 5.1 Two accounts of Alexander's conduct
at Taxila**

*Alexander's conduct towards the Indians was consistent with the behaviour
one expects of military men with an inflated ego. General brutality softened
by conspicuous generosity is the hallmark of such people, and Alexander was
no exception. The following two accounts from European classical writers
bring this out clearly.*

1) Between the Indus and the Hydaspes is Taxila, a large city and
governed by good laws . . . The inhabitants and their king, Taxiles,
received Alexander with kindness, and in return came by more than
they bestowed, so that the Macedonians were jealous, and said it
appeared as if Alexander had found none worthy of his bounty until
he had crossed the Indus (Strabo).

2) As the Indian mercenary troops, consisting, as they did, of the best
soldiers to be found in the country, flocked to the cities which he
attacked and defended them with great vigour, he thus incurred
serious losses, and accordingly concluded a treaty of peace with
them; but afterwards, as they were going away, set upon them while
they were on the road, and killed them all. This rests as a foul blot
on his martial fame . . . The philosophers gave him no less trouble
than the mercenaries, because they reviled the princes who
declared for him and encouraged the free states to revolt from his
authority. On this account he hanged many of them (Plutarch).

Source: A.H. Dani, *The Historic City of Taxila*,
Paris: UNESCO, 1986, 40, 49–50.

the passing of the Macedonian storm' (Vincent Smith, quoted in Briant 1996: 157).
However, the settlement of many of his soldiers all along the north-west of India,
within a number of succeeding Indo-Greek kingdoms, influenced the politics, art,
religion and trade of India in later centuries. The intellectual worlds of both Greece
and India also came to know each other better (Narain 1974: 57–65). Alexander
himself became fond of a naked Indian ascetic, Kalanos (*Kalyana*, or 'lucky'),
whose wisdom and eccentricity were both instructive and amusing for him and
his soldiers (McCrindle 1901/1971: 69–74).

The second urbanisation

The political power of the rulers of various states, whether clan-based or
monarchic, was greatly underpinned by the new economic prosperity that emerged

after 600 BCE. This prosperity was based on the surplus produce from land that the rulers came increasingly to enjoy. Large-scale clearances of forests were taking place in the upper and middle Ganges valley, and even the tracts away from principal water courses were being cleared. The newly developing iron technology helped in the process. There is argument among historians as to how widespread it was, but such implements as iron axes, hoes, ploughshares and nails would have played a part in increasing the efficiency of agriculture. Large areas of marshland were also being drained through inundation channels (Thapar 2002: 142–3); these complemented the terrain that relied on wells and water-lifting devices. Another important factor was the efficient deployment of labour on the farms. The rulers and nobles of the new states came to exercise greatly increased power over labour through such means as the caste hierarchy, the clan organisation and, in the case of the kingdoms, the political legitimacy acquired through the alliance between the royal and Brahmanic authorities. From now on, the vast use of labour, either by state authorities or under the patronage of the rural nobility, came to be an enduring feature of Indian agriculture. Through a variety of taxes, in the nature of either voluntary offerings or royal entitlements, collected by special tax collectors, the *gramabhojaka*, the royal treasuries were greatly augmented (Sharma 1959: 130–42).

The agricultural surplus had a positive effect on the growth of towns during this period. It was this surplus that enabled the rulers of states to encourage relatively large numbers of non-agricultural people to live in towns and pursue their crafts and skills. The surplus fed the townspeople at prices they could afford, which might have been money-based or through barter. This development was most marked in the Ganges valley, and hence historians have described this area as the home of the second phase of urbanisation in Indian history. The first phase had come to an end nearly a thousand years before in the Indus valley with the collapse of such cities as Mohenjo Daro and Harappa.

Evidence for urbanisation: literary and archaeological

Much of our speculation about what the towns in the second phase of urbanisation would have looked like has for long been deduced from such Hindu literary sources as the earlier *Dharmasutras* of this period, along with the epics or the Buddhist *Jataka* stories. These literary sources tell us much about a variety of villages and towns of northern India. The grammarian Panini, for example, identifies in his famous work *Ashtadhyayi* specific types of villages, such as hamlets or herdsmen's camps. Various grades of urbanisation are listed with the designations of terms such as *nigamas* (market suburbs), *purs* (fortified structures) or *nagaras* (towns). The *mahanagaras* (cities) are mentioned in literature as populous, well-defended places where many leading families and their retinues of followers resided. There congregated in the towns and cities all manner of craftsmen: masons, bricklayers, plumbers, carpenters and general labourers for building work; metal workers for producing weapons and tools from copper and iron; and a host of specialist craftsmen who manufactured trade commodities, such as glass, ivory objects, ceramics, beads and textile fabrics. The towns were the principal centres of trade and exchange, and into the towns poured huge amounts of revenue in the form of both agricultural surplus and the profits of trade. They therefore housed the principal treasuries, of grain, silver and gold, which the rich and the powerful commandeered. The secure guarding and the defence of these treasuries set the town apart from the village. Villages do not constitute centres of power and wealth in the way that towns do, and that is why so many types of defensive structures are mentioned in the various texts in relation to the newly developing towns. The gateways, bastions, moats and ramparts were some of the main features of urban defence. With secure defences, the rulers and the nobility embarked on prestigious architectural projects, of which the ruler's palace would have been the chief attraction. Built generally at the intersection of two principal highways, which could be as broad as 25 to 30 feet, the palace was the building around which all the bureaucratic and mercantile operations would be housed (Chakrabarti 1998: 259). Certain towns, such as *Kashi* or Vaishali, also became centres of religious activity and pilgrimage, and Buddhism, particularly, came to have a strong following among the townsfolk.

Although modern archaeology is able to confirm or question our traditional understanding of urban life from ancient literature, we have to accept that it has its limits. The north Indian Ganges valley is today one of the most densely populated regions in the world, but the pressure of population is not something new: it began as early as 600 BCE. Unlike Sind and other north-western parts of the subcontinent, it is also an area of lush vegetation and reasonably consistent patterns of rain. It has therefore been extremely difficult for archaeologists of this region to replicate the successes of their peers in the Indus valley. The fact that there is not a single house-plan available for the pre-Mauryan levels tells us all about the incompleteness of archaeology in this region. Establishing any form of chronological sequence in this situation would have been all but impossible were it not for a strikingly identifiable and abundant material that is available throughout a wide belt of north India: a pottery known as Northern Black Polished Ware (NBPW). The most useful places of study for the archaeologists are the sites where this pottery is located in marked quantity (Allchin 1995: 100–5). The sites of the pre-Mauryan period (covered by this chapter) can be divided chronologically into two historical phases. During the first phase, between approximately 600 BCE and 400 BCE, the NBPW sites show evidence of such potteries as the Polished Grey Ware, Black Slipped Ware and Red Ware that were common during the earlier Vedic period (examined in Chapter 4). This means that the process of development was under way and continuous at these early phase sites. There is also evidence of fortifications and iron at such sites. During the second phase (approximately 400 BCE to 300 BCE) more specialised red ware forms of pottery, used in the making of carinated cooking pots (*handis*) and piriform water vessels, occur at sites in substantial quantity. The phasing of pottery wares has helped the archaeologists to make some sense of the settlement patterns during this period.

Another crucial archaeological contribution has been to establish, in spatial terms, the differences between various types of settlement in a 'hierarchy of settlements' at any particular urban site. As was mentioned earlier, literary sources have made us familiar with such terms as *grama* (village), *nagara* (town), *pura* (defensive-cum-administrative structure), *rajdhani* (capital city) or *mahanagara* (metropolitan city); traditionally, historians and sociologists have used these terms almost casually, on the premise that their meaning can be taken for granted. The contribution of archaeologists to our greater understanding has been to carefully map out and delineate the clusters of settlement spaces at a particular site; then, with the help of the evidence found at actual sites, calculate the concentration of population and the constellation of power which would have been the likely factors determining the evolution of a settlement from a village to a large city. This level of technical rigour has made it easier for us to grasp the precise significance of varied terms in usage. Thus, for example, both intensive and extensive excavations carried out in the Allahabad district, at the confluence of the rivers Ganges and Yamuna, have suggested a pattern of settlement that conformed to the NBPW phases (Erdosy 1995b: 105–10). Different rungs of the settlement ladder have been established for different historical phases. In the early phase, the town of Kausambi was identified as a primary centre, where complex manufacturing processes in the production of luxury items of trade, such as beads, were carried out. Supporting the primary centre in this phase was the secondary settlement of Sringaverpur. By the time of the second phase there were concentrations of population in a variety of sites that were clearly graded in size, with the regular spacing of central places along all major arteries of communication. Many other secondary settlements were either home to such manufactures as those of ceramics, lithic blades or iron smelting, or began to function as administrative and service centres. Surrounding the primary and secondary centres were a host of nucleated villages, where agriculture and pastoralism were the main occupations. The increasing food needs of a rapidly growing urban population led to the felling of vast tracts of forest in this region (Allchin 1995: 105–8).

From the excavations carried out at over 100 sites on which important historic cities of South Asia have developed, archaeological evidence can confirm that there are six definite sites where the remains of walls, gateways and ramparts can be dated to the period around 600 BCE (Chakrabarti 1998: 242–9). They were Taxila, Rupar, Rajghat, Rajagriha, Kausambi and Ujjain. Both the textual and archaeological evidence regarding these sites complement one another (Chakrabarti 1998: 257). The towns were either the capitals of their *mahajana-padas* or else they straddled 'one of the earliest well-defined trade routes of India' (Chakrabarti 1998: 248); their sites have yielded valuable evidence of the NBPW pottery, the hallmark of the quality of life and prosperity after 600 BCE. At all these places they have found the evidence of fortifications on a monumental scale. The fortification at Ujjain, for example, measured 75 metres at the base, reached a height of 14 metres and stretched for 5 kilometres. The manpower needed to build such a structure would have required a high degree of socio-political organisation. Inside the excavated areas of settlements, a variety of articles and artefacts have been recovered. They include such things as furnaces, common agricultural and household tools, coin hoards, a wide range of semi-precious stones, and items made out of ivory, glass, terracotta and even gold. These items confirm to us that the procurement, processing and distribution of key raw materials would have been a key function of the emerging central places in the pre-Mauryan age. Many of the settlements are also mentioned in Buddhist literature, and they correspond to the urban patterns as reconstructed from archaeological evidence. It is possible that further advances in archaeological methods and techniques will confirm, not dispute, the contents of the texts regarding the towns of the subcontinent. Nevertheless, it is advisable not to take some of the descriptions of urban centres in ancient texts too literally, as **Excerpt 5.2** illustrates.

Dissent and heterodoxy

The sixth century BCE was a period that was 'a watershed in the history of speculative ideas' (Ray *et al.* 2000: 248). By this time, at one level, Vedic society had become highly stratified, with gross inequality pervading its structure. There was a feeling of injustice and grievance among the ordinary populace. At the same time, as we have seen, a number of developments that were taking place in the political and economic sphere throughout northern India were impacting upon the mindset of social classes and groups. The stage was set for a greater fluidity and mobility within the social pyramid. The position of the large majority of the lower-caste *shudras* and the Untouchables remained as depressed and subservient as ever, although increased prosperity might have trickled down to some of their artisans (Sharma 1958: 101–2). The *brahmans* retained their monopoly of priestly functions and religious scholarship, while the more enterprising among them were prepared to assume greater political responsibilities, thereby reaping yet more power and prestige. The *kshatriyas*, or the secular ruling elites, benefited greatly as their kingdoms or republics thrived and became richer, but it was the innumerable trading groups, part of the *vaishya* caste, who assumed the role of the bourgeoisie of the Gangetic basin. The *vaishyas* originally controlled land, but were able to convert surplus from land into more mobile forms of wealth production, such as trade. Their newly found wealth gave them the confidence to ignore any humiliation attached to their third place in the ritual ranking within the caste system. They were irked by obsolete restrictions not just in trade but in religion too. Over one particular Vedic practice, the ritual sacrifice of animals, most of them, along with the more liberal of the *kshatriyas*, were opposed to the meaningless cruelty and extravagance displayed by the Brahmanic authorities. As far as they were concerned, it was a senseless and economically wasteful practice that needed to be disbanded (Walker 1968: Vol. 1, 49–50). Although the teachings of Jainism and Buddhism finally helped to put an end to this Vedic practice, animal sacrifice has not been entirely eliminated; even today animals are sacrificed in some Hindu temples. Gandhi's comment in **Excerpt 5.3** below is instructive.

Excerpt 5.2 Description of Ayodhya in the *Ramayana*

Since Ayodhya is a place of great significance for both the Hindus and the Jains, archaeologists have undertaken a number of excavations in the city, in order to retrieve some of the ancient glory in the form of impressive ruins or monuments. Alas, apart from a burnt brick fortification wall, a ditch and some indifferent structures, nothing much of archaeological value has come to light that can directly corroborate the contents of the following beautiful passage from the Ramayana. *The reason for this could be that Ayodhya has been such an established site for so many centuries that it is just too difficult for archaeologists to dig really deeply in the central populated area. Or was Valmiki just imagining rather than describing?*

On Sarju's bank of ample size,
The happy realm of Kosal lies
With fertile length of fair champaign
And flocks and herds and wealth of grain . . .
There, famous in her old renown,
Ayodhya stands[,] the royal town,
In bygone ages built and planned
By sainted Manu's princely hand
Imperial seat[,] and her walls extend
Twelve measured leagues from end to end,
And three in width from side to side,
With square and palace beautified.
Her gates at even distance stand;
Her ample roads are wisely planned.
Right glorious is her royal street,
Where streams allay the dust and heat,
On level ground and even row
Her house[s] rise in goodly show:
Terrace and palace, arch and gate
The queenly city decorate.
High are her ramparts, strong and vast,
By ways at even distance passed
With circling moat, both deep and wide,
And store of weapons fortified . . .
She seems a painted city, fair
With chess-board line and even square.

> **Source:** Ralph Griffith, from *The Ramayana of Valmiki*, Benares, 1915, Book 1, Canto 5; quoted in Niharranjan Ray *et al.*, *A Sourcebook of Indian Civilization*, Hyderabad: Orient Longman, 2000, 222–3.

Excerpt 5.3 Gandhi's comment on animal sacrifices

The most famous vaishya of modern times was Mahatma Gandhi, a man deeply influenced by the philosophy of ahimsa, non-violence towards all living creatures, which he learned partly from the Jains. Gandhi was shocked to witness the practice of animal sacrifices in the great Kali Temple in Calcutta. The practice, which must have been carried on in some form or other all through the ages, repulsed him terribly. He describes in his autobiography what he experienced on his trip to India from South Africa in the year 1901.

On the way to the [Kali Temple] I saw a stream of sheep going to be sacrificed to Kali ... I asked [a religious mendicant]: 'Do you regard this sacrifice as religion?'

'Who would regard killing of animals as religion?'

'Then, why don't you preach against it?'

'That's not my business. Our business is to worship God.'

'But could you not find any other place in which to worship God?'

'All places are equally good for us'.

We did not prolong the discussion, but passed on to the temple. We were greeted by rivers of blood. I could not bear to stand there ... That very evening I had an invitation to dinner. There I spoke to a friend about this cruel form of worship. He said, 'The sheep don't feel anything. The noise and the drum-beating there deaden all sensation of pain.' I could not swallow this. I told him, that if the sheep had speech, they would tell a different tale ... It is my constant prayer that there may be born on earth some great spirit, man or woman, fired with divine pity, who will deliver us from this heinous sin, save the lives of the innocent creatures, and purify the temple.

Source: M.K. Gandhi, *An Autobiography, or The Story of my Experiments with Truth*, Ahmedabad: Navajivan Publishing House, 1940, 171–2. Reproduced with permission of the Navajivan Trust.

Religious ferment was particularly widespread in the towns of the sixth century BCE. A variety of atheistic, amoralist and materialist doctrines were being preached by philosophers, ascetics and hermits, in opposition to Vedic beliefs and rituals, in one form or another. Collectively speaking, the movement that was to bind various heterodoxies came to be known as Shramanism. The *shramanas* were the voices of dissent, opposed to Brahmanism (Warder 2002: 32–41). Thus, the sect of Ajivakas, led by Makkhali Goshala, did not believe that good deeds could affect the transmigration of souls, a key Vedic concept (Embree 1992: 46). They believed that all individual fate was entirely predetermined. The sect of Charavakas, led by a leader called Ajita Kesakambala, believed in pure materialism. They did not believe in any form of afterlife; for them, 'when the body dies both fool and wise alike are cut off and perish. They do not survive after death' (Embree 1992: 46). There was also a school of extreme sceptics led by a certain Sanjaya Belatthiputa, who is reputed to have said:

> If you asked me 'is there another world?', and I believed that there was, I should tell you so. But that is not what I say. I do not say that it is so; I do not say that it is otherwise; I do not say that it is not so; nor do I say that it is not not so.
>
> (Embree 1992: 47)

In other words, there is no certainty of any definable knowledge at all. The presence of such sects is growing evidence of a stimulating intellectual atmosphere in India at the time. The greatest amount of dissidence was in the clan states and, particularly, in the areas of the east, such as modern Bihar and in the marginal lands between India and Nepal. While Brahmanism was much too strongly entrenched in places such as the Punjab, the Gangetic *doab* or the middle Ganges valley, it was far more vulnerable to challenges in the east and along the Nepalese border. Among many ethnic groups there was considerable contempt for Brahmanic sacrifices and caste rigidities. Jainism and Buddhism, although now having matured into full-fledged universalist religions, began life as dissident traditions in the areas that were clan states rather than kingdoms.

Two teachers and their faiths

The founders of the two great faiths of Jainism and Buddhism were north Indians. Mahavira, the twenty-fourth *Tirthankara*, or the teacher of the Jain faith, was born in 599 BCE and died in 527 BCE. There is greater controversy about Gautama Buddha's dates. It is conventionally accepted that he lived between 563 BCE and 483 BCE, but some historians have proposed his date of birth as late as 400 BCE. The life of the historical Gautama Buddha can be studied through art, literature and oral traditions. The earliest evidence of his life narrative comes from *c.* 100 BCE, from the relief carvings on the stone fence at Bharhut in north India. Mahavira's life can be studied from either the extensive Jain texts or through art in Jain temples. Belonging to the noble *kshatriya* families, both Gautama Buddha and Mahavira left settled lives of luxury for a period of renunciation. They went through periods of extreme penances and meditation for a number of years. Buddhism and Jainism are rooted in the idea of renunciation. The renunciatory movements became stronger, ironically, during this period when urban affluence was increasing, because 'the ideology of renunciation presupposed the affluence of possessions, as renouncers were dependent on those who lived the worldly life' (Ali 1999: 39). Each of the two men obtained enlightenment in his own way and then preached for some three decades all over northern India. Both of them believed in the idea of monastic institutions and were received enthusiastically by kings, merchants and ordinary people. Mahavira organised the Jain order of ascetics across the Magadhan state, while the Buddha encouraged the formation of *sanghas*, where the monks may reside and work for the benefit of society. They championed the reform of Vedic Brahmanism by their insistence that people should learn to give up their vices and follies, to adopt right conduct in their daily lives and not be too concerned with rituals and sacrifices, but, at the same time, both of them believed in the key Vedic concept of the transmigration of souls and the process of reincarnation, and the idea of *karma*.

Both the Buddha and Mahavira preached not in scholastic Sanskrit, but in a vernacular such as *Ardha Magadhi*, in order to spread widely their message among

Excerpt 5.4 Contrasting Vedic and Buddhist views on the caste system

The two verses in the hymn of the sacrifice of Purusha, the First Man, in Rig-Veda, *Book X, 90.11–12, continue to be quoted, time and again, by orthodox Hindus in support of the caste system. This is a pity, because caste is thereby legitimised by so-called religious sanction.*

> (11): When they divided Purusha how many portions did they make? What do they call his mouth, his arms? What do they call his thighs and feet?
>
> (12): The Brahman was his mouth, of both his arms was the Rajanya made.
>
>   His thighs became the Vaisya, from his feet the Sudra was produced.

Source: Ralph T.H. Griffith, *The Hymns of the Rig-Veda*,
Vol. 2, Benares: E.J. Lazarus, 1920, 519 and 576.

While the Buddhists learned to live with the reality of caste and class, the pristine message of the Buddha was that character was more important than birth in the shaping of one's life, as expressed in the Buddhist text of Sutta Nipata.

No Brahman is such by birth.
No outcaste is such by birth.
An outcaste is such by his deeds.
A Brahman is such by his deeds.

Source: Sutta Nipata, v. 136; quoted in Ainslee
Embree (ed.) London: Penguin, 1992, *Sources of Indian Tradition*, 139. Copyright © 2016 Columbia University Press. Reprinted with permission of the publisher.

ordinary people. One of the key messages was about non-violence and compassion. The Jain attitude on non-violence was, and remains, extreme and severe; the most accidental killing of even the smallest insect deeply hurts the Jain conscience. Jain monks gently sweep the ground under their feet before walking a few steps forward. The Buddhist attitude is a little more liberal, and Buddhists are not as strict about vegetarianism as the Jains are. This difference between the two faiths may explain why Jains are very few in number compared to the Buddhists, and mostly confined to Gujarat, Rajasthan and Karnataka. Buddhism is a worldwide religion, with its followers numbering in the hundreds of millions. Both faiths also advocate a fair degree of egalitarianism; they have strong reservations about the caste system. The contrast between the Vedic and Buddhist ideas on caste are clearly apparent from **Excerpt 5.4** above.

The credibility of their personal efforts by both Gautama Buddha and Mahavira to improve the life and status of the lower caste people, the *shudras*, is undoubted; they incessantly conveyed the message to their followers that the *shudras* had every right to be teachers or monks, and there should be no discrimination in their treatment in the monasteries. They were not necessarily against the existing socio-economic relations between the classes at that time, and one could even conclude that the dissenting heterodoxies were more interested in benign improvements for the depressed classes rather than in starting a revolution in their favour (Sharma 1958: 133–42). Nevertheless, the two most well-known Indians of the first half of the twentieth century, Mahatma Gandhi and Dr Bhimrao Ambedkar, based their philosophy of life on the spiritual principles of Jainism and Buddhism, the two heterodox systems of thought which challenged the Vedic Brahmanic orthodoxies.

Varieties of literature

The Indic treasury of literature from the Vedic tradition is enhanced and enriched in the post-Vedic age when literature from the Buddhist and Jain systems of thought begins to make its mark. This is also the age of the creation of the two most spectacular epics, whose influence have extended beyond the boundaries of India.

A work of grammar

Of the many works of this period, first and foremost is a grammatical work that has been described as 'one of the greatest monuments of human intelligence' (Cardona 1976: 243). This was the *Ashtadhyayi*, written in about 500 BCE by Panini, a scholar and linguist who lived in *Shalatula*, in the north-western *mahajanapada* of *Gandhara*. The *Ashtadhyayi*, which is a systematic grammar of the Sanskrit language, can be considered one of the earliest works of descriptive linguistics. The Sanskrit language and its various dialects had been evolving for more than a millennium, and, as Panini himself acknowledged, a number of attempts had been made by grammarians before him to systematise the language. Panini called it the living language, or the *Bhasha*, and he was the first great and true codifier of

Sanskrit. Two other grammarians, Katyayana (*c.* 300 BCE) and Patanjali (*c.* 200 BCE) carried forward Panini's work. Panini is the earliest linguist to present a comprehensive and scientific survey of the phonetics, phonology and morphology in Sanskrit or, for that matter, in any other language. In the *Ashtadhyayi*, which means eight chapters, Panini provides formal production rules and definitions of Sanskrit grammar. Basic elements such as vowels and consonants, and parts of speech such as nouns and verbs, are placed in categories. The construction of compound words and sentences follow ordered rules operating on underlying structures, in a manner similar to present-day formal language theory. On the basis of just under 4,000 *sutras* – rules expressed as aphorisms – Panini summarised virtually the entire structure of the Sanskrit language (Katre 1987: ix–xxv). From the *Ashtadhyayi* we can also derive a huge amount of geographical and cultural data concerning regions, towns, peoples, rivers, economic products, historical associations with place names and so on. The data's value is in the way grammatical rules are explained rather than in expounding geographical knowledge *per se* (Schwartzberg 1992: 167–8). When Sir William Jones, the great eighteenth-century scholar and linguist, praised the qualities of Sanskrit (as we mentioned in Chapter 4), he was in a sense paying a handsome tribute to the genius of Panini, the greatest of all the world's grammarians who lived before the twentieth century.

Epic literature

Long before television gave them their current international fame, the two large epics of the *Mahabharata* and the *Ramayana* were known to millions of South and South East Asians. Besides the traditional Hindu versions of them, there are Buddhist, Jain and even Muslim versions. The dim origins of both the *Mahabharata* and the *Ramayana* lie in the Vedic period, when poets and bards recited tales and sang songs in honour of heroic warriors; their composition, however, took place in the post-Vedic age. Transmitted orally for a long time, it took many centuries before we witness their written form. Scholars believe that a series of recensions (revisions) made it inevitable that the process of completion for both epics might have lasted over several centuries.

The *Mahabharata* is supposed to have been compiled by Vyasa, or the arranger, and one could speculate that, in view of the central heroic narrative of the epic and the plots within plots, there would have been more than one arranger for the entire story. It is worth remembering that the whole work has upwards of 100,000 couplets. In all, there are eighteen books, known as *parvans*, containing nearly 100 'little books', the *upaparvans*. Besides the central story of the dynastic rivalry within the clan states, there are sixty-seven fascinating sub-tales, the *upakhyanas*, which have made this epic so appealing to all generations of South and South East Asians over the time span of two and a half millennia. The original story of the *Mahabharata*, prior to 400 BCE, concerned the inter-Aryan tribal warfare between the Kuru and the Panchala tribes (mentioned in Chapter 4), but two later developments need to be noted. Between 400 and *c.* 50 BCE, the story took a new turn with the introduction of five new semi-divine figures, known collectively as the Pandavas, whose struggle against a hundred-strong set of cousins, the Kauravas, became the central event of the epic. Then, in around 100 BCE, beyond the period of this chapter, a great spiritual dialogue between Arjuna, one of the Pandavas, and the god Krishna was inserted in the epic. In this dialogue the hesitations and moral doubts of Arjuna on the eve of the momentous eighteen-day battle of Kurukshetra are confronted by Krishna with explanations about the importance of duty without any regard for reward in this or the afterlife. This dialogue, known as the *Bhagavad Gita* (Song of God), is for millions of Hindus a guide to good living in this world, and it is rightly celebrated by scholars and philosophers as the most concise and coherent statement of Hindu conceptions of duty and virtue.

The *Ramayana*, with its 24,000 *shlokas*, or verses, is a more compact piece of work in terms of its linguistic style and vocabulary, and most of the original composition was the work of one individual poet, Valmiki. The *Ramayana* story, set in the eastern part of the Gangetic basin, with the main plot centring upon a family jealousy and the conflicts between Aryan and non-Aryan, is a straight-forward story of Rama, the hero, who loses the throne of the kingdom of *Kosala*, located in the eastern Ganges plain, through the jealousy of his stepmother, and is exiled to the jungle with his wife Sita and brother Lakshmana for fourteen years. He loses Sita to Ravana, the demon king of Sri Lanka, who abducts her. Since such a demon ruled over a state without a righteous monarch, he is supposed to symbolise the 'disordered' nature of a clan polity. The idea of a kingdom is thus glorified. In his struggle to save Sita, Rama is helped in a number of ways by a host of monkeys led by their chief, Hanuman. He defeats Ravana and rescues Sita, but is then besieged by doubts about Sita's fidelity. Controversially, after returning from exile, he decides to banish Sita in the interest of his reputation as a moral ruler in the eyes of his subjects. After undergoing much ordeal and further exile, Sita proves her chastity and purity by performing a 'truth act' invoking the earth goddess to take her back; the earth opens and the goddess emerges, only to take Sita on her lap and sink below the surface again. Rama is left in a state of grief, but then ruled from his capital, Ayodhya, justly and wisely, for a long period of time. His utopian reign is celebrated by Hindus as *Ramarajya* (the reign of Rama).

For centuries the children of South and South East Asia have not only been entertained by the theatre and puppet shows of the *Mahabharata* and the *Ramayana*, but also have had their value-systems influenced by the moral message of the narratives. These epics raise a plethora of issues of private and public morality, such as succession rights, the conscience of a king, sexism, the honour of the female sex, the morality of warfare and so on; they are also a mine of information for geographical, cultural and social details. The affairs of royalty and warfare serve as the backdrop to the epics, but the call to duty and *dharma*, as interpreted in Vedic Brahmanism, is their core message. With successive revisions over many centuries, both epics have become suffused with Hindu religious imageries. This in fact mattered less in connection with the *Mahabharata* because,

Figure 5.1 A boy playing the part of Sita

although pious Hindus venerate and recite the *Bhagahavad Gita*, they normally consider the text of the epic as a whole 'inauspicious' to read or recite in their homes (Brockington 1998: 1). The *Ramayana* is, however, cherished in every Hindu home, and the gradual evolution of Rama 'from a moral hero to a divine figure' (Brockington 1984: 307) has had dramatic political and social consequences in recent decades in modern India.

Early Buddhist literature

Although much of the great Buddhist literature dates from the middle of the third century BCE, it is worth noting that the earliest sections of it are from our period; they contain some valuable historical material (Singh 2003: 53–9). In line with the dissenting tradition, a large amount of the important, and original, Buddhist literature is in the vernacular language of Pali rather than Sanskrit. The so-called Pali Canon represents the teachings of the oldest Buddhist sect, the *Thera*, or 'ancient', from which is derived the term *Theravadin*. The canon consists of 'three baskets' of knowledge, called *Tripitaka*. The first basket is *Vinayapitaka*, which gives an account of the Buddha's life, his times, his relationship with Ajatsatru, the king of *Magadha*, and the economic conditions of town and country during the sixth and fifth centuries BCE. A section called *Mahavagga* also includes some medical information concerning diseases and their remedies and the importance of hygiene. The second basket, the *Suttapitaka*, contains five collections, or *Nikayas*, which provide inestimable information on economic and social history. Each *Nikaya* has further sub-divisions in the form of whole books. The last of the five *Nikayas* of the *Suttapitaka*, known as the *Khuddaka nikaya*, is itself divided into many different works, of which the most well known are the *Jataka* stories. About 500 such stories narrate in verse form the previous lives of the Buddha, but these stories only become meaningful when they are read in the prose form. Since the Buddha himself was supposed to have passed through thousands of previous existences before achieving the perfect Buddhahood, the idea of accumulated merits of good deeds performed in countless births is very real and meaningful to Buddhists throughout the world. The *Jataka* stories provide moral lessons from all the lives of the Buddha; they also provide clues to economic, social and cultural conditions in ancient India. The stories, originally part of the Pali Canon, have been translated into many languages. The third basket, the *Abhidhammapitaka*, deals specifically with religious and ethical concepts. Tradition has it that the three *Tripitakas* were compiled by Buddha's followers shortly after his death, in 483 BCE, at the first Buddhist Council at Rajagriha; but there is doubt as to whether such an extensive work as the Pali Canon could have been closed so early on. It is more likely that the true progress over the formulation of the *Tripitakas* was made at the second Buddhist Council at Vaishali in 377 BCE.

Early Jain literature

The Jains believe that their earliest literature goes back to some 250 years before Mahavira, and that it originally consisted of sixty texts (Marett 1985: 82). A number of these texts are now lost, but those remaining are classed in five categories: eleven limbs, or *Angas*; twelve secondary limbs, or *Upangas*; ten miscellaneous texts, or *Prakirnakas*; six separate texts, called *Chadasutras*; and two other texts, known as The Blessing, or *Nandisutra*, and the Door of Inquiry, or the *Anuyogadvara*. Although the Jain canon, consisting of these principal texts, was not fully codified until the Council of Valabhi in CE 450, some of the earliest parts of it come from our period. Most of this early literature deals with doctrinal matters, rituals, legends, ethics and Jain philosophy in general, but it also contains fragments of scientific material. The Jains, for example, have had a great fascination for enumerating truly large numbers, and two of the earliest *Upangas*, from our period, the *Surya Prajnapti* and the *Jambu Dwipa Prajnapti*, contain mathematical and astronomical information. The *Tamdula Veyaliya*, which is part of the *Prakirnakas*, discusses physiology, anatomy and embryology (Bose *et al.* 1989: 44). It must, however, be acknowledged that most of the Jain philosophical, scientific and technical literature dates from the later centuries of the first millennium CE.

STUDY GUIDE

Key issues

- Differences between clan states and kingdoms.
- The political and economic importance of *Magadha*.
- Alexander the Great's legacy in India.
- Reasons for religious dissent in Vedic India.
- The significance of Panini's *Ashtadhyayi* as a major intellectual work.

Suggested readings

Allchin 1995: 99–122; Cohen 1978: 31–75; Cousins 1997: 369–444; Dimock *et al.* 1974: 47–80; Omvedt 2003: 23–52; Thapar 2002: 137–73.

INTERNET SELECTION

1) Art History Summary: 'Ceramic and pottery in the ancient art of India'. http://arthistorysummerize.info/ceramic-potteryindia
2) Wendy Doniger (New York Review of Books): 'War and peace in the Bhagavad Gita'. www.nybooks.com/articles/archives/2014/Dec/04/war-and-peace-bhagavad-gita
3) David Jordan: 'A Jataka Tale Retold: Prince Vessantara'. http://pages.ucsd.edu/-dkjordan/scriptorium/fortwo/Jataka.html
4) Salma Mahmud (*Friday Times*, Pakistan): 'The grammar of lions'. www.thefridaytimes.com/beta3/tft/article.php?issue=20130208&page=16
5) Puja Mondal: 'The causes of the success of the Magadhan imperialism up to the reign of Ashoka the Great'. www.yourarticlelibrary.com/history/the-causes-of-the-success-of-the-magadhan

QUESTIONS FOR GROUP DISCUSSION

1) Democracy and freedom of thought are concepts that are conventionally considered as having originated in Europe. To what extent might they have been practised in ancient India too?
2) Examine the ways in which ancient texts can help us to make sense of historical stories. Why are they also inadequate as historical sources?
3) Why does the study of pottery occupy a central place in archaeology? How does one proceed with the study of the history of pottery?

(4) Buddhism began in India, but in the course of time reached many different countries. Make a list of those countries today where Buddhism: a) is the religion of the majority of people; b) plays a central role in public life.

5) In what ways is Jainism either similar to or different from Hinduism?

Note

1   For a theoretical analysis of key factors affecting the rise of early states, consult Cohen 1978: 37–69 (p. 100).

6 The Mauryan state: imperialism and compassion

(321 to 184 BCE)

For a brief period of less than two centuries, from the early fourth to the late second century BCE, an imperial polity held sway over more than three-quarters of the land mass of the Indian subcontinent and the eastern half of Afghanistan. This was the Mauryan Empire. As with any empire, its genesis lay in the economic and military strength of a heartland state and the ability of its leaders to assert their power beyond its frontiers. From their central state of *Magadha*, the first three Mauryan emperors evinced a capacity, never before witnessed in Indian history, to muster extraordinarily large material resources for maintaining an imperial hegemony in South Asia. This hegemony was exercised by two methods of governance that, paradoxically, were contradictory but that helped weld together the many different peoples of the empire. On the one hand, as under any imperial system, the strong buttresses of bureaucratic institutions and administrative diktats gave the people a sense of security and belonging but also demanded strict obedience to the emperor. This remained the style of governance throughout the period of the empire but, halfway through its history, a new element was introduced. Under the third emperor, Ashoka, a unique form of cultural coherence based on the moral values of Buddhism came to be bestowed upon the empire, in the shape of moral exhortations inscribed on stone erected in different parts of India. These messages constituted an ideal norm of benignity, civility and humanity in matters of governance; they are benchmarks of progress in Indian political maturity. The relative prosperity of the Mauryan Empire was underwritten by a huge base of agricultural wealth and extensive commercial networks. It would be a long time before India would experience, nay enjoy, such a bold experiment in imperial sovereignty on this scale. The experiment did not last long, and most of the knowledge concerning the empire was lost. What has made it possible for posterity to appreciate the true scale of the Mauryan achievement is the fact that, for the first time in Indian history, we are able to make use of some contemporary written historical material in addition to archaeological findings. The painstaking researches of the last 200 years, along with accidental discoveries, have given us a new understanding of the two centuries when India made its first debut on the stage of world history.

Chandragupta Maurya and his court

The mystery of Chandragupta

The term 'Maurya' is derived from *moriya* (Sanskrit: *Mayura*), or peacock. According to a Jain tradition, the founder of the empire, Chandragupta, came from a clan of peacock-tamers who owed allegiance to the kingdom of *Magadha*. Until the late eighteenth century there had been much uncertainty about who the first Mauryan emperor, Chandragupta, really was, where and when he ruled, and even whether he ever existed. There were fragments of information about him in the *Puranas*, in the Buddhist text of *Mahavamsa* and in a Sanskrit drama dating from the middle of the first millennium CE called *Rudra-rakshasa*. There was also mention of a king called Sandrocottos, sometimes known as Sandrokoptos, in the works of some of the Roman writers who had learned about him from the writings of Megasthenes, an ambassador representing Seleukos Nicator, one of Alexander the Great's successors, at the Mauryan court. Megasthenes had referred to the majesty and power of King Sandrokottos, who ruled from a city called *Palimbothra*, which lay at the confluence of the rivers Ganges and *Erranoboas*, and the failure of Seleukos Nicator to subdue his Indian rival. The man who made sense of all these disparate references, through his vast knowledge of Greek, Latin and Sanskrit, was Sir William Jones, the Calcutta scholar and judge, who had articulated the idea of an Indo-European family of languages (Chapter 4). He received some help from a Major James Rennell, sometimes known as the 'father of Indian geography', who identified *Palimbothra* with *Pataliputra*, the capital of the state of *Magadha* and very near the modern city of Patna in Bihar. Rennell also used his skills in map-making to identify the River *Erranoboas* with the modern River Son, whose waters merged into the Ganges until as late as the fourteenth century CE. When Jones himself, while studying the Sanskrit drama *Rudra-rakshasa*, came across the name of a river called *Hiranyabahu*, he realised in a moment of inspiration that *Erranoboas* was the Greek form of *Hiranyabahu*. From the same play, Jones also came to learn about how the last king of the Nanda dynasty of *Magadha* was killed by Chandragupta, who then usurped the Magadhan throne. A further close study of Greek, Roman and Sanskrit works brought him close to realising his dream of fixing 'on an Indian prince, contemporary with Seleukos', in order to have a common fixed point in history. In 1793, just a year before his short but highly creative life was to come to an end, he modestly declared at the annual meeting of the Asiatic Society of Bengal in Calcutta (now Kolkata), 'I cannot help mentioning a discovery which accident threw my way' (Allen 2002: 71), and went on to explain how he had worked out that Sandrocottos was the same personage as Chandragupta. By correlating the long lists of kings and dynasties of ancient India in the *Puranas* with the data found in Greek texts he was able to establish a synchronology between the dates of Alexander the Great's invasion of India and the rise to power of Chandragupta, and he also clarified Chandragupta's relationship with Seleukos Nicator. Jones's work credibly established the sequence of events for the beginnings of the Mauryan Empire, and his discovery may therefore be considered 'one of the great chronological anchors of Indian history' (Drekmeier 1962: 166).

Chandragupta was the first true great emperor of India. He is always known as Chandragupta Maurya, to be distinguished from Chandragupta I, the founder of the Imperial Gupta kingdom that was established over 600 years later. After defeating the last of the nine Nandas of *Magadha* (Chapter 5), he assumed power in 321 BCE. By the time his reign ended in 297 BCE, he had, by war, threats of war, and aggressive diplomacy, reduced the kingdoms and republics of north India to impotence. His greatest triumph lay in the north-west. There, after Alexander's death in 323 BCE, the Graeco-Macedonian authority over the Indus basin and the areas to the west had significantly declined. In 305 BCE, Seleukos Nicator, who controlled the eastern or the Syrian part of the old Alexandrine Empire, turned his attention to India to reclaim Alexander's heritage. Chandragupta confronted him, with a victorious outcome – and forced him to surrender the Indus basin, Baluchistan and all lands east of Kabul. Seleukos made a dignified retreat from India in 302 BCE, after giving his daughter in marriage to Chandragupta, establishing diplomatic relations at the Mauryan court in *Pataliputra* and accepting Chandragupta's modest gift of 500 war elephants, which he later used against his western rival Antigonos. The successful campaign in the north-west brought to a close the military career of the emperor, and in his last few years he was much absorbed in the teachings of Jainism. Chandragupta's interest in Jainism is the first significant indication of the influence that the heterodox religions were to have on the future rulers of India for the next few centuries. If Jain tradition is to be believed, Chandragupta ended his life as a pilgrim and recluse in Karnataka, in the vicinity of Sravana Belgola, a major centre of Jain pilgrimage (Raychaudhuri 1996: 262).

Kautilya and the Arthashastra

The key to Chandragupta's worldly successes lay in the help and advice he received from his chief minister, Kautilya. While, after 1793, Chandragupta became a figure of importance in the pages of world history, Kautilya remained, for a further century or more, a marginal figure. In the old Vedic, Jainist and Buddhist sources, and in the later *Itihasa-Purana*, the genealogical records, he was known as Chanakya, the one who was the chief minister of Chandragupta. This was all that was known, and except for a very strange twist of history the memory of his name would have remained confined within those sources! However, one day in 1904, an anonymous *pandit*, a learned man from the Tanjore district, came to the Mysore Government Oriental Library and handed over to the librarian, Dr Shamasastry, a four-centuries-old palm-leaf manuscript of an ancient text. This text, which is now known as *Kautilya-Arthashastra*, was translated by the librarian in the pages of the *Indian Antiquary* in 1905. With the encouragement of the Maharaja of Mysore, in 1909 Dr Shamasastry published the full text as Volume 37 of the Bibliotheca Sanskrita of Mysore. Thus was resurrected the fame of Chandragupta's adviser Kautilya, and his great text, the *Arthashastra*.[1]

The *Arthashastra*, composed and written in Sanskrit, is a very valuable guide to our understanding of the Mauryan state and society. It deals with issues concerning diplomatic skills, political economy and general secular knowledge. It is a guidebook for monarchs and a rulebook for citizens. While it is not a text of political philosophy, it deals with the issues of political craftsmanship in great detail. It is also concerned with civil and political institutions and the ways the ruler can operate them. It is a primer of secular law; after reading the precepts of the *Arthashastra*, no one can claim that ancient India was a lawless place. There is also a huge amount of economic information as regards agriculture, manufacturing, rules of trade, mining, etc. Dr Shamasastry's translation of the Sanskrit text is laid out in fifteen books, each with a number of chapters. The English text has approximately a quarter of a million words. In addition to the names of people and places, the index to the text lists 430 different items and issues, ranging over a wide spectrum of subjects and experiences in which humanity is involved. Although the entire text is concerned with material and worldly issues and contains very little on religious matters, the philosophical premise of the work is entirely Vedic in outlook. The Vedic ideas of a social hierarchy, for example, along with the dominance of the *brahmans* and *kshatriyas*, are taken for granted. Heterodoxy is shunned, as can be evidenced in the following injunction: 'when a person entertains, in dinner dedicated to god or ancestors, Buddhists, Ajivakas, Sudras and exiled persons, a fine of 100 panas shall be imposed.' (Shamasastry 1923: Bk 3, Ch. 20). One of the reasons for this might be that the later revision could have been strongly influenced by a writer well versed in Vedic Brahmanism.

Because of what is written in the *Arthashastra* we can surmise that Kautilya must have advised Chandragupta in the arts of war and peace. There is a great deal of originality in his ideas on the relationship between a monarch and his neighbouring states. For example, he tells us that there are only two forms of policy for a king to choose in his dealings with other kings: war or peace. The operation of these two policies can take six different forms: agreement with pledges is called peace; offensive operation is war; indifference is neutrality; making preparations is marching; seeking the protection of another is alliance; and making peace with one and waging war with another is termed a double policy (Shamasastry 1923: Bk 7, Chs 1–3, 7). Kautilya deals at considerable length with the complexities and duplicities required for a king to pursue his relationships with his peers, as is manifest in **Excerpt 6.1** below. The collecting of intelligence was particularly vital.

Excerpt 6.1 The nature of alliance, according to Kautilya

The cunning methods of realpolitik that Kautilya outlines below have been followed by rulers of many nations in the history of the world.

> Of the two forms of policy, double policy and alliance, double policy (ie making peace with one and waging war with another) is preferable; for whoever adopts the double policy enriches himself, being ever attentive to his own works, whereas an allied king has to help his ally at his own expense . . . One shall make an alliance with a king who is stronger than one's neighbouring enemy; in the absence of such a king, one should ingratiate oneself with one's neighbouring enemy, either by supplying money or army or by ceding a part of one's territory and by keeping oneself aloof . . . A powerless king should behave as a conquered king towards his immediate enemy; but when he finds that the time of his own ascendancy is at and, due to a fatal disease, internal troubles, increase of enemies, or a friend's calamities that are vexing his enemy, then under the pretence of performing some expiatory rites to avert the danger of his enemy, he may get out of the enemy's court; or if he is in his own territory, he should not go to see his suffering enemy; or if he is near to his enemy, he may murder the enemy when opportunity affords itself . . . A king who is situated between two powerful kings shall seek protection from the stronger of the two; or from one of them on whom he can rely; or he may make peace with both of them on equal terms. Then he may begin to set one of them against the other by telling each that the other is a tyrant . . . and thus cause dissension between them. When they are divided, he may put down each separately by secret or overt means . . . Or, he may make friendship with traitors, enemies, and wild chiefs who are conspiring against both the kings. Or, pretending to be a close friend of one of them, he may strike the other at the latter's weak point by employing enemies and wild tribes.

> **Source:** R. Shamasastry, *Kautiliya's Arthasastra*, Mysore: Wesleyan Mission Press, 1923, 320–1.

It was the specific task of officially employed spies, informants and secret service agents; its diligent use was of the utmost importance to the ruler (Shamasastry 1923: Bk 1, Chs 11–12; Bk 13, Ch. 3).

What is generally termed Machiavellian in the context of historic rivalries of dynasties and ruling elites in European history was very much grounded in Kautilya's thinking eighteen centuries before Machiavelli himself (Dhar 1957: 10–12; Drekmeier 1962: 204–8).

A large part of the text is also concerned with the duties of a king. Many of the personal qualities recommended for the king would be considered admirable in any age. The king is advised to avoid betaking to others' women, appropriating others' wealth and injuring others; long sleep, fickleness, falsehood, gaudy dress, associates of low character and unrighteous actions are all condemned (Shamasastry 1923: Bk 1, Chs 7 and 19). This emphasis on the king's personal character is part of Kautilya's wider prescription for the organisation of the state. Capital, labour and land are, in his view, what constitute the wealth of a nation. In order that all the people in the state have some share of this wealth and are thus able to enjoy a measure of prosperity, good governance through strong institutions has to be paramount. For Kautilya, such governance has to be based on ethical principles of fairness and justice. The *Arthashastra* contains numerous references to varied issues of social rights for people; they include, among others, protection of the vulnerable, laws against sexual harassment, illegality of child labour, consumer protection, commercial malpractice and workers' rights to form unions. These rights lead to greater incentives for work and productivity in a country. In any assessment of the *Arthashastra*, however, the ethical prescriptions have to be balanced by a quite harsh and unforgiving environment of rules and regulations to be maintained by an extremely efficient and organised bureaucracy, whose officers wield great authority over every aspect of the lives and occupations of the people. In legal relationships – between husbands and wives, debtors and creditors, employers and workers, masters and servants, traders and customers – a severely retributory regime is invoked as soon as one party is deemed to have broken the contract. The index to the text lists 336 different offences for which fines are to be levied. The offences and fines, in a sense, tell us about one highly placed person's criteria for a well-governed society based on Vedic codes of conduct. His prescriptions concerning crime and criminality, however, are alien to progressive thought in modern times.

The text that we now have has been a subject of great debate among scholars as to its date and authorship. A large number of authorities have taken for granted that, since the author Kautilya (Chanakya) was the prime minister of Chandragupta, the *Arthashastra* has to be considered a contemporary Mauryan document. What may give credence to the *Arthashastra* is the fact that many of the contents in the text do correspond to a number of other Mauryan written, archaeological and numismatic sources. Recent research has, however, strongly challenged this assumption, and there has been much controversy, among scholars, about the dating of the *Arthashastra*. It is now increasingly argued that Kautilya might have composed a central core of the work, drawing upon more ancient sources, but that our present text is a later revised version dating to the second or third century CE. Several scholars believe that the present text is from a later period and that it may also have been written by more than one person. This is an understandable argument, since all ancient writing in many civilisations was subject to what are known as recensions and redactions (revisions and rearranging of texts). Ancient Indian texts were often works of multiple authors; the texts were refined and embellished long after the core sections had been written by the original author. It is therefore quite likely that the text of the *Arthashastra* would have also undergone many revisions in the course of time. This work would have been undertaken with great love and respect for the memory of that original author. Indeed, in the very first sentence of Chapter 1 in Book I, we are told that the *Arthashastra* is made as a compendium of almost all the *Arthashastras*, 'which, in view of acquisition and maintenance of the earth, have been composed by ancient teachers'. Kautilya, therefore, modestly eschews the claim of complete originality. At the same time, every chapter and book in the text ends with the phrase 'Thus ends Chapter X from Book Y of the *Arthashastra* of Kautilya'.

A further complication concerning the *Arthashastra* is the fact that the name of Chandragupta Maurya is not once mentioned in the work. There is therefore an understandable uncertainty among historians whether the *Arthashastra* describes the Mauryan, pre-Mauryan or post-Mauryan society. The temptation must also be avoided of treating this work as an idealistic model of ancient Indian society. It is very doubtful if a state like that of Kautilya's description ever existed in ancient India. However, when the overall message, rather than the technical language, of the text of the *Arthashastra* is closely examined, it is indeed very striking that it greatly confirms the picture that we have of conditions in India during the mid-first millennium BCE, if not the Mauryan world itself. The archaeological and foreign literary sources do corroborate many of the details to be found in the *Arthashastra*.

The 'Indica' of Megasthenes

Our understanding of the early Mauryan world in the reign of Chandragupta is further enhanced if we complement the *Arthashastra* with fragments of the contemporary account left behind by the Greek ambassador at the court. Megasthenes was a native of Ionia (modern Turkey) who represented the diplomatic interests of Seleukos Nicator. During his four years in India, from 302 BCE to 298 BCE, he observed and recorded the varied features of life in India; although his diary, *Indica*, is now lost, its contents were known to later European classical writers such as Strabo, Arrian and Diodorus Siculus, and it is from their writings that we learn what Megasthenes had earlier described. Considerable doubt was cast on both the veracity and the credibility of Megasthenes' writing even by the ancient historians themselves, particularly Strabo (Brown 1973: 142). Megasthenes was certainly wrong on a number of matters. He denied the existence of slavery in the India of the Mauryas, although it undoubtedly existed then as it did in later times. It was perhaps a different form of slavery from that in Greece, and he might have been misled by the fact that the working and living conditions of slaves did not differ much from that of the *shudras*. His erroneous calculations of the area of India and the length of the rivers can be excused by the fact that no one could have done better with the sort of instruments they possessed at that time. He had a most distorted view of India's history before his time: he wrote that 'the Indians had no cities . . . [and] they dressed in the skins of animals and ate the bark of trees' and that it was only after:

> Dionysus came and made himself master of India, he built cities and established laws for them, and he became the giver of wine, for Indians as well as the Greeks, and he taught them to sow the land, furnishing them with seed.

> (Brown 1973: 44–5)

Megasthenes also claimed that there were gold-digging ants in India, that India never suffered famines, that there was a river there on which nothing could float, that winged snakes dropped their urine from above, and that there were men who had no mouths. He was one in a long line of European observers who, through no particular malice, wrote inaccurate accounts about other nations, a tendency that did not go unnoticed, as can be seen in **Excerpt 6.2** below.

Notwithstanding such errors, historians are satisfied that on at least some of the matters Megasthenes was correct in his observations. The first is his social picture of India. He observed that its people formed seven estates. At the pinnacle were

---

Excerpt 6.2 European ignorance of non-European geography

We must forgive Megasthenes for a great number of geographical errors because, even after a millennium and more, European writers of the late medieval and the early modern world were propagating similar types of nonsensical images of the non-European world. The English satirist Jonathan Swift correctly described the way the map-makers of the sixteenth and seventeenth centuries solved the problem caused by the lack of hard facts about Africa in the following lines:

Geographers in Afric-Maps
With Savage Pictures fill their Gaps,
And o'er inhabitable Downs
Place Elephants for want of Towns

Source: Jan Nederveen Pieterse, *White on Black: Images of Africa and Blacks in Western Popular Culture*, New Haven, CT: Yale University Press, 1992, 18.

the philosophers, who, according to him, performed public sacrifices, learned the ancient texts, gave blessings to kings and led a life of abstinence and frugality. Many of them went about naked. In the context of the ritual caste system of India, this class would include the *brahmans* and various groups of sages and mendicants belonging to both Vedic and dissident traditions. The second estate consisted of the majority of the Indian people, the cultivators. Their task was to produce food and remit a quarter of it to the king, who owned all the land. Unlike in medieval Europe, they did not have to fight for him, although this was not strictly true. In the third estate were the herdsmen and the hunters, who had to bring in a certain proportion of their cattle into the cities as tribute, for which, in return, they received free corn. Traders, artisans and the boatmen constituted the fourth estate. The fifth estate was that of the soldiers, who did nothing else but fight and were always paid and maintained, thereby constituting a standing professional army. The sixth estate was made up of spies and intelligence officers, whose work is also described at length in the *Arthashastra*. The seventh and the smallest estate was that of those who constituted the political and imperial establishment. This sevenfold division seems to be a more elaborate classification of Indian society than the ritual hierarchy of the traditional caste system.[2]

Another item of interest in Megasthenes' diary was his description of the Magadhan capital, *Pataliputra*, which he called *Palimbothra*. This is especially valuable, as we have relatively limited evidence for what the cities and towns of India in the third and fourth centuries BCE looked like. While the splendid bricks and the isolation of Mohenjo Daro and Harappa preserved the original layout of those cities for posterity, the cities of the Ganges have suffered from both poor quality materials and periods of great turbulence. That is why Megasthenes' *Pataliputra* is so evocative. Built at the confluence of the rivers Ganges and Son, the palisade defences of *Pataliputra* formed a great oblong, 9 miles long and 1.8 miles in width. All along the palisade were 570 towers and sixty-four gates. Outside the palisade ran a ditch, 60 feet deep and 200 yards wide, serving as both defence and public sewer.[3] Megasthenes describes both the hustle and bustle of the streets of the capital and the peace and beauty of the royal park, and he gives a colourful account of the royal palace, which he considered more sumptuous than those of Susa and Ecbatana in Iran (Raychaudhuri 1996: 242–6). It is also in his accurate understanding of the way in which the municipality of *Pataliputra* was organised by Chandragupta that historians have found Megasthenes most useful. The work of six major committees is described at length. Their duties covered such varied issues as the promotion of arts and crafts in the city, the reception and care of foreigners, the registration of births and deaths, the supervision of weights and measures, the quality control over manufactures and the collection of duties over goods sold. An examination of the departmental details indicates to us not only a high level of bureaucracy but also a certain concern for the quality of life of the ordinary people (Raychaudhuri 1996: 246–60). The greatest of all the Mogul emperors, Akbar, 'had nothing like it, and it may be doubted if any of the ancient Greek cities were better organised' (Smith 1958: 110). When the accounts of Megasthenes are corroborated by the vast number of details in Kautilya's

Arthashastra, our knowledge of the world of Chandragupta Maurya becomes more complete. It was indeed a highly ordered and well-regulated world.

Ashoka and his *Dhamma*

Dhamma is a term in the Pali language, related to the Sanskrit word *dharma*. While Sanskrit was the classical language of the learned in Vedic society, Pali itself began as *Prakrit*, the vernacular of the common masses of north India, and became the scriptural language of Buddhism. *Dharma*, in Vedic thought, implies a sense of universal law or norm, eternal and unchanging. Many Hindus therefore like to call their religion *Sanatana Dharma*, or the religion of the eternal law. In Buddhism, *Dhamma* has varied meanings. One meaning refers to the teachings of the Buddha himself, while another deals with the philosophical aspects concerning the 'nature of things' or what may be termed 'natural'. However, a more practical interpretation of *Dhamma* was provided by the third Mauryan emperor Ashoka himself. The *Dhamma* of Ashoka, or the law of moral virtues, exhorted people to engage themselves in ethical behaviour and good deeds.

Ashoka's grandfather, Chandragupta, had founded the Mauryan Empire in 321 BCE and, under his father, Bindusara, the empire had been consolidated into one of the strongest and most extensive of the political authorities of Asia. A large part of the South Asian subcontinent had been subdued by Ashoka and his predecessors, yet one strategic region on the eastern seaboard, *Kalinga*, had escaped Mauryan control. A vigorous attack by Ashoka, in which hundreds of thousands of enemy troops died, finally subdued *Kalinga*. Witnessing death and destruction on this scale, however, Ashoka felt acute remorse and the imperative of repentance. For him this was a point of catharsis, when he felt he had to purify himself holistically. He became a Buddhist, and came to believe in the pristine tradition that Buddha had bequeathed. He supported Buddhist causes and promoted the founding of Buddhist shrines and cities. He also backed the efforts of a renowned Buddhist monk, Moggaliputta Tissa, in summoning the Third Buddhist Council at *Pataliputra* in 250 BCE and organising Buddhist missions to the Hellenistic kingdoms, Tibet, Nepal, the deep south of India and Ceylon. He was the first king to embody an imperial ideal called *Chakravartin*, the 'wheel turner', which is largely Buddhist in inspiration. The *Chakravartin*, unlike the Vedic warrior king, was to be the promoter of peace and prosperity – leading to a new concept of irenical (peaceful) sovereignty that was later incorporated into Hindu kingship. His main ambition, however, was to establish a *Dhamma* in a society imbued with Buddhist ideals.

The principal method by which Ashoka propagated *Dhamma* was by issuing a set of edicts that were inscribed on the faces of cliffs and hillocks (rock edicts) and pillars (pillar edicts) in different parts of the empire. With a few exceptions, the language used for the inscriptions at most sites was *Prakrit*, the contemporary spoken language of north India. The words were carved in the *Brahmi* script that, along with a parent script known as *Kharoshti*, was in use in India by the time of the Mauryans. One would justifiably presume that a king such as Ashoka, who

Figure 6.1 Ashoka's temple at Bodh Gaya

idealised compassion not conflict (albeit after his *Kalinga* war) and humane values rather than authoritarianism, would be a celebrated figure in the history of India. Although today he is well known as a great figure of history, such was not the case for more than twenty centuries, when he had remained a 'lost' (Allen 2012: book title) emperor to Indians. As time had moved on and Indian history had crossed new pathways, the memory of Ashoka had faded, and his rock and pillar edicts that propagated Buddhist ideas and ideals had been forgotten. In fact, by the nineteenth century, there were hardly any Buddhists left in India.

There are a number of reasons why Ashoka, along with the Buddha, remained a figure of mystery in India for such a long time. First, although Buddhism remained a vibrant religious force in India for another seven or eight centuries after Ashoka, it always faced pressure from Hinduism that, every so often, emerged from the shadows and asserted itself, thus eroding Buddhist confidence (Omvedt 2003: 160–74). While the Buddha himself became part and parcel of the iconography of Hindu deities, his religion came to be received with greater warmth abroad rather than in its homeland. The gems of Buddhist literature came to be nurtured in Sri Lanka, for example, and it was in the literature of Sri Lankan Buddhists that Ashoka was most respected and venerated. Second, whatever was left of the legacy of Buddhism within India came under ferocious assault from the early iconoclastic Turco-Afghan invaders from the eleventh and twelfth centuries onwards (Wink 1997: 147–8, 307–33). Third, since India's climate shows little mercy to both manuscripts and monuments, much had therefore been lost over the centuries. Although some of the edicts had managed to survive and were there for interested observers or travellers, Indian scripts had long moved on since Ashoka's days and had evolved into something very different; therefore, no one in India could make any sense of Ashoka's message. Fourth, while early Indian historical concerns are evident in both historical consciousness and historical traditions as represented by many and varied literary texts such as the great epics or the *Puranas*, it would not be an exaggeration to maintain that history had held out little fascination or interest for scholars in the Hindu world. Ancient Hindus displayed both talent and originality in their approach to such systematic studies as mathematics, grammar, logic or astronomy, yet they produced no outstanding historian who could interpret secular evidence to explain a historical story (Thapar 2011: 553–76).

It was the curiosity and methodicalness of British oriental scholars of the nineteenth century that finally helped to rescue Emperor Ashoka from obscurity. The most important contribution to the de-mystification of both Ashoka and Buddha came from the work of James Prinsep (1798–1839), a gifted engineer, draughtsman and numismatist (Allen 2002: 140–99; Allen 2012: 120–81; ODNB 2004: Vol. 59, 570–2). A man of great energy and enthusiasm, he was admired by all who came to know him, as can be witnessed in **Excerpt 6.3** below.

Excerpt 6.3 In praise of James Prinsep

James Prinsep was entirely dedicated to the task of promoting Indian historical studies; this won him numerous supporters and followers who were equally enthused and inspired by him. Although the deciphering of the Brahmi script on Ashoka's pillars and rocks remains his greatest legacy, he took keen interest in the work of other scholars and greatly encouraged them. Dr Hugh Falconer, who later became the Chief Superintendent of the Botanical Gardens in Calcutta and Professor of Botany at the Medical College there, fell under Prinsep's spell and wrote the following words.

Himself the soul of enthusiasm, he (Prinsep) transferred a portion of his spirit into every inquirer in India; he seduced men to observe and to write; they felt as if he observed and watched over them; and the mere pleasure of participating in his sympathies and communicating with him, was in itself a sufficient reward for the task of a laborious and painful investigation.

Source: quoted in Charles Allen, *Ashoka: The Search for India's Lost Emperor*, London: Little, Brown, 2012, 131.

The early British scholars had come across the Ashokan pillar and rock edicts, but had been unable to decipher the *Brahmi* script of the inscriptions. Most literature in ancient India was transmitted orally. Leaving aside the Harappan script, which remains undeciphered and therefore unintelligible, the first written documents of India were the Ashokan edicts of the third century BCE, carved in two principal scripts of *Kharoshthi* and *Brahmi*. By the third century BCE, *Brahmi* had become the dominant script, which means that its earliest development must be traced back at least 500 years, to the eighth century BCE. It is from *Brahmi* that the scripts for the varied languages of both the Indo-Aryan family and the Dravidian family of languages came to be developed (Fischer 2005: 105–20). It was Prinsep who was able to break the code of the *Brahmi* script after carefully studying the script of certain rock and pillar edicts and comparing it with that on a gateway of an important Buddhist *stupa*, that at Sanchi in Central India. The Mauryan coins that were being discovered at this time were also to prove useful in establishing some pattern in the inscriptions (Prinsep 1858: Vol. 2, 1–34, 55–101). The diverse data collected was then coordinated with the huge amount of information from Sri Lanka that became available after the translation of a major Buddhist text, the *Mahavamsa* or the Great Dynastic Chronicle, by another Englishman, George Turnour, in the early 1830s. The first major breakthrough came with the deciphering of the opening sentence in all the edicts, which proclaimed: '*Devanamapiya piyadasi laja hevam aha*', meaning literally: 'Beloved-of-the-Gods, beloved king, spake thus', commonly translated as: 'Thus spake King Piyadasi, Beloved of the Gods'. Prinsep's work also clarified the confusion caused by the fact that there had been a king of Sri Lanka called King Devanamapiyatissa, who had been converted to Buddhism through the efforts of the Indian king Dharmashoka, the wheel-turning monarch of India. Prinsep stated conclusively that *Devanamapiya piyadasi* referred to Dharmashoka, not to King Devanamapiyatissa of Sri Lanka. The final deciphering of the script in 1837 and the identification of the name of Ashoka within the text of a number of edicts were Prinsep's crowning glory. Like Sir William Jones, he helped to greatly expand our knowledge of Indian history.

The Ashokan edicts

Ashoka's edicts can be classified into three separate groups (Thapar 1998: 250–66). First, there are the fourteen major rock edicts, in a single corpus or in a partial form, inscribed on rock in *Prakrit* in *Brahmi* script. These are found at sites as varied as Kalsi (Himachal Pradesh), Girnar (Gujarat), Sopara (Maharashtra), Yerragudi (Andhra Pradesh) and Jaugada and *Dhauli* (Orissa). At the last two sites there are also inscribed two separate edicts, known as the *Kalinga* Edicts, which may be considered part of the major rock edicts. At two further sites in Pakistan, Shahbazgarhi and Manserah, on the upper Indus, the fourteen edicts are inscribed in *Kharoshthi*, the roots of which are to be found in the Persian Aramaic. Major rock edicts have also been recently found at a place called Sannathi, in Karnataka, and at Kandahar in Afghanistan. Second, three minor rock edicts have been found at nearly twenty different places in the subcontinent, covering areas such as the Deccan, the Ganges valley, the lands east of the Yamuna River, and in Afghanistan. A minor rock edict, recently discovered at Kandahar, was inscribed in two scripts, Greek and Aramaic. Third, there are seven pillar edicts in *Prakrit*, again inscribed as a single corpus or in a partial form, in the *Brahmi* script. They can be seen today at Delhi, Allahabad, Buner in Pakistan, Amaravati on the east coast, and at three sites in Bihar: Lauriya-Araraj, Lauriya-Nandangarh and Rampurva. At Delhi there are two pillars, Delhi-Meerut and Delhi-Topra. They were originally brought down to Delhi from Meerut and Topra (both in Uttar Pradesh) by Sultan Firoz Shah Tughluq in the fourteenth century, and given pride of place in his new medieval Delhi. Finally, there are two minor pillar edicts, one at Lumbini in Nepal, which is known as the Rummindei Pillar Inscription, and another at Kausambi, called the Schism Edict. The geographical spread of the rock and pillar edicts clearly delineates the extent of the Mauryan Empire. The empire's influence spread as far west as Afghanistan but stopped short of penetrating the far south. Also, no rock or pillar edicts have been found in Punjab, Sind, the deserts of Rajasthan or the lands immediately south of the Vindhya hills in central India (see Map 6.1).

Distinguished scholars, from Prinsep onwards, have translated the edicts and pondered over what Ashoka meant to tell his people.[4] Here we shall highlight some particular subjects emphasised in them. First, the rock and pillar edicts are a key to understanding the mindset of Ashoka after his conversion. One major rock edict gives us the context of the conversion by describing the trauma of the *Kalinga* war and Ashoka's agony and remorse. He is truly repentant at having caused enormous suffering to all classes of people, which, he says, 'weighed heavily on [his] mind' (Major Rock Edict 13). Despite this weighty confession, it is interesting that this particular major edict was left out from the rock inscriptions found in modern Orissa. The two *Kalinga* rock edicts emphasise, instead, the king's desire for justice and fairness. The theme of justice is likewise taken up in other edicts. Prisoners, for example, need to be treated humanely (Pillar Edict 4). Ashoka wanted his officers, known as *mahamattras* or *rajukas*, to oversee agricultural improvements in villages and promote law and order in the countryside (Major Rock Edicts 3, 5 and 12; Pillar Edict 4). He went on tours around the empire to monitor their work (Major Rock Edict 8). The edicts also emphasised the emperor's own sense of self-discipline. He refused to spare himself from the rigours of introspection and self-analysis. In one of the pillar edicts he said that the hardest thing for a human being was to recognise the evil that was within his or her own self – only when that was achieved could a genuine conversion to a humanist path begin – and he was aware that he needed to be strict with himself (Pillar Edict 3). For him, the crowning glory lay in his dedication to the service of his people and their welfare. Another major rock edict mentions his effort at securing medical help, from home and abroad, for sick humans and animals, building roads and wells, and planting trees, while a pillar edict mentions the building of rest-houses for travellers (Major Rock Edict 2). The need for non-violent behaviour by humans towards other humans is emphasised again and again. This may be a result of

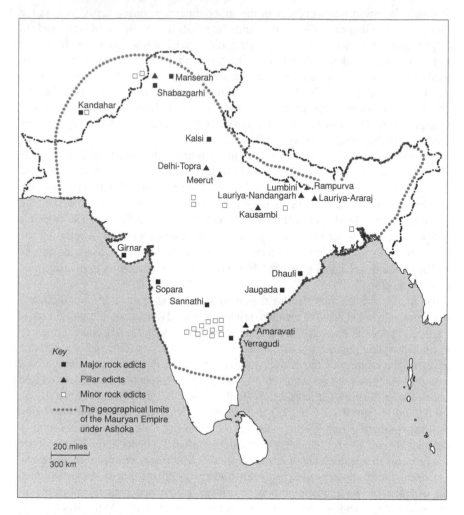

Map 6.1 The Mauryan Empire at its greatest extent and the spread of Ashoka's
inscriptions

extreme guilt over the slaughter of the *Kalinga* war, but it would be somewhat
churlish to doubt his sincerity merely because emperors normally do not develop
such a consistent philosophy of non-violence. For Ashoka, non-violence extended
to humans and animals alike. He exhorted all people to stop killing animals for
wanton pleasure at festivals, and he laid down specific days at regular intervals
when various classes of animals and fish could not be hunted at all. He had enough
knowledge of animal welfare to realise that an animal must not be fed with the
meat of other animals (Pillar Edict 5).[5]

We also need to examine Ashoka's attitude towards religion in general and the
religions of others. He appreciated that, on occasions of birth, marriage, illness

or long journeys, people needed to perform religious ceremonies, however 'trivial and useless', for their own mental satisfaction, but 'if such ceremonies must be performed they have but small results' (Major Rock Edict 9). The *Dhamma* was of greater value than ritualistic religion. This did not imply that Ashoka was necessarily anti-Vedic; he desired that all sects might dwell harmoniously everywhere, for all seek self-control and purity of mind (Major Rock Edict 12). He exhorted his officers to be fair to all, both to the *brahman* priests of the majority Vedic society and to dissenters such as the Buddhists, Jains and Ajivakas (Pillar Edict 7). He shows a profound sensitivity towards issues that arise in a multi-faith society when he urges his subjects to honour other sects and not to disparage or be over-critical of other religious viewpoints, as shown in **Excerpt 6.4** below.

By talking the language of tolerance and understanding, Ashoka made his *Dhamma* 'the common property of all religions' (Bhandarkar 1925: 107). It is also the most appropriate way of binding together a vast and variegated society of the

---

Excerpt 6.4 Ashoka's interfaith outlook

Religious conflicts have torn apart peoples and nations throughout history. Ashoka offered something that is both profound and modern, and greatly worth reflecting upon.

> Beloved-of-the-Gods, King Piyadasi (Ashoka), honours both ascetics and the householders of all religions, and he honours them with gifts and honours of various kinds. But Beloved-of-the-Gods, King Piyadasi, does not value gifts and honours as much as he values this – that there should be growth in the essentials of all religions. Growth in essentials can be done in different ways, but all of them have as their root restraint in speech, that is, not praising one's own religion, or condemning the religion of others without good cause. And if there is cause for criticism, it should be done in a mild way. But it is better to honour other religions for this reason. By so doing, one's own religion benefits, and so do other religions, while doing otherwise harms one's own religion and the religions of others. Whoever praises his own religion, due to excessive devotion, and condemns others with the thought 'Let me glorify my own religion' only harms his own religion. Therefore contact between religions is good. One should listen to and respect the doctrines professed by others. Beloved-of-the-Gods, King Piyadasi, desires that all should be well-learned in the good doctrines of other religions.
>
> **Source:** Ashoka's Major Rock Edict 12, translated by Venerable Shravasti Dhammika, quoted from Charles Allen, *Ashoka: The Search for India's Lost Emperor*, London: Little, Brown, 2012, 412–13.

Excerpt 6.5 H.G. Wells on Ashoka

In the Western world, H.G. Wells's fulsome praise of Ashoka in his worldwide bestseller The Outline of History, *first published in London in 1920, might have made an impact upon the consciousness of readers.*

Amidst the tens of thousands of names of monarchs that crowd the columns of history, the name of Asoka shines, and shines almost alone, a star . . . more living men cherish his memory today than have ever heard the names of Constantine or Charlemagne.

Source: H.G. Wells, *The Outline of History*, London: Waverley, 1920, Vol. 1, 212.
Reproduced with permission of United Agents LLP on behalf of The Trustees of G.P. Wells Deceased.

empire and providing it with a cultural and spiritual value system. Since, for several decades before and after his reign began, the Buddhists had been occupied in much infighting over the nature of their most important institution, the *sangha*, Ashoka took the opportunity, in one of the minor rock edicts and in the Schism Edict at Allahabad, of proclaiming his belief in the unity of the *sangha* and issuing a threat of expulsion to those who created schisms. On the other hand, in the Rummindei Pillar Inscription, at Lumbini village in Nepal, the birthplace of the Buddha, he exempted the villagers from taxes and fixed their grain due at the liberal rate of one-eighth of their produce.

In conclusion, we can say that the powerfully conveyed messages in his edicts entitle Ashoka to be called the greatest of all the kings of India. The lion capital of an Ashokan pillar is the official emblem of the Indian republic, and every Indian child is taught about Ashoka at school. Outside India, too, his name has spread far and wide, and all encyclopaedias of world history list his august name (**Excerpt 6.5**).

The Mauryan world

Agriculture

As during all periods in Indian history, agriculture remained the central activity of the people in the Mauryan Empire. The key unit in the agricultural landscape was the village, and it was the collective effort of people in each village that buttressed the village economy in the empire. It was in the fields around the village that the bulk of the production of crops and the rearing of livestock took place. The ultimate ownership of the land in the village, at the primary level and throughout the empire, depended upon its nature and quality. The state itself owned and controlled, as crown lands, extensive areas of terrain. Some of these were highly fertile and productive, but many others were fallow and wastelands. Fertile crown lands were leased to landlords on the payment of both rent and taxable produce, but only for the duration of their lifetime. Some of these landlords, described in Buddhist sources as *gahapati* or *gramabhojakas*, were both rich and powerful in their own right. They would then sub-lease the land to sharecroppers and tenants against paid rent. As regards the wastelands, the state at first organised the large-scale clearing of desolate areas and then usually settled *shudra* cultivators on those newly reclaimed lands. They would be initially exempt from tax, but once the land began to be cleared the tax was imposed. Slaves conquered in wars were also employed as hired labourers. Although the Greek historian Diodorus, echoing Megasthenes, affirmed that slavery did not exist in India (Ray *et al.* 2000: 265–6), the Indian sources themselves contradict him (Thapar 2002: 186). Although both the slaves and the *shudras* suffered from prejudice, discrimination and a lack of real freedom, their treatment, as employees of the state or of private landlords, was made more humane in the reign of Ashoka through the work of the *rajukas*, the state officials, who were charged with the

Figure 6.2 Farmers worshipping a sacred tree in the Buddhist tradition

task of maintaining harmony and equity in the countryside. The appropriate auditing of the crown lands was in the hands of the superintendent of agriculture, who, in addition to holding seed stocks, hired contingents of labourers to private owners of land (Shamasastry 1923: Bk 2, Ch. 24).

That not all land in the country belonged exclusively to the king is evidenced by the fact that there were many estates that were not crown lands. In his *Arthashastra*, Kautilya has numerous references to the idea of the purchase of land and to the kinsmen, relations and neighbours interested in the purchase; he also provides details of how purchases could be secured, including by auctioning; and he gives priority to kinsmen and creditors in the case of lands sold by private owners facing hardships (Shamasastry 1923: Bk 3, Chs 5, 6, 7, 9, 10, 16). The concept of private landed property was validated: not only were title, ownership and the purchase and sale of private land recognised as ratified in the eyes of law, but even its mortgage was legalised (Saletore 1973: 466–9). In whatever form the ownership of land existed, a range of rural taxes and dues made the Mauryan state a great beneficiary of agricultural production. Taxes included those levied on the area of land cultivated, or on the value of the yield. The assessment was regionally based, and it could range from one-sixth to a quarter of the produce of the land. The arable quality of the land was normally taken into consideration in any assessment. A tax, known as *pindakara*, could also be gathered as a collective sum from an entire village. Shepherds and livestock breeders were taxed depending on the number and produce of the animals. In addition, there was a labour tax, which could be the provision of labour in lieu of a tax. Sometimes, craftsmen had to provide a stipulated amount of free time to the state. There was also a charge for the supply of irrigation water by the state to private owners, by means of reservoirs, tanks, canals and dams (Thapar 2002: 187). Agriculture evidentially enriched the rulers of the empire, but to what extent the ordinary people benefited is uncertain. It may be averred that, while famines, diseases and the lack of advanced medicine and technology would have taken a big toll of the relatively small Mauryan population of 100 million or so (Lal 1988: 33), the rural population was probably better fed than during the British rule in India, a period of enormous famines.

Urban life

Cities and urban centres had once been the pride of the Harappan civilisation, but during the Vedic era, when the Gangetic basin was being opened up, there was only a crude conception of urbanism. In Chapter 5 we observed that, during the three centuries of the pre-Mauryan period, a number of settlements grew and expanded, which we may refer to as towns, but it was really during the Mauryan period that some of these towns developed into cities. From this period onwards we have a clearer idea of the distinctions between the settlements as identified by their sizes. The *grama*, or the village, was, then as now, the most numerous class of settlement, but in size and importance it was being superseded by the town, or the *nigama*, which was a settlement between a village and a city in size but with a specific function, as an administrative or market centre. At the top of the settlement hierarchy was the *nagara*, the city. Cities could be classified into the *mahanagara*, or great city; the *rajadhaniya nagara*, or shortened to *rajdhani*, generally the capital city; and the *sakha nagaraka*, or the branch city or a satellite town. Nearly twenty centres that can be credited as *nigama* or *nagara* have been identified. The Mauryan metropolis, *Pataliputra*, covering an area of 2,500 hectares, or about 12 square miles, was then the largest city in South Asia, while other settlements were less than 240 hectares in size. The cities were political, commercial or monastic centres, all fortified by walls, ditches and ramparts (Allchin 1995: 194–209).

Our understanding of the theoretical ground plan of an ideal city comes from Kautilya's *Arthashastra*, some of the ideas of which might have been based on the ancient architectural manuals, the *Silpa Sastras*. Another textual source of reference is the description of *Pataliputra* by Megasthenes. The ground model in the *Arthashastra* suggests that a typical Mauryan city was built on a grid plan (Shamasastry 1923: Bk 2, Chs 3 and 4; Allchin 1995: 227–8). Along each side of the surrounding wall would be three gates, with the middle one carrying the central entry. The four middle gates would be known by the names of Brahma, Indra, Senapati and Yama. The entire city was divided into sixteen blocks, with central areas taken up by the royal palace and the quarters for the royal functionaries. The *brahman* castes occupied two middle blocks to the north of the palace; the *kshatriya* bureaucrats and officers took up three blocks to the east; the *vaishya* traders and their various guilds were spread out in six blocks, south of the palace; while the *shudras* and other manual workers were confined to three blocks in the west. All crematoria, sanctuaries and quarters for extreme heretics were outside the city moat. The authenticity of the plan in the *Arthashastra* may be testified by Megasthenes' description of *Pataliputra* and its royal palace. Megasthenes, as was pointed out earlier, is completely unreliable when he talks about things and places that he had never seen; however, as ambassador at the royal court in *Pataliputra* he had the opportunity to observe life in the city and the palace, and on those subjects he was certainly not writing up imaginary descriptions.

Archaeological excavations of the remains of this period have not been intensively carried out, but just sufficient evidence has been found to corroborate the accounts in the *Arthashastra* or in Megasthenes' *Indica*. Much of the archaeological effort has been concentrated on three places: *Pataliputra*, the capital, Bhita in the Ganges valley and Taxila in the north-west. The area of *Pataliputra*, as conjectured by the extent of excavations, is not as large as calculated by Megasthenes, but the city was certainly the largest in South Asia in Mauryan times. The foundations of nearly eighty pillars that supported a great hall in the palace have been excavated, providing some indication that the architecture of the palace might owe to the style of architecture in Achaemenid Persia. Fragments of polished stone sculptures and architectural elements have also been found in the city. At both Bhita and Taxila the archaeologists have been able to lay bare complete housing blocks along a number of streets. The houses in Bhita, with nearly fifteen rooms, were arranged on three sides of a large open courtyard paved with bricks. Drains, wells and storage jars have been recovered from the ground. At the Bhir Mound in Taxila, ruins of houses built of stone rubble rather than bricks, streets laid out on a grid pattern and terracotta ring wells were excavated by two great masters of Indian archaeology, Sir John Marshall and Sir Mortimer Wheeler. Varieties of polished black ware pottery fragments, weights made of iron or stone, and Mauryan gold, silver and copper coins of various shapes and sizes have been found at the three sites and many others too.

There can be little doubt that the Mauryan city was a hive of activity and industry for craftsmen and traders, who would have been organised within guilds and allotted portions within towns and cities from which to operate. The products were sold not only locally, but regionally and nationally, as well as abroad. A network of trade routes criss-crossed the subcontinent, covering the hinterland centres of trade

Map 6.2 Urban centres of the Mauryan Empire

as well as ports such as Broach or *Tamralipti*. Both copper and punch-marked silver coins help to provide clues to internal and external trade (Allchin 1995: 218–21). A number of foreign artisans, such as the Persians or even the Greeks, worked alongside the local craftsmen, and some of their skills were copied with avidity. It is difficult for us, after such a long interval, to visualise a Mauryan city, but both literature and archaeology testify to its relatively large size and permanence. Unlike in the Indus cities, however, we cannot be sure what sort of hygiene and sanitation prevailed in the Mauryan city. Although latrines, wells and drainage channels have been identified, it is very likely that public refuse and disease were prevalent. We know that during the post-Mauryan era, when Indian external trade by land and by sea expanded enormously, India exported not only its valuable commodities, which were in great demand everywhere, but also the unwanted dreaded epidemics of plague, tuberculosis, cholera and leprosy (Ponting 1991: 228).

Administration

The Mauryan administration has been studied in great depth by many scholars and much has been written about it. As mentioned earlier, Megasthenes himself has left us an account of the administration of *Pataliputra*, the capital; much can be gleaned from the *Arthashastra*; and the Ashokan edicts give us further clues. Here we shall highlight three particular aspects: the degree of administrative control exercised over a vast territory, the hierarchy of control, and the functions of administration. The cultural and economic diversity of the varied areas of the empire meant that a completely uniform degree of control throughout was impossible to operate. Instead, one should treat the empire as consisting of three zones of culture and economy. The first was the heartland, i.e. the state of *Magadha* and the Gangetic plain. Here there had been a long tradition, going back many centuries, of tight political authority being exercised, almost in the way its concept is described in the *Arthashastra*. This was the zone where power ultimately resided in the royal palace at *Pataliputra*; naturally, a large number of Ashokan pillars are also found in this zone. The second zone consisted of the conquered areas, such as *Gandhara* in the north-west, Karnataka, *Kalinga* or Saurashtra. These were areas of great potentiality in terms of trade, revenue and strategy, but 'as areas brought into the ambit of the Mauryan system they experienced state formation at second remove' (Thapar 2002: 196). In these places, too, numerous Ashokan rock edicts have been found. As conquered areas, they carried the risk to the Mauryan governors of being volatile regions. A gentler and more sensitive style of governance was therefore needed in this second zone. The third zone consisted of isolated buffer areas, where lived nomads, forest people or hill tribesmen. From their lands came valuable resources, such as elephants, timber and precious stones. Inside this third zone it was important for the agents of the empire to create conditions in which a plentiful labour supply was able to exploit and marshal the natural resources for the economic benefit of the empire. The Mauryan state attempted to secure maximum compliance and subservience from the people of all three zones, but the means employed naturally varied. The principles of both direct and indirect rule were attempted.

The empire was divided into a number of provinces, which were sub-divided into districts. A prince or a member of the royal family ruled over a province and a hierarchy of officers controlled the bureaucracy. This stratification must have been extremely elaborate and finely graded, and one can see in it the antecedents of the hierarchy at the court of the great Mogul or the British viceroy. Those occupying the top echelons of power and privilege were far removed from those at the lower grades. It has been estimated that the ratio of the clerk's salary to that of the chief minister or of the humble soldier to the commander was approximately 1: 96 (Thapar 2002: 195). With such a high level of remuneration, it is quite likely that the highest officials of the administrative service would have been required to meticulously oversee a large number of civil and economic tasks and a variety of public works mentioned in contemporary sources. Two of the topmost officers were the treasurer and the collector. The former kept complete accounts for the whole empire, while the latter made the arrangements for the collection of taxes. It was its ability to garner revenues from all classes of people that particularly marks out the special quality of the Mauryan government. The Mauryan taxation bureau scrupulously exacted every *pana* (silver coin of that period) and every *masaka* and *kakini* (copper coins) owed to it, in revenue, from town and country. If the punishments for misdeeds and corruption, as described in the *Arthashastra*, are any indication, it was most unlikely that the Mauryan state could be defrauded by the people or its officials. That is in striking contrast to the taxation regimes prevalent today in South Asian countries.

The large-scale collection of taxes leads us to ask: where did the revenue go? Most of it must have been spent on maintaining the royal family and replenishing its treasury, and on the military establishment and administrative services. The Mauryans encouraged a mixed world of state enterprise and private capitalism that was highly regulated, and their desire to control the 'commanding heights of the economy' meant incurring great expense in the staffing of a bloated civil service. What is significantly missing, however, is the notion of public finances being systematically expended on supporting public services, such as health, education, social security or pensions. The notion of the state undertaking such responsibilities is, however, a relatively recent one, arising out of a more varied and enlightened understanding of a government's functions. The Mauryan government would have neither understood nor accepted the public finance implications of humanism that was preached by Ashoka.

Architecture and sculpture

For at least a thousand years after 1700 BCE, during most of the Vedic period, there is little evidence of architectural creativity in India. Of course, large wooden palaces, halls and barns must have been constructed, but we cannot really tell how durable they were. From 600 BCE, however, with the growth of towns once again, there is a certain change; but it is from the Mauryan period particularly that we first get evidence of the large-scale use of hewn stone as a building material (Allchin

1995: 238–9). There is a lively debate among scholars as to whether the beginnings of stone architecture and sculpture in India from 300 BCE onwards should be associated with the contacts of the Indians with the Persians from the Achaemenid Empire and the Greeks. Both these peoples had built impressive monuments of stone, such as the palace at Persepolis and the Parthenon on the acropolis of Athens, and both the Persians and the Greeks could be found working in various capacities in India at that time. There were skilled craftsmen in stone who could have been mentors of the Indian workers. Another viewpoint challenges this 'Perso-Hellenistic . . . post-Alexandrian' influence altogether and argues for an indigenous evolution of stone architecture from the tradition of wood architecture. Either viewpoint may be correct; the Indians could quite easily have observed and emulated the masonry skills of the foreigners, but what they finally produced was distinctly Indian in both reality and symbolism (Smith 1958: 133–4; Rowland 1977: 67–70; Allchin 1995: 238–9; Craven 1997: 41–2; Daheja 1997: 44–5).

Two particular aspects of Mauryan architecture – secular and religious – need to be taken note of. The first piece of evidence of both stonework and brickwork of the Mauryan craftsmen relates to secular urban architecture. Archaeologists have now been able to locate solid brick or stone defences and ramparts in such places as Kausambi, Taxila, Rajgir and Sisupalgarh. Megasthenes' description of *Pataliputra* and the ideal city plan projected in the *Arthashastra*, both referred to above, have helped archaeologists to identify particular types of ground plans and the layout of domestic houses. Much effort has also gone into excavating parts of the pillared hall at *Pataliputra*, although here the timber framework had perished. The elements of the urban architecture and planning that developed as a process from the pre-Mauryan to Mauryan times, and were later elaborated in texts such as the *Shilpashastras*, persisted for many centuries and gave the cities of India a particular distinctiveness. The Mauryan architects and builders were also the pioneers of a particular strand of religious architecture which was to dominate the Indian landscape for some seven or eight centuries. This was the Buddhist religious architecture, and two of its forms have their roots in the Mauryan period. One was the *stupa*, a massively built dome, housing the relics of the Buddha and Buddhist preachers, standing on a square or circular base with a flattened top and a kiosk. The earliest part of the *Stupa* I of Sanchi dates from the Mauryan times (Tomory 1989: 23) (see Figure 6.3). The second type of structure was the cave form, hollowed out from the living rock, later developing into what is called a *chaitya* hall (see Figure 6.4). The Buddhist monks used the *chaitya* as their place of retreat, and the best of the Mauryan caves are Lomas Rishi (see Figure 6.5) and Sudama in the Barabar Hills (Rowland 1977: 63–5).

Mauryan art was essentially the art of the sculpture (Tomory 1989: 165–8). The Ashokan pillars are beautifully polished monolithic shafts, made from sandstone quarried at Chunar, in Benares, without footings and with carved capitals in the form of lotus flowers with inverted petals, with an animal or animals mounted. The capitals are decorated in relief. The bull capital of Rampurava and the lion capital of Sarnath are the best examples of the animal-figured pillars. Another animal sculpture of the Mauryan period, of equal renown, is popularly called the

Figure 6.3 Stupa of Sanchi

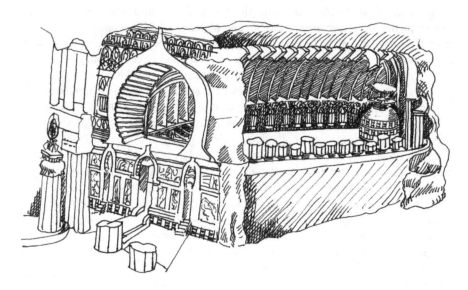

Figure 6.4 Chaitya hall at Karle

Figure 6.5 Lomas Rishi entrance

Dhauli Elephant. With its slightly raised right leg and flowing trunk, this massive elephant, carved *in situ* from the living rock at Dhauli in Orissa, is one of the most impressive sculptures in animal studies anywhere in the world. Yet another achievement of Mauryan sculpture consists of a number of statues of *Yaksha* and *Yakshini*, which are male and female divine spirits. Among them the most polished and sophisticated statue is the *Didarganj Yakshini*, whose beautifully rounded figure with sensuous curves might be called the precursor of the later more famous Mathura *yakshinis*.

The decline of the empire: some causes

A number of causes of Mauryan decline have been identified by historians, but it is difficult to place them in order of importance. One set of issues has to do with the size of the empire at a time when the means of communication were poor. The outlying areas always had a temptation to pull away from the centre, and there is some evidence of the reassertion of regionalism under the fairly autonomous governors and princes within the empire. This pulling-away process would intensify in areas where the people felt oppressed by the system. The Mauryan bureaucracy failed to establish long-lasting popular institutions through which the local people could participate in their own governance. The state used espionage much too frequently for a true bond of trust to develop among the people. One might rightly suspect that the officers appointed by Ashoka to promote harmony in the countryside were not above using spies to collect information. The large-scale economy of the empire also concealed an underlying stress of raising enormous revenues through a near-penal form of taxation. On the other hand, feelings for autonomy grew in some of the conquered areas where substantial development had taken place, such as the provinces of *Kalinga* or *Avanti*. Historians have also suggested that the overtly Buddhist pieties of Ashoka had made a large mass of people subscribing to the Brahmanic traditions antipathetic to the empire, thereby weakening the internal cohesion of the state. This point has been challenged on the grounds that Ashoka dealt fairly towards all in his kingdom. There may be something in another view that holds that Ashoka's non-militarism undermined the strength of the army, leading to disaffection within the ranks. The last Mauryan emperor was stabbed to death by his own commander-in-chief at a military parade: he had been weak and indecisive. All Ashoka's successors lacked force and character, a fact that would certainly have contributed to the decline of the empire. That decline was accelerated by both external and internal threats.

STUDY GUIDE

Key issues

- Scholarly discoveries by Sir William Jones and James Prinsep in establishing the chronology of Chandragupta Maurya and Ashoka.
- The *Arthashastra* as a primary document of Vedic political economy.

- Varied forms in which Ashoka promoted Buddhism.
- The governance of the Mauryan state.
- Main elements of Mauryan architecture.

Suggested readings

Allchin 1995: 187–273; Allen 2002: 42–74; Allen 2012: 120–81; Drekmeier 1962: 189–226; Thapar 1998: 250–66; Thapar 2002: 174–208.

INTERNET SELECTION

1) Burjor Avari: 'Reviews in history – Ashoka: the search for India's lost emperor'. www.history.ac.uk/review/reviews/1286
2) Ajay Goel: 'The Mauryan administrative system'. www.importantindia.com/430/the-mauryan-administration
3) Ven. S. Dhammika: 'The edicts of King Asoka: an English rendering'. www.accesstoinsight.org/lib/authors/dhammika/wheel386.html
4) Khan Academy: 'The stupa'. www.khanacademy.org/humanities/art-asia/beginners-guide-asian-culture
5) Balbir Sihag: 'Kautilya and national security'. www.idsa.in/event/TalkbyBalbir SinghSihagKautilya.html

QUESTIONS FOR GROUP DISCUSSION

1) An *Arthashastra* scholar has described this work to be superior to Adam Smith's *Wealth of Nations* and Machiavelli's *The Prince*. Why, then, is the *Arthashastra* ignored in most Western textbooks of political economy?
2) By what means was James Prinsep able to decipher the *Brahmi* script of Ashoka's edicts? Why was his achievement so crucial for modern India?
3) In the light of Ashoka's edicts, would you consider the Mauryan state to be a 'welfare state'?
4) What were the main challenges that the Mauryan emperors faced?
5) What is the difference between a *stupa* and a *chaitya* in Buddhist architecture?

Notes

1   The version used for this chapter is that by Shamasastry himself, published at Mysore in 1923 (p. 125).
2   For a critique of Megasthenes' sevenfold division, see Thapar 2000: 190–2 (p. 130).
3   For a comparison with recent archaeological results, see Allchin 1995: 200–4 (p. 130).
4   For example, see translations by Bhandarkar 1925: 273–337; Mookerji 1928: 107–207; Thapar 1998: 250–66. Thapar's version is used here (p. 135).
5   This simple piece of safety regulation was disregarded by commercial farming interests in Britain at the end of the twentieth century, causing much suffering to victims of the BSE illness (p. 136).

7 Between the Mauryas and the Guptas

(185 BCE to *c.* CE 300)

Timeline/Key Dates

185–73 BCE	Shunga rule in north India
185–172 BCE	Kharavela's rule in *Kalinga*
180 BCE	Demetrius rules over the first Indo-Greek state in north-west India
166–150 BCE	Rule of Menander, the best known Indo-Greek ruler
c. 50 BCE–CE 236	Satavahana dynasty of the Deccan
CE 78–111	Kanishka rules over north India
CE 130–50	The reign of Rudradaman, the powerful Western Shaka ruler
CE 1st–3rd centuries	Indo-Roman trade at its height
CE 1880	The British Museum acquires the iconic Amaravati art collection

With the fall of the Mauryan Empire came the loss of a pan-Indian authority exercised from *Pataliputra* in *Magadha*. There now arose a number of competing power centres in different regions of India (see Map 7.1). The imperial monarchy was replaced by regional monarchies, and a centralised bureaucracy by regional bureaucracies. These changes had little effect on the continuing hold of the idea of absolutist kingship. Numerous royal eulogies, called *prasastis*, from the various regions, endowed the respective monarchs with superhuman qualities. Many regional monarchs had Central Asian origins, but they too in time conformed to the notions of kingship that had been maturing since late Vedic times and which reached their apogee in the Mauryan period. All monarchies, whether of foreign or indigenous origins, subscribed to the Brahmanic notions of caste and the fourfold *varna* system, although Buddhism provided a relatively easier route for foreigners to become adjusted to the Indian social system. The political diffusion in the post-Mauryan period and the emergence of monarchies with foreign roots, described by one historian as 'chaotic darkness' (Dunbar 1943: 68), might be seen as signs of regression from the heyday of Mauryan imperialism, but, in reality, both the economy and the culture showed much dynamism.

One of the reasons why historians find the post-Mauryan era so absorbing is the huge scale of available evidence for research. The domestic literary evidence can be drawn from the royal inscriptions, the *shastras*, the secular literature, Buddhist religious and secular texts, and the fascinating Tamil anthologies from the south. Foreign literary sources, from China, Syria, Greece, Persia and Egypt, give credence to the political and commercial setting of this period. The clear numismatic evidence available to historians also facilitates the construction of relative chronologies. With sufficient archaeological corroboration, we can be confident that, from about 200 BCE onwards, the study of Indian history takes on a definitiveness that for earlier periods often eludes us. In terms of sources, this is like a transition from the proto-historical to the historical.

New dynasties and new centres of power

The political landscape after the Mauryan collapse in 185 BCE remained confused for about 200 years until the beginning of the Christian era, with a host of dynasties jostling for power. These dynasties were either native Indian or ethnically mixed, such as Indo-Greek or Indo-Scythian. During the first three centuries of the first millennium CE, most of India, except for the far south, was dominated by three systems of authority: the Central Asian Kushan, the Deccan Satavahana and a branch of another Central Asian group, known as the Western Shakas. Incipient kingdoms developed in the extreme south of India too, although our main interest in the southern region in this period concerns the elaborate trading connections it had with different parts of the world and with the flowering of Tamil literature.

The Gangetic heartland: Shungas, Kharavela

The Shunga dynasty, founded by Pushyamitra, the renegade army commander of the last Maurya, controlled the central Magadhan region for 112 years, until 73 BCE. The Shungas were continually at war with their neighbours as well as more distant enemies. Their most dangerous internal enemy was Kharavela of *Kalinga*, whose deeds and activities can be studied from a classic early royal eulogy, the famous Hathigumpha Inscription at the Hathigumpha cave in the Udayagiri hills near Bhubhaneshwar in Orissa (Raychaudhuri 1996: 331–5, 644). Although *Kalinga* had earlier been severely defeated by King Ashoka, Kharavela restored its power. He not only attacked the central state of *Magadha*, but also the Greeks in the north-west and the Pandya kingdom in the south. The somewhat faded Hathigumpha Inscription informs us that although he was a man of war he believed in the non-violent Jain faith and endowed a Jain monastery. He enlarged an irrigation canal originally built by the Nandas, and he was responsible for

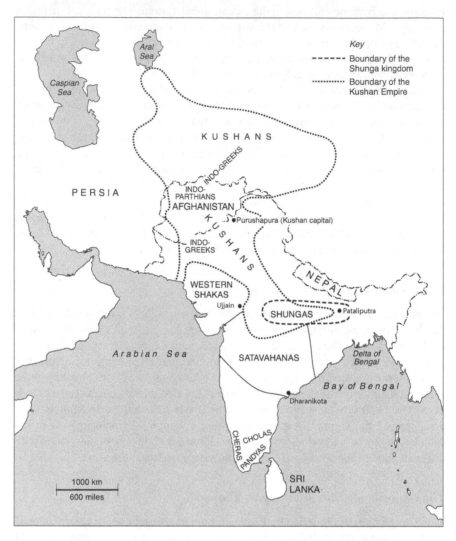

Map 7.1 Post-Mauryan kingdoms

constructing gates, walls and gardens. The inscription neatly summarises his deeds during thirteen years of his reign (185 BCE to 172 BCE). After his death, *Kalinga*'s power waned, giving breathing space to the Shungas. Externally, however, the Shungas faced an ever-present danger from the Indo-Greek and Indo-Scythian kings and warlords of north Afghanistan and north-west India. Pushyamitra and his successors just about kept them in check, although many Mauryan-held lands were lost. Despite the distractions of warfare, the Shungas provided valuable patronage to both Buddhism and Brahmanism and also helped to create a minor architectural renaissance.

The north-west: Indo-Greeks, Pahlavas, Shakas

During the last two centuries before the Common Era, much of the north-west was attacked and occupied by forces from across the border in Bactria, the part of Afghanistan that lies between the River Oxus and the Hindu Kush mountains. Bactria, as part of the Persian conquests of Alexander the Great, had been attached to the Selucid kingdom run from Syria. In the middle of the third century BCE, Bactria, along with another Persian province, Parthia, revolted against the Seleucids. Normally the Greek governors of Bactria were appointed by the Seleucid kings, but after their revolt they called themselves kings in their own right. The first of these rebellious kings was Diodotus I of Bactria (*c.* 250 BCE). His successor, Euthydemos, fought a war against Antiochus the Great of Syria, who, in 208 BCE, accepted the independence of the Bactrian kingdom. The Graeco-Bactrian kings clashed with the Mauryans during their forays into north-west India. They became bolder after the Mauryan collapse and, under a monarch called Demetrius, occupied a large part of the Indus delta, Saurashtra and Kutch (Narain 1957: 12–45; Frye 1996: 111–18). The Shungas were powerless against them. The Graeco-Bactrian kings belonged to various lineages, but those who invaded India and established their tiny kingdoms in parts of its north-west, particularly in *Gandhara* and Punjab, are specifically known as Indo-Greek rulers. One of these rulers was Menander, whose capital was in the rich city of Sialkot in Punjab and who figures prominently in the Buddhist philosophical text *The Question of Milinda*. Indeed, Buddhism became firmly implanted in the Indo-Greek territories, and it was from there that it later spread north and west. All Greeks in India were, however, known as *Yavanas*, and the upper elite of Indians, particularly the *brahmans*, generally held an unfavourable view of them (Thapar 2002: 160). Those tiny territories of the Indo-Greek kings were certainly lively places, where commerce flourished. A vast hoard of coins, with a mixture of Greek profiles and Indian symbols, has helped archaeologists and historians to identify various lines of Indo-Greek kings and dynasties; the coins also indicate a certain level of prosperity. The most well known of the Indo-Greek cities was Taxila, 'the most extensively excavated city site of the subcontinent' (Allchin 1995: 285); some of the sculptures and monumental remains, brought to light by archaeology, point to a rich fusion of Indian and Hellenistic influences (Tarn 1951: 351–408).

Both the Bactrian Greek and the Indo-Greek monarchs faced attacks, during the first century BCE, from the Parthians and the Scythians. After seceding from the Seleucid kingdom, at around the same time as Bactria's revolt, the Persian province of Parthia, which lay to the south-east of the Caspian Sea, went on to become the second great Persian empire (after the Achaemenid), and the power of Parthia spread east as far as the Punjab and even beyond (Boyce 2002a: 99–115). The Indians called the Parthians Pahlavas. Soon, however, the Parthians themselves faced an onslaught of a Central Asian group, the Shakas (or Scythians). The latter had been facing a squeeze in their homeland near the Aral Sea from a nomadic group called the Yueh-chi and had managed to escape towards eastern Iran. Eventually the Parthians tamed the Shakas and, under their leadership, directed them further east. Thus, in the first century BCE, after overrunning

Bactria, the Shakas moved into India too and took *Gandhara* and Punjab. A little later they penetrated the areas around Mathura, the Yamuna valley, the upper Deccan, Saurashtra and Ujjain in Malwa. In Indian history the Shaka rulers are known as Shaka-Pahlava, meaning a mixed group of tribal Shakas and Parthians. Effective Shaka suzerainty in India came to be exercised eventually by two authorities, respectively known as the Northern Shakas of Taxila and Mathura and the Western Shakas of Malwa and Kathiawar (Frye 1996: 121–30).

From the Aral Sea to Kashi: the trans-Asiatic empire of the Kushans

Having avoided the Yueh-chi once, the Shakas came under pressure from a further Yueh-chi wave. This was because, during one of their regular bouts of nomadic warfare, the Yueh-chi in turn had suffered a defeat by a rival tribe, the Hiung-nu, and been forced to move west towards Bactria in around 130 BCE (Yu 1990: 118–49). After overcoming the Shakas and settling down in Bactria, the Yueh-chi gradually evolved from their nomadic roots into a sedentary people (Khazanov 1984: 198–227). They were established in five different groups, one of them being the Kuei-shuang, or Kushans (Narain 1990: 151–76). At around the beginning of the Common Era the Kushans subdued the other four and assumed overall control of most of Afghanistan and eastern Iran, under their leader Kujula Kadphises. His son, Wima Kadphises, entered north India in the middle of the first century CE. All Punjab, Kashmir and the plain of the Ganges up to *Kashi* came to be Kushan-controlled. The whole of the empire, from the River Oxus to *Kashi*, was consolidated by Kanishka, who succeeded Wima (Frye 1996: 133–50; Raychaudhuri 1996: 715–32). There is uncertainty as to when this exactly happened and whether there was more than one Kanishka (Zevmal 1970: 152–5; Kumar 1973: 58–77). We do, however, know that he fought a number of battles, with mixed results, in order to keep his empire secure in his grasp. The Kushans maintained a powerful dominion over north India until at least CE 250, and their trans-Asian empire became one of the great conduits for India's international trade.

Kanishka, however, was more than a soldier and conventional emperor. Although personally 'cruel and temperamental' (Daniélou 2003: 130), he provided the framework of a firm and fair rule of law based on Buddhist precepts. He was also a great compromiser and synthesiser of different ideas. In his empire many religious traditions flourished: Persian Zoroastrian, Greek and Roman paganism, Buddhism, Chinese Confucianism, Jainism and, above all, a whole range of Vedic traditions. His coins bear their proof, because they carry images of deities from the various religions practised in his kingdom. In keeping with the broad Indian political conventions, Kanishka allowed space to differing ideas. Buddhists, however, consider Kanishka as second in importance only to Ashoka Maurya, because under his rule Buddhism had flourished as never before (Zelinsky 1970: 156–7; Liu 1994: 109–10, 117–18). At the Kushana capital in *Purushapura* he built an enormous *stupa*, nearly 700 feet high and 300 feet in diameter, for

Figure 7.1 Torso of King Kanishka

Buddhist pilgrims and travellers crossing the empire (Kumar 1973: 97–102; Liu 1994: 135; Daniélou 2003: 130–31).

Under Kanishka's successors the Kushan hold over India lessened. They lost all real authority in Afghanistan, eastern Persia and Central Asia when the new powerful Sasanian dynasty, under Ardashir, seized power in Persia from the Parthians in CE 226. From then on the Kushans became the minor vassals of the new Persian Empire. In India too their authority increasingly came to be challenged by the Western Shakas and by other minor independent principalities. By the end of the third century CE a variety of tribal republics and monarchical states were reasserting themselves.

The Satavahanas of the Deccan: their prosperity and piety

The history of the lands of northern Andhra Pradesh, northern Karnataka and Maharashtra is very much a part of the history of the Deccan, which, together with the areas of the far south, makes up the great southern half of India. There arose in two particular regions of the Deccan – in north-western Maharashtra and the Andhra region between the rivers Godavari and Krishna – a great dynasty called Satavahana (sometimes known as the Andhra dynasty). These regions had been part of the Mauryan Empire, so the dynasty arose either in the very last years of the empire or shortly after its fall (Allchin 1995: 279–80; Raychaudhuri 1996: 356–72). The most famous of their early kings was Satakarni, who ruled between about 37 and 27 BCE.[1] He is well known in history for his successful campaigns against *Kalinga* and Malwa. He gained Sanchi, the site of the great *stupa*, and an inscription from there refers to him as Rajan Shri Satakarni (Tripathi 1999: 194). His conquest of the Godavari valley and the southern regions gained him further power and status. After his reign the Satavahanas suffered a major defeat at the hands of the Western Shakas and lost their hold on Maharashtra. As the Shaka satrapies denied the Satavahanas access to the western Deccan, the latter were thus forced to concentrate their energies on the eastern Deccan. This situation lasted for about a century, but eventually the Satavahanas turned the tables on the Shakas and reconquered their lost territories. Many Shaka coins found in places such as Nasik in western Maharashtra have their original Shaka images overstruck with those of the returning Satavahana monarchs. Satavahana power reached its zenith during the second century CE, in the reigns of Gautamiputra (113–38) and Pulumayi II Vasisthiputra (138–70). By the time the kingdom perished in CE 236 it had been in power for more than 300 years.

The basis of Satavahana prosperity lay in agriculture and trade. The Satavahana kings were some of the greatest donors of land and land revenue to communities of Buddhist monks, the *brahmans*, and to all who wished to engage fruitfully in agricultural pursuits (Ray 1986: 98–102). Merchants and traders were equally encouraged to open up new trade routes from the hinterland towards the ports. This provided a further boost to the growth of urban centres in the Deccan as a whole, but particularly in the Andhra region (Yazdani 1960: 138–40; Ray 1986: 113–17, 129–32). Part of the evidence for prosperity is to be noticed in the man-made cave sites of north-west Maharashtra, which were once the centres of Buddhist religious piety. The epigraphic inscriptions retrieved from some of the caves provide us with details of religious charities and endowments made not just by the prosperous merchants or local governing elites but also by a whole variety of people belonging to various crafts and professions. Buddhism was the inspiration behind the actions of these people. Dotted all over the Satavahana Deccan were the great Buddhist monasteries that had been established by pious endowments at the significant crossing points of trading routes (Yazdani 1960: 142–3; Ray 1986: 82–9). Into these monasteries came people from all walks of life, for peace, meditation and spiritual care, and bequeathed some of their wealth as charity to support the further material needs of these institutions. The Andhra merchants were some of the greatest donors. It is in this context of prosperity and piety that we can best appreciate the glory that was the great *stupa* of Amaravati, which no longer exists. This monumental structure, built by an army of labourers, masons and craftsmen who lived in the great *entrepôt* city of Dharanikota on the River Krishna, was a true symbol of Buddhist piety and mercantile prosperity (Knox 1992: 9–13). The sculptures from this site, a fine example of the Indian art of this period, will be referred to later in the chapter.

Gujarat and Malwa: the Western Shakas

Of the two Shaka branches mentioned above, the Western Shakas assumed greater dominance. While the northern branch suffered a chequered history, the western one endured until the rise of the Guptas in the fourth century CE (Raychaudhuri 1996: 446–53). It was under their powerful king Rudradaman I (*c.* CE 130–50) that they tightened their grip on Gujarat, Malwa and Sind. Despite the overweening power of the Satavahanas, Rudradaman found ways to coexist with the Deccan giant. His true fame lies in the fact that he left behind, on a rock inscription at Junagadh, a *prasasti* containing a most exquisite account of himself and of his cultural achievements and acts of valour (**Excerpt 7.1** below). Unlike the Ashokan edicts, which used the *Prakrit* language, the Junagadh Rock Inscription was in Sanskrit, which could be interpreted as Rudradaman's way of showing respect to Brahmanic Vedic culture. It must have ensured his legitimacy as a ruler, despite his Central Asian Shaka origins. The monarchs who followed Rudradaman were people of lesser stature, but they nevertheless managed to maintain hold over their territories in central India with determination and tenacity until both the Kushans and the Satavahanas, their main rivals, had perished.

Excerpt 7.1 A fragment of the Junagadh Rock Inscription

The rock inscription in the town of Junagadh in Gujarat celebrates the construction of a lake and a dam. Much of the inscription, however, consists of praises of King Rudradaman. The words below are an example of royal self-importance and lack of humility in the wording of eulogies in ancient India. The kings were endowed with superhuman qualities.

. . . he (Rudradaman) who because, from the womb, was distinguished by the possession of undisturbed consummate Royal Fortune, was resorted to by all castes and chosen their lord to protect them; who made, and is true to, the vow to the latest breath of his life to abstain from slaying men, except in battles; who showed compassion . . . not failing to deal blows to equal antagonists meeting him face to face; who grants protection of life to people repairing to him of their own accord and those prostrating themselves before him; who is the lord of the whole of eastern and western . . . territories gained by his own valour, the towns, marts and rural parts of which are never troubled by robbers, snakes, wild beasts, diseases and the like, where all subjects are attached to him . . .

. . . he who has attained wide fame by studying and remembering, by the knowledge and practice of grammar, music, logic and other great sciences . . . he who has acquired the name of Mahakshatrapa Rudradaman . . .

Source: F. Kielhorn, 'The Junagadh Rock Inscription of Rudradaman', *Epigraphia Indica*, Vol. 8, 1981, 45–9, quoted in Niharranjan Ray *et al.*, *A Sourcebook of Indian Civilization*, Hyderabad: Orient Blackswan Private Limited, 2000, 327–8.

Tamil lands of the deep south

The origins of the Tamil people and other Dravidians in the extreme south of India are a matter of dispute among historians. They are either the descendants of the first humans who reached there from Africa, or perhaps they are later migrants, some of whom are said to have come from the eastern Mediterranean basin. Whatever their ancestry, they were never entirely cut off from the historical movements in north India. The Aryanisation of the south had been proceeding since the Vedic period, and the heterodox religions of Buddhism and Jainism had also penetrated into the south. Megasthenes, the Greek ambassador to the Mauryan court of Chandragupta Maurya, refers to pearl fishing in the southern waters controlled by a ruling group called the Pandyas. The inscriptions of the Mauryan emperor, Ashoka, also mention two other groups, known as the Cheras and the Cholas. It had taken a great number of centuries for these three groups to make the political transition from tribal chiefdoms to kingdoms. However, by the end of the first millennium BCE, we have the first faint outlines of three distinct kingdoms, with the Cheras well established in the far south-west, and the Cholas and the Pandyas on the south-east coast and the tip of India. The movement of people between the north and the south had certainly helped to bring about this development. The consolidation of the kingdoms owed to the economic prosperity of this region. The Cholas were pioneers of southern irrigation schemes, while the Pandyas had ventured far out into the high seas. They made contact with South East Asia and attacked Sri Lanka. The wealth of this region exceeded all expectations once Roman ships began trading there. It was not long before the three kingdoms themselves engaged in bouts of fighting with each other, and the most distinguished Chola king of this period, Karikala, led a number of attacks against not only the Cheras and the Pandyas but also against the rulers of Sri Lanka.

The international trade of India

India was extremely rich and her GDP exceeded that of any other nation or region during this period (Maddison 2003: 259, 261). She was a nation with which people from far and near wished to trade. The beginnings of her international trade can be noticed as early as 2500 BCE, when the Harappan civilisation traded goods with Mesopotamia and the ports of the Persian Gulf. There is not enough historical evidence of any large-scale external commercial contacts during the Vedic age, but from 600 BCE onwards, through a strong interaction with the Achaemenid Persians and the Graeco-Macedonians, a period of great expansion in international commerce, as well as cultural links, set in. The links became stronger during the Mauryan period, but the really significant developments of that period were the growth in the production of goods and the setting up of a sound commercial infrastructure. The post-Mauryan era is particularly well known for the range and volume of international trade that was generated, and this trade, by both land and sea, added enormously to both urban and rural prosperity. Practically no part of India was left untouched by developments resulting from increased foreign trade. Whether one examines the contents of *The Periplus of the Erythrean Sea*, an ancient guidebook for mariners, or the works of Roman historians or the *Sangam* literature of south India, or studies the ground with archaeological skills, the subject of India's international trading connections assumes utmost importance for our understanding of the period under review here.

The commercial infrastructure

A vital aspect of the commercial infrastructure was the guild system. During the post-Mauryan centuries the guilds came to play a crucial role in the success of both domestic and international trade. Known in India as *shreni*, the guilds can be described as associations of professional people, merchants or artisans. They acted variously as trade unions, cooperative organisations, regulatory bodies or even banks. They existed in various crafts and trades; there were, for example, guilds of potters, goldsmiths, bead and glass makers, ivory carvers, musicians and carpenters. The rules of work, quality control over finished goods, the fixing of prices, the recruitment of labour from a specific occupational caste for a particular trade – these were all overseen by each craft guild (Saletore 1973: 528–43). Rich merchants and many ruling dynasties invested in the guilds, making them viable and flourishing. The guilds, in turn, provided large donations to religious foundations and monasteries. The guilds of merchants, who were known as *shreshthins*, acted also as bankers, financiers and trustees. Large sums were loaned out, bearing interest rates of between 12 and 15 per cent, with higher rates carried for the sea trade (Thapar 2002: 252). Another aspect of the commercial infrastructure was the great increase in the minting of coins during the post-Mauryan centuries. For the numismatist, the best of the early coins of India were those struck by the Indo-Greek kings and the Kushan monarchy. Through the foreign influence of the Persians, the Greeks and the Romans, the quality of Indian coins greatly improved over the older punch-marked coins. Made from gold, silver, copper or tin, the variety of coins proved especially useful for variant trading economies in different regions, and the huge quantity of local and foreign coins also made it easier for merchants to engage in forward speculation in goods and capital.

The links by road and river between the main cities and trading towns were an essential element in the general infrastructure facilitating the volume of trade as a whole (Saletore 1973: 349–60) (see Map 7.2). Starting with the north-west, in the centre of the Kushan territories, was Taxila, a city where the merchants of Central and South Asia exchanged their goods and the intellectuals their ideas. Taxila was joined to *Pataliputra* by a major highway; en route was Mathura, which in turn was linked to Ujjain in the Malwa region, controlled by the Western Shakas. Mathura and Ujjain linked the western Ganges valley and the lands of central India. A number of market towns were also developed in the Satavahana kingdom of the Deccan. Centres such as Nasik and Karad in Maharashtra and Nagarjunakonda in the Andhra region were all important trading centres where the farmers, pastoralists and hunter-gatherers from the hinterland congregated to sell their commodities and wares. The routes linking these places sometimes had to follow the gaps and breaks in mountains or the river valleys. All the major routes led to the five main international ports of that period, namely *Barbaricum* in the Indus delta, *Barygaza* on the Gujarat coast, *Muziris* on the Kerala coast, Arikamedu on the Coromandel coast and *Tamralipti* in the Ganges delta. These ports handled the bulk of the sea trade of India with Arabia, the Levant, the Roman Empire and South East Asia (Casson 1989: 21–7).

The overland trade route through the Kushan territories

Since at least 600 BCE the main overland trade route had run from Taxila towards West Asia and the Hellenistic world (Saletore 1973: 372–85). Caravans from India carried ivory, elephants, spices, cloths, salt, musk, saffron and indigo; the returning caravans brought lapis lazuli, turquoise, fine quality ceramics, wines, and gold and silver coins. The first part of the overland route was from *Taxila* to Begram, from where two main routes branched out: the northern route via Bactria, the Oxus, the Caspian Sea and the Caucasus to the Black Sea, and the southern route via Kandahar, Herat and Ecbatana to the ports of the eastern Mediterranean. Once the Kushans came to establish their trans-Oxus empire and controlled all territory between the Aral Sea and the middle Ganges valley, a new dimension was added to the overland trade route. This came to be in the form of a link to the famous Silk Road that connected China with Europe by land (Liu 1994: 2–11, 18–22; Frye 1996: 153–7). The Silk Road began at Lo-yang in China, progressed through Chang'an and reached Dun-huang on the eastern edge of the Taklamakan desert. From there two routes branched, one north of the desert and the other south of it, both reaching Kashgar on the western edge of the Taklamakan desert. From Kashgar the Silk Road entered the Central Asian and Bactrian territories of the Kushans before proceeding through the Parthian Empire towards Syria, the Levant and eventually Constantinople. Through their Kushan connections, the merchants of India could now begin to share in the handling of the products that travelled along the Silk Road, particularly the silk from China. They first did this by taking expensive gifts to the Chinese emperors (Liu 1994: 53, 77). At the same time, during the first and second centuries CE, Buddhist missionaries were making progress in spreading the message of the Buddha among both the Central Asians and the Chinese, and, during the period when the Kushans were dominant, Indian merchants and the Buddhist missionaries forged a powerful alliance of interests. At various junctions on both the northern and southern routes of the Silk Road, skirting the Taklamakan desert, at places such as Kashgar, Yarkand, Khotan, Miran, Kuchi, Qurashahr and Turfan, Indian merchants set up their colonies, while the missionaries established monasteries. As Buddhism spread into China, the demand for Buddhist artefacts from India underwent a manifold increase (Liu 1994: 88–102). During this time the Chinese emperors were becoming concerned by the growing tensions between the Roman Empire and the Parthian Empire, resulting in Parthian impediments to the movement of goods through their territory. They were therefore more than content to entrust Indian merchants with handling the silk destined for the Roman market, taking it via Taxila, whence it would be dispatched southwards to the ports of *Barbaricum* and *Barygaza*, bypassing

Parthian lands. Roman ships would then carry away the silk and leave behind their products, such as coral, glass, silver and topaz. These, in turn, would also be handled by Indian merchants on their overland route to China. The strategic location of the Kushan state between India and China meant that the ruling nobility and the subsidiary elites were heavily involved in this trade; they too wished to partake of the share of luxury goods. However, they were not particularly interested in the handling of the trade itself; they left that to individual merchants and, probably, to the specific merchant guilds. Their benefits came in the form of imposts and levies that they charged on all movement of goods through their territory.

India and Rome

With the founding of the Roman Empire in 31 BCE, India and Rome began a highly successful trading relationship that lasted for more than two centuries. The main reason was the increasing prosperity of the Roman populace and their insatiable demand for certain Indian products and those of China and South East Asia, which could be easily procured for them by Indian merchants. The annexation of Egypt by Rome in 31 BCE was also a factor of great logistical importance, because Rome became the mistress of both the Mediterranean Sea and the Red Sea. The ports of the Red Sea, both on the Arabian and the Egyptian–Ethiopian shores, had had trading relations with India for many centuries, during the post-Alexandrine Hellenistic period and even earlier (Tomber 2000: 624–31). Relatively small Egyptian, Arab, Greek and Indian ships used to ply between those ports and the western Indian ones of *Barbaricum*, *Barygaza* and *Muziris* (Sidebotham 1991: 12–13). Until the first century CE, foreign mariners, with perhaps the exception of the Arabs of Yemen and Hadhramaut, did not fully understand the behaviour of the Indian Ocean winds, which meant that destinations were reached after prolonged detours by ships closely hugging the Arabian and Indian coastlines. This changed after CE 45, when Hippalus, an Alexandrian, worked out the pattern of seasonal winds (the monsoon), thereby helping his fellow seamen to sail through the Arabian Sea during the right season and shortening their journey time. The trade links with south India were to be particularly strengthened by this development.

After 31 BCE, the type of large vessels that used to carry Egyptian grain from Alexandria to Rome began to be built along the Red Sea ports, in order to be fitted out for trade voyages to India. They could be 180 feet in length and weigh 1,000 tons (Casson 1991: 8–11). A large Roman ship, carrying from India compact and costly merchandise of silks, fine cottons, pepper, costus, nard and spikenard, and bringing to India products such as two-handled amphorae, fine ceramics, bronze vases and delicate glassware, represented a 'monumental investment' (Casson 1991: 10) by many traders. As the captains of such ships did not normally sail to the east-coast ports of India, both import and export goods were loaded onto much smaller Indian ships that continually plied between the two coasts. At Arikamedu, for example, the foreign goods brought by these ships would be unloaded, and valuable spice cargoes from both India and Indonesia, along with other Indian goods, would be loaded onto the same ships bound for *Muziris*. This was the legendary *entrepôt* trade of south India (Miller 1969: 177–8; Casson 1991: 10–11). Generally speaking, the overall balance of trade between India and Rome was in the favour of India, and the Romans had to pay for the deficits in the form of bullion (Miller 1969: 217–41; Saletore 1973: 272–9). A large hoard of Roman coins found at Arikamedu and other places in south India, along with the archaeological remains of a Roman colony, testify to the vigour of the Indo-Roman trade. Owing to the absence of local gold coins in south India, Roman gold and silver coins were also used as high-value currency, which would have encouraged hoarding. Only a quarter of the good-quality Roman coin hoards discovered in south India have been found in north India: the Kushan state issued its own gold coins, as valuable in metal terms as the Roman ones, and simply melted down the Roman coins for their metal (Liu 1994: 10). Apart from coins, small hoards of other Roman goods, such as amphorae, bronze vessels and finer quality ceramics and potsherds, have been recovered from a variety of sites in western India, the Andhra region and the south. Much research is also directed at studying whether the excellent Red Polished Ware (RPW) pottery of western India or the rouletted ware of south-eastern India were imitations of Roman or Hellenistic potteries (Begley 1991: 157–96; Orton 1991: 46–81). Another interesting piece of recent research concerns the role of the Indian venture capitalist in the financing of Indo-Roman trade. Until recently, it was widely assumed that the 'initiative of this long-distance sea-borne trade with west was taken by western traders, while the role of India, steeped in agriculture, was only that of the grower of some luxury and prestige commodities' (Ray *et al.* 2000: 609). This view needs to be revised in the light, first, of a recently discovered papyrus document detailing a loan contract between an Indian and a Roman (Ray *et al.* 2000: 607–9) and, second, of the excavations in Egypt pointing to the presence there of Indian settlers and traders (Sidebotham 1991: 23).

New trends in Indian religions

A series of remarkable developments in religious thinking in India took place during the post-Mauryan era. They affected both Buddhism and Vedic Brahmanism. Within both systems particular strands of theism – belief in the existence of God with or without a belief in a special revelation – began to develop, with profound consequences for many millions of people in the subcontinent and beyond.

Mahayana Buddhism

Buddhism was not just the 'central public religion' (Ali 1999: 43) of India; during our period it was also assuming the status of a major world religion. A number of royal dynasties became the patrons and guardians of the religion, as can be witnessed from impressive monuments and inscriptions left behind. The monarchs of Central Asian origin were particularly attracted by its 'catholicity' (Majumdar 1977: 166); the Kushan king Kanishka remains for Buddhists even today the most

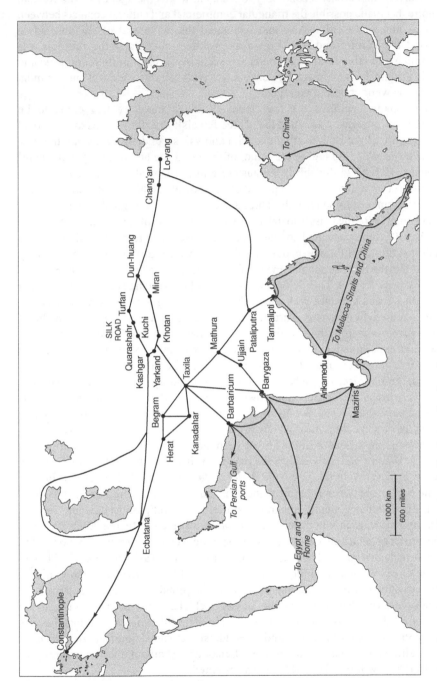

Map 7.2 Land and sea routes of ancient Indian international trade

cherished of monarchs, second only to Ashoka. It was the agency of the Kushan Empire that made possible the triangular commercial and cultural contacts between India, China and Central Asia and facilitated the movement of Buddhist ideas beyond the Pamirs and the Himalayas. Within India itself the religion was becoming attractive to different cults and sects. As a result of both domestic and foreign expansion and interactive encounters with beliefs inside and outside India new ideas were bound to emerge.

Over many centuries the traditional Buddhist ideology had come to be crystallised into what was called the 'Three Jewels': first, the lessons to be learned from the life of the Buddha, the 'one who knows'; second, the *Dhamma*, the 'law of the cosmos . . . the law of the mind, of the good life and of the spiritual path' (Cousins 1997: 374–8); third, the austere and puritanical life in a *sangha*, the monastic community. Now, in a period of new social and historical realities, many Buddhist thinkers argued that the Three Jewels approach was much too intellectual and restrictive for the masses to grasp. It was really a type of 'icy idealism' (Tripathi 1999: 230), quite unsuited to the needs of newer devotees subscribing to the Buddhist faith. While not repudiating the core values of the Three Jewels, they argued that the Buddha could come to life for the masses only when he was elevated to the status of a god. This deification of the Buddha and the doctrine of salvation by faith were at variance with the traditional teaching, because the Buddha had never claimed divine status. Further, he had left the endeavour of achieving bliss, or *nirvana*, to each individual through a rational understanding of his ideas and methods expounded in his Four Noble Truths and the Eightfold Path. The dissenters, however, argued that an individual needed the intercession of divine beings, the *Bodhisattvas*, who were born again and again on this earth because they were prepared to forego their own *nirvana* in order to help ordinary mortals help achieve theirs. The *Bodhisattvas* came to be arranged within the Buddhist pantheon of semi-divinities, which suggests that this new variant of Buddhism was attempting to become more attractive to local sects and cults by incorporating their gods and goddesses within the pantheon. It is also likely that another new idea, that of a saviour to come – the Buddha *Maitreya* – might have had its origins in the contacts between Buddhism and Zoroastrianism, the religion of pre-Islamic Iran. The latter is generally reckoned to be the first religion to develop the idea of a saviour messiah – known as *Saoshyant* (Kotwal and Mistree 2002: 337–65). The cluster of such new ideas provoked a split between the dissenters, who wanted a more inclusive and faith-based Buddhism, to be known as *Mahayana* Buddhism, or the Great Vehicle, and the traditional elders, the *Theravadins*, who clung on to the pristine purity of ideas represented by the principle of the Three Jewels. A pejorative term, *Hinayana*, or the Lesser Vehicle, came in due course to be applied to the *Theravadin* school of thought. The final victory, ultimately, was that of the Mahayanists; their brand of Buddhism remained dominant in India until the twelfth century and, apart from Sri Lanka and Thailand, the vast majority of the Buddhist world today is *Mahayana*-oriented.

Historians of religion have argued that much of the new thinking, particularly in the *Mahayana* tradition, was really like 'old wine in new bottles', simply a reinterpretation of the traditional Buddhist viewpoints (Cousins 1997: 382ff.), but we still need to recognise that there is considerable literature in this period that points to dynamic and radical departures in Buddhist thinking. Some of the key *Mahayana* texts were formulated during the post-Mauryan centuries, although we are uncertain about their exact dates (Liu 1994: 89–102). One particularly interesting text was the *Milindapanha* (the Question of Milinda), the philosophical questions asked by the Indo-Greek king Menander to the Buddhist philosopher Nagasena. In some of his answers Nagasena laid great stress on the divinisation of the Buddha and the importance of relic worship. Another text, the *Buddhacharita*, a biography of the Buddha, composed by the renowned polymath Asvaghosha, also confirms the Mahayanist image of a divine Buddha. From an older and more traditional treatise, known as the *Mahavastu*, the Mahayanists adopted the particular styles of Buddha-worship, with copious use being made of such precious materials as gold, lapis lazuli, pearls, silver, silk, etc., as gifts for gaining merits and rewards from the Buddha. This attitude embodied 'the great influence of commerce-oriented lay worshippers on Buddhism' (Liu 1994: 95) and again demonstrated the importance of the overland trade between India and China. While the bulk of the *Theravadin* texts are in the Pali language, the key works of the *Mahayana* canon, made up of many different books used by different sects, were written in Sanskrit; they are known collectively as the *Vaipulyasutra*. The most important work of the *Vaipulyasutra* is the *Saddharmapundarika* (the Lotus Sutra), a *Mahayana* text greatly revered in China and Japan. This text formulated the concept of the *Bodhisattvas* and provides elaborate details of how a *stupa* should be designed and how the rituals of Buddha worship were to be conducted. Finally, there is the *Prajnaparamita*, a *Mahayana* philosophical text, which lists the various virtues necessary to attain the Buddha state.

Vaishnava and Shaiva traditions

The first manifestations of what we would now describe as popular Hinduism began to emerge during the post-Mauryan centuries. For more than a thousand years, until the sixth century BCE, Vedic Brahmanism had been the principal religion of India. The main elements of this religion, as we have noted earlier, were the supremacy of the *Vedas*, the caste system, the sacrificial rituals for propitiating the powerful Vedic elemental gods such as Indra, Surya, Rudra, Varuna, Vayu, etc., and the monopolistic role of the *brahman* priests in the performance of all ceremonies. From the sixth century BCE onwards, Buddhism, Jainism and various heterodox forms of *Shramanism* launched a challenge to Vedic Brahmanism and gained a relatively large number of adherents. Buddhism particularly secured a powerful ascendancy during both the Mauryan and the post-Mauryan periods. However, during the post-Mauryan age, there came a certain backlash in favour of Vedic Brahmanism at some of the royal courts. What also took place was the beginning of a modified form of Vedic Brahmanism. Two very strongly theistic traditions, which we call the *Vaishnava* and the *Shaiva*, blossomed at this time. They centred round three main concepts: that of a supreme deity in the form of

Vishnu or Shiva; that of salvation being made possible through the supreme deity's grace; and that of attainment of that salvation by the means of intense love and devotion to the deity, the process known as *bhakti*. The two traditions did not break away from Vedic Brahmanism, but rejected some of the practices such as animal sacrifice. The *Vaishnava* form of worship at first focused on three older deities: Vasudeva, a tribal deity; Krishna, the deity of the Yadava clan; and Narayana, referred to as a deity in the *Satapatha Brahmana* (Flood 1996: 117–27). All three deities eventually became identified with Vishnu, originally a Vedic god of lesser importance but now assuming a much greater status in the eyes of its followers (Jaiswal 1967: 1–7, 32–51). The major strand in *Vaishnavism* came through those with the Vasudeva–Krishna connections, known as the *bhagvatas* (Colas 2003: 229–33). Perhaps the greatest spiritual and intellectual legacy they have left to us is the world-famous short dialogue between Krishna, an incarnation of Vishnu, and Arjuna, one of the five Pandava brothers, in the *Mahabharata*. Refuting such practices as withdrawal, renunciation and idle sentimentalism, Krishna enjoins Arjuna to focus his devotion upon him and fulfil his duty according to his place in society, however hard that struggle may be. The *Vaishnavites* intensely concentrated devotion to a personal lord, *Bhagavana*, attracted even some non-Indians. The most well-known testimony to this is the inscription, written in Sanskrit, or at least *Prakrit* showing Sanskrit influences, on a column in central India, known as the Pillar of Heliodorus, mentioned in **Excerpt 7.2** below.

The *Shaiva* tradition rests upon the ancient deity of Shiva and the Mother Goddess Shakti, Shiva's consort. Shiva has an ancient pedigree in Brahmanic mythology. Some scholars have also traced this deity to the Harappan culture's 'Pashupati' seal, which shows a seated horned proto-Shiva figure surrounded by animals, but this is now strongly challenged by others. More convincingly, Shiva was the original god Rudra in the *Vedas*, a god who represented the destructive and malignant forces of nature (Flood 2003: 200–6). Rudra was known as the 'Roarer', but, like Vishnu, he too had been a marginal god in the first instance. However, from the time when he was elevated to a supreme force in one of the *Upanishads*, Shiva has been venerated by millions in India. During the period under review a definite *Shaiva* tradition emerged through the activities of sects such as Lakulin, Pashupata or Maheshvara (Jash 1974: 1–17). Their intense devotion to Shiva was also emulated by great rulers such as Vima Kadphises of the Kushans, who ordered the depiction of the Shiva on his coins. The *lingam* that replaced the Shiva image has in due course been the core of intense devotion by the Shaivites throughout India.

The orthodoxy of the Dharmashastras

While *Vaishnavism* and *Shaivism* may have helped to access the Vedic religion to greater numbers of people, the Brahmanic thinkers nevertheless continued to reaffirm the principles of Vedic orthodoxy in much of the commentorial litera-ture that developed during this period. This literature was part of the great *Smriti* corpus that began with the composition of *Sutras* in the late Vedic and post-Vedic

Excerpt 7.2 The Pillar of Heliodorus

This pillar was erected in 113 BCE by Heliodorus, the Greek ambassador of the Indo-Greek king Antialkidas of Taxila at the court of the Shunga king Bhagabhadra in Besnagar in the Bhilsa district of Central India. Heliodorus must have been a Vaishnavite, because the pillar, which is also known as the Garuda Column, honours Vasudeva (Vishnu), whose symbol in the minds of the devotees is the mythical bird garuda. Many historians have conjectured that the Vaishnavite influence reached up to the far corners of India and that perhaps king Antialkidas and some other Indo-Greek kings of the north-west might themselves have been worshippers of the god Vishnu. The Heliodorus Pillar is a powerful reminder to us of the inter-cultural heritage of India and how Indian history has been shaped by multiple cultural influences of different peoples of the subcontinent. The short verses of the inscription on the two faces of the pillar read as follows:

Side 1: This Garuda-standard was made by order of the Bhagavata . . . Heliodorus, the son of Dion, a man of Taxila, a Greek ambassador from King Antialkidas, to king Bhagabhadra, the son of the princess from Benares, the saviour while prospering in the fourteenth year of his reign.

Side 2: There are three steps to immortality which, followed, lead to heaven, namely, self-control, self-denial and watchfulness.

Source: Archaeological Survey of India, *Annual Report, 1908–9*, Calcutta: Superintendent of Government Printing, 1912, 129.

periods. It deals with a host of issues in society and life generally, with lessons and implications drawn from the *Shruti* literature of the *Vedas* and the *Brahmanas*. Part of this literature consists of nineteen so-called *Dharmashastras*; four of them are paramount: *Manavdharmashastra*, or *Manusmriti*, *Yajnavalkyasmriti*, *Naradasmriti* and *Parasarasmriti*, attributed to sages Manu, Yajnavalkya, Narada and Parasara (Rocher 2003: 109). Their texts are, in the main, normative prescriptions concerned with *dharma*, 'the whole system of Law, moral and legal, that has its foundation in the transcendent order, and the specific systems of rules and regulations under which a given individual lives' (Dimock *et al.* 1974: 83). They are also more than that, because in them we also find a great variety of wisdom literature, morality tales and useful guidance too for ordinary mortals. **Excerpt 7.3** below gives a flavour of this from the *Naradasmriti*.

Excerpt 7.3 Wealth and morality as explained in the
Naradasmriti

The Naradasmriti is one of the great Dharmashastras of the Gupta period.
Like most Dharmashastras, it throws much light on Hindu civil and religious
law. In the following passage it explains the degree of morality behind the
acquisition of wealth.

. . . Wealth is of three kinds: white, spotted and black . . . White wealth
is acquired by sacred knowledge, valour in arms, the practice of
austerities by instructing a pupil, by sacrificing and by inheritance.
    . . . Spotted wealth is acquired by lending money at interest, tillage,
. . . by artistic performance, by servile attendance, or as a return for
benefit conferred on someone.
    . . . Black wealth is acquired as a bribe, by gambling, . . . by forgery,
by robbery, by fraud.

Source: *Naradasmriti*, I, 44–8, translated by Julius Jolly,
in Max Muller (ed.), *Sacred Books of the East*, Vol. 33,
Oxford: Clarendon Press, 1889, 53–4.

The most well-known of the four major *Dharmashastras* is the *Manusmriti*, a
critical text for our period. It might have been composed any time between 200 BCE
and CE 200; the other three are later compositions, falling outside our period. There
is debate in historical circles as to whether the *Manusmriti* is the work of one author
or several; we cannot be certain. The text is very prescriptive and rigid in its thinking,
and became the rule book for orthodox *brahmans*. Its contents, consisting of 2,684
verses divided into twelve chapters, among other things, affirm the divine right of
kings; confirm and rationalise the theory of the caste system; elaborate upon and sing
praises of the so-called four stages of life for Vedic followers; and express grave
reservations about the constancy and capabilities of women. The text was never
universally followed or acclaimed by the vast majority of Indians in their history: it
came to the world's attention through a late eighteenth-century translation by Sir
William Jones, who mistakenly exaggerated both its antiquity and its importance.
However, today, many of its ideas are popularised as the golden norm of classical
Hindu law by Hindu universalists. They are, however, particularly reviled by
feminists and those opposed to the caste system. On caste, the *Manusmriti* emphasises
the dignity of the *brahman* and casts grave aspersions over the *shudras*, although it
does take notice of the fact that greater social fluidity could arise out of the union of
sexes from different castes and the formation of new castes resulting there from. The
great twentieth-century leader of the 'Untouchable' (Dalit) communities, Dr
Ambedkar, had little time and low regard for this text and condemned it outright,
with much good reason (Ambedkar 1989: 100–2, 283–6). On Christmas Day 1927,
he and his followers burned copies of it in public (Keer 1971: 100–1).

Feminists and other educated women feel highly affronted by the strictures on women in this text and, again, rightly so because of the offensive language in which some of the ideas are expressed. The *Yajnavalkyasmriti* is slightly more liberal than Manu's laws, but ultimately both propound ideas that are no longer acceptable to educated and thinking women. Both texts have pious words on how women should be respected and revered; nevertheless, both deny them the freedom to think and decide for themselves. The quotations from the two *smritis*, along with that from the *Naradasmriti*, in **Excerpt 7.4**, provide enough evidence for this.

Excerpt 7.4 Contradictions on women's rights in the *smritis*

The first two quotes below from the Manusmriti *are classic Hindu affirmations of respect, nay reverence, for women. Their positive tone is contradicted by the three subsequent quotes from both the* Manusmriti *and the* Yajnavalkyasmriti *on critical issues affecting the nature or independence of women. The double disadvantage suffered by women of the lower caste is illustrated in quote 6 from the* Naradasmriti. *A more liberal outlook is noticeable in the last two quotes on the theme of a woman's wealth or right to property.*

1. Those fathers, brothers, husbands and brothers-in-law who desire much prosperity should esteem (these) women and adorn them (*Manusmriti*).
2. Where women are respected, the deities rejoice, but where they are not respected, all rituals become fruitless (*Manusmriti*).
3. To corrupt men in the world is women's essential nature (*Manusmriti*).
4. A father protects his daughter (in her childhood), her husband when she is married, and her son in her old age. In their absence the relatives (should look after a woman). A woman cannot have independence (*Yajnavalkyasmriti*).
5. A wife should always listen to her husband. This is the best dharma of a wife (*Yajnavalkyasmriti*).
6. A wanton woman, a non-Brahmin, a prostitute, a servant, or one who is not constrained by her master can be approached if she is of the lower caste but not if she is of the higher caste (*Naradasmriti*).
7. While making the partition after the father's death the widowed mother will be entitled to an equal share with her sons (*Yajnavalkyasmriti*).
8. The brothers should separately give their unmarried sisters something from their own portions, a quarter from each one's share (*Manusmriti*).

Source: Quotes from Mandrakanta Bose, *Women in the Hindu Tradition: Rules, Roles and Exceptions*, Abingdon: Routledge, 2010, 66, 82, 87, 93, 94, 107.

We can thus argue that little advance was made on the position of women from the time of the *Vedas*, which were composed over a millennium before the *smritis* (Chapter 4). One empathetic writer, however, feels that the contradiction in the *smritis* is 'more apparent than real . . . for the emphasis is not so much on the denial of any freedom to a woman as on the duty of her near ones to protect her at all costs' (Embree 1992: 228). This may be so, and Manu's views may not be entirely at odds with views on women held by both men and women not just in India but also in many parts of the non-Western world. Nevertheless, with increasing education, greater awareness of progress in this field made by women abroad, and the lack of safety on Indian streets in recent years, Indian women are now facing up to the challenge of sexism from the male gender.

Secular literature, sciences and the arts

A florescence of cultural creativity is distinctly noticeable during the post-Mauryan centuries. This creativity was partly an expression of the efforts and genius of the Indian people themselves, and partly the result of a cross-fertilisation of ideas from different traditions and cultures. The fusion of native ideas and skills with those borrowed from Persian, Greek, Central Asian or Chinese sources gave a sharper impetus and edge to all cultural products created in India at that time. In due course, the outside world came to admire some of these products. The developments in literature, sciences and the arts will furnish us with appropriate examples of progressive creativity.

Writing became more widespread and diversified during this period. The two early scripts of *Brahmi* and *Kharoshti* might have developed as early as the post-Vedic age, but they were extensively used in the Mauryan period, as we saw in Chapter 6. Now, in post-Mauryan times, we notice the first real signs of regional variations of the two scripts, which may be considered the ancestors of our modern Indian regional scripts. Of the two scripts, *Brahmi* was the more widely used; even in the south of India it was adapted to the phonetic requirements of Tamil. Generally, the language written in this script was the *Prakrit* vernacular, but Sanskrit was also being increasingly used. Bi-lingual coins, such as those with Greek and *Brahmi* or *Kharoshti* scripts, are a good indication of the wider use of writing in this period. *Kharoshti* was most prevalent on the coins of the north-west, but over time it also spread to the Ganges valley as well as Bengal. Some of the early written records of this age are a variety of inscriptions, in Sanskrit or *Prakrit*, to be found in caves, pillars or religious buildings, such as the *stupa*. The inscriptions relate to charitable donations by rich citizens or good and valorous deeds of kings. Three of the inscriptions, those of the Hathigumpha Cave, the Junagadh Rock and the Heliodorus Pillar, have already been referred to.

Sanskrit literature

Sanskrit was the hallowed language in which the most sacred of India's literature had been composed. Although during the age of the Buddha and under the

Mauryan Empire various forms of *Prakrit* – the popular languages – came into prominence, Sanskrit always remained the language that wielded a pervasive influence. Far from being hostile to Sanskrit, the post-Mauryan monarchs, whether Indian or foreign, also provided valuable patronage, and even much of the literature of *Mahayana* Buddhism was written in Sanskrit. The most famous Buddhist writer in Sanskrit was Asvaghosha, whose life of the Buddha, the *Buddhacharita*, was an early gem of Sanskrit biographical literature and 'a work of art' (Sastri 1960: 66). A French scholar, S. Levi, said in 1923 that Asvaghosha 'stands at the starting point of all the great currents that renewed and transformed India towards the beginning of the Christian era . . . in his richness and variety he recalls Milton, Goethe, Kant and Voltaire' (quoted in Majumdar 1977: 187).[2] In fact, during the post-Mauryan period, Sanskrit came to be recognised as the language of the educated and cultured classes, irrespective of their religion. It was the quality of language and its subtle use that preoccupied such people. The *Buddhacharita*, along with another acclaimed work, the *Mahabhashya*, by Patanjali the grammarian, was admired as a fine example of Sanskrit prose literature. However, the most significant of literary developments in Sanskrit came to be expressed through poetry and drama. The poetic genre was the *kavya*, or court poetry. This poetry, in the form of either a grand narrative poem or a short lyric, described vividly such themes as nature, a love scene, a spectacle or praise for the monarch. This last function was particularly sought after by monarchs with an eye to their place in history. Thus, in the famous *prasasti* of Rudradaman, inscribed on the Junagadh Rock, referred to earlier, the king's praises are sung by the poet using various figures of speech and alliteration (Ray *et al.* 2000: 327–9). The *kavya* has exercised a major influence on the Indian poetic tradition generally for more than a thousand years. Parallel to it was the rise of the secular drama, the *natya*. The Indian drama tradition harked back to Vedic times and all early dramas were based on religious themes. In the new Sanskrit drama, however, the issues of morality or conduct in society were explored in plots around a hero or a heroic figure, with much use of sentiment, romance, satire or farce. They were to be more appealing to varied audiences. In the next chapter we shall refer to the contributions of India's greatest dramatist, Kalidasa, but, during our period, a most amazing textbook of dramatic criticism was produced by someone called Bharata. We know very little about him personally, but his work, the *Natyashastra*, rediscovered as late as the nineteenth century, is now considered a most compact compendium of dramaturgy, theatre, acting, costumes, make-up, dance, audience participation and theatre architecture, with pertinent advice and instruction for actors, producers and playwrights. The appropriate use of words, mimicry, gesture and posture are all, according to Bharata, necessary for success in the performing arts, and it is only through this success that the audience's appreciation, or what is known as *rasa*, can be aroused (Embree 1992: 264–8). This notion of *rasa* (literally 'flavour' or 'taste') has remained 'the most important and influential single concept of Indian criticism to this day' (Dimock *et al.* 1974: 130). Further explanation of this is provided in **Excerpt 7.5** below.

Excerpt 7.5 Four millennia of musical ancestry

In the following passage, a practitioner of Indian classical music, the late Dr Mahesh Godbole, explains the development of this ancient art form.

According to Bharata every artist should create a Rasa or a mood. His nine Rasas are wonder, terror, disgust, joy, pathos, anger, love, serenity and valour. It has been said that western music describes a mood, but Indian music creates it. A Raag is a series of five or more notes on which a melody is based. Raag Basant creates joy and Raag Todi grief. Even the drum beats are used to produce a mood, e.g., the 6-beat Dadra inspires a romantic mood, while the 14-beat Dhamar creates a vigorous mood.

The whole tradition of Indian classical music has, in fact, its roots in the Hindu religion. Originally the Vedas were recited, but later they came to be chanted in three musical notes. Samveda developed to a scale of seven notes: Sa, Re, Ga, Ma, Pa, Dha, Ni [the Western major scale C–D–E–F–G–A–B]. These are compared to the cry of the peacock and the calls of the chataka bird, the goat, the crane, the cuckoo, the frog and the elephant respectively. They are said to be always of the same pitch. Later on, four flats Re, Ga, Dha, Ni and one sharp Ma were added. These twelve notes are common to both Indian and western music, but ten more notes (micro-tones) are also used in Indian music. By the end of 1000 BC the Samveda came to be sung to the scale of what we now call Raag Bageshree.

. . . In the caste system the sub-castes produced hereditary guilds, known as Gharanas. Many Raags are produced in a variety of form, style and presentation by the Gharanas.

Source: From a note sent to the author by the late Dr Mahesh Godbole, formerly Secretary of the Indian Classical Music Society in north-west England. For further understanding, read A.H. Fox Strangways, *The Music of Hindostan*, New Delhi: Oriental Books, 1975, and Reginald Massey and Jamila Massey, *The Music of India*, London: Kahn & Averill, 1986.

Tamil literature

The Aryanisation of the Dravidian-speaking peoples during the first millennium BCE had involved an increasing use of Sanskrit in the south. The Sanskritic influence is strongest in three of the southern languages: Telugu, Kannada and Malayalam. Tamil, the principal and most ancient of the Dravidian literary languages, was also influenced by Sanskrit, but on a far smaller scale. It retained its independence and originality, particularly in its technical structure. A fuller appreciation of the political, social and cultural development of the far south can be gained only by studying the most ancient of the Tamil texts. Tamils dominated the early history of the region, and one of their major intellectual traditions was the regular gathering of a large number of poets in a *sangam*, or an academy, at which poems and stories were recited. The so-called *Sangam* Age lasted between approximately 200 BCE and CE 400. Three *sangams* were held, but the works from the first two are difficult to trace. An important grammatical work of the second *sangam*, known as *Tolkappiyam*, is an exception. It gives us, among other things, information concerning the ecology and the environment of the far south, expressed in a particular concept of a geographical habitat, known as *tinai*. A number of habitats are identified: high lands, forests, pastures, dry lands, river valleys or coastal lands. The *Tolkappiyam* tells us about the people who lived in these locales, their relationship with nature and between themselves, and their varied customs (Gurukkal 1995: 242–4). The differences, for example, in the lifestyles of people who lived in the forests and those of the river valleys are brought out by the descriptions of large-scale cattle raids by the former on the lands of the latter. It is from the third *sangam* that the bulk of our literary heritage in Tamil can be drawn. Three major anthologies cover the works from this *sangam*. They are *Patthuppattu* (Ten Idylls, or short pastoral poems), *Ettuthokai* (Eight Collections) and *Padinenkilkanakku* (Eighteen Poems). Two of the Eight Collections of *Ettuthokai* are particularly valuable. One is the *Purananaru*, which contains descriptions of the life of the southern people in that period; the other is *Kurunthokai* (*c.* CE 100), consisting of 400 verses of short love poems, between four and nine lines long, composed by 205 poets (Dimock *et al.* 1974: 171). Among the Eighteen Poems of the *Padinenkilkanakku*, the eleventh, the *Kural*, laid out in 113 sections of ten couplets each, presents in verses a guide to the art of good living. The varieties of *sangam* collections also enable us to understand the differences among the people of the south. Although there was much inequality between the castes and great poverty among the lower-ranked, the overall impression one has of the south is that it was suffused by a relatively peaceful and relaxed communal atmosphere.

Advance in sciences

Astronomy and medicine were two of the main sciences in which steady progress was made during this period (Bose *et al.* 1989: 58–92, 213–35). Indian interest in astronomy dated from the earliest of Vedic times, and much astronomical knowledge can be gathered from the *Samhitas*, the *Brahmanas* and *Sutra* literature. Many reflections and speculations about the sun, the moon, the earth, the planets or the eclipses were interspersed with calculations of the division of time in terms of a day, a month, seasons, solstices, equinoxes and calendars in general. Religious preoccupation and mystical interpretations, however, dominated the astronomical thinking during those centuries. It was with the beginning of the Common Era that a new turning point was reached, with a greater emphasis on a rigorous scientific method of inquiry and interpretation. There also came into use a more sophisticated system of computation, with mathematical concepts such as the integral solutions of indeterminate equations and trigonometry. The positions of the various planets were charted with greater precision, and more accurate calculations of the length of the year or of the day were recorded. The relevant literature for this information consists of a set of *siddhantas*, or the so-called final solutions, each ascribed to a particular astronomer-sage. It is believed that there were originally eighteen such *siddhantas*, but only five of them, codified in the sixth century by the great astronomer Varahamihira, are now available to us. The names of two of them, the *Romaka Siddhanta* and the *Paulisa Siddhanta*, give strong hints of the Greek and classical influences on Indian astronomy. This is a subject of intense debate, but common sense suggests that the strong commercial links of India must also have had their parallel in cultural links (Yano 2003: 388–9).

Ayur-Veda, the ancient medical system of India, is today considered one of the important branches of complementary medicine. Its relative popularity throughout the world is because of its emphasis on a more holistic approach by the physician towards illness in general. The bulk of our knowledge of the system is drawn from the works of Charaka and Susruta, who belonged to this period. Their works constitute the standard material of *Ayur-Veda* and have been handed down to us over the centuries in various revisions. They describe and explain fully eight branches of medical knowledge and practice: therapeutics, surgery, diseases of the sensory organs, mental illness, infant disorders, toxicology, tonics/drugs and sexual virility. The materia medica of *Ayur-Veda* was also extensive, with a variety of substances drawn from the animal, vegetable and mineral kingdoms. As with astronomy, there is debate among historians whether India contributed at all to the Greek and Hellenistic medical systems, or whether these developed independently. In the light of the testimony from Alexander the Great's contemporaries, the accounts of Megasthenes, the export of valuable medicinal plants from India to the Mediterranean lands and the generally more articulate and clearer instructions in Indian medical texts, it is quite possible that Indian medical ideas might have influenced those of the Greeks.

Architecture and sculpture

Despite the political confusion of the post-Mauryan era, the arts developed to a remarkable degree. Progress in architecture tended to follow the Mauryan style, but archaeologists have also noticed the use of burnt brick and tile in the construction of more permanent structures for domestic houses. The most outstanding developments affect religious architecture. The *stupa* became the symbol of post-Mauryan architectural progress. The archetype at Sanchi is the most famous of all such buildings in India, and the entire range of developments in the evolution of the *stupa* can be found there. Under the Shungas, the *stupa* of Sanchi, originally most probably an Ashokan structure, was greatly enlarged and a terrace built around it. A stone *vedika*, or railing, encircled both the *stupa* and its terrace.

Under the Satavahanas beautifully carved *toranas* (i.e. arched doorways) were erected, one at each of the cardinal points of the *vedika*. The stone railings and gateways were adorned with many inscriptions and relief carvings (Figure 7.2).

Other well known *stupas* were built at Bharhut, Bodh Gaya, Sarnath and Amaravati. The style of the *stupas* in the north-west of India, in Taxila for example, was generally Indo-Greek. The Greek influence is particularly noticeable in the use of Ionic order of columns and *pilasters*. No matter where the *stupas* were located, their sacred nature was recognised by all Buddhists. The actual body of the Buddha was identified with the monument, and the *stupa* was conceived as the 'symbolic microcosm of the universe' (Auboyer 2002: 141). From the second century BCE onwards, rock cut cave architecture made great strides too. Impressively carved out Buddhist *chaitya* halls of huge dimensions at places such as Bhaja, Karle and Kanheri in western India are fine examples of rock-cut monumental architecture. Both Jain and Buddhist rock-cut caves are also found in the eastern coastal areas of Orissa and Andhra. We also find, in this period, the building of shrines as places of worship by *Vaishnavites* and *Shaivites*. Some of the earliest of such shrines, dating from the second century CE, have been found at Nagarjunakonda.

The art of the sculpture also took off during this confusing period. There is abundant sculptural material to examine on the *vedikas* and *toranas* of Sanchi *stupa* no. 2 (Figures 7.3 and 7.4). Three types of relief sculpture have been studied in great detail (Gajjar 1971: 109–32; Tomory 1989: 168–74). One is the vegetation design, consisting of lotus flowers on winding stems, trees and garlands of flowers. Another consists of individual figures, such as *yaksha* and *yakshi* (male and female semi-divine beings and life spirits) (see Figure 7.5), deities such as Indra, or soldiers. The most interesting reliefs are those of narrative tableaux depicting various scenes from the Buddha's life, such as the dream of Maya Devi, Buddha's mother, the purchase of the *Jetavana Park* or Buddha's descent from *Trayatrimsa*, and the *Jataka* legends.

The sculptures of the Buddha were most common during the Kushana period (see Figure 7.6). Two major schools produced works of great excellence and beauty

Figure 7.2 Relief from a Sanchi gateway

Figure 7.3 A hip girdle from Bharhut *Stupa*

(Tomory 1989: 181–7; Craven 1997: 81–109). They are known as the schools of *Gandhara* and Mathura. The *Gandhara* school of art was the more cosmopolitan of the two. The sculptures of this school consist principally of the Buddha and the *Boddhisatva* figures that show strong Greek and Roman artistic influences on Indian themes. Early *Gandhara* Buddhas, for example, have Apollonian faces, with their clothing draped in the style of a Roman toga. Some of the finest examples of *Gandhara* art are to be found in the British Museum, Peshawar Museum, Berlin Museum and Indian Museum at Calcutta. The second of the two schools was the Mathura school of art. During the first three centuries of the Common Era, Mathura, 50 miles south-east of Delhi on the River Yamuna, was a great hub

Figure 7.4 A rider on the Bharhut *Stupa*   *Figure 7.5* A *yakshi*

of cultural activity. In contrast to the *Gandhara* school, a more authentically Indian artistic influence is stamped all over the art of Mathura. A whole variety of Buddha statues, in different poses and postures, carved in the red spotted sandstone, are the distinguishing feature of this school. The portrait sculpture of rulers is also a hallmark of this style, the most famous of which is the statue of Kanishka himself. Power and authority radiate from this statue, even though its head and arms are missing (see Figure 7.1).

The sculptures of the great *stupa* of *Amaravati* are in a class of their own. A priceless collection of 133 pieces of this treasure from the Satavahana era has been exhibited at the British Museum since 1880. They are from the site of the *Mahachaitya*, or the great *stupa* of *Amaravati*, located in the lower reaches of the River Krishna in Andhra Pradesh. It was in 1816 that Colonel Colin Mackenzie, later surveyor general of India, and his staff recorded the contents and made the drawings, all of which are preserved at the India Office of the British Library. By 1880 the British Museum had come to possess the larger portion of the collection, with the rest being held by the Madras Museum. The sculptures

Figure 7.6 Buddhas in different art styles

not only tell us the story of the Buddha's life, using a variety of Buddhist icono-graphy and imagery, but they also depict social scenes in a typically busy Indian setting. The crowds of labourers and masons and the performances of musicians and dancers are detailed, with a lively imagination, alongside men on horses, chariots and bullock carts (Knox 1992: 9–42).

STUDY GUIDE

Key issues

- The significance of Indo-Greek kingdoms in Indian cultural history.
- Indian commercial relations with the world.
- *Mahayana* Buddhism and its influence outside India.
- Controversies about the contents of the *Manusmriti*.
- Theoretical basis of *Ayur-Veda*.

Suggested readings

Casson 1991: 8–11; Liu 1994: 89–102; Sidebotham 1991: 12–38; Sivaramamurti 1977: 154–9; Tarn 1951: 351–408; Time-Life Books 1994: 80–110.

INTERNET SELECTION

1) Kathryn Brown: 'Buddhist art and the trade routes'. www.asiasociety museum.org/buddhist_trade/index-html
2) Jennifer Howes: 'A colonial history of sculptures from Amaravati Stupa'. www.academia.edu/3808140/A_Colonial_History_of_Sculptures_from_Amarav ati_Stupa
3) Encyclopaedia Iranica: 'Kushan Empire: a major world power in Central Asia and North India during 1st to mid 3rd century CE'. www.iranicaonline.org/ articles/kushan-dynasty-i-history
4) K. Jaishankar and D. Haldar: 'Manusmriti: A critique of the criminal justice tenets in the ancient Indian Hindu code'. www.erces.com/journal/articles/ archives/v03/v03_05.htm
5) Vrndavan Parker: 'Roman Empire, soldiers, settlements in India 100 BC to 300 AD'. www.pazhayathu.blogspot.co.uk/2009/03/roman-empire-soldiers settlements-in.html

QUESTIONS FOR GROUP DISCUSSION

1) Identify major Indo-Greek kingdoms on a historical map of India. What were their origins? How did they both absorb and enrich India's culture?
2) Examine the extent of the Kushan Empire on the map of Asia. How did this empire help to further Indian trade with the outside world?
3) By means of a drawing, show how the Indian Ocean monsoon wind pattern operates. What was the major complaint of Roman writers about their empire's extensive trade with India?
4) What were the main contents of Sanskrit and Tamil literatures during the period covered by this chapter? In which particular branch of knowledge did those literatures lag behind contemporary Roman writings?
5) What types of drugs does the *Ayur-Veda* medical system use? Can this system be of use to people today?

Notes

1   It should be noted that he is one of the many Satakarnis in the Satavahana dynasty of monarchs (p. 155).
2   It is speculated that the source of the popular Christian legend of Baarlam and Josephat was the *Buddhacharita* of Asvaghosha. Most probably the biography of the Buddha travelled westwards to Damascus by way of the Manichaean Church, 'the most inclusive and pervasive of the Christian heresies' (Allen 2002: 26) (p. 171).

8 The era of the Imperial Guptas

(CE 320 to c. 550)

Timeline/Key Dates

CE 320	Chandragupta I founds the Gupta Empire
CE 335–75	The reign of Samudragupta
CE 375–415	'Nine Gems' at the court of Chandragupta II; Kalidasa writes his *Shakuntala* and other plays
CE 405–11	Fa-Hsien travels through India
CE 425	Nalanda monastic college founded
CE 460	First attacks by Huns
CE 499	The great mathematician and astronomer Aryabhata writes his *Aryabhatiya*
CE 500	Second Hun attack under Toramana
CE 528	The defeat of Mihirkula, the Hun leader

In the fourth and fifth centuries of the Common Era, most of north India was ruled by monarchs of the Gupta dynasty, originally the controllers of a minor principality in the western Ganges plains. The Gupta family's fortunes rose when its third king, Chandragupta I, extended his realms into *Magadha* itself in CE 320. His acceptance among the kings and princes of the eastern Ganges basin was confirmed after he married into the Lichchhavi family, an influential republican clan on the borders of Bihar and Nepal. With Chandragupta's steady consolidation of his hold over the Magadhan heartland the Gupta principality expanded into the Gupta kingdom, and under his son and grandson the Guptas became a formidable power in north India. The extent of their lands was smaller than that of the Mauryan or future Mughal territories; nonetheless, the Guptas ruled over what was essentially an empire of great majesty and consequence. Another astute marriage extended their influence further south. There ruled in the Deccan the dynasty of the Vakatakas, who had been the successors of the Satavahanas, and a politically crucial marriage alliance between a Gupta princess and the Vakataka king in the late fourth century brought the two families closer. Although the Guptas remained the senior partners, the fifth century may rightly be described as the Gupta–Vakataka Age. By the early sixth century, the glory of both had faded, but a number of minor Gupta kings carried on ruling ever-smaller territories right until the eighth century. We must distinguish these later, lesser, Guptas from the earlier powerful ones who are often called the Imperial Guptas.

A number of early Gupta emperors of outstanding character and ability gave India two centuries of unprecedented stability. Despite much internal warfare in the early years and external threats in the last decades of the fifth century, they created a framework of peace and order for their empire that heralded much fruitful progress and activity. The beneficial effects of their benign rule and of their later

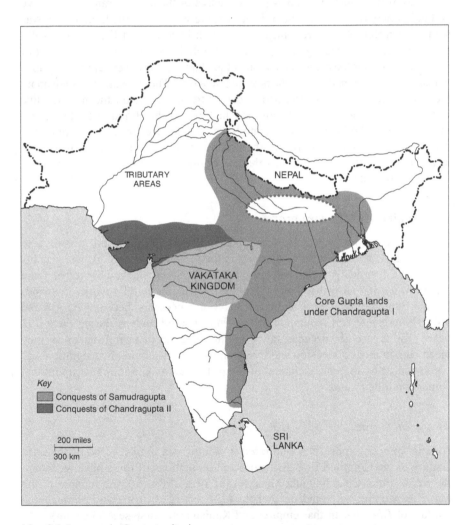

Map 8.1 Increase in Gupta territories

subordinate partners, the Vakatakas, can be evidenced from the many achievements of that era in the varied areas of life, whether political, military, economic,
social or cultural in nature. Those searching for an idyllic Hindu past of India have
tended to glorify the Gupta times as the 'golden age' of Indian history, but there
are also some who have been stern critics of such historical nostalgia.[1] Undoubtedly Gupta India was a far more desirable and creative place in which to live than
the other great civilisations of that era, whether European, Chinese or Persian, but
we must be careful that we do not succumb to the exaggerated notion that it was
an age of well-being for all of northern India's people. We need to ask critically
who benefited most and who did not. Among the former were those who were
most able to seize the opportunities provided by stable conditions. They were either
the elites of the upper and upper-middle classes of the caste pyramid or creative
and gifted people. As far as the ordinary people were concerned, the reality was
somewhat different. The vast majority of them lived a short life, economically
precarious and disadvantaged by social, cultural and gender inequalities. Part of
the explanation for the naive perception of the Gupta era lies in certain assumptions
that are sometimes made about the post-Gupta period. These assumptions are about
the consequences of regionalised and feudal politics in this period, the most negative
of which is considered to be the ultimate inability of the Hindu rulers to contain
the steady inroad of Muslim forces into India from the eleventh century onwards.
The last three or four centuries of the first millennium CE are therefore viewed
as a period of retrogression, rather than deserving to be studied and appreciated
in their own context.

The empire and the emperors

The imperial Guptas rightly begin with Chandragupta I, because it was he who
was honoured with the title of *Maharajadhiraja*, King over Kings, whereas his
father, Sri Ghatotkachagupta, and his grandfather, Sri Gupta, had carried only the
title of *Maharaja* (Raychaudhuri 1996: 468). Chandragupta I's work in expand-
ing the Gupta domain continued under his four successors, between CE 335 and
467. The prestige and reputation of the Guptas stood highest during these 132
years. The next eight decades saw a gradual decline in their fortunes as they
faced both internal dissension and foreign invasions. The final disintegration was
accompanied by the encroachment of minor tributaries and rulers on traditional
Gupta-controlled lands.

Two great Guptas (CE 335–415)

Among the many monarchs who ruled in South Asia until the end of the third
century of the Common Era, the names and reputations of three have withstood
the test of time: Chandragupta Maurya (321 BCE–298 BCE), the founder of the
Mauryan Empire; his grandson, Ashoka (272 BCE–232 BCE), who promulgated
the law of *Dhamma* in that empire; and Kanishka (*c*. first–second century CE),
the great Kushan king. To these three we must now add the names of two

remarkable Guptas – Samudragupta and Chandragupta II – who were the best and the most sagacious of them. Their achievements define the political and social tone of India during the heyday of their rule. Samudragupta (CE 335–75) made the dynasty truly imperial. His strength and wisdom have generally been admired, but we have more definite information about him from the inscription carved on an Ashokan pillar that used to be at Kausambi but is now in Allahabad (Sircar 1971: 1–16). This so-called Allahabad Pillar lists, at length, different classes of kings subdued by Samudragupta; there were kings who were slain and their territories annexed, but there were also defeated kings who were released by the grace of Samudragupta in return for tribute, the provision of military help, loyalty, the granting of their daughters in marriage, etc. Frontier kings paid homage to Samudragupta, and distant kings sent embassies acknowledging his suzerainty. The Gupta domain extended all the way up to the foothills of the Himalayas, ranging over the eastern Deccan and a long stretch of the eastern coastline. Samudragupta's defeat of some fourteen kings of south India and his several victories led the historian Vincent Smith to describe him as the Napoleon of ancient India (Smith 1924: 306). Unlike Napoleon, however, Samudragupta never met his Waterloo, because he refused to overextend himself. In that he showed the wisdom common to many Indian rulers. Great as were his military skills, Samudragupta was also a poet, a musician and an intellectual personality. He was honoured as a poet-king, or *kaviraja*, and he gathered about him a galaxy of poets and scholars, promoting high culture at his court. Though a *Vaishnavite* (Tripathi 1999: 248), he showed much liberality of outlook in employing Buddhist advisers, such as the philosopher Vasubandhu. When Meghavarman, king of Sri Lanka (*c.* CE 350–80), sent a request for help in building a monastery at Bodh Gaya for visiting Sri Lankan monks and scholars, Samudragupta generously donated towards the construction of a building, which eventually housed a thousand monks (Majumdar and Pusalker 1954: 11–12).

Under Samudragupta's son, Chandragupta II (375–415), the Gupta state became more powerful and prosperous. A spectacular conquest and a strategic matrimonial alliance were key factors. The conquest was that of the Shakas of western India. The Shakas, or the Scythians, as will be recalled, had moved into India after the collapse of the Mauryans, but by the fourth century CE their main power base in India was in Malwa and Saurashtra, with their capital at Ujjain. Their defeat at the hands of Chandragupta II opened the way to the Gupta control of key ports in western India, such as Broach, Cambay and Sopara, which produced greater revenues from their overseas trade (Majumdar 1977: 234). The possession of Ujjain led to dominance over the internal trade routes that crossed through that great central Indian city. After his conquest of the Shakas, Chandragupta II came to be known as *Vikramaditya*, or 'Sun of Valour', a title highly esteemed in Brahmanic India. Like his grandfather, Chandragupta II was shrewd enough to understand the value of marriage alliances for enhancing the influence and dignity of his own dynasty. He himself married Kuvera-Naga, a princess from the Naga family, and thus extended his patrimony (Raychaudhuri 1996: 489–90). More importantly, however, he married his daughter Prabhavatigupta to King Rudrasena II of the

Vakataka dynasty of Maharashtra and the western Deccan. When Rudrasena II died prematurely, Prabhavatigupta ruled as regent for her minor sons, thereby bringing the Vakatakas under Gupta influence (Raychaudhuri 1996: 769–77). The strength and prosperity of Chandragupta II's empire are reflected in the fine gold and silver coins issued during his reign. The coins united the emperors with their far-flung subjects. Chandragupta II was also a renowned patron of art and culture. He held three courts – at *Pataliputra*, Ayodhya and Ujjain, but the one at Ujjain was particularly lustrous. It was a court where a circle of poets and intellectuals, commonly known as the 'Nine Gems', is said to have flourished under the patronage of Chandragupta and composed verses in his praise.[2]

Decentralisation and devolution of power

The honorific titles bestowed upon the Gupta emperors leave no doubt as to their belief in the Brahmanic notions of kingship (Majumdar 1977: 414; Thapar 2002: 290). The king's right was divinely ordained and was sanctified by the ceremonies that the *brahmans* performed on his behalf, but his right was only valid as long as he followed a righteous policy towards all his subjects. As the *Markandeya Purana* puts it, 'a king inaugurated in his kingdom must in the first place conciliate his subjects, without obstructing his own duty' (quoted in Ray *et al.* 2000: 386). The Gupta emperors kept to the letter and spirit of this understanding (Dikshitar 1993: 108–39). Instead of governing by absolutist principle, they followed the *rajadharma*, the duty of kings to protect their subjects and to arbitrate in disputes. They also initiated certain changes in the very style of exercise of monarchical authority. For nearly a thousand years the Indian monarchs, whether imperial or regional, had aimed at a concentration of all power in their hands. Absolutist rulers were tempted to subdue provinces and regions to their will through their bureaucracies, and the Mauryans were perhaps the greatest of centralisers. The Gupta dominions were organised on a somewhat different model, the main difference being the principle of decentralised administration (Chattopadhyaya 1995: 314–18). The Guptas consciously devolved power on a variety of people and authorities who were then brought together in a circle of friendship and homage. Instead of bolstering a bureaucratic hierarchy, they helped to develop political hierarchies. This trend could be noticed in the power structures operating in the centuries immediately after the Mauryas, but the Guptas developed it further. To appreciate this model of decentralisation more fully it is necessary to peruse carefully the deeds of Samudragupta as narrated in the inscription of the Allahabad Pillar. Samudragupta did not wish to vanquish his enemies merely for his own gratification. After defeating them he permitted most of them to keep their domains within the empire. They were to be protected by him, while he would share in their wealth. What he was developing was a form of contract between the tributary kings and himself as the overlord. This arrangement did not work for the weaker Gupta emperors of the sixth century, but during the heyday of Gupta power in the fourth and fifth centuries it functioned extremely well and helped to keep peace among the various ruling families. The post-Gupta rulers in future centuries would also, in the measure of their capabilities, adopt the model of tributary ruler-ship. Indeed, in one sense it would be true to say that the model operated right until the end of British rule in India. After the great rebellion of 1857, the British realised that it was far better to make friends of the remaining princes of India than to subjugate them and alienate them further. They were simply following the Samudragupta principle of a network of what were called *samantas*. Over centuries the Sanskrit word *samanta*, literally meaning neighbour, has undergone many changes in its political significance, but during the Gupta period a *samanta* came to mean a neighbouring subsidiary ruler who was a friendly tributary of the Gupta sovereigns.

Imperial organisation

The Guptas avoided an overly elaborate bureaucracy. Part of the reason for this was the decentralisation of administrative authority accompanied by land grants, carrying varied immunities and concessions, to persons and institutions. State rule was lightly exercised. At the royal palace in *Pataliputra* the monarch was advised by a council of ministers led by the *Pradhana Mantry*, the chief minister. He headed the civil administration, but a good number of other ministers and high officials had duties related to military matters. Thus there was a separate junior minister for each of the following departments: peace and war, the police, the palace guards, the cavalry and the elephant corps. This emphasis on defence and security naturally reflected the essential concern of the central government: the maintenance of state power and the security of the people (Dikshitar 1993: 215–26). In the central secretariat, each office had its own seal with which its communications were stamped for authentication. The second layer of administration dealt with the provinces, which were called *bhukti* or *desa*. A class of officers known as *kumaramatyas* headed the provincial councils (Dikshitar 1993: 239–52). The district, generally called *pradesha* or *vishaya*, and its council, headed by another group of officers, the *ayuktakas* or *vishayapatis*, were the concern of a third layer of administration. In the fourth layer were grouped the villages and towns. For each village there was a village assembly consisting of village elders, guided by a village headman (Dikshitar 1993: 271–8). In the towns and cities there were corporations or guilds consisting of many representatives of guild merchants (Dikshitar 1993: 265–71). These were headed by a chairman, the *nagarashreshthin*, who was helped in his work by the chief scribe (Schwartzberg 1992: 28). All substantive decisions affecting each town or village were taken at the local level, reflecting the decentralising policies of the state. We do not have any evidence of voting procedures, but there can be no doubt that decisions would have been arrived at after robust discussion, in the true Indian fashion. The *kumaramatyas* and the *ayuktakas* functioned as serving intermediaries between the centre and the periphery. This model of organisation was replicated in many of the lands of the *samantas*. In addition to peace with the *samantas*, the Gupta policy of general devolution of power helped, in the long run, to create layers of responsibility among the Indian people, in their villages, towns, districts and provinces. It allowed for self-governing communities to progress within the framework of their empire. The mildness of Gupta rule exerted a cohesive and beneficial effect upon the social classes of India. It was a highly pluralist world that was being created, a world in which groups of people came together to define their common interests or activities; the well-heeled ones formed associations, solicited patronage and proceeded with creating prosperity for themselves. The Gupta state was there to guide and help, not to coerce.

Gupta power maintained intact (415–67)

From the end of the fourth century CE, the superpower of Europe, the Roman Empire, was in great difficulties. Far from Rome, in the lands north of the Black Sea and to the north-west of the Caspian Sea, a nomadic people from central Asia, the Huns, had established themselves in an aggressive federation. Their presence destabilised another group of people living nearby, the Goths, whose various tribes then broke through the eastern boundaries of the Roman Empire. The empire could not be defended integrally, and in 395 it divided into western and eastern halves. The fifth century proved to be a period of horrendous difficulties for the Western Roman Empire. Alaric, the Goth leader, sacked Rome itself in 410, and the ancient provinces of Gaul, Spain and North Africa were seized by the Goths, the Franks and the Vandals. The province of Britain was also conquered, by the Angles, Saxons and Jutes. In the meantime, the Huns had moved further west, established their new headquarters in Hungary and found a new leader in Attila. Under him, in the 440s the dominance of the Huns attained its peak and, although Attila's hordes were finally defeated in the early 450s, the fate of the western empire was sealed (Previte-Orton 1971: 45–59, 77–102; Collins 1991: 45–57). Roman civilisation and the Pax Romana wilted away from the soil of Europe. In contrast, during this period, the Gupta state in north India maintained its commanding position. The reign of Kumaragupta I (CE 415–55) was a period of consolidation of the state structure, with its refined administration reaching out benevolently into the grass-roots villages of north India to ensure peace and prosperity, which came to be symbolised by the monarch's highly elegant gold and silver coins (Maity 1957: 165–78). The chaos and confusion of the collapsing Roman Empire seemed far away indeed, although not for long!

The Huns who damaged Roman Europe were but one branch of the federated Hun family of the Hsiung-nu (Schwartzberg 1992: 179–80). Originally migrating west from the borders of China during the first two or three centuries of the Common Era, the Hsiung-nu had divided into two branches, one moving towards the River Volga and the other towards the River Oxus. What the Volga Huns did to the Romans and Goths, the Oxus Huns were to repeat in north-west India during the late fifth and most of the sixth centuries. From the name of their rulers' family, the Huns of the Oxus valley came to be known as the Hephthalites, or the White Huns as the Greeks referred to them. In India, specifically, the term 'Huna' is used instead of Hun. From the Oxus valley the Huna (the White Huns) advanced towards both India and Persia, and in 460 they occupied *Gandhara*. Their advance, however, was stalled by the Gupta emperor Skandagupta (CE 455–67), who proved to be more than a match for them. Their defeat at his hands not only gave north India another thirty years of respite from the Huna incursions but also deflected them towards launching further attacks into other parts of Eurasia.

Guptas in decline (467–c. 550)

With the death of Skandagupta in 467, the line of illustrious Imperial Guptas comes to an end. From now on, until about 550, we note a succession of weak and ineffectual rulers. The liberal and benevolent polity that the Gupta state had been for nearly two centuries was now going to be a plaything for its enemies, internal and external. Despite being checked in 460, the Hunas remained the most dangerous foreign enemy. Around 500, under a leader called Toramana, they again invaded north-west India, Rajasthan and the western Ganges basin. Toramana's domain stretched from Persia to Khotan, with its capital at Sakala. Toramana was, however, more than a mere warlord. In areas of India under his control he brought much trade and encouraged groups of merchants to make donations to religious foundations (Ray *et al.* 2000: 615–16), and his rule was not an unmitigated disaster. In 510 he was succeeded by his son, Mihirkula, who made further and deeper inroads into Indian lands. Eventually, in 528, a powerful confederacy formed by the Gupta king Narasimha Gupta Baladitya and the ruler of Malwa, Yashodharman, checked Mihirkula and forced him to take refuge in Kashmir (Raychaudhuri 1996: 518–19). While Mihirkula, like his father, also gave grants and donations, most sources confirm his legendary reputation as the most aggressive Huna leader. He betrayed the ruler of Kashmir, perpetrated great massacres and visited wanton cruelties upon the Buddhists (Wink 1990: 227; Jha 2004: 207). On his death in 542, north India gave a sigh of relief. The days of Huna glory were finally over by the 570s, when another group of nomadic Central Asian Turks defeated the Oxus Huns and invaded Afghanistan. Although the Hun danger had passed, the legacy of their incursions into India was bloody and tumultuous. The decentralised administration of the Gupta state could not take the strains imposed by the large-scale military counter-measures required against the Hunas. The quality of life in north India, which had attained a high level of refinement in the fourth and fifth centuries, suffered considerably in the resulting period of economic instability. While most of the Gupta revenue was drawn from land taxes, a significant part of it was obtained from India's lucrative trade, by land and sea, with West Asia, the Levant and the Mediterranean basin. The Hun incursions virtually destroyed the land trade, depriving the Guptas of valuable foreign currency; the latter were dealt a further blow when the ports of Gujarat strayed out of their control into the hands of their local rivals (Schwartzberg 1992: 180). The sizeable diminution of their wealth is indicated by the paucity of inscriptions recording the various grants of lands and gifts traditionally conferred by them. The real death blow to the empire, however, came from the internal crisis of the Gupta dynasty: the weak and inept emperors were confronted with the assumption of their right to hereditary rule by provincial governors and imperial feudatories, and were powerless to check it. In fact, among the scanty records of the sixth century, we notice the rise of a new phenomenon: the self-asserting inscriptions issued by heads of regional families who once paid homage to the Guptas. By about 550 the empire had become a pale shadow of its former self.

Gupta society: a world in transition

Fa-hsien, a Chinese pilgrim, visited India in the early fifth century during the reign of Chandragupta II. His aim was to collect Buddhist manuscripts and relics and to seek the knowledge of Buddhism in the places of its origin. He had left China in 399, crossed the Gobi Desert, the mountains of Khotan, the Pamir plateau, Swat and *Gandhara*, and stayed in India for nearly seven years, visiting such places as Peshawar, *Kanauj*, *Kashi*, Kapilavastu, Kusinagar, Vaishali, *Pataliputra* and several other Buddhist sites. He left India by sea from the port of *Tamralipiti* and visited Ceylon and Indonesia on his homeward journey. Fa-hsien never had an audience with Chandragupta II, and neither was he interested in the politics of his kingdom. His main concern was Buddhism (Liu 1994: 127–36). Nevertheless, some of his recollections about India, which were translated by French scholars only in the nineteenth century, are worth noting. He called India the 'Middle Kingdom', a term normally used in reference to China, and he vividly describes the free and liberal society of India that he found practically everywhere. The two particular matters that clearly impressed him were, first, the facilities of welfare and care for the weaker members of society and, second, the ordinary people going about their daily life in an atmosphere of peace and order, with little interference from the state. There was no capital punishment, and public officers were held to be non-corrupt. People lived with moderation, abstaining from alcohol and meat-eating. This portrayal of Chandragupta II's India is uncritical and adulatory, and we need to be more circumspect before accepting his observations as reliable: he only saw what he wanted to see. For example, there is evidence for the prevalence of alcohol-drinking and meat-eating (Auboyer 2002: 195–7). Fa-hsien's work does not help us to understand some of the deeper changes that were taking place in Gupta society. The varieties of inscriptions, whether on temple walls or copper plates, are far more useful for this purpose. From much detailed research now available, we can see that the achievements of the fourth and fifth centuries did not take place in the climate of enduring stability of Fa-hsien's imagination; there was also a considerable change coming over society. It could indeed be argued that the entire Gupta era was one of gentle transition, a transition that can be witnessed in the changes severally occurring. The age of Gupta transition acts also as a pointer to the new realities on the ground during the succeeding centuries. We select here three areas in which there were clear signs of change taking place.

Land grants and the early beginnings of feudalism

The idea of the *samanta* becomes even clearer when we examine the characteristics of the Gupta land policy. In contrast to the Mauryas, who acquired as much land as possible under their officers, the Guptas actively gave away much land in the form of land grants (Maity 1957: 43–7). This practice was prevalent in its nascent form even during the early centuries of the post-Vedic era, when the kings were enjoined to give gifts to their *brahman* priests or royal officials. It became more widespread under the Satavahanas of the Deccan, the Shakas of western India and the Pallavas of south India, but the Guptas made it a substantive part of the discharge of their responsibilities. Three important types of land grants were made by them: the religious grants to *brahmans*, individually or collectively, known as *brahmadeya* grants; grants to institutions such as temples and monasteries, known as *devagrahara* or *devadana* (Sharma 1959: 202–5); and secular grants to crown officers, craft guilds or, on rare occasions, military commanders. The motive for the grants, particularly for religious grants, was the gaining of religious merit in an age of social and moral crisis that was commented upon in the *Puranas*; however, a more pressing reason might have been the contraction of the monetary economy as a result of the shrinking of the previously very large international trade with Rome and the Levant. Since the shortage of funds made it difficult for the Gupta kings to maintain an elaborate bureaucracy, they could make more efficient use of their lands. Land was something that technically belonged to the king, and he could dispose of it in any way he thought fit. The land grants to individual *brahmans* were more or less permanently alienated to the donees, thereby affirming their hereditary rights over the lands. No rents were charged and all revenues that could be derived from the produce of the cultivators could be retained by the new landholders. The *brahman* landlord was expected to improve his land and to contribute to rural prosperity. The cultivators became his possessions; as long as he did not wilfully mistreat them he could use their labour in any way he preferred. There is evidence that the new *brahman* owners made efforts to improve their estates (Thapar 2002: 291–2). Sometimes entire villages with their people were alienated by the Gupta kings either to a collectivity of *brahmans* or to the temples. The grants were rent-free, but carried an obligation to collect taxes due from the cultivators to the state. The relative lack of monetary resources would definitely explain the rationale of secular grants to officers and admin-istrators. These land grants were in lieu of cash salaries for military and administrative service. Their privileges included also the hereditary alienation of land and rights over its produce, along with a variety of legal and administrative immunities. The various categories of cultivators were again to lose the protection of the monarch and his officials, and we can be sure that the attendant evils of forced and bonded labour would have increased considerably in these altered situations (Maity 1957: 141–54).

The Gupta land grants created a class of feudatory intermediaries in the countryside. There was a limit to what the state could achieve for the countryside, but by creating layers of intermediaries the Guptas gave opportunities to various people to become proactive in the management and improvement of rural estates. While the state lost a certain amount of revenue and power, it had in the new donees a class of people who would act as its support mechanism. Some historians have described this development as a form of Indian feudalism (Sharma 1959: 202–33; Sharma 1985: 19–43). They have recognised in it some of the features found in the full-blown feudalism of the type that was prevalent in Europe in the Middle Ages, when lord and vassal, at various levels of the social pyramid, were bound together in a chain of protection, homage and service. Other historians have raised doubts about the applicability of the European feudal model to India, and there has been a contentious debate engaged by scholarly protagonists on both sides of the argument. This will be further discussed in Chapter 9. What is indisputable is that the small-scale programme of land grants that the Guptas inherited and further encouraged became greatly accelerated in the post-Gupta centuries, and land grants created ideal conditions for some form of feudalism to flourish in India. In that sense, Indian feudalism predates European feudalism. From the time of the Guptas until the mid-twentieth century, feudalism remained a persistent factor in Indian political and social life. Even today, in much of rural India, a feudal mindset prevails, despite television sets and mobile phones.

Varying fortunes of faiths and sects

The period of Gupta transition affected the religions of India in different ways. Buddhism had been a powerful presence before the Guptas, partly owing to the favours the Buddhists had won from sympathetic monarchs. The Guptas, who were truly pluralist and broad-minded, continued with the established traditions of patronage and support to the Buddhist monasteries and institutions of learning. For most of the Gupta period Buddhism was to enjoy a healthy and robust life throughout most of India. Both the *Mahayana* and the *Theravada* schools flourished in different parts of the country, and great philosophers such as Vasubandhu, Dignaga and Dharmakirti either provided masterly expositions of the founder's teachings or expounded fresh ideas and developed new schools of thought. Some of the finest Buddhist caves of Ajanta were built under the patronage of the Vakatakas of the Deccan, the allies of the Guptas. There was, however, an ominous cloud hanging over the horizon, which was that, despite their widespread generosity, the Gupta emperors were essentially followers of the Brahmanical religion, particularly of the theistic schools of *Shaivism* and *Vaishnavism*. This meant, for the Buddhists, intense competition for monarchical patronage. They could not take for granted the quality and volume of support that they were accustomed to from previous monarchs. *Shaivism* and *Vaishnavism* were also appealing to a broader range of kings, besides the Guptas, in both north and south India, and that was bound in the long run to have a deleterious influence on Buddhist fortunes throughout the country. A much more serious and immediate danger for them in the declining decades of Gupta rule was that of the horrendous destruction wreaked on their monks and monasteries by the Hunas. What also perturbed them was the support given to the Hunas by the *Shaivite brahmans* of Kashmir, who expected to receive land grants from the Huna chief, Mihirkula (Thapar 2002: 287).

The oldest tradition in the country, Vedic Brahmanism, had been experiencing a gradual revival in the pre-Gupta centuries, but it was under Gupta patronage that it secured the opportunity to establish itself more firmly in the religious life of the people. The influence of heterodox ideas in Indian society over many hundreds of years had, however, been sufficiently strong to prevent the return of full-blooded Vedic Brahmanism. For example, one of its major planks, the highly elaborate and sometimes bizarre ritualistic sacrifices in propitiation of the old Vedic gods, was being gradually dismantled. These sacrifices incurred much expense and many resources; even the *Dharmashastra* of Yajnavalkya recommended that an expensive sacrifice such as that of the *Ashvamedha* could only be performed when there was 'a provision for three years in one's store' (quoted in Kachroo 2000: 365). There were now those who wished to modify and reform the sacrifices, while affirming their faith in the supremacy of the 'authorless and eternal' *Vedas* and other essential belief systems of Vedic Brahmanism (Ali 1999: 45). For the *Shaivite* and *Vaishnavite* theists, neither the reformed sacrifices nor the eternal supremacy of the *Vedas* were of any consequence when compared with the power and majesty of the one supreme deity, either Shiva, Vishnu or Shakti (the goddess Devi). Both the theists and the reformist sacrificers, sometimes called *Smartas*, operated under the umbrella of Brahmanism, but in their own distinct ways. In both *Shaivism* and *Vaishnavism* the ceremony of the *puja*, with an image of Vishnu or Shiva as the focus of worship, superseded the Vedic sacrifice. In the matter of the conduct of worship, the orthodox Vedic Brahmanists remained wedded to the role of the priest as being central to the performance of all the rituals, while the theists greatly emphasised individual devotional worship, or *bhakti*, without the necessity of priestly intercession. In the long run, all parties eventually settled down to accepting a compromise. The upper castes continued a number of Vedic rituals short of full-blown sacrifices, along with a respect for theistic devotionalism. The mass of the people, under the influence of *Shaivism* and *Vaishnavism*, became increasingly devotional-minded in their religious attitudes. It is the genius of Hinduism that has permitted myriad sects to develop without causing existential conflicts.

One of the most important means by which millions of unlettered common people, and particularly women, came to be imbued with a strong passion for devotional worship was through the readings of a set of texts called the *Puranas*, composed by the learned among the *Shaivites* and the *Vaishnavites*. While their earliest compositions might have begun in pre-Gupta times, and the later works continued to be composed long after the Guptas, the *Puranas* are essentially a product of the Gupta age (Rocher 1986: 101). They are also a marker of the transition that we witness in the fourth and fifth centuries. In them are to be found numerous stories of deities and their missions, and the explanations for the origins of the world and the process of time. The idea of the Divine is made manifest for the masses of people by reference to holy sites, the use of music, dance and drama in worship, vows, austerities and pilgrimages, along with much advice on the importance of detachment, sacrifice, abstinence and peacefulness. Personal worship can take the form of a *mantra*, whereby the name of the particular deity, whether Vishnu or Shiva, is continually recited, as demanded by god Vishnu in the *Bhagvata Purana*, as explained in **Excerpt 8.1** below.

Excerpt 8.1 Devotion to Vishnu in the *Bhagavata Purana*

Of the eighteen major and eighteen minor Puranas, the one which is most popularly cherished by Hindu worshippers is the Bhagavata Purana. *Its main subject is the god Vishnu, who, in different incarnations, comes again and again to eliminate evil and restore virtue in the world. Here Vishnu urges the worshipper to show complete devotion to Him.*

> One should engage himself in singing of Me, praising Me, dancing with My themes, imitating My exploits and acts, narrating My stories or listening to them . . . Whenever and wherever one feels like worshipping Me in images, etc., one should do so. I am, however, present in oneself and in all beings; for I am the soul of everything . . . Thus worshipping me with Vedic and Tantric methods, one attains through Me the desired welfare here and in the hereafter.

Source: Quoted in Ainslee Embree (ed.),
Sources of Indian Tradition, London: Penuin, 1992, 328.
Copyright © 2016 Columbia University Press.
Reprinted with permission of the publisher.

This devotion to Vishnu was a powerful psychological tool in securing the loyal adherence of the intellectually unsophisticated devotees, which has sometimes helped to bolster a form of religious sectarianism. The *Puranas* became a primer of religious education for the masses. Written in an accessible style, and containing a mixture of morality, history, genealogy, folklore and practical wisdom, astrology, geography, medicine and countless other subjects, including humour and irony, the eighteen major and the eighteen minor *Puranas* became the key agencies by which the *Shaivites* and the *Vaishnavites* drew the people towards them and away from both Buddhism and orthodox Vedic Brahmanism. The rationale of what we nowadays call folk Hinduism is best studied through the Puranic writings. Within the current 'Indological scholarship', too, these writings 'have regained . . . the central place they have always occupied in living Hinduism' (Klostermaier 1994: 94). The *Puranas*, like the *Mahabharata*, can be useful to historians and scholars of ancient India, because they contain long lists of kings and dynasties. The two terms frequently mentioned are *Suryavamsha* (solar lineage) and *Chandravamsha* (lunar lineage). Often there is an urge to over-interpret whatever historical evidence there may be in the *Puranas*; serious historians have to resist that temptation because the Puranas can never be considered as systematic historical chronicles. The bulk of their contents are concerned with religion and mythology, but they are still one of the great literatures of India and a treasure house of the Indian creative imagination at its best.

Caste mobility

The caste system has remained a notable feature of Indian religious and social life until the present. So it was too during the Gupta period. At the same time, we also notice some indications of mobility and fluidity affecting the system during this period. The first signs can be detected from the readings of the various *Dharmashastras* that contain ample references to the caste system. These normative sources contain much to explain the condition of the *shudras*, slaves and various categories of labourers. With increased political decentralisation, economic expansion and the liberal use of land grants, large areas of the country had become more accessible, with the result that many tribal groups who had formerly lived very isolated lives were now brought within the caste system. One might say that the detribalisation of India proceeded apace during Gupta rule. Similarly, the older foreign groups, such as the *Yavanas*, the Shakas and the Kushans, were also being acculturated into the caste hierarchy. There is also evidence that the principle of caste endogamy was not as rigidly applied as in earlier times. Different marriage conventions were approved and socially recognised, despite the various strictures in the *Dharmashastras* (Trautmann 1981: 271–7). There was also a certain weakening of the links between a caste and its vocation, as instances of the *brahmans* and the *kshatriyas* following the occupations of lower classes and of the *vaishyas* and the *shudras* adopting the occupations of superior classes have been recorded. In a period of mobility it was natural that some castes improved their standing, others stood still or rose marginally and some sank in social standing. The *brahmans* maintained their status through their ability to read, write and recite, but members of lesser castes could also improve theirs by performing any type of scribal work. Traditionally the *kshatriyas* were power-holders and power-brokers. However, with the rise of many non-*kshatriya* ruling houses, it came to be gradually recognised in the *Dharmashastras* that the king need not be a *kshatriya* by birth, and that the *kshatriya* status was an 'achieved, not an ascribed, rank' (Stein 1998: 99). The *vaishyas* retained the third ritual hierarchical layer, but their influence grew with numbers of *jatis* with useful trades and occupations multiplying and flourishing. The *shudras* made a definite leap forward for themselves. The relative improvement in the status of the *shudras* in Gupta society can be evidenced by a number of developments among them. They increasingly went into farming in capacities other than labourers and turned into sharecroppers and peasants; they became craftsmen; they joined the army; and some got themselves educated (Sharma 1958: 231–8). They came to be granted definite legal rights that they did not previously possess. While the *Dharmashastra* of Manu adopted a harsh tone in relation to the punishments to be meted out in cases of *shudra* transgressions, the later *Dharmashastra* of *Yanavalkayasmriti* took a much more humane and pragmatic line in this matter (Sharma 1958: 268, 273). Their forward movement, though limited in scope, was a significant marker of social mobility, but it was naturally counter-balanced by the growth of new outcaste groups, generally known as the Untouchables. The latter were assigned the most demeaning and polluting occupations, and they, along with the slaves, constituted perhaps the lowest stratum of Indian humanity. Even Fa-hsien, who showered so much praise on the India of his day, admitted that the *Chandalas* or the Untouchables had to sound a 'clapper' (Thapar 2002: 303) in the streets so that the caste people would be warned of their presence, and that an upper-caste person would have to take a ritual bath in the event of close proximity with an Untouchable (Sharma 1958: 261–5). The Untouchables had also become Unapproachables.

Indian achievements in the Gupta period

In January 2000, an international seminar was held at Tiruvanthampuram (Trivandrum), Kerala, India, to honour the 1,500th anniversary of the writing of *Aryabhatiya*, a seminal mathematical treatise by Aryabhata I, the great mathematician-astronomer of India, who was born in CE 476. Many Indian and international Sanskrit scholars and historians of mathematics read papers explaining Aryabhata's mathematical insights and the relevance of his work even today. The time during which Aryabhata lived has been labelled by historians as the Classical period of Indian history. The term 'Classical' implies unsurpassed intellectual and aesthetic excellence – a norm against which all other similar achievements can be judged. Although there was much creativity in India in both earlier and later times, many historians feel that the Brahmanic–Buddhist–Jain civilisation that had been maturing for many centuries reached a particularly splendid height under the Guptas. The American historian William McNeill

Figure 8.1 The idea of the Classical in the Indian context

described the Gupta period as one of the 'flowering' of Indian culture (McNeill 1967: 173). As the Guptas were the dominant power over more than half of India, the historians talk of a Gupta Classical culture. Although this could be misleading, because Indian creativity was not confined to the peoples and territories controlled by the Guptas, there is no doubt that the liberal patronage of the Guptas and their allies for the aspiring writers, artists, poets and thinkers of all castes and creeds helped to promote excellence in general.

Mathematics and technology

Long before the Guptas came to power there had been steady progress made in Indian mathematics (Joseph 2010). Such problems in mathematics as arithmetical operations, the geometry of altars, algebraic equations and the number theory had already been investigated in earlier sources such as the *Satapatha Brahmana*, the *Sulbasutras*, Jain mathematics and the *Bakhshali Manuscript*. The Indian number system, with ten symbols representing one to nine and the zero, and the decimal place-value system, were also utilised, although the earliest documented symbol for zero dates from the Gwalior inscription of the ninth century. A considerable body of astronomical knowledge, using mathematics, was additionally contained in texts called the *Siddhantas*. Indian astronomy began with the need, first, for accurate calendars for use in religious rituals and for predicting rainfall patterns; it developed further with the rapid expansion of Indian trade, with the charting of high seas necessitating the exact knowledge of tides and stars. Mathematical intervention was therefore crucial. However, despite such progress made before the Guptas, we do not know of any one person whom we can recognise as an iconic figure in Indian mathematics or astronomy. Aryabhata I was the first great mathematician and astronomer to whom this honour must be accorded; he lived at a time of great flux and dynamism in Indian science as a whole. Whether in medicine or metallurgy, music or mathematics, pharmacy or astronomy, new observations were being made and ideas rigorously tested, with their results codified and synthesised (Bose *et al.* 1989: 584–93). Aryabhata's own work was neither prolific nor exhaustive, but it was he who not only summed up, in a concise way, the precedent mathematical achievements but also provided new insights which later proved to be vital to the development of mathematics. Practically all ancient Indian mathematical and astronomical concepts were expressed in verse form, in *sutras*, in what might be termed mathematical Sanskrit. The mathematical ideas in the *Aryabhatiya* of Aryabhata I were also expressed in a *sutra* form, and only those few people closely acquainted with both Sanskrit and mathematics can decrypt the meaning of these *sutras*.

Traditionally, the learned people disseminated ideas through written commentaries on original mathematical works, and further commentaries on the commentaries were also made available.[3] There was therefore much elitism and, perhaps, intellectual exclusivity. During the Classical period, however, owing to greater openness of outlook and exchange of ideas, schools of mathematics and astronomy began to flourish at places as far apart as Kusumpura, Ujjain and Mysore, where useful mathematical exchanges took place. Aryabhata himself might have been a native of Kerala, but he worked at both Kusumpura and Nalanda. In the *Aryabhatiya* there are four chapters, or *Padas*: *Gitika Pada, Ganita Pada, Kalakriya Pada* and *Gola Pada*. The *Ganita Pada*, consisting of thirty-three verses, is the critical mathematical text. It includes references to such concepts as squares, cubes, square-roots, cube-roots, areas of triangles, the volume of prisms, areas of circles, the volume of spheres, areas of quadrilaterals, the circumference of circles, elementary trigonometry of series-figures, triadic rules, the reduction of fractions and the theory of pulveriser. An example of the problems that Aryabhata might have asked his students to solve is illustrated in **Excerpt 8.2** below.

Excerpt 8.2 A problem attributed to Aryabhata by Bhaskara I (*c.* CE 600), one of the most able commentators on his work

Ancient Indian mathematicians formulated their problems with a human touch, as can be shown in the following example.

Oh beautiful maiden with beaming eyes, tell me, since you understand the method of inversion, what number multiplied by 3, then increased by three-quarters of the product, then divided by 7, then diminished by one-third of the result, then multiplied by itself, then diminished by 52, whose square root is then extracted before 8 is added and then divided by 10, gives the final result of 2?

The solution offered is elegant and simple:

we start with the answer 2 and work backwards. When the problem says divide by 10, we multiply by that number; when told to add 8, we subtract 8; when told to extract the square root, we take the square; and so on. It is precisely the replacement of the original operation by the inverse that gives the method its name of 'inversion'. Thus

$$((2)(10)-8)^2 + 52 = 196$$
$$\sqrt{196} = 14$$
$$\frac{(14)(3/2)(70(4/7)}{3} = 28 \text{ Answer}$$

Source: A problem sent in a note to the author by Dr George Gheverghese Joseph, whose book *The Crest of the Peacock: Non-European Roots of Mathematics*, Princeton: Princeton University Press, 2010, contains a number of examples and problems from ancient Indian mathematics.

In order that mathematical information could be conveyed in poetic form, Aryabhata I developed the alphabet-numeral system of notation, by which specific numbers are allocated to specific letters of the alphabet. He provided the methods to solve simple quadratic equations, which, in the words of one historian, allowed him to earn 'for himself the credit of founding the science of Algebra' (Sarasvati 1986: 64). From the other *Padas* we learn about his belief that the earth was a sphere and that it rotated on its axis, and that eclipses were caused by the shadow of the earth falling on the moon. His calculations of the *pi* ratio and the length of the solar year were remarkably close to recent computations. It would be a few

Figure 8.2 Sultanganj bronze Buddha

more centuries before the works of Aryabhata and his illustrious successor, Brahmagupta, would first be closely scrutinised and then approvingly appropriated for development within the Islamic mathematical tradition, which in turn eventually influenced European developments in mathematics.

Skilled craftsmen, working through their guilds, produced good-quality jewellery, ivory carvings and artefacts, ceramics and textiles, but the essential technology of the Gupta period was concerned with metalwork in copper and iron. A seventh-century bronze statue of the Buddha (see Figure 8.2), weighing 1 ton, found in the ruins of a Buddhist monastery at Sultanganj, Bihar, in 1864, and now housed in the Birmingham Museum, is the finest example of copper metalworking that began during this period using the *cire perdue* technique, which has been described in some of the contemporary texts (Bose *et al.* 1989: 299). The so-called Iron Pillar of Delhi, a shaft 24 feet high and weighing more than 6 tons, showing no signs of erosion or rust since about CE 400, is the best example of iron technology in that period (Bose *et al.* 1989: 299–303). For many centuries, excepting China, India led the world in metal technology.

Sanskrit literature

Sanskrit literature flourished in the Gupta period. A large body of Brahmanic religious literature, whether consisting of the epics or the *shastras*, was embellished and augmented by learned commentaries and critiques. Buddhist literature was systematised, and so was Jainist knowledge. Not all Sanskrit literature was uniformly attractive or valuable, but certain works have left an indelible impression on the mind and consciousness of the outside world. One outstanding example is the collection of animal fables, known as the *Panchatantra*, the five strategies for gaining wisdom. A whole variety of animals – lion, bull, monkey, crocodile, mongoose, deer, tortoise, jackal, mouse, crow, dove, owl, etc. – are the main characters, and their dialogues have given pleasure and insights to generations of Indians across so many centuries. **Excerpt 8.3** provides an example of a typical fable, whose simplicity conceals much political and moral wisdom.

Through the increased contacts of Classical India with the Middle East and the Levant, the fables reached Persia, the Arab lands and eventually medieval Europe. Subtle changes in the characterisation of animals took place as the fables moved outward from India; a number of revisions within India and the translations into other languages also twisted the stories around. Although it is reasonably fair to argue that many European fables have their origin in Indian fables, it would be difficult to provide an exact number of European folk tales that are truly derived from India. No two stories are precisely alike. The degree of similarity required before a particular tale can be considered genuinely derivative from another one will differ from one researcher to another, as explained in **Excerpt 8.4** below. It is also valid to argue that the *Panchatantra* fables might well have derived their inspiration from Aesop's fables from the ancient Greek world, in the same way as the Romano-Greek art style affected the *Gandhara* school of art in the northwest of India.

Excerpt 8.3 Thousand-wit, Hundred-wit and Single-wit

Two fishes lived in a pond. One was called Satabuddhi (with the under-standing of a hundred); the other one was known as Sahasrabuddhi (with the understanding of a thousand). The two of them had a frog for a friend, whose name was Ekabuddhi (with the understanding of one). One day, some fishermen came with nets and dead fish. They were keen to catch more fish, but the water in the pond was very low: so they agreed that they would return the next morning. The two fishes and the frog now consulted each other as to whether to stay or flee. Sahasrabuddhi, with the understanding of a thousand wits, urged the others to stay and he assured them that with his powers of understanding he would be able to guide them to safety. Satabuddhi agreed, and said: 'Everything can be solved through intelligence. We should stay; we must not abandon our place of birth'. Ekabuddhi, the frog, now said: 'I have only one wit, and it is advising me to flee. On this very day I shall go with my wife to another pond'. The next day the fishermen returned and caught all types of fish in the pond. Despite trying their level best to avoid being caught, both Sahasrabuddhi and Satabuddhi were also caught. One of the fishermen carried Satabuddhi on his head, while Sahasrabuddhi was tied to a string and dragged along by another fisherman.

The frog, Ekabuddhi, who had climbed on to the bank of his pond, said to his wife: 'Look dear, Mr. Hundred-wit lies on someone's head, and Mr. Thousand-wit is hanging from a string. But Mr. Single-wit, my dear, is playing here in the clear water'.

Source: Adapted and abridged from D.L. Ashliman (ed.),
A Selection of Tales from Ancient India, University of
Pittsburg, 1996–2006, www.pitt.edu/-dash/folklinks.html

Excerpt 8.4 Indian fables in European literature

It is often assumed that many European fables have their origin in Indian fables. The following passage may help to serve as a corrective to this perception.

It would be difficult to make an exact account of the European folk tales which are truly derived from India . . . In 1957 Laurits Bodker, summing up the results of decades of folklore research, asserted that, of about 500 animal tales recorded from modern European oral tradition, only about 20 had close Indian counterparts. Interestingly, the count goes much higher in the case of literary fables: the Panchatantra is the most prolific source of Indian stories found in Europe.

Source: Jean W. Sedlar, *India and the Greek World*,
Torowa, NJ: Rowman and Littlefield, 106.

A Sanskrit work that has received the unqualified praise of the literary world since the end of the eighteenth century is Kalidasa's *Shakuntala*. Kalidasa, one of the 'Nine Gems' who constituted the circle of poets in the reign of Chandragupta II, wrote three plays, but *Shakuntala* is considered his greatest work. As an admiring critic has said, 'Of the arts the best is the drama; of dramas, *Shakuntala*; of *Shakuntala*, the fourth act; of that act, the verses in which Kanva bids farewell to his adopted daughter' (quoted in Rawlinson 1965: 137). The story, adopted from the *Mahabharata*, is touching in its simplicity, and yet most memorable. King Dushyanta of Hastinapur, while out hunting in a forest, felt grief after Shakuntala, a forest girl, who lived as the adopted daughter of the sage, Kanva, lovingly attended to a deer that the king had killed. Shortly, the two fell in love, and married according to the *gandharva* marriage ceremony by mutual consent, with Mother Nature as the chief witness. On his departure for the capital, Dushyanta gave Shakuntala a parting gift of a ring and promised to return. Meanwhile, Shakuntala fell foul of a hermit, Durvasa, when she absent-mindedly forgot to offer him the water that he was asking for; Durvasa put a curse on her, saying that the person whom she was thinking about would forget her. Hearing this, Shakuntala begged for forgiveness and requested the hermit to lift the curse. This was not possible, but the hermit consoled her by saying that if she showed her lover something he had given her he would remember her. A pregnant Shakuntala went to meet the king in the capital but, while crossing a river, accidently dropped her wedding ring in the water, which meant that the king was unable to recognise her, owing to the original curse of the hermit. She returned to the forest and gave birth to a son, naming him Bharata. When a stray fisherman accidently found the royal ring inside the fish he returned it to King Dushyanta, who then suddenly remembered Shakuntala. Returning to the forest, the king was united with Shakuntala and Bharata. The latter eventually became the supreme king of the Aryans, according to the *Mahabharata* (referred to in Chapter 4). Sir William Jones was the first to translate the play into English from its Bengali version and to publish it, in 1789. The real impact of the play was felt most on a long line of German Romantics, great geniuses such as Schiller, Goethe and Herder; through their writings, the glory of *Shakuntala* was laid bare before the world. Famous European composers have produced ballets and operas based on its plot, and even today the play attracts large audiences both inside and outside India.

Another enchanting work of classical Sanskrit literature, and now an international bestseller, is the *Kama Sutra* by Vatsyayana. Although a great textbook of erotic love, it is unfortunately much misrepresented and grossly maligned. This is partly because of the inadequate translation of its depictions into English by Sir Richard Burton, one of the reckless adventurers and philanderers of the nineteenth century. Burton's translation gave the *Kama Sutra* a reputation of being a pornographic work. The *Kama Sutra* fell victim to Burton's own infantile and orientalist fantasies, and even today the general public frankly feigns embarrassment at the mention of this powerful work. A fresh translation, along with a new psychoanalytical interpretation of the text, has recently been published, allowing us to appreciate the *Kama Sutra* for what it was intended: an account of the untainted and sublime beauty of erotic pleasure, entirely separated from the 'crude purposefulness of sexual desire' (Doniger and Kakar 2002: xxxix). A fascinating section of the text, called 'The lifestyle of the man about town', gives us an insight into what it was like to be a sophisticated rich young man in the Indian urban culture of the fifth century CE. Such a man needed training in the arts of love through flirtations and liaisons with courtesans, mistresses and even prostitutes. A woman who wishes to be a courtesan of a refined man is also enjoined to learn a host of skills, as shown in **Excerpt 8.5** below.

On the issue of marriage, the *Kama Sutra* text wholeheartedly recommends love match as the best form of marriage, 'because its essence is mutual love' (quoted in Doniger 2010: 331). In contrast to the more mean-spirited assertions about, and injunctions on, women that one finds in a *Dharmashastra* such as the *Manusmriti* (Chapter 7), the *Kama Sutra* displays a refreshing openness and liberality towards the female gender as a whole. Thus, for example, on the issue of women's access to household funds, the *Kama Sutra* takes it for granted that the wife should control the home budget and gives practical advice as to how to look after it. Instead of blaming the adultery by women on their evil nature, as described in some of the Brahmanic texts, the *Kama Sutra* locates the cause for such a situation on the inadequacy of men. It also has no particular problems with the re-marriage of widows. Diverse patterns of sexual orientation in humans, whether it be homosexuality, lesbianism, bi-sexuality or trans-gender, are accepted as 'third nature' in sexual behaviour (Doniger 2010: 331–4). The assumptions and attitudes of the *Kama Sutra* are in marked contrast to the sexual repression and sexism (e.g. the current plague of rapes) that have existed within Indian society for countless centuries. Having said that, it should be understood that this particular text is concerned with the life of only well-to-do urban people in the Gupta period, not the masses. As urbanisation spreads across modern India, hopefully there might take place a renaissance of liberal and tolerant sexual attitudes among the people.

Dissemination of knowledge: the Nalanda monastic college

The greatest of all the educational institutions of India during the second half of the first millennium CE was the Buddhist college at Nalanda, Bihar. It first gained its status as a major centre of higher learning in the reign of Kumaragupta I (415–55), and the year CE 425 'is the most approximate date' of its establishment (Sankalia 1972: 57). For a long time before that there had existed a Buddhist monastery on the Nalanda site, and Buddhist monks were trained there. Nalanda's transformation into an academic centre was a result of several fruitfully interacting factors during the Gupta era. If one of the purposes of such a centre is to help young minds to understand, absorb, interpret and disseminate knowledge, then ancient India was uniquely the land where there was no dearth of knowledge. By the time of the Guptas, the amount of knowledge available in India, albeit mostly oral, had reached a critical mass in terms of its range and depth. The first huge

Excerpt 8.5 Exposition of the arts

The following is a fascinating list of skills that, according to Vatsyayana, the author of Kama Sutra, *are required of a cultured woman if she wishes to win over the hearts of men. This list is different from another set of sixty-four arts of love that Babhravya, the author of an earlier textbook of love, had advised men to be good at in order to enjoy maximum sexual pleasure. The list below is a testimony to both the richness of social life among the well-to-do people in Gupta India and the range of activities that women could engage themselves in. The term 'courtesan' generally applied to a prostitute, but on accomplishing the sixty-four skills below such a woman was given the special title of Courtesan de Luxe.*

The sixty four arts that should be studied along with the Kama Sutra are: singing; playing musical instruments; dancing; painting; cutting leaves into shapes; making lines on the floor with rice-powder and flowers; arranging flowers; colouring the teeth, clothes and limbs; making jeweled floors; preparing beds; making music on the rims of glasses of water; playing water sports; unusual techniques; making garlands and stringing necklaces; making diadems and headbands; making costumes; making various earrings; mixing perfumes; putting on jewellery; doing conjuring tricks; practicing sorcery; sleight of hand; preparing various forms of vegetables, soups and other things to eat; preparing wine, fruit juices and other things to drink; needlework; weaving; playing the lute and the drum; telling jokes and riddles; completing words; reciting difficult words; reading aloud; staging plays and dialogues; completing verses; making things out of cloth, wood and cane; woodworking; carpentry; architecture; the ability to test gold and silver; metallurgy; knowledge of the colour and form of jewels; skill at nurturing trees; knowledge of ram-fights, cock-fights and quail-fights; teaching parrots and nymph birds to talk; skill at rubbing, massaging and hairdressing; the ability to speak in sign language; understanding languages made to seem foreign; knowledge of local dialects; skill at making flower carts; knowledge of omens; alphabets for use in making magical diagrams; alphabets for memorizing; group recitation; improvising poetry; dictionaries and thesauruses; knowledge of metre; literary work; the art of impersonation; the art of using clothes for disguise; special forms of gambling; the game of dice; children's games; etiquette; the science of strategy; and the cultivation of athletic skills.

A courtesan who distinguishes herself in these arts
And who has a good nature, beauty, and good qualities
Wins the title of Courtesan de Luxe
And a place in the public assembly.

The king always honours her,
And virtuous people praise her . . .
Luck in love comes
From learning the arts . . .
Source: Vatsyayana Mallanaga, *Kamasutra*, translated
and edited by Wendy Doniger and Sudhir Kakar, Oxford:
Oxford University Press, 2002, 15–16.
By permission of Oxford University Press.

area concerned the three religious systems themselves – Brahmanism, Buddhism and Jainism – and the similarities and differences between them. The second was that of philosophy and logic. Many philosophical ideas had, by now, come to be crystallised into six major schools of thought, called *darshans* or 'points of view', and there were intense intellectual debates centred on their validity. The third area concerned grammar and epistemology. From Panini onwards we know of a number of grammarians who had been analysing, recording and classifying the vocabulary and grammar of Sanskrit, and other scholars similarly worked in the *Prakrit* languages. Besides the trinity of theology, philosophy and grammar, there existed much practical knowledge in areas as varied as medicine, music, agriculture, astronomy and mathematics. For a college or an academic institution to impart knowledge usefully it needs able and learned scholars who are not narrow or biased in outlook. At the Nalanda monastery, the highest standards were set by the Buddhist scholars and managers who comported themselves like true academics. Scholars of other faiths were always made welcome and given the opportunity to introduce and discuss intellectual issues. The style of teaching was unpedantic and non-didactic. It was very much in the form of dialogue or discourse, respectfully conducted through a series of propositions about the various qualities and theories of knowledge and their refutations, and great philosophers such as Dignaga, Asanga and Vasubandhu were teaching complex ideas at Nalanda (Sankalia 1972: 123–6). When the monastery received a large land grant, with rent eventually drawn from nearly a hundred villages, from the *Vaishnava*-oriented Kumaragupta I, its financial affairs and future became secure (Majumdar 1977: 453). It was to last until about 1205. The range of subjects taught, the quality of the academic staff, the very high standards demanded from the students, and the great renown of the institution within and outside India – all these factors enable us to describe Nalanda as a multi-functional college. Long before the Western world came to embrace the idea of a college as an institution and as a centre of instruction from the scholars of the Islamic world (Makdisi 1981: 224–80), everything that a college was ideally capable of was being realised at Nalanda. The size of the silent ruins of the Nalanda campus today allows us a glimpse of its glorious past.

The Vakataka achievement at Ajanta

Among the many great productions that have taken place over the years at the Royal Opera House, Covent Garden, London, perhaps the most enchanting one for connoisseurs of Indian arts must have been the Ajanta Ballet of 1923 (Keay 2001: 148–55). Performed by two of the twentieth century's greatest dancers, Anna Pavlova and Uday Shankar, the choreography of this ballet was based on the dance gestures of the fresco figures and images in the Ajanta caves of Maharashtra. The ballet was, in a sense, the culmination of a hundred years of the art world's fascination with the caves and their contents since they were 'rediscovered' by a hunting party of British soldiers in 1819 (Allen 2002: 128–34). What we see in Ajanta today is a mute but eloquent testimony to the beauty and vigour of the Buddhist art and architecture of India over a period of 700 years, between about 200 BCE and CE 500. The site of Ajanta was strategically placed at the crossing of merchants' and travellers' routes that ran alongside it, and Buddhist monks and monasteries were richly supported by that merchant class. Ajanta was only one, although the most noble, of the many Buddhist caves of this period. Here, cut through the living rock of the Deccan, around the bend of the River Waghora, are twenty-nine man-made caves (see Figure 8.3, which shows twenty-eight of these).

We can see the two main features of all such caves: the *Chaityas* and the *Viharas*. The *Chaitya* caves are huge preaching halls with horseshoe-shaped windows pierced above the entrance porches. The *Viharas* were like monastic cells, sometimes

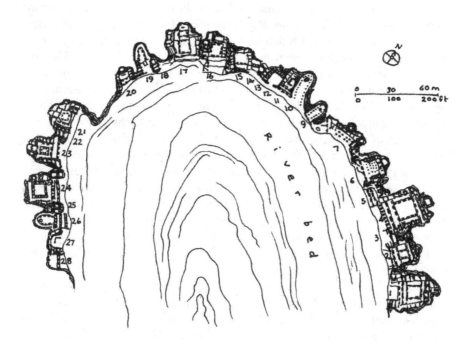

Figure 8.3 The plan of the Ajanta caves

Figure 8.4 An Ajanta façade

two or three storeys high. The great bulk of the excavation and construction had ztaken place during the first phase of 400 years after 200 BCE, but the most spectacularly creative portions were completed in the very short second phase of less than two decades in the second half of the fifth century CE. This later phase coincided with the reign of the Vakataka king Harishena (460–78), the last great patron of Ajanta.

The Vakatakas had been, for the most part, subsidiary feudatories of the Imperial Guptas, but with the waning of Gupta power they came to enjoy a brief, if truncated, spell of true independence and expansion of their territory. It was indeed good fortune for Indian art that Harishena was not only wealthy but also truly dedicated to further embellishing the Buddhist art at Ajanta. New caves were hewn, and it was chiefly on his orders that the most beautiful frescos came to be created, depicting both divine and human scenes and associated legends. More than the architecture, it is the Ajanta paintings that have captured universal imagination. These paintings, executed with masterly skill in the use of materials and colours, portray Vakataka court scenes and the *Boddhisattava* manifestation in its full glory, along with the narration of stories from the *Jatakas*. We can confidently assert that 'the architecture, paintings and sculpture that emerged and evolved in Ajanta (in the Gupta–Vakataka Age) were to leave an impression on all subsequent Indian, Central Asian and Far Eastern Art' (Sengupta 1993: 15).

Figure 8.5 Shiva and Parvati at Ajanta

Figure 8.6 Head of Bodhisattava at Ajanta

STUDY GUIDE

Key issues

- The differences in size and governance of Mauryan and Gupta empires.
- Samudragupta's relations with neighbouring kingdoms.
- Literary and intellectual works of originality.
- The importance of *Aryabhatiya* in the history of mathematics.
- Hindu-Buddhist synthesis at Ajanta.

Suggested readings

Dikshitar 1993; Dimock *et al.* 1974: 81–114; Doniger 2010: 375–8; Doniger and Kakar 2002: xxxix–xlv; Drekmeier 1962: 181–8; Mittal and Thursby 2004: 97–115; Sivaramamurti 1977: 172–7; Thapar 2002: 306–17.

INTERNET SELECTION

1)   All India Council for Technical Education: 'Ancient universities in India'. www.aicte-india.org/downloads/ancient.pdf
2)   D. Almeida and G.G. Joseph: 'Kerala mathematics and its possible transmission to Europe'. www.muslimheritage.com/article/kerala-mathematics-and-its-possible-trans
3)   Indian Review: 'How did Kalidasa's works reach Germany?' http://indian review.in/indian-literature-how-kalidasa-reached-germany
4)   San Diego State University: 'World history for us all: unit 5.1 – centuries of upheaval in Afro-Eurasia'. www.worldhistoryforusall.sdsu.edu/units/five/land scape/05_landscape1.pdf
5)   Sanskriti: 'Puranas in Indian Sanskriti part 1'. www.sanskritimagazine.com/ indian-religions/hinduism/puranas-in-indian-sansk

QUESTIONS FOR GROUP DISCUSSION

1)   How did Emperor Samudragupta shape the imperial policy of the Gupta Empire? In what ways did this policy differ from that of the Mauryas?
2)   By how much did *Vaishnavism* and *Shaivism* modify Vedic Hinduism?
3)   Examine critically the claim that the Gupta period was the 'golden age' of ancient Indian civilisation.
4)   What can we learn about Indian sexual mores during the Gupta period from the *Kama Sutra*?
5)   With reference to the religious history of India, what could have happened to the Ajanta caves before they were discovered in the early nineteenth century?

Notes

1   Compare and contrast the works by Majumdar and Pusalker 1954, Mukerjee 1958 or Tripathi 1999 with those of Thapar 2002 or Jha 2004. For a concise and balanced judgement, see Ray *et al.* 2000: 618–19 (p. 182).
2   The 'Nine Gems' included Kalidasa (dramatist and poet), Varahamihira (astronomer and mathematician), Harisena (the court poet who inscribed a poem on the Allahabad Pillar inscription), Vetala Bhatta (poet), Vararuchi (grammarian), Amarsinha (lexicographer), Kahapanak (astrologer), Dhanvantari (possibly a physician) and Shanku (architect) (p. 184).
3   To understand the general context of the mathematical work in one part of India – Kerala – for example, see Joseph 2010: 418–26 (p. 195).

9 Feudal north India

(*c.* CE 600–1200)

Timeline/Key Dates

CE 606–47	The reign of Harsha
CE 711	Arab invasion of Sind
c. CE 725–1018	Gurjara-Pratihara dominance in north India
c. 765–1155	Pala kingdom of Bengal
CE 9th century	The golden age of the city of *Kanauj*
CE 1000	The first of the Turco-Afghan raids into India under Mahmud Ghazni
CE 1026	Mahmud Ghazni desecrates the temple of Somanatha
CE 1192	Prithviraj Chauhan defeated by Muhammad Ghuri at the Second Battle of Tarain: Hindu power severely weakened in north India
CE 1197–1205	Bakhtiyar Khalji conquers Bengal and Bihar
CE 1206	The establishment of the Sultanate of Delhi

With the decline and fall of the Imperial Guptas came the demise of the imperial idea. It was in north India that this idea had had its greatest potency and diffusion through the great empires built over many centuries by outstanding personalities such as Chandragupta Maurya, Ashoka, Kanishka and Samudragupta; it was therefore in north India that the impact of its passing was most felt. From the middle of the sixth century onwards, large and small regional kingdoms were to dominate the north Indian political and state apparatus, and their authority was to last for several centuries (Maps 9.1 and 9.2). Individual kings dreamt about the attraction of pan-Indian control, and many of them, out of sheer egotism, adopted pompous titles, but just one of them, Harsha, in the seventh century, came near to realising such control, and that only for the duration of his reign. Regional kingdoms are one of the main characteristics of this era. In this chapter we are essentially concerned with political and socio-economic aspects of these north Indian kingdoms between the end of the Gupta era and the beginnings of the Sultanate of Delhi. It is in the last chapter of this book that we shall examine the cultural history of this period across the subcontinent as a whole, in relation to religion, literature and art.

The political narrative of the regional kingdoms and their dynasties are presented in the first section of this chapter. As feudalism, the beginnings of which we noticed during the Gupta period (Chapter 8), was now becoming an entrenched feature of the new regional states, the six centuries between CE 600 and 1200 may be described as the period of early medieval feudalism in north India.[1] The idea of kingship and strategies for dynastic survival in a politically competitive world are discussed in the second section. The third section is concerned with aspects of the economy and society that went hand in hand with feudalism. In pursuit of their parochial interests the feudal kingdoms dissipated their energies and gravely weakened themselves. The vital area of Sind was lost to the Arabs in the early eighth century, but it was from the early eleventh century onwards that the Hindu states would begin to face Turco-Afghan aggression, first in the form of plunder, and then by an existential threat to their survival. The demise of Hindu power in north India will be the theme of the fourth section of the chapter.

Our historical knowledge of feudal north India is dependent on a variety of interlocking interpretations drawn by historians, linguists, archaeologists and anthropologists. The historians and linguists have concentrated on numerous inscriptions that either speak for themselves or need interpreting, along with both contemporary historiographical material, such as the biography of the young king, Harsha, by the writer and poet, Banabhatta, and later historical sources. A rich analysis of such issues as feudalism, feudal attitudes and the nature of kingship itself is now also becoming increasingly available. Some of the literature of this era will be reviewed in Chapter 11. Perhaps one of the most fascinating contemporary works, *Si-Yu-Ki*, is a travelogue written by Hsuan Tsang, the famous Chinese Buddhist monk and pilgrim who travelled around India in the early seventh century. His text, which grips our imagination even today, contains all the rich details of life in the India of that era and must be classed among the great geographical and social documents of the ancient world.[2] We learn about the conditions in several towns and villages, the social structure, the economy and character of the people of India, their different laws and punishments, their religious events and their festivals. While all the details naturally will not meet our modern criteria for historical verifiability, this book is an indispensable asset for the historians of India. Further reference will be made to *Si-Yu-Ki* in Chapter 11. Another set of useful sources are the Islamic records that provide details of the invasion of Sind by the Arabs and the wars of aggression by Turco-Afghan warriors such as Mahmud of Ghazni and Muhammad Ghuri.

The dynastic landscape

A number of dynasties became engaged in fierce competition for control of north India during this period (Majumdar and Pusalker 1954: 60–95). It began in the middle of the sixth century, with the later Guptas struggling against not only the Hunas but some powerful regional families too. Independent kingdoms began to spring up in different places on the borders of the empire. Such kingdoms as *Valabhi, Gauda, Vanga* and *Kamarupa* asserted their autonomy at the margins of their empire, while the Gangetic heartland was itself subjected to undue strains. In the latter area two great dynasties were finally to supplant the weaker Guptas of the sixth century: the Pushyabhuti, based at Thaneshwar in *Sthanivishvara*, and the Maukhari, based at *Kanauj*, controlling the prime estate of north India, the *doab*, or the land between the rivers Ganges and Yamuna. A marriage alliance between the two royal houses was followed, however, by a war waged upon them by the kings of Bengal and Malwa, resulting in many tragic killings (Devahuti 1970: 56–81). Eventually, the Pushyabhuti prince, Harsha, became the ruler of both houses, with his capital in *Kanauj*, and controlled a substantial portion of the former Gupta territories. Although *Kanauj* now began its period of glory, it also was to become a bone of contention among many rival dynasties.

Harsha's kingdom

Harsha's kingdom lasted from 606 to 647. We know much about it from accounts left by two of his greatest admirers: his friend, courtier and biographer, Banabhatta, and the great Chinese traveller Hsuan Tsang. From their writings, along with his own literary works, we can discern that Harsha played three different roles: as a conqueror, an administrator and a man of intellect and culture. Leaving aside the last two roles for consideration later in this and the last chapter, Harsha was, first and foremost, a man of power whose conquests were wide and far-reaching. After he had unified the Pushyabhutis and the Maukharis and transferred the capital to *Kanauj*, giving him the overlordship of the Maukhari domains in the central Gangetic heartlands, he went on to conquer Bengal, Bihar, Orissa, Gujarat and Punjab. Although he met defeat on the River Narmada at the hands of the Chalukyan king Pulakeshin II, he came to be recognised as the master of what was termed 'the five Indies' (Beal 1884: Vol. 1, 213). An inscription at Aihole in Karnataka, although outside his realm, describes him somewhat exaggeratedly as the ruler of the whole of north India (Devahuti 1970: 93). On defeating his rivals, he too, like the Guptas, adopted the neighbourly policy of the *samanta*. So successful was this policy that even the powerful kings of Kashmir, Nepal and *Valabhi* counted among his tributaries. Tai Sung, the Tang emperor of China, was particularly friendly to Harsha, owing to the latter's closeness to Hsuan Tsang and extreme generosity towards the Buddhists (Devahuti 1970: 207–29). Shortly after Harsha's death in 647 his kingdom broke up. No one of comparable stature appeared on the scene, and the ensuing anarchy lasted for more than seven decades.

Yashovarman and Lalitditya

In the second quarter of the eighth century, power in north India came to be strongly contested by two great protagonists. One was Yashovarman, who acceded to the

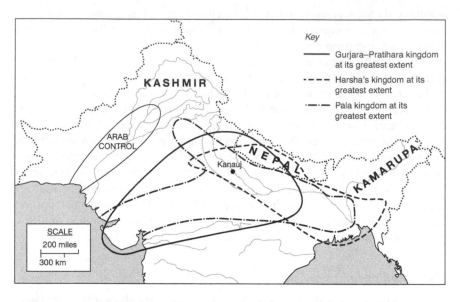

Map 9.1 Major post-Gupta north Indian kingdoms

throne of *Kanauj* after the post-Harshan anarchy and who ruled between about 725 and 752. Yashovarman's ambition was to conquer the whole of India, and his armies penetrated as far as Bengal. He embellished the city of *Kanauj* and established it as a symbol of his power and authority. He was a great patron of arts and letters, and at his court resided the famous playwright Bhavabhuti (Majumdar and Pusalker 1954: 308). Yashovarman, however, faced hostility from the other protagonist, Lalitditya Muktapida, the ruler of Kashmir between about 724 and 760. Much conflict resulted between them, and other parties also became involved in the fray: the Chinese, the Tibetans, the Arabs and the rising Rajput dynasty of Gurjara–Pratihara. Each of these groups had strategic agendas of their own, creating much confusion (Wink 1990: 44–5, 241ff.). Lalitditya was able to keep Yashovarman in check and deftly negotiated his way through the north Indian political and military morass, but ultimately he perished with his army while fighting the Tibetans in Sinkiang. With the passing of both Yashovarman and Lalitditya, north India became the scene of rivalry among three great dynasties of the Gurjara–Pratiharas of *Madhyadesha*, the Palas of Bengal and the Rashtrakutas of the Deccan. The first two, being part of the north, are discussed here; the Deccani Rashtrakutas of the south, although they also sought to control the north, will be examined in the next chapter.

The Gurjara–Pratihara kingdom

From the middle of the eighth century, the dominance over the Gangetic heartland of *Madhyadesha* became the ambition of two particular clans among a tribal people in Rajasthan, the land of desert hill forts and fastnesses (Figure 9.1). The two clans were those of the Gurjaras and the Pratiharas. They were both part of a larger federation of tribes, some of which later came to be known as the Rajputs.

There has been much controversy about the origin of the Rajputs, as to whether they were the descendants of the indigenous inhabitants of India or of the Central Asian Hunas (the White Huns) who had attacked north-west India during the later Gupta period (Chattopadhyaya 1994: 57–64; Thapar 2002: 418–21). It is difficult to arrive at a firm conclusion, but what we do know for certain is that the various Rajasthani tribes, including the Gurjaras and the Pratiharas, who were originally a nomadic and pastoral people, underwent a major social transformation between the late sixth and the ninth centuries CE. A process of assimilation into the Aryan Hindu fold gathered strength at this time throughout north India, and the Pratiharas particularly vaunted their martial qualities, in order to be recognised as the *kshatriya* Rajputs (Wink 1990: 281–3; Thapar 2002: 418–21). With their enhanced status, the Gurjara–Pratiharas made a significantly tactical move by transferring their capital from Bhilmal in Rajasthan to *Kanauj* in *Madhyadesha*, a move made as a result of the latter being perceived as both a spiritual and a geopolitical heartland. It also became clear that whoever held the city of *Kanauj* would enjoy a pre-eminence over north India. From this city it was easier to subdue most of the Gangetic valley. Control of this fertile and resource-rich region, with its busy water transport system and considerable trade, has throughout history been essential for raising revenue for all Indian rulers. Under Harsha (606–47), *Kanauj* had gained metropolitan status as both an imperial seat and a centre of north India's finest culture, but its star shone brightest after the Gurjara–Pratiharas made it their capital in 815 and held a brilliant court there, becoming the envy of their neighbours. A ninth-century Persian traveller, Abu Zayd of Siraf, wrote of numerous *brahman* 'poets, astronomers, philosophers and diviners' in *Kanauj* (Wink 1990: 290). The feudal court of the Gurjara–Pratiharas acted as a patron of learning and scholarship; the artistic and literary community from both within the kingdom and outside was encouraged and supported, as can be evidenced from **Excerpt 9.1** below.

Honouring their earlier commitment to defend India against all foreign invaders, the Gurjara–Pratiharas put strong pressures on Sind that had been captured by the Arabs in the early eighth century; in a contemporary Arab account from 851 about the greatest of the Pratihara kings, Raja Mihir Bhoja, we read that 'among the princes of India there is no greater foe of the Muslim faith than he [Bhoja]'; but there 'is no country in India more safe from robbers' (cited in Majumdar and Pusalker 1955: 32). In his tenth-century description of the land of al-Jurz (the Arabic name for Gujarat, part of the Pratihara kingdom) the Baghdad Arab writer Al-Masudi also expressed the Arabs' concern about the hostility of the Pratiharas towards them. He, however, exaggerated their strength, because the military realities on the ground were exceedingly complex. The Arabs were not the only enemy that the Pratiharas had to deal with. Their two Indian rivals, the Palas and the Rashtrakutas, were far more dangerous, and did their utmost to deny them the monopoly of power in *Madhyadesha*. They did not succeed, however, because in

---

Excerpt 9.1 The promotion of scholarship and scholarly exchanges

From the advice given to his monarch by a great poet and pandit, Rajashekhara, who was based at the Gurjara–Pratihara court of King Mahendrapala, we can surmise that cultural activities were held in high esteem in the India of the ninth century CE.

A king should find an 'Association of Poets'. He should have a hall for the examination of poetical works. The scholars at his court should be satisfied and maintained at his court. Deserving people should be awarded rewards.

Exceptionally good poems or their authors should be properly honoured. A king should make arrangements for establishing contacts with scholars coming from other lands, and show honour to them as long as they stay in his dominions.

Source: M.A. Stein, *Kalhana's Rajatarangini*, New Delhi:
Motilal Banasidass, [1900] 1961, Book 1: 5, 7, 8, 10.
Read also A.L. Basham, *Studies in Indian History and Culture*, Calcutta: Sambodhi, 1964, 45–56.

---

the late eighth and ninth centuries six of the ablest Pratihara monarchs, particularly Bhoja (840–85), fought them to a standstill.

The Pala kingdom of Bengal and beyond

Bengal played a leading role in Indian politics between the eighth and the eleventh centuries. This was the age of the famous Pala dynasty, some of whose rulers were the ablest in ancient India. For nearly a century after Harsha's death in 647, Bengal had been subjected to much interference and disruption by its near and farther neighbours. The respite came in 765 with the election by the people of an able leader, Gopala, who was neither a *brahman* nor a *kshatriya*. The dynasty prospered under Gopala's successors, Dharamapala and Devapala. The Palas realised the importance of *Madhyadesha* in the Indian political world, and fought hard to gain power and influence there. Their main rivals, of course, were the Gurjara–Pratiharas and the Rashtrakutas, although with the latter there were useful marriage alliances. All three dynasties ultimately exhausted themselves in the triangular contest over *Madhyadesha* and *Kanauj*. However, the fact that the Palas were ever-present, asserting their right to reorder affairs to their advantage, meant that Bengal was no longer on the margins of the Indian polity.

Commerce and religion linked the fortunes of Bengal, Tibet and Nepal. There was also the desire for territorial power. The Palas were forced to pay attention to their northern frontier by keeping a wary eye on Tibetan aspirations. Nepal was the principal bone of contention between Tibet and Bengal. From the seventh century onwards, the Tibetan resurgence had begun to overawe Nepal, and for nearly two centuries Nepal remained within the political shadow of Tibet (Wink 1990: 258–9). At the same time, Nepal could not escape the Sanskritic influences and the Buddhist missionary work that continued to arrive from Bengal. Through Nepal also ran a major trade route between Tibet and Bengal. Although Nepal herself broke loose from Tibetan hegemony in 879, the general Tibetan domination was a fact of life that the Palas could not ignore. While Tibet maintained very close commercial and Buddhist links with Bengal, on a number of occasions her armies invaded Bengal and posed a major threat to the Pala supremacy. Some of

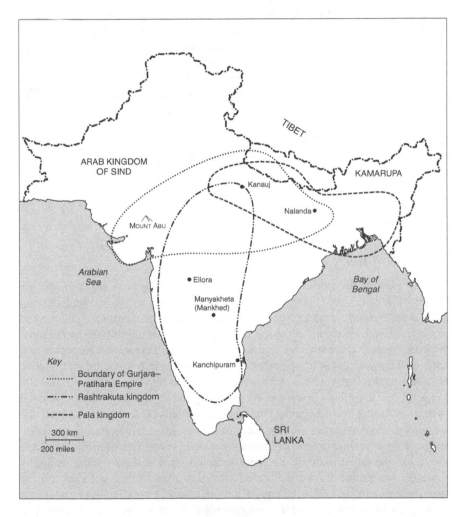

Map 9.2 The struggle for *Kanauj* among the three titans

the Tibetan sources, in fact, talk of a kingdom extending from Mongolia down to the mouth of the Ganges (Wink 1990: 266). It may be surmised that the Tibetans ultimately contributed to the collapse of the Palas.

Bengal under the Palas had interests in Assam, Burma and South East Asia too. Assam was known as *Kamarupa* or *Pragjyotisha*. Here there were many Mongoloid-featured people, who had migrated from such areas as Nagaland and Burma, and between CE 350 and 800 two Mongoloid dynasties ruled over Assam. However, just as in Bengal, the Sanskritisation process had been under way throughout the first millennium of the Common Era. Assamese monarchs had dominated Bengal until Dharamapala reversed the situation and extended the Pala suzerainty in Assam. The key factor that made Assam a vital area for the Pala monarchs was its strategic position, lying on the main trade routes between Bengal and China and between Bengal and Burma. Assam was the entry point into the north-east then, and is so today. Bengal's relations with Burma were both commercial and cultural in nature. Both kingdoms drew together, particularly whenever they faced challenges from the Chola kingdom of the south. The most important power in South East Asia during the heyday of the Palas was that of the Shailendra dynasty, which ruled over the Malay peninsula and the Indonesian archipelago, including Sumatra, Java, Bali and Borneo. The Shailendras were the followers of *Mahayana* Buddhism and derived their religious inspiration from Bengal, which was then the chief centre of the *Mahayana* and *Tantric* traditions. They had extensive diplomatic relations with the Palas, and there was much cultural traffic between Pala Bengal and the Shailendra Empire.

Pala suzerainty in Bengal and eastern India lasted until the end of the eleventh century, when they were succeeded by the Senas, who, in turn, lost out to the Turkish Khaljis in the thirteenth century.

Patchwork of Hindu kingdoms

Over a period of nearly two centuries, the three great kingdoms of the Gurjara–Pratiharas, the Palas and the Rashtrakutas of the Deccan had been fighting internecine dynastic wars for the control of the Gangetic heartland. This was to weaken them all. Politically speaking, by the year CE 1000, north India had become truly fragmented. There emerged nearly twenty north-Indian regional kingdoms, and none of them was going to be powerful enough to be able to mount an effective resistance to the Turco-Afghan intrusions that were to begin from the year CE 1000 onwards. A few of them deserve to be especially noted, and they may be grouped as follows. Of the two substantial Himalayan kingdoms of Kashmir and Nepal, the former was more important than the latter, and, as outlined earlier, its famous earlier leader, Lalitditya Muktapida, had briefly wielded power over *Madhyadesha* and *Kanauj* in the eighth century. Kashmir occupied, as it still does today, a highly strategic geographical zone that acted as a link route between India and the surrounding countries of Tibet, Nepal, China and Central Asia; it also lay along one of the great trade routes between these countries. Nepal had been intermittently in contact with India since before the Mauryan times but, as mentioned above, was greatly affected by stressful relations between Bengal and Tibet. Next, we have a group of Rajput kingdoms. In addition to the Gurjara–Pratiharas, a number of Rajput dynastic kingdoms were spread out across the northern plains and the central regions. In *Madhyadesha* and surrounding areas such as Bundelkhand, the successors to the Gurjara–Pratiharas were the dynasties of the Gahadavalas, Kalachuris and Chandellas. The last-mentioned was particularly lustrous in its glory. A tour around the Khajuraho temples, built under the patronage of the Chandellas, should be enough to dispel any notion that a small Indian kingdom in this period lacked wealth or flair. Further west, there was another cluster of four Rajput kingdoms, including those of the Chahamanas or the Chauhanas of eastern Rajasthan, the Tomaras of the Delhi region, the Parmaras of Malwa and western Madhya Pradesh, and the Chalukyas (not to be confused with the Deccan Chalukyas) or Solankis of Gujarat. The Chahamanas were the final bulwarks of defence against the later Turco-Afghan Ghurid invaders, and the tragic fate of their brave king, Prithviraja Chauhan, evokes great emotion among many Indians. Still further to the west, there was the kingdom of Sind, occupied by the Arabs since 711, but in the north-west and along the frontier area, and earlier extending deep into Afghanistan, there was also a small kingdom of the so-called Hindu Shahis. Originally they had been the rulers of Kabul and the surrounding area where there were many Buddhists too. It needs to be remembered that both Brahmanism and Buddhism had a strong presence in Afghanistan before Islam. By the time of the Islamic penetration of Afghanistan, the Hindu Shahi rulers had transferred to the Punjab; they were the first of the Indian rulers to be destroyed by the Turco-Afghan conquerors. At the opposite end of the map, in Bengal, the great Pala dynasty was nearing its end by the middle of

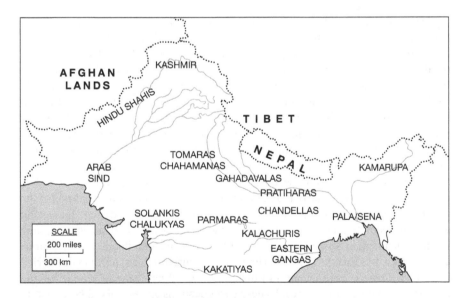

Map 9.3 Political fragmentation of north India *c.* CE 1000 to 1200

the eleventh century, and from 1080 the Sena dynasty was to control Bengal. Further to the north-east there existed the Assamese kingdom of *Kamarupa*, which, like Nepal, had not only come under the influence of Brahmanism and Aryanisation but was also facing pressures from the rulers of Bengal.

Kingship in the feudal age

Modern historical studies in India first began during the time when the British ruled India. It was therefore inevitable that Indian historians were profoundly influenced by many of the concepts, methods and terminologies that had been employed in the study of British and European history. One of the key concepts was that of feudalism. A detailed study of the characteristics of society in Western Europe after the fall of the Roman Empire had led Western historians to conclude that the collapse of overarching Roman imperial authority resulted in political fragmentation and the upsurge of feuds between various warlords and princes across Europe. This development created a new form of society, in which people in various localities learned to serve their local lords in order to get protection from them. The people in the countryside were particularly affected by the changing relationships. A very systematic analysis of the differences in modes of production and social relationships between this feudal age and modern industrial civilisation was made by the great nineteenth-century thinker Karl Marx. In European history, feudalism takes centre stage during the so-called Middle Ages (medieval). In India too, both the imperial British and the Indian historians, copying the pattern of European periodisation, divided its history into three parts: ancient, medieval and modern. However, this carried a certain political undertone, because while the ancient was conceived as the golden age of Hindu culture and civilisation and the modern was equated with progressive Westernisation of India, the medieval tended to be dismissed as the backward era of absolutist Muslim rulers, with perhaps the exception of the reign of Emperor Akbar (1556–1605). This suited the political instincts of both the Hindu nationalist historians and their imperial British peers. It took many decades before a group of Indian historians, who had intensively studied the writings of Marx and other economic and social historians of Europe, challenged the prevailing periodisation. In their view, the medieval included the centuries of both Hindu and, later, Muslim kingdoms between the end of the Gupta period and the end of the seventeenth century. One of the most distinguished of these historians, R.S. Sharma, also provided both a strong theoretical framework and empirical evidence for the presence of feudalism in the context of Indian medieval history, particularly in relation to the post-Gupta Hindu kingdoms of the north. Although his thesis sparked a still-ongoing controversy, there is increasing agreement about its general validity. One of the most important elements explaining Indian feudalism, in Sharma's view, was related to kingship itself. Two questions are central to the issue: how did the Hindu royal dynasties of the north in this period legitimise themselves in the eyes of their subjects? What were their political and economic strategies for survival? These two questions are examined here first, to be followed by a brief discussion on the debate about feudalism.

Kingdom formation and dynastic legitimation

A great variety of regional kingdoms flourished in this era. They arose for a number of reasons (Chattopadhyaya 1994: 17ff; Chattopadhyaya 1995: 332–5; Ludden 2002: 47–50). Quite often, those whose ancestors had originally received land grants from a previous ruler broke loose from the existing kingdom and formed new polities. On certain occasions, as utility lands were being increasingly wrested from forested terrain, new territories emerged under new names, with local chieftains sometimes assuming a dominant role and, sometimes, forming alliances with existing kingdoms. The forest-dwellers, who normally lived in a pre-state situation, were being increasingly drawn into the processes of state formation through interaction with sedentary peasant societies, thereby fostering a new state. Once a kinship group or a clan acquired power over a defined territory and control over the economic resources of that region, then it was not too difficult for its power-holders to initiate the process of forming a new state. In practically all the states the caste system was to retain its grip wherever Brahmanic influence remained pervasive (Ghoshal 1955: 231–9). This meant that the kingdom model, based on the girder of the *brahman–kshatriya* alliance, became the standard for all states. The boundaries of kingdoms never remained static, because the ambitions of their rulers led to either the expansion or the diminution of their territories, depending upon their capabilities. Nevertheless, there was an enduring association of a particular kingdom with a distinct geographical or cultural zone. The dynasties that controlled them had, in some cases, a long and distinguished lineage, but a majority emerged out of their feudatory status (Thapar 2002: 444–5). It is of course a mistake to assume the continuity of a kingdom merely because a branch lineage bearing the name of the original royal family appears in its genealogical records. Taking an example from south India, the family name Chalukya, for example, was applied to three sets of dynasties, but it would be far-fetched to imagine that the Chalukyas of the eleventh century were the controllers of the same territory ruled by the Western Chalukyas of the seventh and eighth centuries.

Generally speaking, most Indian kingdoms of this period were hierarchical in nature. Harsha's kingdom was a case in point. The legitimacy of the political sovereignty of his kingdom was derived from the concepts articulated in such famous texts as the *Upanishads*, the *Mahabharata*, the *Arthashastra* and the *Manusmriti*, written before the fourth century CE, or more recent texts such as *Katyayanasmriti* (*c*. CE 400–600), *Haritasmriti* (*c*. 400–700) and Kamandaki's *Nitisara* (*c*. 400–600), which contained useful advice on kingship (Devahuti 1970: 111–24, 129–35). Of great importance was the concept of *dharma*, the moral law. There might be different types of kings and conquerors – righteous, greedy or plain demonic – but they were all obliged to follow *dharma*. The king, however, had a powerful tool at his disposal, which was the threat of *danda*, or punishment. Both *dharma* and *danda* were the backbone of kingship, but successful kingship also depended upon the close alliance of the *brahman* and the *kshatriya* (Thapar 2002: 120–1, 128–9, 148–9). Most kings were genuinely *kshatriyas* or contrived to be so; however, the legitimacy of their power also rested on the *brahman* support mechanism. Once secured, that power became real, and exercised through a variety of means, including bureaucracy. The rulers could control taxation and maintain large centralised armies. The land grants, made either to the *brahmans* or to the feudal vassals, reduced the king's actual control over land, but did not affect his ultimate exercise of sovereignty. Thus, a ruler such as Harsha continued to exercise real control, even while devolving power over many of their lands to their subordinates.

Each new dynasty wished to acquire full legitimacy in the eyes of the others. The case of the Gurjara–Pratiharas provides a good example of the extraordinary lengths taken to achieve this. Originally a nomadic and pastoral people, the Gurjaras consciously underwent a major social transformation between the late sixth and the ninth centuries by assimilating into the Aryan fold, relinquishing pastoralism and taking up agriculture. The Pratiharas became specialised in military skills, and demonstrated their prowess by keeping a wary check on the Arabs who had captured Sind in 711. They became the dominant partner. To call themselves *kshatriya*, they first underwent, in 747, a major purification ceremony before a great sacrificial fire on Mount Abu, in the presence of *sadhus*. This made them 'fire-born' *kshatriya* Rajputs (Wink 1990: 277–81, 291–3). The Pratihara status among the monarchs of north India rose greatly from then on. The symbolic ceremony on Mount Abu was only one of the ways of legitimising their power and social status. Another was keeping a record for posterity. This was achieved by claiming genealogical links with the most ancient recorded *kshatriya* families, forging marriage links with the existing members of such families, granting lands to the *brahmans* as an act of piety, and registering such facts in *vamshavalis*, which were the histories of ruling families, or the *charitas*, which were eulogies of particular kings. It could be said that, to a certain extent, the genealogical pedigrees thus constructed by the Pratiharas were purposefully fabricated, intended to enhance their royal status and obliterate their own pastoral and nomadic origins from popular memory.

The mandala and the samanta

Inter-state relations among the Indian states of that period, like those of Harsha, were organised on the principle of what is generally called a *mandala*. This principle, articulated in the *Arthashastra* of Kautalya and the *Nitisara* of Kamandaki, presupposed a circle or orbit of states around any one kingdom; the circle normally consisted of twelve states, including the dominant kingdom. Starting with the nearest state and moving outwards, the five states with shifting allegiances in front of the kingdom were presumed to be the enemy, the friend, the friend of the enemy, the friend of the friend, and the friend of the friend of the enemy. Similarly, at the rear of the kingdom, again in the order of location, would be positioned the rearward enemy, the rearward friend, the friend of the rearward enemy, and the friend of the rearward friend. Somewhere in the orbit, but fairly close to the kingdom, as well as to the enemy, there was posited an intermediary state; finally, a neutral state was situated somewhere well beyond the territory of all the other states. Although a theoretical construct, bearing only a notional relationship to events 'on the ground', the *mandala* principle allowed 'political elites to make sense of the shifting events of their political world and to formulate theories of "diplomatic action"'.[3] It was evidently enunciated on the basis of a common-sense observation of the political state system in post-Vedic India. The kings were encouraged to be active participants of the *mandala* by adopting certain key strategies at appropriate times. These would include making an alliance, declaring a war, being neutral, preparing for attack without declaring a war, seeking protection from another state, or making use of a 'double policy', which was making peace with one and waging war against another. Each king had to try to secure his position in the *mandala* by adopting one or other of the six strategies. Headstrong kings, such as the great Chalukyan ruler in the south, Pulakeshin II, simply went for total domination of their *mandala* by being always aggressive or adopting aggressive stances, until in the end they dominated wholly for a while or were then themselves consumed by a great defeat, as Pulakeshin himself was. Wiser rulers, such as Harsha, followed in the footsteps of the great Gupta monarch Samudragupta, who won many conquests but never exulted over the vanquished. These rulers normally created the *samantas*, those defeated peers who continued to maintain their dignity and honour even as they became lesser tributaries paying homage to the conqueror (as mentioned in Chapter 8). Harsha's *mandala* became a less intimidating circle of states for him, because it consisted of friendly *samantas* or *maha-samantas* who acknowledged him as paramount sovereign (Devahuti 1970: 152–4).

However benign the concepts of *mandala* and *samanta* may appear to us, they were essentially linked to the principle of hierarchy that governed the Hindu monarchy from the time of the Guptas onwards. A twelfth-century manual of architecture from Gujarat, the *Aparajitaprccha*, goes into great detail about what a palace of a mighty king who headed a *mandala* of many minor kings and *samantas* should look like. Such a palace, located in a square, walled city, would have principal gateways, archways, watch towers in the shape of curved chariots, columns of glory for flying banners, ornamented pillared pavilions, ornately sculpted roof and walls, and a throne room with canopy draped with white silk and ornamented with precious stones. Rows of elephants, horses and men surrounded the pedestal upon which the throne was mounted (Inden 2006: 136–7). The massed ranks of aristocrats surrounded the king.

Political and economic strategy behind land grants

We observed in the previous chapter that the Imperial Guptas had increasingly followed the ancient practice of donating state land as grants to *brahmans* or to some of their officers. The programme of land grants accelerated during the post-Gupta centuries, and the royal dynasties saw in it a means of demonstrating their power and authority. Specific evidence is available for Harsha's land grants to *brahmans* or religious institutions from just a few inscriptions, along with the references in *Harsha-charita* or *Si-Yu-Ki*; one of his religious endowments was a donation of 100 villages of 1,000 ploughs each to *brahmans* (Devahuti 1970: 169). Such a grant, known as the *agrahara*, meant that the *brahmans* and/or religious institutions, such as Buddhist monasteries or Hindu temples, often acquired both revenue and judicial rights over the peasant cultivators on their newly granted lands. Secular land grants to royal officers and various grades of *samantas* also came to be adopted by post-Gupta rulers, partly owing to the relative decline of the monetary economy in this period. Historically, there had been a continuing argument among the political and social thinkers of India as to whether the king had the sole right of ownership of all land, in his kingdom or merely the entitlement to collect taxes; nevertheless, during the medieval period, the king was assuming a clearer right of ownership of land, and in many cases new interests in land were created by him. The general assumption was that all waste land or uncultivated terrain was state property and kings could confer those lands upon whom they pleased. During his travels through Harsha's kingdom, Hsuan Tsang observed that royal land was divided into four categories assigned to four items of expenditure, namely expenses relating to government and state worship, endowments to ministers, rewards to persons of great ability, and charity to various faiths and sects. Land was generally measured in terms of ploughs, drawn by a given number of cattle, to till a certain amount of acreage. Therefore, when the kings donated their income from land they declared the extent of arable territory in plough measures. A minor *samanta* in Harsha's time would be entitled to an average village of 1,000 plough units, or 1,333 acres of land (Devahuti 1970: 203). Different conditions applied to different beneficiaries: some were granted outright gifts with all the assets of the land, including peasants, as in **Excerpt 9.2** below; others could enjoy the revenue but had to pay a land tax; while yet others were expected to provide a certain amount of service.

From the perspective of the medieval royal authority, one of the main advantages of land grants was that the state did not have to bear the responsibility of collecting taxes throughout the countryside by its revenue officers and then disbursing them in cash or kind. Those who received the grants – the *brahmans*, powerful soldiers, administrators, educational institutions or temples – were now responsible for collecting dues from peasants or workers under their charge. On the other hand, the cultivator's rights often came to be adversely affected. The bestowal of ownership rights on those who received the land grants could result in the appropriation of former ownership rights; established tenants could be evicted and replaced by new. The creation of so many landed intermediaries meant a diminishing share of his own produce for the cultivator (Ray *et al.* 2000: 443–4). However, there can be no doubt that both religious and secular land grants during these early medieval centuries provided a major boost to the growth of feudalism and a feudal mentality in north India.

The debate on feudalism

Despite various dissenting views among historians, the inscriptions of the period provide strong evidence of the way feudalism linked the states with their

Excerpt 9.2 A land grant in Bengal

Thousands of land grants have been found recorded on copper plates all across India. It was an old tradition, but the bulk of the evidence comes from the Gupta and post-Gupta centuries. The inscriptions are engraved on one or more plates of copper varying in size, between 6 and 20 inches long. The plates were prepared with great care in order to protect the writing from damage or wear and tear. Often the edges were raised to prevent the plates from rubbing together, and sometimes the outer plates or faces were left blank. Multiple plates were bound by one or two rings inserted through holes in the plates. As many as a dozen plates could be found joined, carrying as much as 200 pounds of weight. A typical inscription had a preamble that included an invocation, the place of issue, the grantor's name and ancestry, address. This was followed by the specification of the gift, names of the grantee(s), the purpose of the grant and the reason for it. There would be a word or two of exhortation to respect the grantor's command. The names of people witnessing the grant would also be recorded. The following partial extract is a typical example.

[T]he prosperous Rajabhanja Deva, of the earth-conquering race inhabiting Kotta . . . says greetings to the princes of the earth-conquering race.

Bounded by the suburbs of the northern divisions and appertaining to the estate of Brahmanavasati is the village denominated Brahmanavasati (also); this village as far as its boundaries are hitherto known bestowed by us (in gift) for his merit to the generalissimo named Buddha, son of Mundi Samanta, free of all rents and encumbrances and by means of this copper plate edict. So long as there are virtuous men on earth, this must be observed by you, princes of the earth-conquering race . . .

Source: Quoted in Niharranjan Ray *et al.*, *A Sourcebook of Indian Civilization*, Delhi: Orient Blackswan Private Limited, 2000, 446.

economies. Feudalism would long remain a persistent factor in the shaping of Indian society and its mindset, although its characteristics would undergo much transformation in succeeding centuries. Karl Marx described feudalism as the precapitalist stage of development in the social and economic history of Europe. It was a stage in which the mode of agricultural production was based on the relationship between the lord and the peasantry. In this relationship the peasants owed the lord labour service for being allowed to till the soil and eke out a subsistence living. They also had to accept extensive judicial powers over their lives as a measure of protection by the lord. Historians have also debated over feudalism as a method of maintaining order at a time, particularly between the tenth and the fourteenth centuries in Western Europe, when public institutions were in a state of crisis and flux. In that situation, private relationships had become crucial, and one of the key manifestations of this relationship was the arrangement by which a tributary lord attached himself to a liege lord for protection through homage, tribute and military service.

Whichever way feudalism may be understood, it was essentially 'a system based primarily on the exploitation of the peasantry', as Frank Williamson, a dedicated communist thinker of recent years, has put it (Williamson 1999: 85). One of the noted social features of any system of exploitation is the obsequiousness shown by the humble towards their superiors. R.S. Sharma has argued that the political, social and economic development of India during the period examined here can be characterised as feudal too.[4] He sees the subservience of the lower classes of people and their servile mentality as arising out of the oppression of their superiors. He traced this essentially to the decentralisation of royal power by the creation of a great number of new landlords who had been the main beneficiaries of land grants. The evidence for such grants, along with the varied immunities and perquisites for the beneficiaries, was clearly found in what was written in the charters of the grants. The necessity for grants had, according to Sharma, arisen out of the loss of public revenues through the decline of trade and debased coinage in the post-Gupta period. The grants, however, worsened the oppression of the humble by the newly empowered lords and feudatories. Evidence of many rural riots and the descriptions in the *Puranas* of general disorientation within contemporary society convinced Sharma that the old order of loyalties and certainties was breaking down in the post-Gupta centuries. The rise of the new Hindu religious and devotional movements reflected changes within society.

Sharma's thesis has not gone unchallenged. It has been argued that, far from being an age of political decentralisation, the post-Gupta period in fact witnessed a growth in state power through a continual series of state formations in the form of new regional kingdoms. The land grants were not a sign of the sovereign's weakness but a method of legitimising his authority, and a question may also be posed as to whether the land grants could be said to be responsible for the increase in the oppression of the peasantry, when in fact the peasant subjugations increased from the thirteenth century onwards under the Delhi Sultanate, which made comparatively few land concessions. It has also been pointed out that the decline of trade and the paucity of coinage have also been much exaggerated; different channels of trade were continually appearing as opportunities for traders, as will be noticed in the next section. Finally, there is the need to acknowledge that the conditions on the ground in the Indian and European countryside in that period were in fact very different. The fertility of land in India was greater than in Western Europe; nature permitted the Indian peasants to subsist at a much lower level of production than those in Europe, and the Indian peasants had always enjoyed a certain measure of freedom that was denied to the European peasants under the manorial system in medieval Europe.[5]

While the counter-arguments against the feudal thesis are increasingly being articulated on the basis of new research, there is still a core of evidence that lends support to the essentials of Sharma's analysis. Land was the critical resource for the potentates of a pre-modern society. Other resources included control over manufacturing and trade, but they could not match in importance the land factor. The inscriptions from our period, containing huge amounts of information about the nature of lands, the range of people receiving the grants, fiscal and judicial rights over taxes and rents, and a variety of contracts stipulating that the beneficiaries of grants could collect revenues and rents from the peasants while being released from the obligation to pay taxes themselves, amply illustrate the Sharma thesis. At a higher level of decision-making, large grants of land were conferred by monarchs to dynastic collaterals for maintaining princes within the orbit of their influence. The subordinate princes, as feudatories, bore certain responsibilities, for example, to raise levies for the king's armies, to consent to marriage alliances, or to attend court with appropriate pomp and pageantry. The king assured for himself a continuing check on these feudatories by creating titular posts as indicants of their place and status in the overall scheme of things. Of course, the feudatory princes became all-powerful in their own domains, enjoying luxurious lifestyles in their palaces and castles. They, too, in turn, created a subordinate layer of lesser feudatories, and in this way the feudal structure and power spread from our period onwards (Kondo 2002: 56–77; Thapar 2002: 444–5; Ali 2006a: 70–4). The magnificence of the famed courts of the Indian *maharajas* of later centuries derived directly from the feudal princely courts of this earlier period.

Aspects of northern economy and society

Agriculture

Notwithstanding the debate on feudalism and the condition of the peasantry, agriculture in the north remained robust and relatively prosperous, as attested by a number of sources. The late Gupta encyclopaedia and lexicon the *Amarakosha*, for example, has much information on the forests and gardens, as well as the trees and plants, of India (Majumdar and Pusalker 1954: 585–6). Another useful source is the travelogue of the Chinese pilgrim Hsuan Tsang. He mentions the cultivation of cereals such as rice and wheat, with the region of *Magadha* producing a most fragrant variety of rice called 'rice for grandees'; there were also rich and extensive orchards of delicious fruits such as mangoes, melons, plums, peaches, apricots, grapes, pomegranates, sweet oranges, apples, jackfruits and coconuts (Beal 1884: Vol. 1, 88–9). Another source, Banabhatta, mentions the fertility of the soil in Harsha's kingdom, and refers to plentiful crops of sugar cane, vines and a variety of beans. The yields were so abundant that whole cart-loads of fruits and vegetables were sent regularly to the nearest towns. At the same time, it has to be remembered that most peasants possessed very small parcels of land that had to feed their whole families. One interesting feature about the boundaries of fields was that they were established not only along the lines of natural obstacles but also according to mysterious landmarks that were kept a secret within the peasant family. Anyone who removed or displaced the landmarks was liable to severe punishment (Auboyer 2002: 66). For generating greater revenue from land, the Indian kings encouraged the sciences of agriculture and animal husbandry (Devahuti 1970: 201ff.). They also employed specialists to construct reservoirs for the regular supply of water. The state was meant to provide facilities for cattle-breeding and for controlling plant and cattle diseases. Then, as now, the more or less guaranteed and seasonally regular natural supply of water ensured a flourishing agriculture on the vast plains of north India, from the Punjab down to Bengal. The one limiting factor was that, with crops grown through undemanding labour, the north-Indian peasant was content with a minimal level of agricultural technology. An exception to this may be found in a dry region such as Rajasthan, where irrigation by wells and water-tanks was more common, and where evidence exists of a primitive form of technology prior to the Persian wheel (Chattopadhyaya 1994: 43–4). Whatever the level of technology, agricultural production continued to increase, partly as a result of the opening up of new lands through the land grants, and partly because of the availability of newly constituted peasant labour. This meant that there was an ample surplus for external trade.

Dimensions of trade

The fall of the Western Roman Empire and the disappearance of the flourishing trade with Rome meant a certain definite decline from the end of the fourth century in the value and volume of Indian international trade. One indicator of this was the paucity of metallic money from the late Gupta period onwards. That was certainly a time of turbulence, but it would be wrong to assume that international trade suddenly collapsed and society relapsed into ruralism. In fact, during this entire period, new prospects for long-distance maritime trade were emerging, and, almost until the beginning of the eleventh century, Indian international trade remained substantial. As far as the western Indian Ocean trade was concerned, it is worth noting that the Eastern Roman Empire had not fallen to the Huns or the Goths, and Greek and Byzantine mariners were now jointly venturing with Ethiopian traders in activating and promoting the Indian Ocean trade (Wink 1990: 47). Another major maritime power, in direct competition with Byzantium, was Persia. Before the rise of Islam, the pagan Arabs, Persian Zoroastrians and Persian Christians had all plied the trade routes of the Arabian Sea and the Persian Gulf under Persian suzerainty. However, with the sudden emergence of Islamic power after 622 and the spectacular defeat of Persia by the Arabs in 651, the new masters of the Indian Ocean were all now Muslim. This control enabled the Muslims to link the Indian markets with the Islamic world. From now on, for many centuries, the Arabs were to be the main controllers of north India's maritime connections with the lands to the west. A distinct imperial Arab Muslim identity had been built up by the Umayyad dynasty, which ruled the extensive Islamic Empire between 661 and 750. Under the Umayyads, Arabic became the standard language of administration and a uniform Islamic coinage was instituted. From their capital in Damascus, the Umayyads encouraged trade and enterprise throughout the Islamic world (Risso 1995: 14–15). With the capture of Sind in 711 the Arabs gained a most valuable piece of Indian territory. Sind had become extremely rich through its trading networks, and, although initially the Arab invaders had raided its vast treasures of gold and silver, they ensured that the commercial edge of the province was not blunted. The Umayyads lost power to the Abbasids in 750, and Baghdad became the new metropolis of the Islamic world. As the centre of Islamic power shifted from Syria to Iraq, the Persian/Arabian Gulf became the vital trade artery in the Islamic Empire (Wink 1990: 53ff.; Risso 1995: 15–16). Muslim mariners and merchants enjoyed a full monopoly over the Red Sea and Arabian Sea routes and a near monopoly in the Mediterranean, and they were to create an integrated Islamic trading system that would shape the global economy almost until the end of the Middle Ages. The products of India were in great demand throughout the Islamic world and, although India imported certain specialised commodities, the general balance of trade was tipped in her favour, which meant that she received large quantities of gold and silver bullion from the Muslim merchants. The gold *dinar* and the silver *dirhem* were the dominant currencies in the Abbasid Empire. Apart from Sind, the ports of Gujarat received and sent the imports and exports of north India. Gujarat, however, belonged to the southern kingdoms of either the Chalukyas or the Rashtrakutas, and Arab mercantile connections with the latter particularly will be reviewed in the next chapter.

Besides the oceanic trades, the land routes also continued to be used. According to Hsuan Tsang's testimony, the medium of exchange in trade consisted of such items as gold, silver, cowries and small pearls (Watters 1904: Vol. 1, 177–8). India–China land trade flourished as well as it had in the post-Mauryan centuries, particularly during the period of the Chinese Tang dynasty, and Chinese silk was always highly prized. It may be noted, however, that both the Chinese and the Indians suffered as a result of the Byzantines surreptitiously learning the art of cultivating silkworms (Wink 1990: 51, 221). Fine steeds and horses were the main item of import from Central and West Asia (Devahuti 1970: 147).

The influence of overseas trade was felt in nearly every region of north India. In Kashmir, for example, tens of thousands of alloy coins have been found, providing evidence for a brisk trade with such people as the Soghdians. Kashmiri metal art objects from the ninth century have been found in far-off Scandinavia, and by the eleventh century there were Jewish and Muslim merchants trading in Kashmir. The Arab traveller Al-Idrisi wrote that in Kashmir there were places 'inhabited by people and merchants from all parts the world' (Wink 1990: 247). While the coinage of Kashmir might be debased, the great historian Kalhana talks of gold ornaments and gold hoards in his history of the region, the *Rajatarangini*. Bengal was another region of India from where much overseas trade was conducted. The evidence for such trade lies in large numbers of gold and silver coins found in a region that has no native gold or silver mines. The main sources of these precious metals were south China, Burma and South East Asia. The Pyu and the Pagan kingdoms of Burma, exporters of such valued minerals as gold, silver, amber and serpentine, along with the so-called 'goldbearing' sands from the Irrawaddy river basin, were at the centre of extensive networks of trade between Bengal, China and South East Asia. The commodities from Bengal included aloe-wood, pottery, rice and both fine and coarse textiles. A greatly extended range of commodities and products were available for export from different regions of India. Luxury items such as ginger, turmeric, cotton, coconuts, perfumes and indigo went hand in hand with items of daily usage, for example, wheat, pulses, sugar, salt and oil.

The extraordinary amounts of gold and silver bullion that flowed into India from abroad in exchange for the extensive range of her products were deposited in the vaults of the Hindu temples in both northern and southern India. It was this wealth that caught the attention of the Turco-Afghan warlord Mahmud of Ghazni, whose seventeen expeditions of loot began in the year 1000.

Urbanisation

One of the key arguments used for characterising our period as feudal has tradition-ally been the notion of commercial decline and deurbanisation. The historic towns and cities that had developed during the second phase of Indian urbanisation, between the sixth century BCE and the fourth century CE, appeared to have lost their vitality and importance from the Gupta period onwards. The principal reason for this was considered to be the drying up of the profitable Indian trade with Rome and the extreme dearth of coinage. Hsuan Tsang's observations of urban decay during his travels in the seventh century are generally cited as evidence of the increase in ruralisation (Chattopadhyaya 1994: 150–2). More recent research casts doubt upon the validity of this theory of decay. The epigraphic information concerning the mercantile classes, market centres, interest rates, merchant associ-ations and the rates of levies and cesses belies greatly the notion of commercial wane (Chattopadhyaya 1994: 131–47). On the other hand, whatever little that archaeology has yielded us from the post-Gupta sites has indeed confirmed a marked decay in urban architecture, particularly in north India. The historic cities of the earlier second phase, having grown from an epicentre, were located in the older imperial territories. They were centres of political power or of Buddhist patronage, with deep hinterlands and situated along the main trade routes. With the fading away of the imperial idea, the decline of Buddhism, the growing importance of the coastal areas and the opening up of new hinterlands in different regional kingdoms, it was inevitable that the older cities would suffer decay.

The decay of historic cities, such as *Pataliputra* and Taxila, was not a reflection of a malady affecting the very idea of urbanism in general. It did not prevent a new phase of urbanism in our period. In fact, it is this third phase of Indian urban-isation, along with the incorporation of subsequent Islamic notions of urbanism, that gave rise to the pre-modern towns and cities of the Indian subcontinent (see Map 11.1). It is true that archaeological confirmation is lacking, but we do have numerous regional inscriptional records. The methodology of interpreting these records has already yielded us fresh insights into the new phase of urbanism (Chattopadhyaya 1994: 162–5). First, we discover that the hierarchy of settlements, as symbolised by such terms as *grama, pura, nagara* and *mahanagara*, that we examined in Chapter 5, for example, did not change substantially, and the Indians of this period were perfectly aware of the differences in urban scale of, say, a *pura* settlement and a *nagara*. Second, the details specified in the charters of land grants give us a spatial context of the land that was being gifted: whether it was a purely rural space or a mixed rural–urban one. In the case of the latter, it would include such features as a market exchange point, residential quarters or manufacturing units. If these predominated in a kingdom's land grants, then that would allow us to determine the scale of urbanism. Third, the records tell us about the various types of exchanges and, indeed, guilds of merchants and craftsmen. The market exchange in north India was generally called a *hatta*, and in the south it was the *nagaram*. The presence of market exchanges implied an urban population density, and exchanges could meaningfully continue trade only in the context of urban centres. Both barter and money were in common use. Fairs too could only be held in some sort of urban centre, however small (Chattopadhyaya 1994: 172–8). Fourth, the inscriptions give us copious information about places of pilgrimage and temples. Our period is profuse with the northern- and southern-style regional temples, and royal patronages were continually creating new sacred spaces that drew in people from the hinterlands. People generally like to live near a great cathedral, a mosque or a temple, and so it was in this period too; the sacred spaces also represented the continuity of an older tradition of sacred towns from the very early centuries of the second phase of Indian urbanisation (Stein 1998: 123–5). In conclusion, therefore, we can say that, although the older towns and cities declined, the newer ones always arose, and some of these were to become even more bustling and busy during the following six centuries of the Sultanate and Mogul eras.

Caste and competition

The caste system became entrenched during this period, particularly among the Rajput kingdoms. In the north, as a whole, the idea of ritual ranking, with its neat categorisation of society into four *varnas* – the *brahmans, kshatriyas, vaishyas* and *shudras* – was generally accepted, although there was a great degree of competition by certain groups wanting a higher status for themselves. Just as the Gurjara–Pratiharas had been interested in status-seeking, many intermediate groups desired *kshatriya* status, and the presence of terms denoting various titles, such as *ranaka* and *thakkura*, in the inscriptions of kingdoms illustrates the nature of caste hierarchy (Thapar 2002: 462–3). Even among the *brahmans* there were demarcations. Thus, the Kanyakubja (*Kanauj*) *brahmans* were considered the most learned and most devout of their caste, while the untutored *brahmans* elsewhere, performing lower-grade rituals in temples, were granted little esteem. Among the intermediate groups were various categories of merchants, artisans or even semi-professional people such as scribes. The various grades of scribes, for example, came to be collectively known as the *kayastha* caste (Jha 2004: 196–8). All sought higher ritual status. With the increasing complexity of society and the growth of multifarious occupations, each *varna* contained many people who were involved in tasks that were far removed from the prescribed function of a *varna* member. The groups involved in a variety of occupations, the *jatis*, nevertheless strove to ensure for themselves as high a place as they could secure within the *varna* framework. The crystallisation of *jatis* was a tolerable process while the general Brahmanic society remained manageably small in terms of aggregate numbers, but it became far more complicated when, with the opening up of new lands for the expansion of agriculture, large groups of non-caste people were being exposed to Brahmanisation and Aryanisation. The result was that more and more such people, consigned to the lowest occupations, swelled the ranks of the *shudra* caste. Thereupon began a major shuffle within the *shudra* ranks; the more dynamic of them came to be known as *sat-shudras* or pure *shudras*, whose members were quite often upper-level merchants and peasant landowners, while those who performed the most menial and servile jobs, such as scavenging, or who were employed as bonded labour, were beyond the pale and became part of the untouchable groups. Their large numbers ensured the relative comfort of all those above them, and this helped to give feudalism a strong lease of life (Chattopadhyaya 1995: 330). In the final analysis, feudalism was, and remains, an oppressive system of exploitation.

Sati: a gender horror

It was during this period that we begin to come across a great number of cases involving the practice of *sati*, the sacrifice of widows by burning in the funeral pyres of their dead husbands. An important piece of evidence from this time and later is the presence of so-called *sati* memorials, in the form of pillars and stones that contain brief inscriptions praising the dead widows for their sacrifice (Pal 2008: 96–7). Historians have provided a number of explanations for this gruesome custom. First, the term *sati* itself is closely associated with Sati, the consort of the god Shiva in the Hindu religion and mythology. She was hurt when her father did not treat Shiva with due courtesy or respect, leading her to an act of self-immolation. Although technically Sati's sacrifice could not be described as an act of *sati*, since the god Shiva was impervious to death, the episode is always quoted as an illustration of a wife's love for and devotion to her husband. From their childhood, the vast mass of Hindu women before the nineteenth century were brainwashed into accepting the story of Sati and Shiva as literally true. When this is reinforced by the stories of Sita, Rama's wife in the *Ramayana*, going through the fire more than once or the burning of widows in the *Mahabharata*, a powerful message is conveyed to Hindu women, which is that the heavenly award would go to a wife who is solely devoted to her husband and burns with her dead husband's corpse in the funeral pyre. This has to be considered the main reason for quite voluntary acts of self-immolation by misguided but pious Hindu women (Altekar 1959: 136–7). These women were immune to arguments opposing the practice.

Most of the Hindu religious texts, including the *Rig-Veda*, have little to say about the custom itself, but these texts and their commentators, like the law-giver Manu or, later, Medhatithi, not only give out mixed and confused messages about women in general, but adopt a highly sexist and selective approach to the female gender (Bose 2000: 23–4). The widow, for example, has to put up with a host of disadvantages and restrictions that are not meant to apply to widowers. It was considered natural that a man who had lost his wife should be able to remarry, while for a widow to remarry was shameful. For a young widow to remarry was considered particularly scandalous. The widow's life was to be one of unending misery, privation and seclusion. The patriarchal feudal family generally showed little sympathy for the plight of a widow in the household, and she was thought of as an economic burden. On the other hand, in a place such as Bengal, where the widow was entitled to her rightful share of inheritance, the greed of those around her could not bear to see her enjoy this right (Pal 2008: 99). It was no wonder, then, that a combination of ideology and family pressures helped to push the widows to

Excerpt 9.3 Bana's attack on *sati*

The poet Bana (Banabhatta), who lived during the reign of Harsha in the seventh century CE, was an ardent opponent of the practice of sati. In his biography of Harsha, the Harsha-charita, *he records the grief of the future king's mother, Yasomati, on the deathbed of her husband, King Prabhakavardhana, and her subsequent plunge into the fire, despite the entreaties of Harsha. In another of his works, the* Kadambari, *he condemns unreservedly, and very rationally, the custom; he thinks of suicide as sinful and he gives many instances of women, such as Rati, Kunti, Uttara and Dusala, who did not commit self-immolation.*

To die after one's beloved is most fruitless. It is a custom followed by the foolish. It is a mistake committed under infatuation. It is a reckless course followed only on account of hot haste. It does no good whatsoever to the dead person. It does not help him in ascending to heaven; it does not prevent him from sinking into hell. It does not at all ensure union after death; the person who has died goes to the place determined by his own karma; the person who accompanies him on his funeral pyre goes to the hell reserved for those who are guilty of the sin of suicide. On the other hand, by surviving the deceased, one can do much good both to oneself and to the departed by offering prescribed oblations for his happiness in the other world. By dying with him one can do no good to neither.

Source: From Bana's *Kadambari*, adapted slightly from the original English translation, in A.S. Altekar, *The Position of Women in Hindu Civilization*, Delhi: Motilal Banarsidass, 1959 (2nd ed.), 124–5.

volunteer to burn themselves rather than suffer the indignities of widowhood. It has also been suggested that the *sati* custom began within the military groups of people who formed the *kshatriya* caste of warlords and bureaucrats. The Roman historian Strabo mentions that Alexander the Great's soldiers witnessed the self-immolation of a widow of one of the Indian commanders who had been killed by them. The custom became widespread in Kashmir, perhaps for the reason that Kashmir had to face the onslaughts of invasions by the Central Asian Scythians, among whom the tradition of *sati* had also been prevalent (Altekar 1959: 127). In another part of India, Rajasthan, the Rajputs developed a version of *sati*, the *jauhar*, when they faced continuing onslaughts from Turco-Afghan invaders from the eleventh century onwards. The *jauhar*, or mass suicide, however, involved the entire family in the event of a household facing an intrusion of an outsider, not just the widow. Unfortunately, even after the Turco-Afghan invasions had ceased, the practice of *sati* continued in places like Rajasthan and Bengal, for no other reason than the misogyny of the patriarchy.

The fact that, despite the continuity of tradition, the overall number of *sati* cases remained relatively low in proportion to the vast population of the country suggests to us that there were people who opposed the practice (see **Excerpt 9.3** above), and that most Hindu widows were far too intelligent to passively accept their fate. Finally, it was in 1829 that the East India Company took stern steps to eradicate the practice. Yet, even as late as 1987, it was reported that an eighteen-year-old woman, Roop Kanwar, died in the funeral pyre of her twenty-four-year-old husband (Bose 2000: 21–32). This was an exceptional case, because the practice has now died out.

Arab and Turco-Afghan invasions of the north

Muslim contacts with India first came about through trade, not invasions. Long before the rise of Islam, Arab and Persian mariners and traders had been engaged in Indian Ocean commerce. Their conversion to Islam made no difference to their trading activity in India. It was initially in order to protect their trade from pirates operating in the waters off the Indus river delta that the first Muslim invasion of a part of India, Sind, took place in CE 711 under the military forces of the Arabic Umayyad Empire, based in Damascus. The Arabs successfully conquered Sind, but were unable to expand further into India. Sind remained their sole possession. The second Muslim invasion of India came in CE 1000, when Mahmud, the Turkish ruler of Ghazni in Afghanistan, made the first of his many lightning strikes against the kingdoms of north India. With this initial Turco-Afghan intrusion by Mahmud there began a chain of invasions from Afghanistan that lasted for centuries. The end result of these invasions was the creation of a Muslim India.

Sind under the Arabs

The successful conquest of Sind, by land and sea, was the work of a dynamic young Arab commander, Muhammad bin Qasim, who took orders from his patron, the Umayyad governor of Iraq, Al-Hajjaj. A relatively small and highly mobile naval task force, equipped with some deadly siege artillery, enabled Muhammad first to take Debal, the commercial port. From there, after crossing the River Indus, he marched upon Brahmanabad, where, in a major battle, the Hindu king, Dahar, was killed. Muhammad then married his widow, Rani Ladi. With Lower Sind taken, Muhammad moved up the Indus, towards Upper Sind, and eventually reached Multan. Sind had thus become part of the Umayyad-controlled Islamic Empire. With the fall of the Umayyads in CE 750, however, Arab authority in Sind came under the control of the Abbasids of Baghdad. The Arabs retained control of the province until CE 1025, when Mahmud of Ghazni wrested it from them.

The native population of Sind consisted of both Hindus and Buddhists. Differing religious beliefs separated them to a certain extent, but the main tension between them was caused by dynastic rivalries. The Buddhists felt aggrieved that Dahar and his father, Chach, had usurped the throne from the Buddhist Rai dynasty. The Buddhists and the Hindus also had divergent socio-economic interests in Sind. Most of the inter-regional and maritime trade was in the hands of the Buddhists in the urban centres of Lower Sind, while Hindu farmers and villagers were predominant in Upper Sind. After the invasion, Arab commercial and financial interests were basically focused on Lower Sind, where the Buddhists had the greatest influence. With power, the Arabs secured an edge over the Buddhist merchants, and the latter found it increasingly hard to remain competitive in business. The Buddhists were indeed facing a covert form of discrimination by Arab merchants against non-Muslims. Feeling a sense of relative deprivation, they more than likely concluded that a simple process of conversion to Islam was the most convenient and practical route to retaining their families' fortunes and well-being. This conversion was a steady protracted process rather than a single event, but by the end of the tenth century CE there was hardly any trace of Buddhism left in Sind. In contrast, the Hindus of Sind remained a resilient community, with their faith protected by the seclusion of the villages of Upper Sind that held no particular attraction for the Arabs (Avari 2013: 26–8). The Hindus remained a vital section of the Sind population until the partition of 1947.

The Arab religious policy in Sind was relatively liberal. According to the instruction issued by Al-Hajjaj to Muhammad bin Qasim, the enemy was to be killed, not because he was a non-Muslim but because he was offering military resistance. The choice was not between Islam and the sword, but Islam and the so-called *jizya*, a form of poll tax (Maclean 1989: 40). The liberalism of Muhammad bin Qasim was a product of contemporary thinking regarding the treatment of conquered people. From the second quarter of the seventh century, the Arabs had begun a series of military campaigns that eventually established their domination over the Middle East and north Africa. A new social and cultural order, based on the principles of Islam, was forged in the conquered territories. The early Muslim philosophers and theologians conceived of the ordered world as the 'House of Islam' (*dar al-islam*), which, according to them, was their world of peace. Those who lived beyond that world lived in the 'House of War' (*dar al-harb*), or 'foreign territory'. From the earliest period of their own internal struggles within Arabia, and across many centuries, the believers battled to bring the infidels into the 'House of Islam'. Only defeats, sheer exhaustion or internal decay could stop them. From the very beginning, however, the promoters of the Islamic Empire faced a major problem, which was how to reconcile their aspirations with the realities of the world. It is important to appreciate that, however impassioned the religious rhetoric behind the projection of the Islamic Empire might have been, Muslim leaders and men of action on the ground were never entirely swayed by it and, more often than not, exercised their authority either pragmatically or rationally. For example, the arrangements and treaties made with their potential enemies created for Islamic jurists a new legal category of the 'House of Truce' (*dar al-ahd*, or *dar as-sulh*), which meant that an Islamic ruler could be reconciled to a ruler, a people or a state that was not Islamic but was at peace with him (Wink 1990: 197). Over the question, too, of the treatment of unbelievers, the scriptural injunctions were flexibly interpreted by most Muslim rulers. Originally, the status of the 'people of the book' (*ahl al-kitab*) was granted to the Jews and the Christians, and they were therefore 'protected subjects' (*ahl adh-dhimma*). However, since the same status had been earlier granted to a people called the Sabians, most Muslim rulers appreciated that the Zoroastrians of Iran and the Hindus of India, both people with their own extensive scriptural heritages, should also qualify for that status. Such flexibility was displayed by the conqueror of Sind, Muhammad bin Qasim, in his dealings with the various power groupings in that province (Avari 2013: 25–6). The so-called Brahmanabad Settlement in **Excerpt 9.4** below explains this very clearly.

The relative liberalism demonstrated above did not, however, create a safe environment for political life in an Islamic setting. Indeed, to our own day, Muslim politics has remained a personally hazardous undertaking for those who take part in it. The promoters and rulers of the Islamic Empire were often victims of circumstances caused by internal squabbling and civil wars. These disturbances were called *fitna*, and they often resulted in horrendous dynastic and family killings. The idea of a constitutional monarchy remained an alien concept in such an atmosphere. Many a good Muslim ruler in history was a victim of *fitna*, leading to his destruction. Just four years after his conquest, Muhammad bin Qasim himself became such a victim and forfeited his life (Wink 1990: 206ff.). It is therefore important not to exaggerate the absolutism of medieval Islamic rulers. In the control of Sind by the Arabs for nearly four centuries we have a good example of both the power and the limitations of those rulers.

The background to the Turco-Afghans

After having defeated the Persian dynasty of the Sasanians, the Arab armies sped towards the northern and north-eastern frontiers of Iran. Beyond these frontiers lay the terrain of the nomadic Turkic-speaking tribes of Central Asia, which had, throughout their history, faced constant harrying over land and land rights from their various neighbours, enemy confederations and, above all, from the Mongols. Migrating into Iran and Afghanistan had been their traditional response; however,

Excerpt 9.4 The Brahmanabad Settlement

The following is an exchange of correspondence between Al-Hajjaj, the reputedly cruel Umayyad governor of Iraq, and Muhammad bin Qasim, the first Muslim invader of India. In this exchange the latter tells the governor what the Hindus of Sind want and hope for; the response of the governor provides a good example of early Islamic liberalism.

The Hindus said: 'In this country, the existence and prosperity of towns depends on the Brahmins, who are our learned men and philosophers. All our affairs, on occasions of mirth or mourning, are conducted and completed through their medium, and we agreed to pay the tax, and to subject ourselves to scorn, in the hope that everyone will be permitted to continue in his own religion. Now, our temples are lying desolate and in ruins, and we have no opportunity to worship our idols. We pray that our just commander will permit us to repair and reconstruct our . . . temples . . .'

Governor Al-Hajjaj replied: 'With regard to the request of the chiefs of Brahmanabad about the building of . . . temples, and toleration to religious matters, I do not see (when they have done homage to us by placing their heads in the yoke of submission, and have undertaken to pay the fixed tribute for the Khalifah and guaranteed its payment) what further rights we have over them beyond the usual tax. Because after they have become dhimmis we have no right whatever to interfere with their lives or their property. Do therefore permit them to build the temples of those they worship. No one is prohibited from or punished for following his own religion, and let no one prevent them from doing so, so that they may be happy in their own homes'.

Source: M.K. Fredunbeg, *The Chachnama: An Ancient History of Sind*, Lahore: Vanguard Books, 1900/1985 reprint, 168–9.

after these countries came under the control of the Abbasid rulers of Baghdad from the mid-eighth century onwards, these migrants came to be seen in a different light (Wink 1997: 67ff.). The Abbasids and their client rulers saw in them a ready supply of 'slave' soldiers for their armies. Bought as children, they were given military training, initially for service against the Mongols but also against other enemies of the Islamic Empire. They were taught the skills of archery and horsemanship. Although remaining slaves, they could rapidly rise within the ranks of the army, suffering little in the way of racial discrimination. Since they had embraced Islam, their status was higher than that of slaves, but they could not easily leave the army. They won rapid recognition in the Islamic Empire; in time, they became as ardent defenders of Islam as the Arabs had been earlier. At the same time, however, there was the danger that the various groups of these soldiers could plot rebellions against the Abbasid caliphs, thereby gravely weakening the integrity of the Islamic Empire.

Mahmud of Ghazni's raids

A hundred miles south-west of Kabul there lie today the ruins of Ghazni, which, in the tenth century, had been a part of the Samanid Empire of Iran. In 933, a Turkish slave of the Samanids, Alptigin, in the rebellious way many slave soldiers behaved, seized the lands around the town and established a small kingdom there. In turn, another risen slave, Sabuktigin, who served in Alptigin's army, instead of rebelling against his master, contrived to marry his daughter. On the death in 977 of his father-in-law and master, Sabuktigin became the king of Ghazni, while continuing to offer nominal allegiance to the Samanids. Thus was established the Ghaznavid dynasty, which lasted from 977 to 1186 (Wink 1997: 112–35). Sabuktigin's major military achievement was to weaken the Indian kingdom of the Hindu Shahis, who controlled the lands east of Kabul, including the Punjab. By the time he died, in 997, he had exposed the vulnerability of the kings of north-west India. His son, Mahmud, who ruled from 997 to 1030, pressed his advantage further against the Hindu Shahis, whose ruler, Jayapala, preferred suicide by self-immolation rather than humiliating subjection by paying a ransom to Mahmud. With Jayapala's demise, Mahmud's confidence grew, and for the next quarter of a century he launched seventeen separate raids deep into north-western and northern India. Neither the now-weak Gurjara-Pratihara nor the other Rajput kingdoms deterred Mahmud, partly because his strategy was simply to carry out lightning raids on cities, temples and monasteries rather than engage the Indian forces in set-piece battles. The bulky Indian armies, more accustomed to conventional static warfare, were no match for Mahmud's mobile horsemen recruited from among the varied Turkic and Afghan ethnic groups. Mahmud avoided the temptation of permanent conquests, even after he had taken the city of *Kanauj*, the capital of the Pratihara kingdom, in 1019. He was focused, basically, on ensuring a secure position for his city of Ghazni within the nomadic milieu that he knew best, which was the Turco-Afghan political and social world; his raids into India were just a means to achieving this end. The transfer of Indian wealth to the treasury of Ghazni was Mahmud's key motive, because only with money could he continue to secure support for the Ghaznavids among the chiefs and warlords. Some of his ill-gotten wealth was spent on a spate of constructions in Ghazni, with the building of libraries, mosques and palaces. Most of the bullion was minted down for the purpose of financing more trade. The Indians had accrued their wealth through centuries of profitable trade balances with other countries, but this wealth was now scattered in West Asia. The economic damage for India was limited, because Indian international trade continued to be buoyant. Mahmud's Islamic iconoclasm, which was given vent in his plunder of temples, is, however, something that is still alive in Indian memories.

The Ghurid conquest of north India

The Ghaznavid raids did not cease after Mahmud's death in 1030. The economy of Ghazni depended upon the continuous supply of funds from India, and it became ever more necessary to attack the wealthy cities of *Madhyadesha*, such as *Kanauj* and Benares. Although Ghazni itself faced a major challenge in the mid-twelfth century from the nearby province of Ghur, the Indian vulnerability to Turco-Afghan attacks remained constant. Situated between Ghazni and Herat, the territory of Ghur was ruled by a local Iranian/Tajik family of Shansabanis, who, though initially subordinate to the Ghaznavids, began to encroach upon Ghazni from the 1150s onwards. By 1186 their control over the city was complete when two brothers in the family, Ghiyasuddin Muhammad and Muzuddin Muhammad, seized all power there. By agreement within the family, Muzuddin became the king of Ghazni – in the Indian context, he is generally known as Muhammad Ghuri. The financial depredation of the Indian lands was a temptation that Muhammad Ghuri could not resist; however, his ambition was not just to raid, but also to annex lands. He evolved new military strategies and introduced a number of innovations in the army (Wink 1997: 137–41). The cavalry, with their well-mounted archers, was widely introduced. The army recruited from a broader range of ethnic groups with military skills, such as the Damghanis of northern Iran, the Tajiks, and the Seljuq and Ghuzz Turks. Two separate units, the advance guards and the reserve forces, were formed in every Ghurid army. The slave soldiers were granted the highest privileges in Muhammad's army, as their military prowess was recognised. Muhammad also decided to streamline the procedures for the procurement of foodstuffs by attaching officially recognised grain dealers and pastoralists, later known as *banjaras*, who, with their massive bullock carts, ensured steady supplies for his mobile forces (Thapar 2002: 459). With his preparations complete, in 1191 Muhammad Ghuri launched a massive attack, through the Punjab, into the territories of the Chahamana kingdom, but was repulsed with great losses by its ruler, Prithviraja Chauhan. It is remembered as the first battle of Tarain. The second battle of Tarain was fought the very next year, but this time Prithviraja and his army were completely overwhelmed by the Ghurid forces. Prithviraja was taken prisoner and executed.

Many reasons have been advanced for Prithviraja's defeat, but a few need to be especially noted. Prithviraja was a traditional Rajput ruler, steeped in the heroic traditions of his people and dependent upon the feudal levies, but these were notoriously unreliable in comparison with the permanently committed centralised Turkish standing armies (Stein 1998: 136–7). The Indian forces had huge numbers of poorly armed and poorly positioned infantrymen who just could not withstand the cavalry charges of the Turco-Afghans (Wink 1997: 87–110). Prithviraja had asked for help from the other Rajput rulers, but none of them felt particularly threatened from across the border at the time and thus failed to come to his assistance, betraying a grave lack of foresight and reliable military intelligence. And at least one Rajput ruler – Jayachandra of *Kanauj* – was so jealous of Prithviraja that he is even supposed to have invited and encouraged Muhammad Ghuri (Daniélou 2003: 200). If Prithviraja had followed up his first victory by pursuing Muhammad, the latter might have been sufficiently intimidated not to return; but Prithviraja's complacency and inaction led to his undoing at the second crucial battle.

After Prithviraja there was no credible north Indian ruler who could withstand the Ghurids. The Ganges valley and *Madhyadesha* fell into Turco-Afghan hands within a few years, and the smaller kingdoms of the Ghadavalas and Chandellas lost all real authority in the province. Between 1197 and 1205, a non-slave commander of the Ghurid army, Bakhtiyar Khalji, conquered Bihar and Bengal. Although Muhammad Ghuri himself was assassinated in 1206, probably for Islamic sectarian reasons, the Turco-Afghan hold over north India could not be shaken. This was just as well for the slave captains of Muhammad Ghuri, because in Ghur itself a new Iranian power of the Khwarizm Shah was coming to the fore. With Ghur fallen, what remained to the Ghurid slave generals was the north Indian heartland that they had conquered. In 1206 Qutb-ud-din Aybak, Muhammad Ghuri's faithful slave general, became the first king of the slave dynasty and inaugurated the Delhi Sultanate (1206–1526).

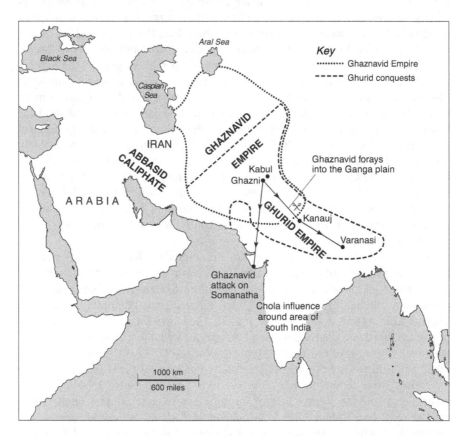

Map 9.4 Turco-Afghan intrusions into India

Evaluating the Turkish impact

The Central Asian Turks were a people whose nomadism was to dominate the socio-cultural milieu of the Islamic Empire and the Middle East in general (Wink 1997: 8–23). The trend towards nomadism was further accelerated when the greatest of all the nomads of Inner Asia, the Mongols, swooped down upon the Islamic Empire and crushed the Abbasids forever. Baghdad, the queen of Islamic cities, was destroyed in 1258, with vast numbers of her people being put to death. A number of factors, however, prevented the triumph of nomadism in India. Here, first, the Indian peasantry remained the foundation of the sedentary lifestyle, and the attacking Turco-Afghans learned to respect the immutable ways of the peasants and their toil on the land. Second, the invaders came to appreciate the rich variety of Indian trades, crafts and occupations, only made possible by complex networks of kinship and caste arrangements unique to India. While militarily triumphant, the Turco-Afghans nevertheless had to make compromises with Indian realities, and over time they became integrated in Indian society. Through their Delhi Sultanate they were eventually to become the greatest bulwark in the defence of India against the Mongols (Daniélou 2003: 203–5).

Over the sensitive issue of religion, the picture is mixed for the eleventh and twelfth centuries. Muslims generally have a proclivity to convert the non-Muslim, but in those two centuries there was hardly any conversion by the Turco-Afghans. Whatever conversion was taking place was in the marginal areas such as the Malabar coast or Sind, and that was mostly undertaken by the Arabs. The Turco-Afghans did, however, indulge in a great deal of Islamic iconoclasm. The example was set by Mahmud of Ghazni, whose greatest act of destruction was the breaking of the sacred idols of the Brahamanic/Hindu faith at the Somanatha Temple on the Gujarat coast. Where Mahmud had led, his successors followed, and during the two centuries the great temples of Mathura, *Kanauj* and Benares were destroyed. It is interesting to note that after the consolidation of Turco-Afghan rule in 1206 there were hardly any great Hindu temples built in north India; most of the temple building was carried on in the south (Wink 1997: 294). The irreligious behaviour of Mahmud and other Turco-Afghan rulers might have been due in part to their own misplaced understanding of their faith, in the manner of zealots in all religions, but also in part from their desire to please the fanatics within the Islamic clerical establishment. Their actions were neither harshly criticised nor critically scrutinised in any of the Indian writings in the centuries that followed (Thapar 2002: 430), but they must have been remembered sufficiently well, with the memories of their misdeeds passed on among the succeeding generations of *brahmans* and *kshatriyas*, for a deep well of resentment to arise in their hearts. The British imperialists of the nineteenth century, ever searching for reasons to justify their own rule over India, were not above instigating anti-Muslim sentiment whenever it suited them, and this has had its perverse effects within modern India. With the growth of a strong Hindu identity since the mid-nineteenth century, one of the negative effects has been the nurturing of a historical myth that all India's misfortunes began with Mahmud of Ghazni and his successors. It needs pointing out that Indian kings themselves drained away much of their wealth and resources in many a pointless struggle against one another; that they too destroyed temples and monasteries during their own bouts of sectarian hatreds; and that, while he might have been an anti-Indian iconoclast, Mahmud was certainly not an ethnic cleanser of Indians. His raids had hardly any effect, one way or the other, on Indian demography (Wink 1997: 4). And he also pursued his Muslim enemies in the same vengeful manner, either because he considered them to be too powerful or because they were Shiite, the sect that he, as a Sunni, opposed. It is also worth pointing out that, despite a very long period of Muslim authority in India, Islam had managed to convert only a third of the subcontinent's population by the twentieth century; furthermore, vast numbers of Muslim converts were actually drawn from the marginalised and disenfranchised groups, such as forest tribes, pastoral groups and the Untouchables, who had remained outside the Hindu religious and social system.

STUDY GUIDE

Key issues

- The establishment of varied kingdoms in north India after the Guptas.
- The importance of land grants in feudal politics.
- Controversies over Indian feudalism: e.g. Sharma versus Mukhia.
- Controversies over the extent of trade and urbanisation in north India.
- The nature of Muslim and Islamic intrusions into India.

Suggested readings

Avari 2013: 17–56; Chattopadhyaya 1995: 309–46; Jha 2004: 183–212; Mukhia 1981: 273–310; Mukhia 1985: 228–51; Sharma 1985: 19–43.

INTERNET SELECTION

1) Chinese Buddhist Encyclopedia: 'Xuanzang or Hsuan Tsang'. www.china buddhismencyclopedia.com/en/index/php/Hsuan-Tsang
2) Koenraad Elst: 'A debate with an eminent historian'. www.hinduhistory.info/ a-debate-with-an-eminent-historian
3) Ram Puniyani: 'Mythification of history and "social common sense"'. www. milligazette.com/Archives/01122001/40.htm
4) Reshma Rai: 'Short essay on the debate on feudalism in ancient India'. www. preservearticles.com/2011101715483/short-essay-on-the-debate-on
5) Pratik Sharma: 'Changes found in the Varna system from 6th century onwards in India'. www.historydiscussion.net/history-of-india/changes-found-in-the-varna-sy

QUESTIONS FOR GROUP DISCUSSION

1) What are the main characteristics of feudalism in general? In what circumstances did feudalism develop in India?
2) Why and how did Muslim merchants come to control both the land and sea routes that were vital to Indian trade?
3) What did the competitiveness within the caste system indicate?
4) Why were the Turco-Afghans able to overrun north India, while the Arabs had been unable to advance beyond Sind?
5) What were the long-lasting effects of Mahmud of Ghazni's iconoclasm?

Notes

1   Although feudalism continued to exist in some form or the other as late as 1947, when all the princely states were abolished, it would be justified to call the period of five centuries between 1200 and 1700 as that of later medieval feudalism (p.210).
2   The translations consulted are those by S. Beal 1884 and T. Watters 1904 (p.210).
3   Quoted from a note sent to the author by Dr Daud Ali, formerly based at SOAS, University of London (p.221).
4   Sharma has been a prolific writer on Indian feudalism, but for a succinct summary of his views, consult Sharma 1985: 19–43; Chattopadhyaya 1994: 7–14; Chattopadhyaya 1995: 319–25; Ray *et al.* 2000: 624–8; Shrimali 2001: 1–5; Thapar 2002: 442–52 (p. 224).
5   For a summary of views opposed to Sharma, consult Mukhia 1981: 273–310; Mukhia 1985: 228–51; Wink 1990: 219–24; Chattopadhyaya 1994: 14–17; Chattopadhyaya 1995: 325–31 (p. 224).

10 The ascendancy of the south

(*c*. CE 600 to 1200)

Timeline/Key Dates

CE 600	Revival of the Pallava kingdom by Mahendravarman
CE 525–757	Chalukyas of Badami
CE 609–42	Pulakeshin II of the Chalukyas begins the great rivalry with the Pallavas
CE 752–982	Rashtrakuta kingdom
CE 765–920	Pandyas of Madurai
CE 814–80	The reign of Amoghavarsha, the most famous Rashtrakutan king
CE 846–1173	The growth of the Chola kingdom
CE 914–28	The Rashtrakutan king Indra III captures *Kanauj*
CE 973	The defeat of the Rashtrakutas by the Chalukyas of Kalyani
CE 985–1014	Rajaraja I extends Chola power in the south
CE 1025	Rajendra Chola's naval expedition to *Sri Vijaya*

The history of the great southern peninsula of India, which consists of the plateau of the Deccan, the plains further south, and the mountain *ghats* bordering the eastern and western coastlines, is almost as old as that of northern India. There is some evidence to show that one of the earliest groups of African humanity might have crossed the seas and landed in south India nearly 50,000 years ago (Chapter 2). There is also speculation that some of the post-Harappan communities might have moved towards the Deccan via Gujarat (Chapter 3). The long process of Aryanisation of south India began as early as the middle of the second millennium BCE. This would have implied at least a partial Sanskritisation of the southern culture in general. Buddhism and Jainism also took root very early in the south. We also know that the Pandya, Chera and Chola kingdoms, the earliest political entities of the peninsula, had established strong mercantile relations with Rome, Levant and Egypt as early as the time of Christ and even before. The Satavahana kingdom of the Deccan was an important political entity during the first three centuries of the first millennium CE. The southern culture was, and is, dynamic and vibrant. A great variety of literary, poetic and philosophical works were being written in Tamil, the most ancient southern language, during the *Sangam* Age, which began as early as 200 BCE and ended in around CE 400.

Despite these facts, it is the story of the north that has seemed to have essentially captured the attention and imagination of historians from the eighteenth century onwards, when systematic study of Indian history and historiography began with the pioneering efforts of Sir William Jones and other Western scholars. Many of the spectacular archaeological discoveries concerned the links of the north with the civilisations of Central and Western Asia. The early epigraphical studies also focused on sources in Sanskrit, an Indo-European language, rather than the Dravidian Tamil. The culture, literature and the Vedic religion of the Aryans became the focus of historical and religious studies throughout the nineteenth century. The political history of the north was also a popular theme to explore, since it was in the north, particularly the Gangetic valley, that the formation of early states took place, giving rise to great empires. With the exception of the Satavahanas, the southern kingdoms had remained small and localised. The south seemed to be marginalised in historical writing. The situation has, however, changed since the mid-twentieth century. The history of the south is now studied with great intensity by historians, both Indian and foreign. The fascination for the striking way Hindu culture has manifested itself in the south may provide a clue to this development.

The political history of the south assumed greater prominence from the seventh century CE onwards. The rise of a number of important kingdoms, some of them with far-reaching influence, brought an end to the political obscurity of the south. There was much conflict among them, but not on the scale witnessed in the north, where the post-imperial fragmentation eventually led to over twenty small states. Politically speaking, the north was locked out of the south for over six centuries after the Gupta Age. Also, the fact that until the fourteenth century CE the southern states were able to keep at bay Muslim interference in their development became a very critical factor. The Arabs had traded in the south even before they had been converted to Islam, and Muslim traders were an ever-present sight in the towns and ports of the peninsula, but Hindu power and the Hindu culture remained firmly imprinted on the southern landscape during the seven centuries between CE 600 and 1300. Although, after the fourteenth century, many parts of the Deccan came under Muslim rule, the core Tamil lands remained firmly Hindu. This was to be highly consequential for the future, because south India as a whole did not experience the violent turbulence of Hindu–Muslim conflict in the north.

This chapter begins with an overview of the major southern kingdoms in the first section. The ideology of kingship and the authority of the state in the southern context will be discussed in the second section. Select economic and social developments are the topics of the third section. The focus of Chapter 11, the last chapter in the book, will be on matters pertaining to cultural developments in the areas of religion, literature and art, across both the north and the south in early medieval India.

The dynastic landscape

In the Deccan, the two mighty kingdoms of the Satavahana and the Vakataka had exercised uninterrupted power after the Mauryas (Chapters 7 and 8). The period between the third and the seventh centuries CE is sometimes called the Kalabhra Interregnum, owing to the fact that a dynasty of local Tamil rulers, called Kalabhra, caused much havoc and disorder in the Deccan. Three powerful kingdoms, however, arose by about CE 600: those of the Chalukya, Pallava and Rashtrakuta dynasties. These dynasties had humble beginnings, going back a number of centuries, but their power grew as each of them successfully met the Kalabhra challenge. It was then their rivalry that was set to shape the fortunes of the south as a whole. Their geographical base of power varied between the Deccan lands of Karnataka, Andhra Pradesh and Maharashtra. From there they waged wars for the control of the whole of the south, and one of them, the Rashtrakuta kingdom, even fought for hegemony in the north itself. They were prosperous kingdoms, to the extent that they had a strong commercial tradition and profited greatly from the links with Arab and Persian merchants and mariners.

From the *Sangam* literature of the Tamils we learn that, as early as the third century BCE, there were three distinct kingdoms in the south of India: the Chera kingdom of the south-west coast in Kerala, the kingdom of the Pandyas in Madurai region and the Chola kingdom of the south-east coast. For many centuries just before and after the Christian era, while experiencing increasing Aryanisation, Brahmanisation and Sanskritisation, south India had enjoyed relative prosperity through a rich base of agriculture and international trade. This can all be evidenced from the *Sangam* literature (Ray *et al.* 2000: 279–87). The three kingdoms themselves, however, registered little impact upon the overall Indian political scene. Their territorial interests were generally parochial, except in relation to Sri Lanka, whose capture always appeared to them a tempting prize. In the deep south of India, while the Aryanisation process over many centuries had been making a considerable social and religious impact on the life of the people, the imperial idea had not grasped the peoples' imagination, partly because of the enormous distance separating the far south from the imperial heartland in the Gangetic basin. State foundation and the rise of kingdoms in the far south came much later than in the north, but their development arose out of factors unique to southern culture and its geography. Between the third and the seventh centuries CE the southern kingdoms also suffered a number of setbacks owing to attacks on them by the Kalabhras. Each of the three kingdoms had to deal with the Kalabhras in their own way, and from the seventh century onwards, drawing strength from their prosperous agrarian base, their profitable commercial links with the outside world and their powerful temple cultures, they created and imprinted their own styles of authority and governance.

When the Turkish plunder of the north was at its height, during the eleventh and twelfth centuries, the south flourished under the great Hindu Chola dynasty, and, when the Cholas declined, other Hindu kingdoms such as the Hoysalas and Vijayanagaras took their place. While the fabulous wealth of the north Indian cities and temples was being drained away to Afghanistan, south Indian wealth was at the same time increasing phenomenally through the commercial and maritime endeavours of the Cholas. As was mentioned in the introduction to this chapter, south India remained obstinately Hindu, even while Muslim power and authority were spreading there through the future centuries. This is just one example of the complex plurality of India that makes a nonsense of periodising Indian history on the basis of religion.

The Chalukyas

The Chalukyas originated from the Kadamba region of the Karnataka, which remained their main base (Majumdar and Pusalker 1954: 227–54). They also pushed into the lands where the Satavahanas and the Vakatakas had once dominated. Three distinct families of the Chalukyas eventually emerged: the Early Chalukyas of Badami (CE 525–757), the Eastern Chalukyas of Vengi (CE 624–1020) and the Later Chalukyas of Kalyani (CE 973–1200); in terms of relative importance, the Early Chalukyas were the most significant. Their real power began with Pulakeshin I (543–66); it reached its zenith in the reign of Pulakeshin II (609–42) and it was consolidated by strong-minded rulers such as Vikramaditya I (654–68), Vijayaditya (696–733) and Vikramaditya II (733–44). The last ruler, Kirtivarman II (744–57), was overthrown by another regional power, the Rashtrakutas. History's most famous Chalukyan monarch was Pulakeshin II. During his reign of thirty-three years he made aggressive moves against all the rulers who surrounded the Chalukyan heartland. He established suzerainty over Gujarat and Malwa, and frightened off King Harsha sufficiently for the latter to confine himself to the overlordship of the lands north of the River Narmada. The importance of this encounter with Harsha was that there was to be no further military intrusion from the north for many centuries. Pulakeshin II brought the Andhra region into his family's patrimony, which eventually gave rise to the dynasty of the Eastern Chalukyas of Vengi. His great victories are honoured in the renowned Aihole *prasasti* by his court poet, Ravikirti, and inscribed on a slab of the eastern wall of the great Meguti Temple of Aihole in Karnataka. The Chinese traveller Hsuan Tsang also paid tribute to his courage and valour, and said about his army that 'if a general loses a battle they do not inflict punishment, but present him with women's clothes, and so he is driven to seek death for himself' (Beal 1884: Vol. 2, 256). Pulakeshin II overreached himself, however, when he attacked the other rising power, the Pallava kingdom, resulting ultimately in his defeat and death in 642.

The Pallavas

We are uncertain about the origins of the Pallava dynasty, but two possibilities have been suggested by historians. One theory is that they were the descendants of a group of Parthians from Iran; this is not entirely incredible, in view of the fact that there has always been a movement of Iranian peoples into India during various periods of history. Another theory describes them as the descendants of north Indian *brahman* migrants who might have been part of the movement of Aryanisation of the Deccan during the post-Vedic period (Majumdar and Pusalker 1954: 255–7). No one can be entirely certain, but, whatever their origins, their first settled place in the south was Andhra Pradesh. This fact, and a large slab of land in the Deccan that they came to control, made them initially a Deccani dynasty. Their dramatic rise, however, began in the sixth century when they came to occupy a core region of the Tamil south called *Tondaimandalam*, which today corresponds to the northern portion of Tamil Nadu. Kanchipuram, the main urban centre of that area, became their capital. Their dynasty dated itself as early as CE 275, but its great epoch straddled the seventh and eighth centuries, when rulers such as Narasimhavarman I (630–68), Parameshvaravarman I (670–700) and Narasimhavarman II (695–728) left their mark on contemporary history.

The Pallavas and Chalukyas held sway in adjacent territories. They had much in common in terms of religion, society and economy, and had many overlapping cultural traditions and rituals. Yet they were unable to live in complete peace with each other. In fact, a hundred years' war raged between them, and the inscriptions of both dynasties provide long lists of conquests by their rulers. The first round in the interminable Chalukya–Pallava conflict had gone to Pulakeshin II, whose victories are recorded in the Aihole inscription. The Pallava revenge, however, came with Narasimhavarman I's attack on Badami in 642, resulting in the death of Pulakeshin II. The Chalukyas were for a time overshadowed by the Pallavas, and their dynasty also faced a succession crisis. However, from 655 onwards, under Vikramaditya I, they commenced the second round of warfare against the Pallavas and captured their capital city, Kanchipuram. Once more, the Pallavas took their retribution. And so it went on, the Chalukya–Pallava conflict, year after year, during the late seventh and early eighth centuries CE. The last great attack by the Chalukyas on the Pallavas took place during the short reign of Vikramaditya II (733–44). In a major campaign of 740, Kanchipuram was again captured. As if to safeguard his reputation and the honour of his people for posterity, Vikramaditya II ordered an inscription to be carved on a pillar of the city's newly built Kailasanatha Temple, recording both his conquests and his generosity towards the people of the vanquished city. This inscription was left unerased by the Pallavas when they regained the city (Keay 2000: 173–4). This type of conflict could, on certain occasions, be very barbaric, resulting in death and destruction on a horrendous scale, particularly if the army commanders on both sides were especially cruel. At the same time, it is worth noting that most inter-Indian conflicts in this period took the form of low-intensity warfare. The final outcome of their hundred years' war, however, proved to be destructive for both the Chalukyas and the Pallavas. The former had always been the initial aggressors, and had therefore aroused the envy and hatred of many of their neighbours. By the middle of the eighth century, with their energies sapped, they became ready prey to the rising power of the Rashtrakutas. The Pallavas survived for a century more, but they too had exhausted themselves by their wars with the Chalukyas and the Pandyas of Madurai. In the ninth century they would be overwhelmed by both the Rashtrakutas and their older rivals, the Cholas.

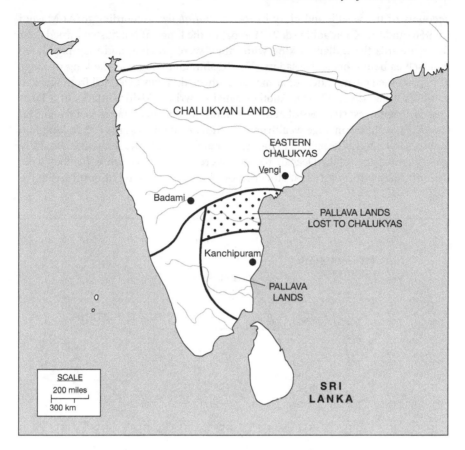

Map 10.1 Chalukya–Pallava conflict

The Rashtrakutas

The word 'Rashtrakuta' means 'peaks among kingdoms'. It was used as an epithet for a dynasty of rulers who carried the Sanskrit title of *Vallabha-Raja* and who ruled from their capital at *Mankir*, or *Manyakheta*, now called Malkhed, southeast of Sholapur in Maharashtra. The title of *Vallabha* meant 'beloved'. It was from a *Prakrit* term, *Ballaha-Raya*, that the Arabs came to call the Rashtrakutas *Al-Ballahara*, and in Arab historical sources the Rashtrakuta kings were thus known (Wink 1990: 303). The dynasty was founded by Dantidurga, who called himself *Prithvi-Vallabha*, 'the beloved lord of the earth', but it truly prospered under his successors. It lasted until the end of the tenth century and produced some of the most outstanding monarchs of India: Krishna I (760–75), Dhruva (780–93), Govinda III (793–814), Amoghavarsha I (814–80), Indra III (914–28) and Krishna III (939–67). The Arab travellers of the ninth and tenth centuries have left us vivid accounts of the wealth and glory of the *Al-Ballahara*. According to Al-Masudi (d. 956) and Ibn Khordadbih (d. 912), most of the kings of Hindustan turned their faces towards the Ballahara king while they were praying, and they prostrated themselves before his ambassadors. The Rashtrakuta king was the king of kings who possessed the mightiest of armies and whose domains extended from Konkan to Sind (Wink 1990: 304–5). Another Muslim writer, Al-Idrisi, talks of a large kingdom, with vast stretches of cultivated lands, abundant commerce and plentiful resources, resulting in huge wealth and revenue. And this was the Indian kingdom that was to be most hospitable to the Arab merchants. The Rashtrakutas naturally fought for mastery of the Deccan, but they were unique in the sense that they were the only southern dynasty that stretched out into the heartland of north India, the

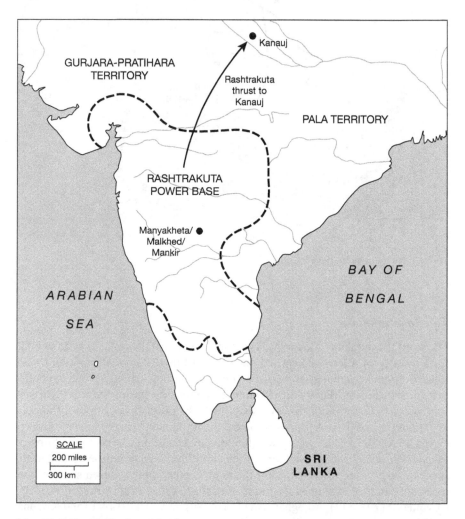

Map 10.2 The Rashtrakuta kingdom

Madhyadesha. The main aim, in all northern campaigns, was the capture of *Kanauj*, which was finally achieved in the early tenth century by Indra III. In the south, the enemy was the Chola kingdom, whose rulers were crushingly defeated in the middle of the tenth century. Despite these victories, the Rashtrakutas confronted the same challenges that all Deccan monarchs always faced: they had to be careful to balance their gains in the north with the possible losses in the south if they tarried overlong in the north, and vice versa. Continual fighting drained their resources and, in the eleventh century, they were overthrown by a feudatory who established a new dynasty, known as the Western Chalukyas of Kalyani.

The Cheras

The Cheras were a Dravidian royal dynasty of Tamil origin; their kings, called Cheraman Perumal, ruled over most of what is now known as the state of Kerala. The antiquity of this state can be evidenced by reference to the term *Keralaputra* as early as the third century BCE, on Rock Edict 2 of King Ashoka. Trading vessels from the Roman Empire frequently called at the ports of the Malabar coast of this state, and Christians, Jews and, later, Arabs all made this little part of India their home. The first major period of power wielded by the Cheras was during the *Sangam* Age, approximately between the third century BCE and third century CE, when, in addition to Kerala, they also controlled the western areas of Tamil Nadu. They ruled from two capitals, at *Vanchi* on the Malabar coast and *Karur* in Tamil Nadu. Then followed many centuries of defeats at the hands of the more powerful Deccani and southern rulers, before a second kingdom was established in the early ninth century CE by a Tamil king, Kulashekhara Alwar, who is now celebrated as a Hindu *Vaishnavite* saint of the devotional *bhakti* tradition. The capital of the second kingdom was *Mahodhyapuram*. The last Cheraman Perumal (king) of the second kingdom, Rama Verma Kulashekhara, was defeated by the neighbouring Cholas, and it is said that he embraced Islam and left for Mecca, never to return. From the twelfth century onwards Kerala became a politically fragmented state, with the petty kings of smaller units drawing their legitimacy from the land grants granted to their ancestors by the great Cheraman Perumals of the past.

The Pandyas

In the furthest south there ruled a dynasty with renowned fame in the ancient world. This was the dynasty of the Pandyas, named after the Tamil word '*Pandu*', meaning 'old'. During the *Sangam* Age, before and around the turn of the Common Era, the Pandyas had built extensive commercial and maritime relations with such far-flung countries as Egypt under the Ptolemys, China, Greece and Sri Lanka, and in CE 361 an embassy from their kingdom was received by the Roman emperor Julian. They were mentioned by Megasthenes, the Greek-Macedonian ambassador at the Mauryan court of Chandragupta Maurya, and, in the Middle Ages, by Marco Polo. Their early rivals were the Kalabhras, whose intention was to raid the Pandyan wealth, but the kingdom survived and went on to establish, through its prodigious wealth gained by trade, a small empire of its own in the deep south between the sixth and the ninth centuries CE. The Pandyan monarchs, known by the titles of Jatavarman or Maravarman, were initially followers of Jainism but, during our period (CE 600–1200), had moved on to accept Hindu *Shaivism*. Their capital was first at *Korkai*, but this was later replaced by Madurai, where their greatest architectural legacy, the Meenakshi Temple, is today a thronging place of worship. From the middle of the ninth century CE, they came under intense pressure from the rising Chola power and, between the tenth and the twelfth centuries, they became a feudatory of the Chola Empire. The Chola decline, however, led to another revival, and the second Pandyan Empire enjoyed a period of economic prosperity during the thirteenth and fourteenth centuries.

The Cholas

The eastern seaboard of southern India is known as the Coromandel coast, the term derived from the *Cola-Mandalam*. On this coast and in its fertile hinterland, a Tamil-speaking people, the Cholas, established a south Indian state with a particular identity and style of governance for nearly three centuries. Although mentioned, along with the Pandyas and the Cheras, in the *Sangam* literature of the Tamils dating back to the beginning of the Common Era, the Cholas emerged as a substantial power only in the late ninth century when they defeated the Pallavas. By the early tenth century they ruled practically the whole of the far south, excepting the Chera kingdom in Kerala. One of the important reasons for their ascendancy was the prosperity of their agriculture, based on the technology of efficient sluices in irrigating the land (Frasch 2006: 2). Their supremacy, however, came to be resented by the Rashtrakutas, who inflicted a crushing defeat on them in 949. The rest of the tenth century saw the Cholas in a state of steady decline, and it seemed that they were past their peak (Satianathaier 1957: 252–5). The picture changed dramatically, however, with the accession of a dynamic king, Rajaraja I, in 985.

Rajaraja I (985–1012) was the first great leader of the Cholas. Under him they adopted a highly aggressive posture against their smaller neighbours, such as the Pandyas, the Cheras and the rulers of Sri Lanka, basically for economic reasons. Rajaraja also attacked the Chalukyas of Kalyani, who had supplanted the Rashtrakutas in the Deccan. History, however, would have been less than kind to him if bloody warfare had been his sole achievement. In fact, he is considered a king who solidified Chola identity through an elaborate royal administration and bureaucracy, along with the promotion of the cult of god-king at an iconic temple that he built at Thanjavur (Champakalakshmi 1996a: 425–37). His son, Rajendra I (1012–44), was equally dynamic. It was in his reign that Chola imperialism asserted itself powerfully. All of Sri Lanka was conquered, and control in south India was consolidated more fully than before. It was the north, however, that particularly fascinated Rajendra. The lure of the lands of *Aryavarta*, and the powerful symbolism of the holy River Ganges, meant that Rajendra, a great southern ruler, had to tame the north to become a universal ruler. His territorial ambition rashly led him to send an expedition to the Pala kingdom of Bengal and, although it did not really gain him any material benefits, he nevertheless turned it into a symbolic triumph by ordering his commanders to bring back jars of Ganges water, so that he could claim token ownership of the ancient land of *Aryavarta*. At Gangaikondacholapuram he built a magnificent temple, surrounded by a huge lake, called *Chola-Ganga*. Rajendra also sent a naval expedition to the kingdom of *Sri Vijaya* (southern Malay peninsula, Java and Sumatra) to protect the existing India–China trade route across the Malay Straits (Sastri 1977: 183–4). The Chola rulers continued to enjoy the gains made under Rajaraja I and Rajendra I, and in the reign of Kulottunga I (1070–1118) the Chola kingdom reached new heights of prosperity and maturity. The kingdom became the symbol of southern classicism, and the cultural levels achieved at that time became the benchmarks for southern culture in general. The Chola kingdom survived for about a hundred years after 1118, but from the early thirteenth century onwards it came under great pressure, not only from the new Deccan kingdom of the Hoysalas but, more severely, from its older rivals, the Pandyas of Madurai.

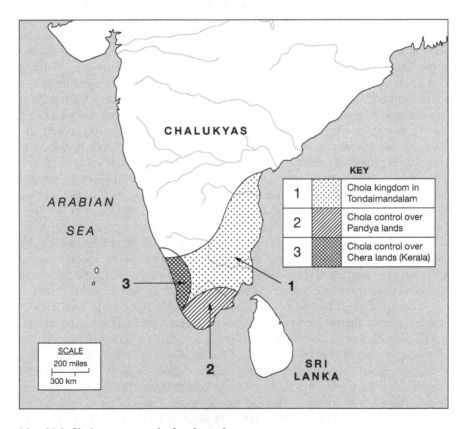

Map 10.3 Chola supremacy in the eleventh century CE

Kingship and authority in a southern kingdom

It is important to understand the background underpinning the political system that operated in the south. Without this understanding we shall remain confused about the true nature of authority in a southern kingdom. In this section we examine two issues that mattered politically in such a kingdom: the ideals of kingship and the exercise of authority.

Kingly virtues

A typical south Indian king, whether in the Deccan or in the southern plains and coastal lands, was always expected to possess certain ideals and virtues if he were to be able to rule his kingdom with both efficiency and popular support. This expectation became embedded in the psyche of south Indian people, owing to the wider proliferation of literary and religious source materials, during the time-period of this chapter (*c.* CE 600 to 1200). There were a number of ways by which a king could demonstrate his virtues.

The first of the virtues emphasised was personal. **Excerpt 10.1** below gives a poetic account of the virtues required of a southern king. Of these, the most essential was manly bravery. This was a quality that was stressed again and again in ancient Tamil sagas and poems composed by bards, minstrels and wandering entertainers. The compositions, about love and heroism, were brought together by the learned of the Tamil society during the *Sangam* Age. In a society that accepted violence as a norm and that had not yet developed non-violent constitutional means of containing conflict, all disagreements were expected to be settled by warfare. War was endemic even within close families. Every family in the land needed a brave warrior to fight for its survival and, above all, the king had to be particularly fearsome and destructive while waging wars in the defence of his kingdom. The king was expected to enhance his dynasty by glorifying his line of descent, and memorials or hero-stones were placed in different places in the kingdom for passers-by to honour and worship his ancestors. The king was regaled by symbols of his authority, such as an umbrella, a sceptre or a royal drum. The kings of the three Tamil kingdoms of the Cheras, Pandyas and Cholas had their own flower-tree or animal emblems, and these highly honorific symbols could not be insulted by anyone. The poets and bards did not ignore other important virtues, such as generosity and the idea of reconciliation. A great feast after a successful battle was considered an appropriate marker of liberality, rather than the redistribution of the booty captured from the enemy. A king who simply resorted to war without examining other alternatives to settle disputes was considered lacking in judgement.

The second set of virtues that the king had to demonstrate consisted of a number of rituals that needed observing. Most of the rituals were part of the Brahmanic Vedic system, much emphasised in the religious literature of the *Vedas* and the *Dharmashastras*. Certain kings of the Deccan and the three Tamil kingdoms were devout followers of Brahmanism, and they were most assiduous in maintaining the rituals. The various inscriptions left behind either by the kings themselves or by their noble courtiers give us varied details of such rituals. The kings and the

Excerpt 10.1 Saluting kingly virtues in the southern tradition

The royal virtues listed in the poem below come from one of south India's most important literary texts, the Tirukkural.

An army, people, wealth, a minister, friends, fort; six things
Who owns them all, a lion lives amid the kings,
Courage, a liberal hand, wisdom and energy: these four
Are qualities a king adorn for evermore.
A sleepless promptitude, knowledge, decision strong:
These three for aye to rulers of the land belong.
Kingship, in virtue failing not, all vice restrains,
In courage failing not, it honour's grace maintains.
A king is he who treasure gains, stores up, defends,
And duly for his kingdom's weal expends.
Where king is easy of access, where no harsh word repels,
That land's high praises every subject swells.
With pleasant speech, who gives and guards with powerful liberal
    hand.
He sees the world obedient all to his command.
Who guards the realm and justice strict maintains,
That king as god over subject peoples reigns.
The king of worth, who can words bitter to his ear endure,
Beneath the shadow of his power the world abides secure.
Gifts, grace, right scepter, care of people's weal;
These four a light of dreaded kings reveal.

Source: *The Sacred Kurral of Tiruvalluva-Nayanar,*
Book II, 381–90, translated by G.U. Pope,
New Delhi, 1980, 57–8.

brahman priests worked in tandem in the successful completion of rituals in the task of propitiating Hindu gods and goddesses. The temple was the sacred space where the great sacrificial ceremonies took place, involving the lighting of the fire, the chanting of the Vedic hymns, and the use of varied natural objects and products symbolising fertility and growth. The *brahman* priests legitimised the rule of the king with ceremonies, but they were not the only partners whom the king had to keep satisfied. A host of local community and village chiefs, heads of important families in the kingdom, and many ranked groupings within the caste hierarchies also deserved honour and pride of place at the rituals.

In the south, Brahmanism was challenged less by Buddhism than by Jainism. The Jain influence was particularly strong in the Karnataka region of the Deccan, where the site of Sravana Belgola was, and is, a great centre of Jain pilgrimages, but, until the rise of *Vaishnavism* and *Shaivism*, it was also influential in the Pallava kingdom and other parts of the south, particularly in the central Tamil plain of *Tondaimandalam* and the southern plain of the Madurai region. Wherever in the south Brahmanism was challenged by the Jain heterodoxy, the kings were exhorted to display a third set of virtues, which were essentially moral in character. The Jain conception of kingship can be studied from three important texts: the *Tirukkural* by Tiruvalluvar in the sixth century CE and the tenth century CE texts of *Civakacintamani* by Tirutakkadevar and *Nitisara* by Somadeva Suri. In these texts, the ritual of sacrifice is not considered a crucial matter for the reputation of the king; it was his moral character that determined whether he would be considered a hero-king. The Jain king is a perfect moral being who does not have to rely on priestly ritual specialists or the kinship and community groups; he was the supreme *chakravartin*, who exercised independent sovereignty and moral authority. An important marker of Jain kingship, as evidenced in a large number of inscriptions and Jain literature in general, is the concept of *dana* or gift. The gift normally took the form of land grants to the most humble of peoples and institutions; such land grants did not have a transactional character of the more customary feudal land grants either to minor princes or *brahman* priests.

Royal authority and local autonomy: the controversial Chola model

There are three important models for understanding how authority was exercised in the states of India during this period. The first model is that of a centralised state, the character of which was based upon those ruled by the Mauryans (Chapter 6) and the Imperial Guptas (Chapter 8) before our period. Such a state was usually a unitary state, centralised with a strong ruler who controlled the social, economic and religious resources of the state. It was also highly bureaucratic. The second model is that of a feudal state, in which the king operated within the fief system, by which land grants were made to *brahman* priests, warriors or nobles. Some of the great kings of dynasties such as the Gurjara-Pratiharas, Palas, Chalukyas, Pallavas or Rashtrakutas, across both north and south India, ruled their states in that fashion. In this feudal model we see a network of interest groups in a state of transaction with the royal authority. The main disadvantage of this model was that, with the increasing number of land grants, the territorial base of the monarch was shrinking all the time and the lower strata of administration and nobility could start to appropriate royal power. A series of minor chiefdoms arose out of that situation, resulting in political fragmentation, as we saw in the north on the eve of the Turco-Afghan invasions at the beginning of the eleventh century CE. The third model is that of what is called a segmentary state. This model has been put forward as an appropriate way of describing the operation of authority in the kingdom of the Cholas.

By any criterion, the Chola kingdom of the eleventh century was one of the great political structures of India, if not the world. The organisation of that kingdom was based on sound principles of administration and management, the evidence for which lies in detailed inscriptions and revenue records. A valuable set of inscriptions, discovered as late as 1905, and consisting of 816 lines of writing on thirty-one sheets of copper bound together, along with a seal-ring, is the so-called Order (or *sasanam*) of King Rajendra I. The purpose of this copper plate was to record the transfer of a grant to *brahmans* in a particular village to the temple itself. However, the recording of the event is perhaps not as important as the eulogy to the Chola rulers and the articulation of Chola grandeur; it expresses the belief that the space the Cholas ruled was the 'sphere of a world ruler' (Ali 2000: 206). All the early historical studies therefore came to the conclusion that the success of the kingdom lay in the exercise of powerful royal authority through a firm bureaucracy (Wink 1990: 315; Champakalakshmi 1995: 271, 294–6). The monarchs of the calibre of Rajaraja I and Rajendra I provided the role models for royal authority in action.

This particular understanding of Chola royal authority came to be challenged, in time, by the segmentary state theory that was proposed by a group of American historians led by Burton Stein, whose research interests lay in comparative anthropological studies of rural societies. Having studied the way authority worked in African peasant cultures, Stein came to the conclusion that there was much similarity between those cultures and the peasant communities of south India (Champakalakshmi 1995: 273–4). What made them similar was the idea that in both societies power was not centralised; it was vested in local communities. This concept had been operative in the Pallava kingdom; the Cholas more or less continued the Pallava traditions, and it was the Chola kingdom that was the focus of Stein's research. The segmentary state theory argued that in the feudal world of the eleventh century the Chola king did not truly exercise political sovereignty throughout his kingdom; his real political power was confined to the central core area, while in all the outer areas the king exercised only ritual or symbolic authority. True power actually lay with the assemblies of agricultural micro-regions called *nadus* or with the *brahman* lords and local chiefs who had received land grants from the king for varied reasons (Ludden 1985: 34–6; Champakalakshmi 1995: 270–5; Champakalakshmi 1996a: 41–5). Numerous copper-plate and stone inscriptions of the Chola rulers should be viewed, in Stein's opinion, as evidence of ritual sovereignty rather than actual political control. In fact, 'the Chola state existed as a state only as hundreds of *nadus* of its realm recognized the overlordship, the ritual sovereignty, of Chola kings' (Stein 1985). The king did not control a central system of taxation or a central army. If he wished to raise resources, more often than not the Chola king launched plunder raids on the neighbouring states. It was further argued that both the Pallavas and the Cholas built temples as a means of reaffirming their ritual sovereignty in the peripheral areas; the sponsoring of temples was a way of keeping the *brahman* elites compliant, thus preventing any disruption to their nominal authority.

Much controversy has been generated by the segmentary state theory. Further extensive research in Tamil records has, in turn, led a more recent group of historians to challenge the ideas behind the theory. It is accepted that the *nadus* were key units of authority, but the notion that the Chola kings held merely ritual sovereignty outside their core area of *Cholamandalam* is rejected on the grounds that they in fact made subtle use of some of the existing institutions to integrate their kingdom and to place definite limits on the power of the *nadus*. The most vibrant of these institutions were, respectively, the *brahmadeya*, the *nagaram* and the temple (Champakalakshmi 1995: 279–85; Hall 2001a: 85–116). None of them was permitted to displace the *nadu*, which remained the basic agricultural unit; but the *nadu*'s power was significantly moderated by them. Through their land grants to the *brahmans*, the Chola kings extensively encouraged the creation of *brahmadeyas*, which had the potential for raising agricultural productivity and the general income of the kingdom. The *brahmadeya* elites were also to be the eyes and ears of the king. The *nagaram* was the market centre and a place where powerful commercial organisations and merchant guilds operated; the kings realised that the latter too were creators of wealth, and ensured that the *nadu* assemblies did not in any way hinder their work. Since a *nagaram* might serve a number of *nadus*, no one particular *nadu* could impose arbitrary levies on the merchants. The temple, the third institution, was more than a place of worship for the Chola kings (Champakalakshmi 1995: 281–5). It held great commercial and economic advantage for them. Vast donations were made to the temple by the rich and the poor, and huge quantities of foodstuffs were moved into the temple precincts from the hinterland. The temple could thus act as a threshold for the king's intervention in the countryside. The temple, with its iconography and its sacred space for the *Shivalingam*, for example, was the central arena where the king, through his enormous powers of patronage, could demonstrate more than ritual sovereignty. Chola centralism also effectively institutionalised the various religious cults associated with the popular *bhakti* movement in south India, and temple patronage was a key element in this aspect of the imperium (Champakalakshmi 1996b: 135–63). The temple proclaimed to the world the Chola state's ideology (Champakalakshmi 1996a: 425–37). As a further precaution, the Chola kings ensured that the *nadus* did not remain stationary and unchanging. The *nadus* were not just places where all property was to be communally held. Various types of private ownership were being encouraged by royal officials. Continual reorganisations, mergers and rationalisations were effected, and larger revenue or political units, called *valanadu*, *periyanadu* or *tanyiur*, were being created for the purpose of defining and redefining agricultural regions and revenue organisation by the will of a royal authority (Champakalakshmi 2001a: 68–84). Once again, the central bureaucracy was gaining ascendancy over the local rights of the *nadus*. With these divergent versions of the nature of Chola authority that we have summarised, no wonder this kingdom continues to fascinate modern-day students of history.

The economy of the south

Agrarian self-sufficiency

Two distinct geographical landscapes have shaped the agricultural history of the southern peninsula (Ludden 1999: 57–9). The interior of the Deccan plateau has a semi-arid landscape, because of low rainfall and a relatively small volume of water carried by southern rivers. Securing a sufficient supply of water has been the perennial problem for the Deccan farmer. On the other hand, there is available much underground water trapped by volcanic rocks and boulders. In the landscape of the deeper south we find river valleys, plains, deltas and interfluvial flatlands. The tropical monsoon rains that lash down on this land make it extremely fertile. The coastal lands of the south are also home to fishery ecology.

Over many millennia the peasants and farmers of south India have shown much ingenuity in the use of soils, seeds and water. Among a great variety of specific implements and tools for land tillage were the ox-drawn ploughs, pick-axes, hoeing adzes, weeding adzes, other weeding devices and sickles (to peel coconut and cut plantain). A particular device, known as Manmoti, was used in the rice belt for digging, levelling and shifting soil from one place to another in the fields (Krishna and Morrison 2009: 28). Planks were used to level the field before puddling and transplanting. These tools were a vital aid to increasing the production of foods, alongside the use of organic manure, including animal manure, cow dung and farm-yard manure, and a liquid fertiliser formulation. South Indian agriculturists had a good understanding of the genetic variability of crops, and they selected different cultivars to suit agro-climates and soils, in accordance with human preferences and economic considerations. The literary and archaeological records point to a variety of rice crops, with the 'golden cooked rice', rich in Vitamin A, being one of the choice foods of the masses (Krishna and Morrison 2009: 14). Peasants partitioned lands systematically for cereals, legumes, oil crops, for example, mustard or linseed, vegetables, spices and fruits. The rich array of foodstuffs grown required water on a very large scale, and it was the care and effort taken to increase the volume of available water that was the key to success in farming.

South Indian records demonstrate much knowledge of the variability of seasons and precipitation patterns, and methods to quantify precipitation were widely in use long before our period. Ancient Kannada literature, for example, mentions three main sources of water: rain, rivers and tanks. Almost since Neolithic times have southern peasants engaged in providing various forms of irrigation schemes to water their land and in practising mixed-farming. There is an entire Tamil taxonomy of terms to describe wells, canals, tanks, reservoirs and artificial streams. There is also available a historical list of irrigation facilities in the area that is now covered by the modern state of Tamil Nadu for the whole of the first millennium CE (Krishna and Morrison 2009: 33). It is also known that the earliest political states in the south levied a tax on all irrigation, which was valued at one-fifth of the produce. Wells of varied depth were built in the northern parts of the Deccan, while tanks were more useful in Karnataka and further south (Ludden 1999: 58). Many of the rivers, particularly the Kaveri River, were dammed, and inundation canals were built in order to utilise excess water collected in tanks and embankments. The largest of the irrigation tanks, or man-made lakes with earthen walls (*eri*), built on tank land (*eripatti*), were built by the kings of the Pallava dynasty (Ludden 1985: 21). The Pallava kingdom was constituted from twenty-four localities of *Tondaimandalam*, called *kottams*. Each *kottam* was a unique zone of agrarian, pastoral and village-based economy, supported by irrigation based on reservoirs and small lakes (Champakalakshmi 1995: 279–80). The advanced skills required in the building and maintenance of these tanks would have been provided by the *brahman* entrepreneurs and settlers in the *brahmadeya* villages (Ludden 1985: 34–41). The Pallava inscriptions provide us with details of the use and care of these earthwork tanks, as explained in **Excerpt 10.2** below. There is also evidence of sluice mechanisms being used in the Pallava irrigation schemes (Frasch 2006: 8). The large volume of wetland rice production in this part of India dates from this period.

The Chola rulers continued the work of the Pallavas. South Indian inscriptions clearly show that the keen interest taken in irrigation works by kings, nobles and the *brahmans* had three aims in mind: increasing revenue, earning religious merit and gaining social prestige. This was, of course, not the whole story as far as the quality of life of the huge mass of rural people was concerned. The Pallavas and the Cholas were making substantial endowments to the *brahmans*, partly owing to the increasing spread of Brahmanisation throughout Indian society during this period, so the *brahman* influence was paramount in the villages of local political units, such as *nadus*. The Pallavas and the Cholas needed the *brahmans* to confirm the legitimacy of their rule through the use of rituals, but they also appreciated

---

Excerpt 10.2 Agricultural innovations in the Tamil country

An eminent specialist of the agricultural history of India explains the way the Tamils learned to practise agriculture in a fairly harsh natural environment.

Technologically, two processes over the centuries formed the agrarian landscape [of the Tamil country] that we see today. On the one hand, people dug and shaped the earth to manipulate water, to put surface and sub-soil moisture to work. Tamil people built their civilization around irrigation. On the other hand, they adapted an enormous array of crops, seed varieties and cropping techniques to exploit the potentials of different soils and variable water supplies . . . Irrigation has throughout Tamil history provided a proven means to raise land productivity. Not surprisingly, Tamils divided agriculture into two main categories, whose lands connote goodness and poverty, respectively. Irrigated wet land is 'nanjai', and un-irrigated dry land is 'punjai'. Each of these two categories of cultivation supports its own staple grain – rice or millet – and, in Tamil cultural tradition, one embodies the good life, the other meagre subsistence.

Source: David Ludden, *Peasant History in South India*, Princeton, NJ: Princeton University Press, 1985.

Figure 10.1 South Indian tank scene

the valuable role the latter could play in increasing land productivity. However, by their patronage of the *brahmadeya* villages and the granting of entire villages to *brahmans*, they were further adding to the inequalities of the hierarchical caste system. The *brahmans* not only kept the revenue arising from the labour of the peasants, but also did not pay any tax (Champakalakshmi 1995: 279–81; Champakalakshmi 1996a: 38–42; Thapar 2002: 387–9). The peasant had little to gain from this arrangement; he and his family could at best eat what they produced on their small plots, but had little else to look forward to. Human exploitation was no less cruel in the south than in the north.

Temple urbanisation and commerce

The first stage of urbanisation in the southern peninsula was during the time of the *Sangam* Age, when maritime trade in spices and other commodities was brisk. It was in the port settlements of the Malabar and the Coromandel coasts that we notice the early signs of urban culture and organisation. Over the succeeding centuries such urbanisation flourished or decayed in proportion to the growth or decline of overseas trade. With the resurgence of new, and the revival of old, kingdoms from the seventh century CE onwards, we encounter a new, second phase of urbanisation in the region, linked to both agriculture and religion. Agriculture had essentially remained the bedrock of the prosperity of the kingdoms throughout the southern peninsula. However, when the optimum yield from agriculture was reached and enough surplus became available, the impetus for commerce began in earnest and, out of that development, came urbanisation. On the other hand, with the increasing influence of Hinduism, at the expense of Buddhism and Jainism, the southern kings were engaged in encouraging and promoting the recruitment of *brahmans* from the north to settle in their kingdoms. Large areas of land were endowed to the *brahmans*, leading to the rise of the *brahmadeya* village settlements within the administrative areas of *nadus*. The *brahman* control of land led to greater productivity and large-scale surpluses. With few exceptions, most *brahmans* were rooted to their land, but the surplus from their land gave rise to two important classes of people in the south: the craftsmen and the merchants. The *brahmadeya* village settlements became the focus of their activities. Out of these settlements grew small and large towns. We first notice this development within the Pallava kingdom, but it was in the Chola kingdom, which flourished between the ninth and the thirteenth centuries CE, that we find it at its greatest extent.

The Chola kingdom's strength and prosperity came out of a remarkable intertwining of rural and urban interests underpinned by a common religious ideology that was devoted to the worship of the Hindu god Shiva. Within the *nadus* of the kingdom (and previously in the Pallava kingdom too), Shiva temples, great and small, were dotting the landscape of the *brahmadeyas* and their countryside. These temples were in themselves like great landed magnates. The most magnificent of the temples, such as those at Thanjavur, Madurai and Chidambaram, served as royal chapels, and their adornment required resources on a vast scale. The most important human resource consisted of an army of *brahman* priests, whose needs for the upkeep of temples were many and varied (Hall 2001a: 101–14). A huge quantity of foodstuffs, along with many different artefacts, was necessary for efficient maintenance, and the systematic procurement of these was only possible through the role that the merchant class played, as middlemen who bought food from the farmers of the *brahmadeya* villages and manufactured goods from the craftsmen. The Chola economy was becoming increasingly monetised, and the use of currency rather than barter was the preferred method of settling trade deals. A great number of inscriptions, found on the walls of the temples and in their basements, indicate extensive donations by merchants to the temples, in the form of gold, commodities or coins. These temple donations no doubt expressed their personal dedication to Lord Shiva, but they also served a practical purpose of keeping the royal authority on their side. The temple was at the heart of the rural–urban nexus; there was no conflict between the town and the country in the Chola kingdom, which provided social and cultural stability to its people for over three centuries.

One of the most important agencies in the urban context of the south in general and the Chola kingdom in particular was the corporate body called the *nagaram*, which could be construed either as a market centre or an association of merchants, specialised craftsmen or artisans. Historians sometimes call such an association a guild. Each *nagaram* had its own code of conduct for its members, and membership was restricted to a select few in each profession. The craftsmen and artisans wished to maintain their professional standards and reputation on behalf of their association, while the guild of merchants specialised in local and overseas trade. The merchants who dealt in inter-country trade across the south were known as *swadeshi* merchants, while those dealing in trade abroad were called the *nanadeshis*. One of the most well known of merchant associations was the so-called Ayyavole 500, a body of the 500 most influential merchants involved in both local and overseas trade (**Excerpt 10.3** below). It had originated in the town of Aihole in the kingdom of the Chalukyas of Badami, but it had access to

---

Excerpt 10.3 The guild of Ayyavole 500

The Ayyavole 500 was one of the main south Indian guilds of merchants who were the controllers of the Chola overseas trade. They dealt in a variety of commodities sought by foreign merchants, and their influence throughout south India was wide-ranging. Some of the guild's activities are described in the following passage:

> The chief source of information on Ayyavole ... is the corpus of inscriptions [which] are generally recorded on stone and also occasionally on copper plates ... and often located in or near temples and are intended as records of the taxes in cash and in kind levied for the benefit of the temple, from merchant groups and from townspeople, on commodities produced in the area, or on goods in transit. Occasionally they recorded public services in villages or urban areas which are initiated or maintained by merchants. And on a few occasions they record details of what appears to be an agreement between ruler and merchant, demarcating merchant townships, or in one case, a contractual agreement recording trading rights granted to a group of foreign traders, as well as to local trade groups.

As with most Indian inscriptions, the charter generally began with a eulogy to the ruler, known as the prasasti; *its usefulness is explained thus:*

> Both from the standardised phrases and from the newer interpretations one obtains indications of intricate factors such as the relationship of merchants with the state or ruler, or the position of the guild to other corporate bodies, or the religious affiliation of its members at a particular time and place.

Source: Meera Abraham, *Two Medieval Merchant Guilds of South India*, New Delhi: Manohar, 1988, 3–4; see also 156–81.

any region, irrespective of the boundaries of kingdoms. It also cut across caste lines, because some of its members were *brahmans* with enough wealth to invest or to speculate with.

The *nagarams* were especially valued by the kings of the Chola and other dynasties for their generous donations to temples. The financing of all rituals and worship, alongside that of temple expansion, was generally managed by a *nagaram* based in the locality of the temple. The records of donations of varying nature and size can be studied from hundreds of inscriptions within the precincts of great southern temples (Heitzman 2001: 129ff.). The fact that the *nagarams* enjoyed a considerable measure of independence within the autonomous space of the *nadus* was partly due to royal manipulation of the Chola kings, who never ceded more than necessary control to the *nadus*. On the other hand, when the occasion demanded, the kings made sure that merchants did not avoid paying taxes. A great range of taxes was levied in the southern kingdoms, on craftsmen, artisans and other occupations; a land tax and labour dues were enforced in the countryside; and there were a number of toll collections. Merchants and guilds had to pay tolls and customs duties, which were levied on all imports and exports. While the Chola kings were appreciative of generous donations from merchants, they made sure that merchants did not escape paying tax. The zeal of the royal collectors of tax was often resented by the *nagarams* (Heitzman 2001: 139–48).

Muslim role in west-coast overseas commerce

After *c*. CE 600, the western coast of India, from Gujarat down to Karnataka, was controlled by a number of Deccani dynasties, the two most powerful being those of the Chalukyas and the Rashtrakutas. South of the Karnataka coast was the Malabar coast, which belonged to the Kerala-based kingdom of the Chera dynasty. The active involvement of Muslim mariners and merchants in the overseas commerce of this entire coastline contributed substantially to the prosperity of the kingdoms mentioned.

In terms of wealth and economic strength, the most illustrious of the Deccan kingdoms was that of the Rashtrakutas. Its power did not just prevail in the core Deccan lands of Maharashtra and Karnataka; it reached as far north as the city of *Kanauj* in the Gangetic basin and further south even in parts of Kerala. The natural resources, including foodstuffs and minerals, from such a vast area of land immeasurably enriched the kingdom and sustained it for nearly three centuries. The Rashtrakuta administration was systematic and well organised, which helped to produce sufficient tax revenues. Domestic business was organised on the lines of corporations and guilds. These powerful bodies, made up of people from a number of interest groups, regulated the trade of the kingdom, with the help of their own militias and banks. They were the most active economic agents of the kingdom in port towns along the Gujarati, Konkan and Karnataka coasts, and also in the interior regions. On these coasts were located ports, such as *Kambaya*, *Saymur* and *Baruj*, that served as outlets for the deep hinterland depots. The region of Gujarat was vitally important for the Rashtrakutas, because through its ports they were able to control the overseas trade of north India with the lands of the Middle East and further west (Wink 1990: 306–7).

The Rashtrakutas showed great hospitality to foreigners, and especially to Muslim traders from Arabia and Iran. The latter were permitted to settle in the kingdom's domains; and, according to the Arab traveller, Al-Masudi, nearly 10,000 Muslims lived in the district of *Saymur* and were known as the *bayasiras*, or 'Muslims born in Al-Hind of Muslim parents' (Wink 1990: 69). The Rashtrakutas and their deputies in Gujarat encouraged and facilitated Muslim trade, if for no other reason than their own interest in securing a share of the mercantile profits. When, as a result of the overthrow of the Umayyads by the Abbasids in CE 750, the centre of gravity of the Islamic Empire moved from Damascus to Baghdad, the sea route from Basra and the Iranian ports to Gujarat and the Konkan coast through the Persian Gulf became an important passageway. It remained so until the tenth century. During the heyday of the Abbasid Empire, the demand for Indian goods increased at a rapid pace. The huge range of products exported out of India included cottons, muslins, calicos, hides, indigo, incense, betel nuts, rice, coconuts, sandalwood, timber, sesame oil, bamboo, red kino, myrobalan plum fruits (used in dyeing), ginger and ivory, but perhaps the most valuable Indian resource for the Abbasid naval establishment was the teakwood from the forests of the Rashtrakuta kingdom. The Arab shipbuilding industry depended upon securing this wood from India. From outside, into India, arrived the imports of such items as pearls, gold, wines, glass, slaves and horses. Since their value was not large enough to pay for Indian exports, the Muslim world made good its trade balance with India with gold and silver coinage and bullion. Islamic coins, such as *dinar* and *dirham*, were the universal gold and silver coinage of that era, and the Rashtrakuta kingdom was the agency that integrated India and the Indian Ocean trade into the Islamic world economic system (Wink 1990: 306–9).

The power of the Rashtrakutas waned at around the end of the tenth century CE, and one of the reasons for this might have been the waning of the Abbasid Empire at around the same time. The displacement, within the Islamic economic world, of the Abbasids based in Baghdad by the Fatimids of Egypt, based in Cairo, had a profoundly negative impact upon trading links between the ports of the Persian Gulf and the Rashtrakuta-controlled ports of western India. The Fatimids did not entirely ignore the Persian Gulf trade, but their main interest was to promote the Red Sea route from Egypt to India (Wink 1990: 56, 175, 215–16). They were far more interested in the Malabar coast in the west and the Coromandel coast in the east than in the Gujarati, Konkan and Karnataka coasts of the west. The Fatimid sailors and merchants were, so to speak, restoring the old Roman trade links with India; they were also helping to create the first global economy of the Middle Ages by linking the Indian Ocean trading networks with those of the Mediterranean and the African and European hinterlands. One reason for the success of this trade was the simultaneous revival of the European economies in the tenth and eleventh centuries: spices, textiles, cloths and timbers from south India were being sold at great profit in the fairs and markets of Europe (Wink 1990: 35–8). Carefully following the monsoon-regulated timetable of boats arriving at the Egyptian port of Alexandria with their tropical cargo, sea captains from Venice and Genoa would sail into Alexandria at the right moment, to buy a share of the cargo for the European market. This cargo was not entirely Indian in origin. It included goods and commodities from South East Asia and China that would have arrived at the ports of the Malabar and Coromandel coasts, as well as Sri Lankan ports.

The Fatimid trade between south India and Egypt was handled in both places essentially by Jews and Muslims. Although the presence of Jews in Kerala goes a long way back (see Chapter 11), the most substantial Jewish migration came about through the agency of the Islamic Empire from the eighth century onwards (Wink 1990: 86–104). Jewish traders and entrepreneurs, whether domiciled in Damascus, Baghdad or Cairo, facilitated a huge amount of commerce within that empire (Goitein 1973: 3–21, 175–91). Their agents and mariners also came to Kerala, where many later settled, seeking goods produced in south India and South East Asia, in exchange for some of the luxury products from other parts of the empire. We can learn much about their ventures and trade deals from a set of rather stray and miscellaneous papers and letters that are now collectively called the Cairo Geniza documents, named after the area of Cairo where they were first discovered. These documents give us a graphic picture of the extent and scope of the India trade and the multifarious relationships that the Jewish traders in Egypt, Yemen and India had with Arabs and Indians. Although there were great profits to be made, the documents also tell us about the risks of losses at sea. A typical hazard at sea is described in **Excerpt 10.4** below.

Muslim Arabs were the more numerous foreign community in Kerala. Their numbers steadily increased from the tenth and eleventh centuries onwards. The poorer among them have for long been known as the Mapillas of Kerala, descendants of Arab merchants and Keralan women from marine and fishing castes, and may be considered the first authentic group of Muslims in India (Wink 1990: 71–2; Heffening 1993: 757–9). The steady process of Brahmanisation within the Chera kingdom was, at that time, leading to an increasing emphasis within the Hindu population on purification rites and caste rituals, resulting in the exclusion of the majority from maritime activities. This gave the Mapillas a unique opportunity to control harbours and long-distance shipping routes (Wink 1990: 72–5). Those Muslims who belonged to the more wealthy and cosmopolitan merchant class were the true controllers of the overseas trade of the kingdom. They ran their own commercial organisations and guilds of trade. Familiar with both Tamil and Malayali languages, they possessed a strong sense of self-identity, owing to unity within their organisations, high levels of literacy, and being in touch with the Islamic heartlands by regular pilgrimages to Mecca. The wealth of this class of people was also much appreciated by the Chera rulers; they could call upon its members for financial assistance whenever they felt their authority to be under threat in the countryside. The rulers considered the profitable duties and taxes that they earned from the flourishing trade conducted by Muslims to be indispensable for their own security.

Excerpt 10.4 Dangers in travel and shipping

The ships travelling between Egypt and India generally made a stop at the port of Aden in Yemen. The Arabian Sea and the Indian Ocean can be very capricious, and countless ships were lost in sea wreckage. Since ships often travelled in convoys, passengers on one boat sometimes witnessed the floundering of another. Records were often kept. Thus, for example, the Jewish authorities at Aden confirmed the death of an Egyptian merchant, whose ship sank a few days after setting sail for India, in the following words.

These are the details of their drowning. The ship they were in, that is the Kulami, sailed from Aden together with the other ships that set sail. This ship and the Baribatani were in the same position. The two of them travelled together for about four days from Aden. On the eve of the fifth day, the sailors of the ship Baribatani heard the cries of the sailors of the ship Kulami and their screams and shrieks in the night as the water inundated them. When morning came, the sailors of the Baribatani did not encounter any trace or evidence of the Kulami ship . . . Any ship that sinks in the environs of Aden . . . never surfaces, nor does anyone who was in it survive at all, because of the turbulence of the sea and the distance from the shore and the abundance of sharks.

Source: S.D. Goitein and Mordechai A. Friedman, *India Traders of the Middle Ages: Documents from the Cairo Geniza*, Leiden: E.J. Brill, 2008, 160–1.

Chola commercial influence in South East Asia

If the Arabian Sea and the western Indian Ocean provided India with maritime links to the Levant and the Mediterranean countries, the Bay of Bengal was the gateway to the countries of South East Asia. Merchants and seafarers, from very early times, sailed eastwards towards Burma and the south-east from the ports on the eastern coast of India that stretched from Bengal downwards to Cape Comorin. By the seventh century, a number of kingdoms had been established in South East Asia, such as *Kambuja* and *Funnan* (Cambodia), *Champa* (Vietnam) and *Sri Vijaya* (the southern peninsula of Malaysia, Java and Sumatra). There had been a strong Indian cultural and commercial influence in these kingdoms for many centuries, and during the heyday of Roman trade, for example, the Indian merchants and shippers had brought spices from there to India for trans-shipment to Rome in exchange for some of the Roman wares. Later, the Pallava rulers built dockyards and developed a navy, which enabled the south Indian mariners to enjoy a near-monopoly of trade until the Muslim maritime challenge in the eighth century (Thapar 2002: 342). This ancient maritime commerce of south India was given a further significant boost in the tenth century when the new dynamic Sung dynasty came to control China (CE 960). At the end of that century there also came to the throne of the Chola kingdom the first of their powerful rulers, Rajaraja I (CE 985), who wished to take advantage of building strong commercial links with Sung China. He therefore first set about bringing both the Malabar and the Coromandel coasts under effective Chola control. The main reason for his attack on the Chera kingdom in Kerala, for example, was to seize the lucrative maritime trade of the Malabar coast after the displacement, within the Islamic economic world, of the Baghdad-based Abbasid Empire by the Cairo-based Fatimids. He and his equally powerful successors also greatly strengthened their hold over Sri Lanka and the Maldive Islands as part of an ongoing effort by them to ensure that their merchants were not disadvantaged.

The main prize for the Cholas was the promise of great riches from the trade with China through South East Asia. For centuries the Chinese had been trading there, and a string of Chinese settlements was established in the islands and the mainland of the region. Indian merchants too had built up their own maritime trading connections with Malays, Javanese, Sumatrans and the Chinese. This maritime trade took place on a fairly modest scale, until the rise of the Sung dynasty in China in CE 960. From then on, a profound economic transformation began to take place within China (Wink 1990: 327–34). The Sung emperors, determined to make their country a global economic player, invested huge resources into the economy. During the eleventh century their country was several centuries ahead of any other part of the world in such fields as steel manufacture, the armaments sector, transportation networks and techniques, the issue of bank notes and paper money, the management of credits and finance, and the specialisation of production in general. Hundreds of Chinese commodities started entering the international market owing to the rapid expansion of the merchant fleet built up by the Sungs. Prosperity greatly increased inside the country, and a large class of wealthy consumers came into being. This class, in turn, demanded luxuries imported from abroad, which resulted in China running up a large balance-of-trade deficit. The gold that China paid out for her import–export deficit led to greater economic activity in the recipient countries. The countries of South East Asia, along with Japan, even stopped minting their own currencies, using Chinese gold as coinage. The opening up of China and China's interests in the world beyond her seas were seen by the Chola rulers and the commercial associations and guilds, such as the Ayyavole 500, as a great opportunity for furthering their trade. A wide variety of materials and commodities – raw cotton and manufactured textiles (in which China was, at this stage, far behind India), spices and drugs, ivory, amber, coral, rhinoceros horn, aromatics and perfumes – were shipped out from ports on the Coromandel coast. Ultimately, however, the success of the India–China sea trade depended, to a large extent, upon the goodwill of the rulers of *Sri Vijaya*, a Malay kingdom of South East Asia, straddling the Malay peninsula and the Indonesian island of Sumatra and controlling the Malacca Straits. This key waterway passage is today one of the world's most important international shipping lanes, as it was in the eleventh century. The Indian merchant marine used this waterway to shorten the journey from the southern ports of India to China. In order to increase their share of the profits from the India–China trade and its customs dues etc., the *Sri Vijaya* authorities decided that all ships had to terminate their journeys in the straits and that their middlemen would trans-ship the goods to their respective destinations. This was much too irksome for the merchant organisations in the Chola state, and Rajendra I (r. 1012 to 1044) decided to use his substantial naval force to punish *Sri Vijaya* in 1025. There was no imperial motive for this; it was solely a matter of safeguarding the shipping lane for the Chola-sponsored merchant fleet. With nearly thirteen ports captured, the supremacy of *Sri Vijaya* in South East Asia was broken (Wink 1990: 333). The Cholas ensured for themselves direct access to China and her valuable markets and regularly sent embassies to the Sung court.

Caste and gender in the south

Caste differentiations

It is inadvisable to understand the caste system in the southern kingdoms through the prism of the northern model. Although the historic roots of the caste system were perhaps in the north, some of the earliest *Sangam* literature of the south also mentions features of the caste system. Originally, in the south, there were agriculturists, pastoralists and hunters, but they did not see themselves partitioned into *varnas* (Gurukkal 1995: 245). From about the later centuries of the first millennium BCE, when the northern *brahmans* began to settle in the south and disseminate the Aryan and Sanskritic culture, with the idea of caste implicit therein, we can see the faint beginnings of an incipient caste system taking shape. All through the first millennium CE, the kings of south India, whether Pallavas, Pandyas, Cheras or Cholas, encouraged and supported the *brahmans* in order to gain enduring legitimacy for themselves. They conferred increasingly large land grants to the *brahmadeyas*, or to the temples, which were the *devadanas*. The *brahmadeyas* and the temples perforce became the main centres around which the southern model of the caste system would evolve and be established (Champakalakshmi 1995: 279–85). This model possessed its own distinctive characteristics. It conceived of society as being made up of two segments: the *brahmans* and the rest, collectively called *shudras*. Being far more numerous than the *brahmans*, the *shudras* contained diverse groups of non-*brahman* people. The most dominant and the wealthiest of these groups, known as the *vellalars*, was made up of prosperous landowners and rich farmers. Having no choice, the *brahmans* accepted the *vellalars* almost as equals. The members of both groups shared their responsibilities as managers and functionaries of the temples whose substantial resources and assets they oversaw. The non-*vellalar shudras* followed a host of occupations, ranging from various trades and crafts to the most menial tasks. With the increasing complexity and mobility of the southern society in general and the emergence of new trades, the non-*vellalar shudras* could no longer be treated as a homogeneous group. Instead of being given a traditional *varna* ranking after the northern model, the south Indians newly devised a twofold division called the Right Hand and the Left Hand, known as *valangai* and *idangai* (Champakalakshmi 1995: 285–8; Thapar 2002: 389–91). The idea of the left/right caste divisions originally began with the description of units in the Chola armies, but later on became marked by occupational status. The Right Hand came to contain relatively more superior occupational groups than the Left Hand. It used to be believed that the Right Hand groups were those who were involved in stable agricultural occupations and the Left Hand groups were mostly different types of artisans; however, this would be to oversimplify the purpose of the division. This division should be seen as a particular form of cultural tool to resolve the problem of status or ranking in a complex situation where different groups of people – newly emergent Sanskritised hill people, forest people and tribals, craftsmen and merchants, traders and pedlars – competed for space and position within the social system. In the south Indian model of the Cholas, therefore, we had the *brahmans*, *vellalars*, and the Right Hand and Left Hand groups. It might be thought that this was a more rational and less oppressive system, but, alas, it was not to be. There were always to be some groups of people whose status could not be assigned even to the extreme left of the Left Hand, because these were the people whose oppression was a *sine qua non* for the comfort and prosperity of the society above them; these people, in the south Indian context, were the *paraiya*, the lowliest of the low – truly pariahs – those who were not only Untouchable but unworthy of approach. As far as oppression was concerned, the south Indian model was no different from the northern one. It was only in 1924 that the issues raised by Mahatma Gandhi's famous Vaikkom Satyagraha, over the question of temple entry for the Untouchables of the south, gave impetus to initiate serious discourse on this subject among the thinking people of both north and south India (Joseph 2003: 19, 158–82).

Women: deconstructing a single tradition

In Chapter 4 we referred to a number of ideas concerning women's honour and obligations as are found in the early Vedic literature. Then, in Chapter 7, we examined the impact of the *Dharmashastras*, like the *Manusmriti* or the *Yajanavalkyasmriti*, on the position of women and how those commentaries confirmed and asserted the Vedic world view of female gender. The ideals, norms and ideologies, as found in the *Vedas* and the *Dharmashastras*, inform us about a model based on a single Hindu tradition that normally placed great emphasis on patriarchy, the patrilineal family, devotion of a wife to her husband, restrictions on women's economic role and limited property rights. Throughout the ancient period, after the completion of Aryan conquests and the establishment of their settlements, patriarchy became well entrenched in north India, and remained a pervasive influence in the social life of the people there. It was further reinforced under the Turco-Afghan rulers who came to rule the north after CE 1200. This does not mean that patriarchy was absent in the south, since those who held power there and articulated about the social morality of the south had also been strongly influenced by Aryanisation, Sanskritisation and the Vedic and Shastric texts. Moreover, although the further south remained strongly Hindu in character, Muslim rule eventually came to be established in many parts of the Deccan after c. CE 1400 and, as a consequence, women suffered further disadvantages of patriarchy. The south, however, does present to us a somewhat complex and diverse picture of women's position.

A present-day reality in one part of south India – Kerala – is a testimony to this complexity and diversity. This is the matrilineal family structure that is found among the predominant Nayar community there, as well as among the Muslim Mapillas. The system had ancient roots, but became common after the seventh century CE. Matrilineality should not be confused with matriarchy. The latter, being the opposite of patriarchy, means the exercise of power by women. This was, and is, not so in Kerala, because men still command power in the public space; in fact, it is impossible to find a functioning matriarchal system anywhere in the world. In the matrilineal system, however, women play a leading role in family life, because the family unit consists of descendants of a common ancestress in the female line. The children acquire their rights through the mother's family, not the father; and property is passed on from mother to daughter. Although males are assigned the task of being the guardians of property, they are not permitted to alienate any part of it. A newlywed bride continues to stay in her ancestral home, and it is her husband who comes to live with her. Since the husband is not the head of the family, he has to behave in accordance with the norms of the wife's family, and there was no question of a wife bringing a dowry to him or to his family. If or when he died, the wife did not have to suffer the misery of widowhood or the horror of *sati*, since she would continue to stay in her own home. The older the woman in a matrilineal family, the greater the respect and honour she would be entitled to. The matrilineal custom, although not universally practised in Kerala, has continued to help women in contemporary Kerala to feel more emancipated and independent in outlook than many other Indian women.

A more significant method of appreciating the greater independence of women in south India is by studying ancient Tamil inscriptions. It has been estimated that there could be as many as 20,000 Tamil inscriptions from the period CE 700 to 1700 (Orr 2001: 205). Perhaps the most prolific study of these inscriptions was carried out by the Japanese historian Noboru Karashima, who, in his time, inspired a whole generation of scholars of Tamil and south Indian studies to research into and interpret the inscriptions (Hall 2001b). Their results have provided us with fascinating details of actual situations and activities in which Tamil women found themselves. Some of them, originally recruited as slaves or captives from wars, entered the royal palaces, learned the etiquette of courts and consequently acquired distinct privileges and positions for themselves (Ali 2006b: 44–62). Others became known as temple women, originally from disadvantaged castes and classes of people, who were supposed to be wedded to the gods in the temple; known as *devadasis*, they involved themselves in all the rituals of the temple, and learned to be highly skilled dancers and musicians, in order to please and propitiate the gods. The vast majority of the women in inscriptions were, however, ordinary people of varied ranks. The inscriptions tell us about the extent to which they donated gifts to temples and other institutions and were involved in property sale and transfers (Orr 2001: 198–234). These donor women's social identity and access to property are revealed in the inscription texts. In contrast to a patriarchal situation, the women donors' identities are not defined by caste, but rather by their place of birth or a place where they had land rights. Many of the women donors are also not identified as wives. Often, identities are defined wholly independently of women's relationship to their natal or marital families. The model of the husband–wife relationship that is found in the *Vedas* and the *Dharmashastras*, with the in-built economic inferiority of the wife, is not borne out in Tamil temple inscriptions. Instead, we find that Tamil women enjoyed considerable social autonomy and independence from male-dominated family structures. Their rights included the ownership and alienation of property, the selling of land in their own right, signing documents and deeds, donating gifts to institutions in their own name irrespective of their husband's wishes, and the issuing of inscriptions in their name. Many of them acquired prestige within their kin group by divesting themselves of wealth rather than receiving it. There were also opportunities for women to interact and compete within the numerous local and cosmopolitan religious, social and political frameworks that existed at the time. Such rights and privileges meant that these women would most probably have enjoyed more freedom and higher status within their families than their northern counterparts. The greater freedom that women in the south enjoy in our own times has its deep roots in the past, particularly in the 'enduringly vital social roles' the Tamil women have played since ancient times (Orr 2001: 230).

STUDY GUIDE

Key issues

- The role of central and local governments in the Chola kingdom.
- Irrigation methods in south Indian farming.
- The role of guilds and foreign merchants in south Indian trading systems.
- The triangular relationship between the Chola kingdom, China and *Sri Vijaya*.
- The role of the Hindu temple in south Indian economic and social life.

Suggested readings

Champakalakshmi 1995: 266–308; Ludden 2002; Orr 2001: 198–234; Stein 1985: 228–51; Thapar 2002: 357–62; Wink 1990: 219–302.

INTERNET SELECTION

1) R. Champakalakshmi: 'Cholas in all their complexity'. www.thehindu.com/ books/cholas-in-all-their-complexity/article3346426.ece

2) James Heitzman: 'State formation in south India 850–1280'. www.uio.no/ HIS2172/h11/undervisningsmateriale/HIS2172_Heitzman.pdf

3) Dipesh Karmarkar: 'From a "Musaffir" to the "Mariffat" of urban change: the Arabs and the urban cultural landscape of coastal western India'. www. academia.edu/1899296/From_Musaffir_to_the_Marifat_of_urban_change

4) Helmut Lucas: 'Theories of Indianization: exemplified by selected case studies from Indonesia (Insular Southeast Asia)'.www.oeaw.ac.at/isa/files/working_ papers/suedostasien/soa001.pdf

5) Leslie Orr: 'Women of medieval south India in Hindu temple ritual: text and practice'. www.academia.edu/3804666/women-of-medieval-south-india-in-hindu-temple

QUESTIONS FOR GROUP DISCUSSION

1) How accurate is it to describe the Chola Empire as a 'segmentary' state?
2) How different is south Indian agriculture from that in the north?
3) What were the economic consequences for India of the displacement of the Abbasids by the Fatimids?
4) How did the Cholas pursue their maritime interests?
5) What historical factors have helped women in south India to be more independent than their sisters in the north?

11 Across north and south: cultural unity and diversity

(*c.* CE 600 to 1200)

Timeline/Key Dates

CE 630–45	Hsuan Tsang's travels in India
CE 760	Krishna I, the Rashtrakuta king, orders the building of the gigantic Kailashanatha Temple at Ellora
c. CE 788–822	The philosopher Shankaracharya
c. CE 800	Harun al Rashid, the Abbasid ruler of Baghdad, orders the translation of the Indian medical corpus *Susruta Samhita*
CE 849	Privileges granted to St Thomas Christians in Kerala
CE 936	First Parsi/Zoroastrian settlement at Sanjan in Gujarat
CE 950–1050	Khandariya Mahadeo Temple built at Khajuraho
CE 985–1012	Brihadiswara Temple at Thanjavur (Tanjore) built in the reign of Chola Rajaraja I
CE 1030	Al-Biruni in India
CE 1048	Kalhana writes *Rajatarangini*
CE 1169	Jayadeva writes *Gita Govinda*

The main themes of Chapters 9 and 10 concerned political and socio-economic issues in the great Hindu kingdoms of north and south India. Our focus in this chapter is to be on cultural developments, specifically in relation to religion, art and architecture, and literature. We shall examine the ways in which these three areas demonstrate, on the one hand, an integral unity across the subcontinent and, on the other, their diverse manifestations in different regions of India. The location of each of the main religious and cultural centres in India between *c.* CE 600 and 1200 will be found in Map 11.1. The last section of the chapter will deal with some of the Indian cultural influences abroad during this period.

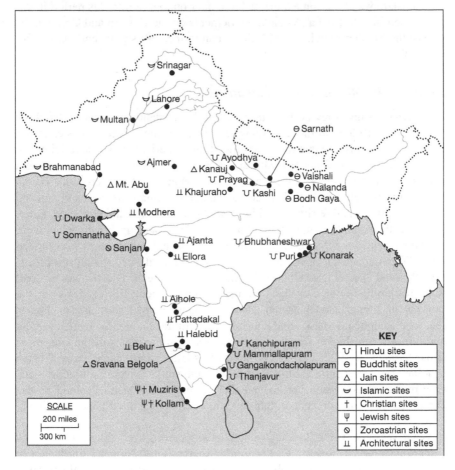

Map 11.1 Principal religious and cultural centres, CE 600 to 1200

The religious landscape

A number of shifts took place in the religious history of India between CE 600 and 1200. This was the period when Buddhism, a powerful religious force for nearly a thousand years, began its long decline in India, almost into oblivion. Hinduism, both in its Vedic form and through its diverse sects and schools of thought, became increasingly dominant throughout the subcontinent. Jainism, with relatively few adherents, continued to exert its influence in Indian society and culture throughout this period. Four non-Indic religions also made their presence felt in those parts of the country where they had clusters of adherents. Among them, Judaism and Christianity had long been rooted in south India, while Zoroastrianism came for refuge in Gujarat owing to the Islamic conversion of

Persia. Islam was to become a major force later on, but during this period it was mostly confined to Sind and smaller settlements on the western and Coromandel coasts; the Muslim population of India began to increase significantly only after CE 1200.

Decline of Buddhism: some explanations

In the centuries under review here, there was still a substantial number of Buddhists in the north-east and north-west, along with some of their large monasteries and monastic sites. It is true that from the time of the Imperial Guptas the religion had been in decline in the Gangetic heartland of *Madhyadesha*, but even in the seventh century, according to the inveterate Chinese Buddhist traveller-monk Hsuan Tsang, who travelled in India between 630 and 645, King Harsha was organising grand assemblies and festivals at which Buddhism was feted and honoured. Later, in the eighth and ninth centuries, Buddhism was also looked upon with great favour by the Pala rulers of Bengal. Buddhist institutions and endowments proliferated under Dharamapala, Devapala and other Palas. To Bengal came Buddhist scholars, travellers and visitors from all the different regions where the Buddha was revered: Sind, Kashmir, Ceylon and Nepal within the subcontinent; Burma, Laos and the Indonesian islands; and China and Tibet. King Dharamapala continued to support the great Buddhist monastic and educational institute at Nalanda, while building another centre of higher learning at *Vikramshila* on the banks of the Ganges in Bihar (Samaddar 1922: 119–41). While to this latter centre came many Tibetan scholars, Nalanda continued to attract monks and students from South East Asia. One might correctly say that under Pala patronage Buddhism obtained its last chance to retain its influence in India before a newly resurgent Hinduism finally crushed it.

Whatever benefits the Buddhists might have received from King Harsha or the Bengal Palas, their position was becoming increasingly fraught with danger in our period. Hsuan Tsang himself observed that in many parts of India the religion was in great decline, with the ruins of monasteries and *stupas* testifying to the decay. Over the centuries that followed, things only got worse for the Buddhists, and by 1200 all their vitality had gone. Among a number of lines of argument advanced by historians for this sudden decline, four need to be looked at more closely.

First, it has been argued that the Buddhist laity had lost its passion and lacked any sense of organisation. Each person, according to the Buddha, had to undertake his or her own journey towards salvation, and no amount of sacrifice or ritual could help towards reaching that final goal. As it was, this was not easy advice to follow, but its simplicity had made Buddhism popular among both the poor and the socially and commercially mobile during the earlier centuries. The laity, however, could hardly be expected to retain that sense of loyalty to the Buddha's pristine message in an age when the ideologically revived Hinduism, with its myriad rituals and caste etiquettes, could more easily draw the Indian masses into its embrace. Besides, the Buddhists themselves had increasingly become highly attracted towards the *Tantric* practices that were being incorporated particularly into the *Mahayana* form. Fewer and fewer Indians were being convinced of the distinctness of Buddhism. A church without laity is like a university without a student body, and with the rapid dissolution of its laity the Buddhist church in India soon became an empty shell (Wink 1997: 335ff.).

Second, it has been argued that Indian Buddhism lacked the political skills of survival in a changing environment. The *sanghas*, the communities of monks, had been obliged to maintain a puritanical lifestyle, although dependent for sustenance on the laity. In the age of the benevolence of rulers such as Ashoka and Kanishka, the *sanghas* could continue with their traditional calling. However, all institutions need sound political 'antennae' if they wish to maintain their position. Unfortunately, the Buddhist *sanghas* lacked any sense of the shifting winds of politics. Many of their monasteries were situated along the trade routes, rather than being close to the cities, where political news travels faster. All this mattered little wherever the local ruler was sympathetic to the Buddhists. After the fifth century CE, more often than not, the rulers favoured Brahmanism or its offspring, *Shaivism* or *Vaishnavism* (Omvedt 2003: 174–81). The latter two had begun in the earlier centuries but, during our period, their influence grew enormously, particularly in south India. The 'simple-hearted' (Majumdar and Pusalker 1954: 327) devotees, or *bhaktas*, sometimes known as saints, were the *Shaiva Nayanars* or *Vaishnava Alvars*. Their songs, poems and hymns, all glorifying either Vishnu or Shiva, were utilised principally in the process of weaning the south Indian masses away from the heterodoxies like Buddhism. The *bhakti* movement can also be seen, in that sense, as a reaction against the contemporary power structures and elites within the south Indian kingdoms, such as those of the Pallavas (Flood 1996: 170).

Third, it has been argued that, in an age of Buddhist decadence, the flexible and fairly tolerant broad church that was Hinduism offered a real home for the assimilation of Buddhists. There was supposed to be no harassment or persecution of the Buddhists, and the Buddha himself was incorporated into the Hindu pantheon of gods (Majumdar 1977: 429). This is a somewhat questionable proposition, because it was not unknown for Buddhists to be persecuted by kings inclining towards *Shaivism* and *Vaishnavism* (Wink 1997: 310–11; Omvedt 2003: 169–70). In a number of *Puranas*, too, the persecution of many non-Brahmanic groups, including Buddhists, was considered praiseworthy (Omvedt 2003: 169). We can only guess why it should be that the history of Buddhism in India can be studied solely with the help of Brahmanic or foreign sources, such as Tibetan, Sri Lankan or Nepali; it must be because there are hardly any original surviving Buddhist documents from the Indian mainland (Omvedt 2003: 165–7). Of course, many valuable manuscripts would have been taken away by the fervent and devoted Chinese and Tibetan travellers, but a good number must have been destroyed in the Brahmanic persecutions or the later Turkish attacks on the monasteries. From the ninth century onwards, the Buddhists themselves began to rationalise their assets; they transferred their most important manuscripts and treasures to larger monasteries (Wink 1997: 343). Through the help and favours granted by the Palas, monastic institutions such as Nalanda and Vikramashila were enabled to continue.

Fourth, there is the argument that the Buddhist demise was the result of Muslim persecutions. This is debatable, partly because, as we saw in Chapter 9, the Buddhists of Sind converted en masse to Islam for economic reasons; it was Arab commercial rivalry, not Arab persecution, which was responsible for the conversion. The Turco-Afghan invaders, who raided India in the eleventh and twelfth centuries and started ruling north India from the thirteenth century onwards, were more rapacious than the Arabs. Wealthy monasteries, such as Nalanda, were certainly pillaged and destroyed; nevertheless, it would be wrong to presume that the Turks carried out genocidal massacres of the Buddhist populace at large. They did not, and did not need to, because the relatively few Buddhists who were left in India at the end of our period posed no particular threat to them (Omvedt 2003: 174–81). Buddhism had been dying in India long before the advent of the Turks.

Diversity within Hinduism

Although by far the largest number of people of India would have been the adherents of Hinduism, it is most unlikely that they would have described themselves by the term 'Hindu' (Thapar 2002: 438–41). This was a term that came into popular usage from about the thirteenth or fourteenth century onwards, and, although its origins are to be found in the ancient Persian geographical references to the land that lay east of the River Indus, it was the Muslims who gave it wider circulation when they used it as a blanket term to describe those whom they considered to be idol-worshippers (Wink 1997: 328). These so-called idol-worshippers would, most probably, have described themselves by either their own caste and *jati* term or a faith term such as *Vaishnava* or *Shaivite*. Buddhists, Jains and various groups of heretics from the Brahmanic fold were generally called the *Shramanas*.

Three broad strands had shaped Hinduism before it encountered Islam and post-Enlightenment Europe. The first and the oldest, Vedic Brahmanism, almost 3,000 years old by this period, had developed a most amazing framework of beliefs and practices, and it commanded at least the nominal loyalty of the vast majority of the people for many centuries. They were guided by the *brahman* priests, who inculcated into them such ideas as the supremacy of the *Vedas*, sacrifices to the Vedic gods, the caste system, the rituals of the 'rites of passage', and the divine right of the monarchy to rule benevolently. In addition to the *Vedas*, commentaries such as the *Brahmanas* and the *Upanishads*, the epics of *Ramayana* and *Mahabharata*, the *Dharmashastras* and the *Dharmasutras*, and the six schools of philosophy – which taught such subjects as logic, cosmology, causation, atheism and the idea of the self – all these were contained within the philosophical, intellectual and theological framework of Vedic Brahmanism. However dominant a heterodoxy such as Buddhism and Jainism might have appeared during certain periods of time after the sixth century BCE, it did not pose an existential threat to Hinduism.

The second strand developed from the fifth century CE onwards, when a new fervour came to permeate the spiritual aspirations of the people. This was the *bhakti* tradition, as referred to in Chapter 7, which sprang from the Puranic religion formed around the *Vaishnava* and *Shaivite* schools, and which demanded from its followers intense devotion to personal gods such as Vishnu or Shiva. Led by the *Alvar* and *Nayanar* saints and poets, this tradition swept through India like a whirlwind in the later centuries of the first millennium CE and was to remain a potent force for centuries into the next millennium. Vedic Brahmanism was not displaced, but faced a daunting challenge from the Puranic ideology, and it was by their intellectual genius that philosophers, such as Shankaracharya (788–822), Ramanuja (1017–1137) and, a little later, Madhava (1197–1276), managed to bridge the differences between the two strands and not precipitate a destructive separation between them. Royal power in the regional kingdoms navigated skilfully between upholding the core values of the older strand while supporting the devotionalists, who represented the growing popular forces of the time. The role of the temples, which were the symbols of royal patronage, was particularly critical in accommodating the two strands (Stein 1998: 122–3; Thapar 2002: 356–7).

It was in this same spirit of understanding and reconciliation that the third strand, that of the local cults, also became part of the developmental process of Hinduism. With the formation of new regional kingdoms and the opening up of hitherto inaccessible territories, remote groups of people were newly being brought into the Brahmanic fold. Many of these people followed inchoate beliefs and practices that existed at the village level, often involving goddess worship, animal sacrifice and animism. Vedic Brahmanism, being the repository of the conservative tradition, naturally remained cautious in its approach to cults, but the Puranic religion learned to embrace them and assimilate their deities into the Hindu fold (Jha 2004: 205). The most powerful cults, known as Devi or Shakti, were those that worshipped the Mother Goddess and her super-power for doing good or evil to the world (Hinnells and Sharpe 1972: 52–4; Flood 1996: 174–97). In the Hindu pantheon, the goddess Uma, or Parvati, was the Mother Goddess showing her beneficent nature, while as Durga, Kali or Shitala she assumed her demonic form (Flood 1996: 193–5). The female gender is also accorded much strength and respect in the various *Tantric* cults, based on magic and mystical formulas, although some of their practices include 'elements of sexual perversion' (Sen 1961: 70). As many non-caste and lower caste people followed the cults, it was vital to incorporate at least some of their beliefs into Hindu practice. Hence we see, during the eleventh and twelfth centuries, a great increase in image worship and the individual worship of a deity in their human aspect. The mythologies of deities also came to be popularised through regional languages and oral recitations (Thapar 2002: 483–4).

The resilience of the Jains

The Jains did not suffer the same fate as the Buddhists. Their numbers might not have been large, but they were able to preserve and maintain their religious identity. A number of reasons might explain their survival instinct. They were a highly literate trading community, with a finely developed sense of business enterprise, which was valued by monarchs who appreciated the commercial gains.

They maintained a strong theological discipline among themselves, and much of their asceticism and orthodoxy came to be admired by the Hindus. While keeping close to the Hindu doctrine of salvation, they rejected any notion of adopting theistic ideas of *Shaivism* and *Vaishnavism*, which helped them to preserve their distinctness. Laity and monks monitored each other closely (Wink 1997: 352). While the Buddhist laity was losing its fervour, the Jain fold took upon itself the task of upholding the values and rituals of their religion. Unlike the Buddhist monk, the Jain monk did not spend most of his time in monastic establishments. Jain monks were expected to mix with the general public and be truly wandering mendicants. By the eleventh and twelfth centuries, the Jains had only a limited foothold in the Gangetic basin, but they were reasonably secure in Rajasthan, Gujarat and Karnataka. In Rajasthan and Gujarat they suffered persecution at the hands of the Turks, but nevertheless survived and continued to flourish in business and banking. In Gujarat, particularly, the twelfth century was a golden age for the community. A great Jain intellectual, Hemchandra, provided a powerful impetus to the growth and development of the Gujarati language through his numerous writings (Yashaschandra 2003: 567ff.). In Karnataka it was their involvement in the Arab mercantile trade that won the Jains favourable royal patronage. In the long run, however, their influence in Karnataka waned during our period owing to the rise of the *Lingayat* sect of the *Virashaivas*, led by a saint known as Basav. The *Lingayats* were extremely anti-Jain (Jha 2004: 207–8). Occasionally, the Jains also came under severe persecution at the hands of the *Shaivites*. The Chola rulers in the deep south were *Shaivites*, but supported the Jains, probably because the latter were important benefactors of the merchant guilds, such as the Ayyavole 500, that were based in the *nagarams* (Champakalakshmi 1995: 289–90; Heitzman 2001: 128; Champakalakshmi 2001b: 326–43;).

Non-Indic faiths

By the year CE 1000, in addition to the Hindus, Buddhists and Jains, the adherents of four Middle Eastern faiths had settled in diverse parts of India. The Arab Muslims were the largest group and, with their conquest of Sind in CE 711, Islam became the religion of the state in that region. As we noted in Chapter 9, Arab authority in Sind was not unduly oppressive; the Buddhists converted voluntarily, but the majority Hindu population was not forced to convert during our period. The Turco-Afghan invaders, being extremely iconoclastic, destroyed many Hindu and Buddhist sacred places, and carried away much loot to Afghanistan. There was, however, little effort at conversion by Turco-Afghans during this period. The Arab Muslims took up trading and maritime activities on the west coast of India, particularly in Kerala (Chapter 10). They had few inhibitions about arranging temporary marriages (*muta*) with Indian women (Wink 1990: 71) and, although initially they did not go out of their way to convert the Indians, they made sure that their offspring considered themselves Muslim.

Kerala was also the place where a visible Christian presence had been evident for several hundred years. According to a commonly held Keralan tradition, the earliest Christian church was established by St Thomas, an apostle of Christ, in CE 52 (Menon 1990: 34–7). Doubts felt by Western Christians about this claim have centred upon two issues: the lack of written testimony and the hazards of long sea journeys. Modern historical research into the many oral traditions within the Kerala church has put the first doubt to rest. Also, since Roman and Egyptian ships were trading regularly with Kerala in the first century CE, there was no reason why St Thomas could not have travelled on one of those ships. The Kerala church had no direct contact with Rome; in fact, from the fourth century onwards, its main link with the Christian world was through the merchants and immigrants who came to Kerala in Persian trading ships. Many of them were West Asian and Levantine Nestorian Christians who owed allegiance to the Persian state, and whose prelates and bishops lived in the Persian Empire of the Sasanians. Their liturgy was in the Syriac language, a variant of Aramaic, the language of Christ and his apostles.[1] It is through this Levantine connection that the St Thomas church came to be known as the Syrian church (Menon 1990: 58–61). While these Christian immigrants helped to familiarise the Syrian church with the various revisionist dogmas of Christianity that were convulsing Europe and the Middle East during the first Christian millennium, the essential strength of the church lay in the numbers of converted natives. A regular series of conversions of some of the most high-caste and influential *brahman* families of Kerala not only provided numerical strength but also helped to Indianise this church in a way realised by no other Christian church in India (Joseph 2003: 19–20, 27–8). In the period covered by this chapter, the most reliable documentary evidence of the influence of the St Thomas church comes from three inscriptions on the so-called Tarisapalli Copper Plates of the year CE 849. The inscriptions record a set of privileges granted to the Syrian church at Quilon by the then local ruler, placing the Christians on an equal footing with the Hindus of Kerala (Menon 1990: 61–3).

As with the Christians, it was again Kerala that was the main hosting society for the followers of yet another Middle Eastern faith: Judaism. The Keralan hospitality went back, according to Indian and Jewish traditions, to 1000 BCE, when King Solomon's fleet was supposed to have traded in Indian waters (Menon 1990: 64). The Jews were in Kerala at the time of Christ, and, again according to tradition, thousands of Jews landed at *Muziris* after the destruction of the second temple of Jerusalem by the Romans in CE 70. The Jewish connection with south India was strengthened by the rise of the Fatimid caliphs, as mentioned in Chapter 10. The Jewish merchant houses in Cairo promoted extensive trade with India. The Chera rulers of Kerala appreciated the financial gains and economic activity generated by the Jews and occasionally, as testified by **Excerpt 11.1** below, granted gifts and privileges to their leaders (Menon 1990: 65–8; Wink 1990: 100).

With the introduction of Islam in Persia after the decisive Arab victory there in CE 641, the state religion of Zoroastrianism was left rudderless. While the mass of the Persian people abandoned their Zoroastrian faith for Islam out of both fear and expediency, substantial numbers of staunch Zoroastrians continued to survive there during the next few centuries. Their position fluctuated between extreme vulnerability and insecure coexistence with the Muslims (Boyce 2002b: 229–45).

Excerpt 11.1 Privileges granted to Jews in Kerala

Among a number of copper plates belonging to the Jewish synagogue in Cochin, Kerala, the one that is most well known is the Jewish Copper Plate of CE 1000, the inscription on which indicates a bond of friendship between the Chera monarch Bhaskara Ravi Varman (r. CE 962–1019) and the local Jewish merchant, Joseph Rabban.

Hail prosperity! This is the gift that His Majesty, Sri Bhaskara Ravi Varman . . . is pleased to make . . . We have granted to Joseph Rabban, the ancuvannam (guild) tolls by the boat and carts, ancuvannam dues, the right to employ day lamp, decorative cloth, palanquin, umbrella, kettle drum, trumpet gateway arch, arched roof, weapon and the rest of the seventy two privileges we have remitted duty and weighing fee . . . Moreover . . . he shall be exempted from payments made by other settlers in the town to the King, but he shall enjoy what they enjoy . . . To Joseph Rabban, proprietor of ancuvannam, his male and female issues, nephews, and sons-in-law, ancuvannam shall belong to them by hereditary succession.

Source: M.G.S. Narayanan, 'The Jewish Copper Plates of Cochin', in *Cultural Symbiosis in Kerala*, Trivandrum: Kerala Historical Society, 79–82.

According to a tradition recorded in a sixteenth-century poem written in Persian, the *Quisse Sanjan*, a band of these Zoroastrians, from the Khorasan province of Iran (Parthia), landed on the Gujarat coast near Sanjan as refugees in 716. It is, however, more likely that they came as late as 936, when they were welcomed by a local ruler, Jadi Rana, who, most probably, was a feudatory of the Rashtrakuta king (Mistree 2002: 413–14). The Parsis, as they have come to be called by the Gujaratis, have lived in India ever since as a minuscule but distinct faith community.

While many nations in the world today are still struggling with the challenges and contradictions of multi-faith societies within their boundaries, the long historical presence of the above four non-Indic religious communities within India is a testimony to the strength and vigour of Indian multi-culturalism.

Art and architecture

For nearly thousand years before CE 600, it was Buddhism that inspired the creators of Indian art and architecture. After CE 600, the inspiration derived from Hinduism. Hindu art and architecture were in the ascendant throughout India for at least seven centuries. After the fourteenth century, Islamic art and architecture predominated in north India, but the Hindu tradition continued in the south long afterwards. The origins of Hindu stone architecture and temples are to be traced in just a few structures found at many scattered sites that were once the capitals of dynasties or sacred places which had attracted pilgrims for many reasons. The classic Hindu temples of India post-CE 600 may be classified into three styles of architecture: Deccani, southern and northern. All of them have common features, such as the *vimana* (sanctuary), the *garba griha* (inner chamber for the idol), the *shikhara* (tower) and the *mandapa* (pavilion), but there are some key differences. The towers of the northern-style temples are curvilinear or bulging, while those of the southern style are pyramidical. The Deccani towers, while pyramidical, are lower than in the northern style. The southern-style temples also have extensive enclosures and great *gopurams* (gateways), while the Deccani temples are star-shaped or polygonal rather than square, as in the other two styles. The northern-style temples developed somewhat later than those in the Deccan and the south. In all regions of India, the temples were constructed under the supervision of the *sutradharas*, the architects, who designed religious precincts in strict accordance with the geometrical rules laid down in the ancient *Shilpashastras* (Ray *et al.* 2000: 537–9; Thapar 2002: 476). Ancient Indian art and architecture incorporate, in their own terms, a set of ideal canons of form. Strict principles of proportion, clearly laid down in ancient prescriptions in manuals of written and diagrammatic formulae, guided both the architects and the artists.

In the Deccan

The Deccani styles began with the Early Chalukyas of Badami (535–757) and developed further under the Later Chalukyas (tenth to fourteenth centuries) and the Hoysalas (twelfth to fourteenth centuries). The Chalukyan culture revolved around the temples, and what remains of the striking architecture of that kingdom cannot fail to impress upon us the significance of a richly endowed Brahmanic religious culture in their part of the Deccan. The main monuments are clustered around three sites in the Karnataka: Aihole, Badami and Pattadakal (Figure 11.1). Each was the centre of royal power in its turn. Aihole was the first capital; here, for many centuries, the Chalukyan craftsmen perfected the styles of the first built temples, as distinct from those carved out of solid rock. An interesting feature of the Karnataka temples built during the various Chalukya dynasties, and continued under the Hoysalas, was the enormous polygonal, star-shaped base on which a typical temple structure stood. The best examples during the eleventh and twelfth centuries are to be found at Belur and Halebid. The oldest of such temples is the Meguti Temple, built in CE 634 according to an inscription by the court poet Ravikirti (Sivaramamurti 1977: 484). The first dated reference to Kalidasa, the author of *Shakuntala*, as provided by Ravikirti, may also be seen in this temple. Badami was the second capital. Here there are some extraordinary temples with immensely vivacious sculptures of gods and goddesses. The Melagitti Shivalaya Temple provides one such example. Inside a large number of many other temples can be seen the valuable inscriptions detailing the victories of a regal hero such

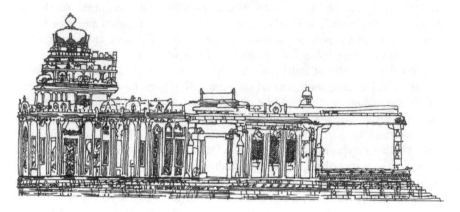

Figure 11.1 The Deccani-style temple of Pattadakal

as Pulakeshin II or treaties and relationships between the Chalukyas and their rivals, the Pallavas (Chapter 10). The temples, small but 'superbly conceived' (Bradnock and Bradnock 1998: 972), were built to supplicate the gods for victory in battles. The Hoysaleswara Temple in Halebid, begun in the twelfth century, took more than a hundred years to complete, but the richness of its frieze carvings, and particularly that of a line of 650 elephants, and of the various jewels and ornaments worn by gods and goddesses provides ample evidence of the skills of the builders and sculptors of the Deccan (Evans 1997: 195–211).

Temples carved out of living rock, the cave temples, began to be constructed during the height of the Rashtrakuta power in the Deccan (CE 760–967). The most concrete physical expression of the grandeur of this dynasty is the eighth-century World Heritage site of the Kailashanatha Temple in Ellora, Maharashtra (Figure 11.2). This massive monument, dedicated to Shiva and representing his mountain fortress, Kailasha, is the world's largest single free-standing structure, carved out of living rock, and covering an area wider than the Parthenon of Athens. The distinguished art historian Percy Brown has described it as 'the most stupendous single work of art ever executed in India' (Sengupta 1993: 21). His wonderment is perfectly understandable, for there is nothing in all of Hindu religious art that can compare with the vastness of Kailashanatha. It is only one of the thirty-four rock-carved cave temples of Ellora. Half of them are Hindu caves, twelve are Buddhist and five are Jain. Kailashanatha is cave number sixteen, the best known and most visited. All the essential symbols of Hindu religion and religiosity are represented in the images of the temple, and, for this, nearly three million cubic metres of rock had to be excavated from the cliff – a stupendous effort (Tomory 1989: 211–14; Sengupta 1993: 19). The temple, which is still standing and protected by UNESCO funds (Nicholas 2003: 122), is a tribute to both the vision and the imagination of the Rashtrakuta king Krishna I and his chief builder, and the craftsmanship of masons and labourers of the eighth century.

Figure 11.2 Tourist Sam Badni on the upper gallery of Ellora

In the far south

The southern temples began with the Pallavas during the seventh and eighth centuries CE, and reached their apogee under the Cholas (CE 900 to 1150) and the later Pandyas (CE 1100 to 1350). Here we shall deal with only the first two dynasties. Two main centres of population, the capital city of Kanchipuram and the port city of Mamallapuram (Mahabalipuram), were at the hub of Pallava culture and influence. Kanchipuram is one of the seven sacred cities of Hinduism, dedicated to both Shiva and Vishnu and renowned as a great seat of learning and philosophy in all Tamil Nadu. Among the great free-standing temples the Pallavas built in the city, the most beautiful are the Kailashanatha Temple and, slightly ahead of our period, the more famous Vaikuntha Perumal Temple (Mahalingam 1969: 139–42, 184; Sivaramamurti 1977: 508–9). Inscriptions narrating the history of the Pallava kings and eulogising their glories formed part of the panelled sculptures on the temple walls. At the port city of Mamallapuram are further testimonies to the Pallava contribution to culture and architecture. The Five Rathas, named after the five Pandava brothers, are miniature temples demonstrating the evolution of the southern temple style (Sivaramamurti 1977: 513–17; Craven 1997: 148–50). The *Mahabharata* episode of Arjuna's penance and the flowing of the River Ganges from Shiva's hair are depicted in an enormous frieze, which is cut into a flat, granite rock face, 28 metres long and 12 metres high (Craven

Figure 11.3 Shore Temple at Mamallapuram/Mahabalipuram

1997: 145–7). The most glorious monument of Mamallapuram is the famous Shore Temple, facing the Bay of Bengal and renowned throughout the civilised world (Figure 11.3). The mythological relief carvings in caves or rock-faces have a restrained elegance, a feature of Pallava art, which originally drew inspiration from the Buddhist Amaravati sculptures (Chapter 7).

Religious architecture and art greatly flourished under the Cholas. The two most iconic of their temples are those at Thanjavur and Gangaikondacholapuram. The first, the Brihadiswara Temple, built by Rajaraja I, in the Chola capital of Thanjavur (Tanjore), is one of the grandest in India (Figure 11.4). With its 62-metre-high *vimana*, a dome carved from an 80-ton block of granite and, mounted on the tower, the innumerable carvings of dancers along with the sculptures of Shiva, Vishnu and Durga, and a gigantic Nandi bull guarding the entrance, this World Heritage site is expressive of Chola religious piety at its best. Among the many buildings within the temple complex were housing blocks for nearly 400

Figure 11.4 Brihadiswara Temple at Thanjavur

devadasis, or temple dancers, who, along with the priests and the musicians, were an integral part of the Chola temple community (Orr 2001: 198–234). Modelled on this temple was the second temple, built by Rajaraja's son, Rajendra I, at Gangaikondacholapuram, to commemorate his expedition to the sacred River Ganges and its water that was brought all the way from Bengal. This too is an extremely large site, 100 metres long and 40 metres wide. Its *mandapa* (assembly hall) and the sanctuary inside the compound were raised on a high platform, while its *vimana* soars 55 metres into the sky. It too contains a fabulous array of sculptures (Bradnock and Bradnock 1998: 808). The Chola artists specialised in both stone and metallic sculptures, and the most prominent figure portrayed was the god Shiva. The so-called Chola bronzes are well known in the art world. The bronze sculptures consisted mostly of icons, ranging from almost life-size to a few inches high, of Hindu deities. The most significant of them were sometimes dedicated as 'portraits' of members of the royal family in the guise of gods, and they were generally meant to be carried in procession. There were many images of Hindu saints in adoration; the best known among them represents the god Shiva as the beautiful 'Lord of the Dance', *Shiva Nataraja*. This sculpture, originally from Tiruvalangadu, has been described by the French sculptor Rodin as 'the most perfect representation of rhythmic movement in art' (Tomory 1989: 231). It is also worth noting that the Chola bronze art deeply influenced the art of South East Asia.

In the north

Notwithstanding the iconoclasm of Mahmud of Ghazni and other marauding Turco-Afghans, the eleventh and twelfth centuries were a time of remarkable progress in temple-building in the north. That the architecture of the northern-style temples reached its culmination and maturity during those centuries can be testified by some of the finest examples to be found at four different site complexes. The largest concentration of such temples is to be found in Orissa, dating from the seventh to the thirteenth centuries. The eleventh-century Lingaraja Temple in Bhubhaneshwar is the most famous (Figure 11.5). With three aligned halls, its architecture is characterised by motifs of human, animal and vegetable life-forms and by lofty spires (Tomory 1989: 92, 95). The Black Pagoda of Konarak, which is an unfinished or ruined temple of the sun, is another iconic structure in Orissa. Most of the Orissan temples were decorated with illustrations on narrow strips of palm-leaf.

Another complex of northern temples has been left to posterity by the Chandella rulers of Bundelkhand at Khajuraho in Madhya Pradesh (Figure 11.6). The largest, and sculpturally the most notable, of the nearly twenty-five temples still standing in the area is the Khandariya Mahadeva, which enthrals the eye with its fine statuary and decoration (Desai 1975: 135–7; Tomory 1989: 102–6). Built between *c.* CE 950 and 1050, this temple has a profusion of sculptural figures cut in deep relief; these are adorned with necklaces, hip girdles, head ornaments, bangles, anklets, etc. It is also possible to make out the fragments of wall paintings inside the temple. Owing to their distance and remoteness, the Orissa and Khajuraho temples might

Figure 11.5 Temple styles of Bhubhaneshwar

have escaped despoliation by the Turks. This was not the case at the Rajasthan and Gujarat sites, where the Turks did cause much damage. Nevertheless, we still have some fine examples from both areas to enrich our senses. The most exquisite Rajasthani examples are the Dilwara Jain temples on Mount Abu, especially the Vimala Vasahi, which was built in the eleventh century by Vimala Shah, a wealthy Jain merchant, and dedicated to the first *Tirthankara*. With its forty-eight pillars in the main hall and a richly carved dome of eleven rings, the Vimala Vasahi is a remarkable showpiece of Jain religious philanthropy (Marett 1985: 70–1; Tomory 1989: 206–7). The carving in this temple is that of the Solanki style, named after the dynasty that ruled both Gujarat and Rajasthan in the eleventh and twelfth centuries. The best surviving example of the Solanki temples on the Gujarat site is the *Surya* temple at Modhera, the beauty of which so moved an art historian that he called its creator 'a weaver of dreams' (citation in Nicholson 1993: 163). Rich and refined Solanki carving is one of the key features of this beautiful sandstone temple sited beside a stepped tank.

Figure 11.6 Temple scene from Khajuraho

Literature and thought

The literary source material for the history of the six centuries between CE 600 and 1200 lies in numerous inscriptions of varying significance in relation to state and religion in both north and south, historical biographies, chronicles and *vamshavalis*, along with contemporary historical accounts. Drama, poetry and religious writing are also part of the literature of the period. The two main languages in which much of the literature was written were Sanskrit and Tamil. There are also the first indications of literature in vernacular languages, and Persian and Arabic writings are also available. There is no shortage of material for primary researchers and scholars to probe and analyse, and new interpretations are always forthcoming as more material is closely studied.

Sanskrit literature

Sanskrit continued, during this period, to be the language of courtly, refined and elite literature. In the seventh century it was the great north-Indian king, Harsha, himself, who set high standards in his Sanskrit writings. In Chapter 9 we referred to his leadership qualities and administrative prowess, but he saw his role extending beyond the onus of waging wars and conducting affairs of state. His literary refinement is well known, and some scholars have even found in his signature the quality of that refinement. A poet, connoisseur and a man of considerable literary talent, Harsha wrote three Sanskrit dramas himself. His masterpiece, *Ratnavali*, dealt with the story of the marriage of King Udayana and Ratnavali, the daughter of the king of Sri Lanka. The second work, *Priyadarshika*, had a similar theme, but also contains a play within a play, which is called *garbhanka*. His third drama, *Nagananda*, deals with the themes of self-sacrifice and love. All three dramas made a contribution to the evolution and development of Sanskrit literature after Kalidasa (Sastri 1960: 107–8). He led the way for other Sanskrit dramatists such as Bhavabhuti and Bhatta Narayana and served as inspiration for the Pallava king Mahendravarman, who composed a farce called *Mattavilasa*. The best example of Sanskrit prose in this period comes from the pen of Bana (Banabhatta), Harsha's biographer. Bana is admired by Sanskrit scholars because of the intensity and vivaciousness in his use of language. He has a unique gift for portraying all manner of situations and circumstances in the India of his day, whether domestic or public; his eye for detail shows in his depiction of themes as varied as war, love, revenge, faith or plain daily life (Cowell and Thomas n.d.: vii–xiv; Keith 1928: 314–19, 326–30; Sastri 1960: 134–5). His biography of Harsha, the *Harsha-charita*, is what is called an *Akhyayika*, in contrast to a *katha* or a romance based on a purely poetic creation. It would not be wise to rely on it for a systematic historical account of Harsha's reign, but there is sufficient information in it for us to form a strong mental picture of the personality and character of this great king (Pathak 1997: 30–55; Singh 2003: 90–6). It is a very positive image that we receive, as Harsha is Bana's hero; and Bana's admiration is reflected in his prose.

Following Harsha's example, both northern and southern monarchs provided much royal patronage to Sanskrit poets and dramatists. One of the styles of writing that was experimented with by later Sanskrit dramatists was called *Champu*, a mixture of prose and verse, particularly popular with monarchs, whose praises were sung sometimes in a sycophantic manner (Devasthali 1955: 187–8). Unfortunately, this form of secular literature was far too stylised, pedantic or didactic, and lacked 'specificity with details of time, place and person' (Dimock *et al.* 1974: 11), thus betraying a distinct lack of originality. There was, however, an important exception, which was in the area of poetic theory. A number of literary critics had, in the past, explored the characteristics of Sanskrit poetry in terms of figures of speech, style or sheer aesthetic pleasure. In the ninth century, however, a critic known as Anandavardhana analysed a new element in poetry, which he termed *Dhvani* or suggestiveness. In his famous work *Dhvanyaloka*, he stated that all poetic work is endowed with three powers: denoting in a factual way, implying something obliquely, or suggesting an imaginative vista (Devasthali 1955: 192–3; Dimock *et al.* 1974: 136–43; Pollock 2003: 44). His work was further refined by the Kashmiri philosopher Abhinavagupta (975–1025), and the *Dhvani* theory of suggestiveness was recognised by the distinguished French critic Jacques Lacan as particularly valuable for his work in psychoanalysis (Pandit 1996: Internet).

A very fine example of Sanskrit poetry is to be found in a lyrical poem, *Gita Govinda*, written by Jayadeva, the court poet at the court of Lakshmansena, the Sena king of Bengal (1178–1205). This poem, combining words and music, has become one of the great sources of religious inspiration in both medieval and contemporary *Vaishnavism*, and millions of people in Bengal and Orissa have, over the last 800 years, sung the songs embedded in the poem in their homes and at the great *Vaishnavite* fairs and festivals. Described as 'a dramatic, lyrical poem' (Miller 1977: 17), the *Gita Govinda* celebrates the passion of Krishna, the 'cosmic cowherd lover', for Radha, the *gopi*, and it deals with the concept of love by exploring what might be called 'sacred profanities' (Siegel 1978: 1–13), in the same way as the artwork of the temples of Khajuraho may be said to fuse eroticism with religious experience (Desai 1975: 188, 191–5). It uses all the techniques of good poetry that were known in India: alliteration, lyricism, and grace of image for effect. In later centuries it inspired the Bengali saint Chaitanya and the artists of the *Kangra* and *Pahari* schools of painting.

Perhaps the most famous Sanskrit historical work in this period is the *Rajatarangini*, 'River of Kings', a historical account of Kashmir written by Kalhana, a Kashmiri poet-courtier of the twelfth century. Using diverse sources of evidence, such as royal eulogies, coins, land grant records and temple inscriptions, Kalhana wrote 7,826 verses in eight books. While the author does not strictly follow the modern historical method and quite often beautifies or idealises the past, he is able to conceptualise the spirit of secular historical writing, as shown in **Excerpt 11.2** below. The *Rajatarangini* does provide us with a credible history of Kashmir, particularly in its last five books (Singh 2003: 113–22). The narrative depicts the history of the region as one of gradual decline, as the virtuous kings of the beginning give way to wicked kings whose courts are filled with corruption as part of the decline of the *Kali Yuga*. As a backcloth to its history, however, Kalhana does provide a sound ecological and environmental perspective of the Kashmir of his day (Thapar 2002: 415–16).

Sanskrit should not be considered the monopoly of northern literature. It remained a language of high culture in the south too. Literary culture there was promoted in the early stage by the educational institutions and monasteries run by the Jain and Buddhist monks and scholars, many of whom specialised in Sanskrit. With the advance of *Vaishnavism* and *Shaivism* through the region, essential Brahmanical learning in Sanskrit came to be provided by an institution called a *matha*, which was like a boarding school. The Pallava kings of the south were no mean donors to the cause of education and culture, and the city of Kanchipuram housed many educational and cultural centres. Sanskrit enjoyed royal patronage, and all the early Pallava inscriptions are in that language. While later inscriptions were in Tamil, the *prasastis* were nevertheless composed in Sanskrit. To the Pallava courts, both in this period and earlier, came famous Sanskritists such as Dignaga and Dandin, the great writer on poetics, and there can be no doubt that the Pallavas were patrons of such literati.

Excerpt 11.2 Kalhana as a historian

Although Kalhana cannot be considered a historian in the modern sense, his Rajatarangini *does provide evidence that he had a certain definite sense of what a good historian should or should not be. In his opinion, a historian must have a vision, he must be impartial, he should present his version of the story from his own perspective, and he must be able to synthesise a number of previous accounts into a coherent whole.*

If the poet did not see in his mind's eye the existences which he is to reveal to all men, what other indication would there be of his possessing divine intuition?

That noble-minded poet is alone worthy of praise whose word, like that of a judge, keeps free from love or hatred in relating the facts of the past.

If I narrate again the subject matter of tales which others have treated, still the virtuous ought not to turn their faces from me without hearing my reasons.

What is the skill required in order that men of a later time should supplement the narrative of events in the works of those who died after composing each the history of those kings whose contemporaries they were? Hence my endeavour is to give a connected account where the narrative of past events has become fragmentary in many respects.

Source: M.A. Stein, *Kalhana's Rajatarangini*, New Delhi:
Motilal Banarsidass, 1900/1961, Bk 1, 5, 7, 8,10.
See also A.L. Basham, *Studies in Indian History and Culture*, Calcutta: Sambodhi, 1964, 45–56

Tamil literature

While Sanskrit was promoted as a language of high culture, Tamil nevertheless remained the key medium of instruction in the far south. Its confidence was far greater than, for example, that of Kannada in the Chalukya kingdom, which was, at this stage, still considered a somewhat poor relation to Sanskrit. Lyric poetry and great epics were composed in Tamil. Just before our period the great epic of *Shilappadikaram*, produced by Ilango Adigal, had appeared (Pollock 2003: 295–301); in contrast to the earlier stories of heroic violence, it extolled the virtues of non-violence and duty. The very famous text of *Tirukkural*, composed by Tiruvalluvar, again a little before the period covered by this chapter, was also part of the rich tapestry of Tamil literature (Pollock 2003: 292–5). In its early stages, this literature was more secular than religious. The Tamil poems were suffused with rich descriptions of both country and town and the activities and lifestyles of people engaged in different spheres of work; and it has been said that 'compared with classical Sanskrit literature, the early Tamil literature was closer to the realities of life' (Jha 2004: 156). From the sixth century CE onwards, however, the religious consciousness began to gather strength and momentum. During the time of the Pallavas, the hymns, the devotional songs and the *mantras* chanted by the *Nayanars* and *Alvars* and their devoted followers of *Vaishnavism* and *Shaivism* were collected into a volume that came to constitute a major branch of Tamil literature. In fact, one could say that the best of Tamil literature of this period is almost wholly influenced by the religious movements in the south. The religious literature that was born out of the *bhakti* tradition of intense devotion and surrender to personal gods lay at the heart of worship in the great temple centres of the south (Champakalakshmi 1996a: 60–5; Flood 1996: 129–32). An unfortunate aspect of it, however, was the growth of sectarianism and sectarian rivalry among its diverse following (Champakalakshmi 1996a: 61).

The beginnings of vernacular literature

For many centuries, Sanskrit had been cherished as a language of perfection and purity by those with facility in it. Some innovative work apart, however, there were ominous signs for the future of Sanskrit in our period. Just as at one time *Prakrit* languages such as Pali, Sauraseni, Magadhi and Maharashtri acquired their own autonomy, so after the *Prakrits* a new phase set in along the development of Indian languages, called *Apabrahmasha* (Jain 1955: 212–19; Pollock 2003: 61–75). The term signified decadence born out of change. Those Sanskrit authors for whom the language was so perfect and so well defined viewed any change in its usage as a decline in standards. This attitude eventually led to the stagnation of Sanskrit; it began to be abandoned by both the elites and the masses because it failed to serve as a useful tool of communication. Its shortcomings have been correctly identified by an eminent historian in **Excerpt 11.3** below.

As the Jain polymath Hemchandra said, good literature could also be written in both *Prakrit* and *Apabrahmasha* (Pollock 2003: 567). While voluminous literature had of course existed in Sanskrit, *Prakrit* and Tamil, it was through the medium of the *Apabrahmasha* languages that the various regional languages of India evolved their own literatures. The development of regional literatures took place over a period of nearly 700 years after the eighth century CE. During the period we are examining, it was a Dravidian regional language, Kannada/Kanarese, which first acquired a literature of its own. It borrowed heavily in style and form from Sanskrit, but it was distinct in its own right, exploring themes and issues within the social and political parameters of Karnataka. The first great literary figure in Kannada was the Rashtrakuta king Amoghavarsha (CE 814–80), who wrote an important manual of poetic theory, *Kavirajamarga*, in which he laid down certain critical tests, with examples, by which the greatness of a poem could be judged (Iyengar 1955: 219–26; Nagaraj 2003: 323–9). Other regional languages, such as Telugu and Gujarati, also evolved at this time. Regional writers commanded royal patronage and found favour at the various feudal courts. They wrote poems,

Excerpt 11.3 The imperfections of Sanskrit

The great historian D.D. Kosambi explains some of the deficiencies of Sanskrit that need to be taken into account by uncritical admirers and religious zealots who wish to re-introduce the language as a universal means of communication within contemporary India.

> Even at its best, [Sanskrit] does not give the depth, simplicity of expression, the grandeur of spirit, the real greatness of humanity that one finds in the Pali Dhammapada, the Divina Commedia, or Pilgrim's Progress. It is the literature of and for a class, not a people . . . The language suffered from its long, monopolistic association with a class that had no direct interest in technique, manual operations, trade agreements, contracts or surveys . . . There is no Sanskrit word of any use to the blacksmith, potter, carpenter, weaver, ploughman . . . The distinction between Sanskrit and Arabic in this respect should also be considered. Arab works on medicine, geography, mathematics, astronomy, practical sciences were precise enough to be used in their day from Oxford to Malaya . . . The 'Arab' literati were not primarily a disdainful priest-caste.

> **Source:** D.D. Kosambi, *An Introduction to the Study of Indian History*, Bombay: Popular Prakashan, 1975, 283–5.

histories, dictionaries, grammars, plays and manuals of science and medicine. It is difficult to be excited by the intellectual rigour or the originality of these numerous and voluminous works, but a start had been made.

Islamic literature

The early Islamic literature concerning India was written in either Arabia or Persia. Most of the evidence was collected second hand. The major breakthrough came with the setting up of a royal court in Lahore by the Ghaznavid rulers in Punjab during the eleventh and twelfth centuries. In Lahore were also established innumerable Persian *madrasas* and, through them, 'the study of the Persian language became wider and more popular day by day among the people of upper Hindustan' (Ghani 1941: 195). The royal court became the meeting point for many poets and writers who excelled in Persian. Two of them are well known in the history of Persian poetry in India. Abul Faraj Runi (d. 1091) composed *ghazals* that became models for compositions both in India and Iran. Following a Sanskrit poetic tradition, Masud Saad Salman (1046–1131) created a new genre of *baramasa* poems that celebrated festivities associated with each month of the year (Schimmel 1973: 11–12; Alam 2003: 135–7). Also at the Lahore court was Abul-Fazl Bayhaqi (995–1077), who wrote the *Tarikh-e Masudi*, a well-researched and systematic account of the reign of Sultan Masud (r. 1030–40). The most famous literary figure at the Lahore court was the Iranian scholar, scientist and traveller Al-Biruni, who came to India with Mahmud of Ghazni in 1017 and stayed on until 1030. During his thirteen years in India he mastered Sanskrit and went on to study all the religious, philosophical, scientific and mathematical literatures of India. He had a great respect for much of the Indian knowledge, although in his celebrated account of India, the *Kitab fi Tahqiqi ma li-l Hind*, written in Arabic, he had harsh words to say about some of the Indian intellectuals' lack of critical scrutiny, as described in **Excerpt 11.4** below. He was also a keen observer of the Indian social scene, and wrote about the innumerable customs and traditions of the Hindus. Although a devout Muslim, he did not disparage the Hindus, and he blamed both Hindus and Muslims for their inability to empathise with each other (Dani 1973: 1–2, 5–6). He was also bold enough to write that his master's numerous raids were nothing short of barbaric (Sachau 1888: Vol. 1, 88). When

---

Excerpt 11.4 Al-Biruni's assessment of the Indian intellectual scene

Al-Biruni had great admiration for Indian mathematics and astronomy. It was only after he had completed a thorough examination of Indian life and learning that he felt compelled to make some highly critical comments about Indian society and scholarship. They point to the decline of Indian intellectual life since the time of the Imperial Guptas.

Folly is an illness for which there is no medicine, and the Hindus believe that there is no country but theirs, no nation like theirs, no king like theirs, no religion like theirs, no science like theirs . . . Their haughtiness is such that, if you tell them of any science or scholar in Khurasan and Persis (Iran), they will think you to be both an ignoramus and a liar . . . The Indian scribes are careless, and do not take pains to produce correct and well-collated copies. In consequence, the highest results of the author's mental development are lost by their negligence, and his book becomes already in the first or second copy so full of faults, that the text appears something entirely new, which neither a scholar nor one familiar with the subject, whether Hindu or Muslim, could any longer understand . . . I can only compare their mathematical and astronomical literature . . . to a mixture of pearl shells and sour dates, or of pearls and dung, or of costly crystals and common pebbles. Both kinds of things are equal in the eyes (of the Hindus), since they cannot raise themselves to the methods of a strictly scientific deduction.

Source: E. Sachau, *Alberuni's India*, Vol. 1, London: Trubner, 1888, 18, 22, 25.

one compares Al-Biruni's work with that of some nineteenth-century British commentators of India, such as James Mill, for example, one is struck by the detached and independent outlook of the Iranian scholar in contrast to the blatant racism that perverted the minds of so many nineteenth-century British and European historians and intellectuals (Sen 2005: 142–50).

Philosophical works

A unique intellectual tradition that guided the philosophers of ancient India consisted of providing commentaries and reflections upon the *Vedas* and other Vedic knowledge. Unlike some of our modern intellectuals, ancient Indian thinkers were never obsessive about their own original insights or contributions; rather, they took pride in the fact that they were privileged to comment upon the thoughts of the earlier texts (Hayes 2000: 387). The commentaries became the vehicles through which, in time, philosophical ideas came to be articulated and gained maturity. The ideas came to be grouped into several schools that dealt with such philosophical concepts as epistemology, logic, perception, inference, ontology, causation or human nature. Six formal schools of thought eventually came to be recognised: *Nyaya*, concerned with right reasoning and logic, as explained in **Excerpt 11.5** below; *Vaisheshika*, or atomism, concerned with the method of

Excerpt 11.5 The idea of debate in the *Nyaya* tradition

In the following passage, by a contemporary philosopher, we are to the rational and logical way of conducting a debate proposed a long time ago in ancient India.

What counts as winning a debate? If the debate is a victory-at-any-cost-sort, and a debater wins when his opponent is lost for words or confused or hesitant, then the best and the most rational way to proceed would be to employ such tricks as play on the opponents' weaknesses, like speaking very quickly or using convoluted examples of referring to doctrines of which one suspects one's opponent is ignorant. In the other sort of debate, the truth-directed sort, 'winning' is a matter of persuading one's opponent, and also an impartial audience, that one's thesis is true, and the rational debater must find some other methods. Nothing is more persuasive than an argument backed up by well-chosen examples and illustrations. And so, when the Naiyayikas come to codify the form of rational debating demonstration, the citation of examples was given at least as much prominence as the citation of reasons.

Source: Jonardon Ganeri, *Philosophy in Classical India: The Proper Work of Reason*, London: Routledge, 2001, 28.

dealing with particular matters; *Mimamsa*, concerned with knowledge proceeding from Vedic exegesis; *Samkhya*, a dualistic philosophy concerned with theory of knowledge and the evolution of the cosmos; *Yoga*, or practice; and *Vedanta*, a metaphysical philosophy which considered itself to be the essence, or 'end', of the *Veda* and focused its exegesis on the *Upanishads* (Hinnells and Sharpe 1972: 42–51; Clear 2000: 353–4).

Shankara, or Shankaracharya, perhaps the subtlest Indian thinker of the ancient world, is considered the greatest exponent of the monist strand of the *Vedanta* school (Fort 2000: 792). Monism is the doctrine of ultimate principle or being (*Brahman*), which denies any duality of matter and mind (Gupta 1995: 215–16). The ideas of the *Vedanta* school were derived from the great commentary on the *Upanishads*, which was the *Brahma Sutra* of Badarayana (fifth century BCE) (Pereira 1995: 170–4). Shankara, according to traditional dating, is said to have lived between about 788 and 822 and wrote a massive commentary in his *Brahmasutra Bhashya* on Badarayana's work. He argued that there was only one non-dual reality (*Advaita Vedanta*); that the world was a product of illusion and false appearances, in the way that ignorant or gullible people mistake a snake for a rope; that the individual Self can realise the ultimate reality, or *Brahman*, through the path of knowledge; and that it is only when the Self has realised the *Brahman* that the ultimate goal of human life is reached (Sen 1961: 82–4; Gupta 1995: 214–19; Flood 1996: 239–43). This purist position stands in contrast to the qualified non-dualism (*Vishisht Advaita*) or dualism (*Dvaita*) stated by later philosophers such as Ramanuja and Madhava. Shankara's purist position has attracted most Westernised Indians, and in modern times its popularity has been enhanced by such figures as Swami Prabhavananda, Gerald Heard and Christopher Isherwood, who have promoted the *Vedanta* school and its ideas (Isherwood 1952: ix–xiv, 1–19). Despite the rigour of his intellectual position, Shankara was a man who reached out to all groups of people. Although brought up within the *Shaivite* atmosphere of a *brahman* family of Kerala, he influenced the *Vaishnavites* too. He respected both Buddhists and Jains, although he rejected their heterodox ideas and regarded 'Buddhism as Hinduism's chief enemy' (Sastri 1960: 428). He travelled the length and breadth of India, engaged in lively debates with thinkers from other schools, and made it his mission to educate the *brahman* priests into strict monism. Perhaps imitating the Buddhists, he also founded four great monasteries, at Badrinath in the north, Sringeri in the south, Puri in the east, and Dwarka in the west, places still revered by Hindu pilgrims (Sen 1961: 67–8; Flood 1996: 92).

Cultural influences abroad

Indian intellectual and cultural influences were felt far and wide during this period. Although clear evidence of the lines of transmission is not always easily available, we are on fairly certain ground in relation to three regions of the world: China, Persia and the Islamic world, and South East Asia.

With the rise of the Tang dynasty in China in CE 618, Indo-Chinese diplomatic and cultural contacts increased apace. The Chinese monks, including Hsuan Tsang, arrived in India to learn about Buddhism; they were particularly excited by the idea of spending some time at the Buddhist educational centres, such as Nalanda. On the other hand, the Indian Buddhist missionaries and scholars in turn were increasingly to be seen in the principal cities of China. Learning each other's language was the great passion of the period, and Hsuan Tsang led the way in this venture. He translated seventy-four different Indian works, consisting of 1,335 chapters (Majumdar and Pusalker 1954: 609–10). On his return journey to China he needed twenty-two horses to carry all the manuscripts (Beal 1884: Vol. 1, xx). Prabhakaramitra, the Nalanda-based scholar and professor, reached China in 627 and, with the help of nineteen Chinese scholars, was engaged in translating Indian Buddhist texts into Chinese (Majumdar and Pusalker 1954: 609–10). Another savant, Bodhiruchi, went to China in 693; with the help of the Chinese board of translators, specially set up for him by the royal court, he translated fifty-three volumes of Indian texts before his death in 727. Apart from Buddhism, the Chinese were interested in Indian mathematics, medicine and astronomy. A Sui dynasty catalogue of about CE 600 lists Chinese translations of Indian works in these three subjects (Joseph 2010: 19). Indian astronomy was also taught at an official Chinese centre for astronomical education. In both India and China, at that time, there was much mathematical work being pursued independently, but there was a good possibility of the transmission of ideas and knowledge in both directions. Their renditions were the most important means to achieving the success of the transmission.

In order to appreciate the extent of Indian influence on the Islamic world, we have to first examine the contacts with Persia before it became Muslim. The last great non-Islamic dynasty of Persia was that of the Sasanians. As inheritors of the famous Achaemenid and Parthian dynasties, the Sasanian rulers held a high conception of their role and power. Their imperial ideology was based on the Zoroastrian doctrine that all knowledge that is useful, wise and sacred emanated from Ahura Mazda, the Lord of Wisdom, and to promote that ideology the Sasanians spared no efforts in collecting, recording and editing historical and religious texts and treatises from wherever they could be found (Rypka 1968: 34ff.). King Shapur I had inaugurated an academy of learning at Jundishapur as early as the third century CE, but it was another Sasanian king, Khosrau I Anushirvan, who, in the sixth century, encouraged translations of Greek, Syriac, Indian and Chinese scientific and literary works into Pahlavi (Middle Persian). It was under Khosrau's patronage that his minister Burzoy travelled around India meeting learned people, one of whom introduced him to the *Panchatantra*, which he translated into Pahlavi (Chapter 8); from then on, this book of Indian fables became highly popular through numerous translations (Edgerton 1965: 12; de Blois 1990: 40–4, 81–2, 88). While we lack the names of particular scholars, we can be fairly certain that a number of Indian mathematicians, astronomers and medical practitioners also went to Jundishapur to disseminate their knowledge. Reliable Arab-Islamic sources of later centuries confirmed this and noted the importance of both the Jundishapur academy and the Indian contribution there (Wickens 1976: 111–19). It should also be noted that the game of chess originated in India, and it moved to Iran in the seventh century.

The most important centre of intellectual life in the Islamic world during this period was Baghdad. The Abbasid rulers of that city soon realised that their people had only a rudimentary knowledge of such sciences as astronomy, mathematics and medicine. They looked to India and Persia for enlightenment. The control of Sind gave the Abbasids a vital route to tap into Indian ideas and expertise. Two independent Arab writers, Ibn al-Adami and Abu Mashar, have recorded the visit of Kanaka, an Indian astronomer-mathematician and diplomat from Sind, at the court of the caliph Al-Mansur (754–75). With his curiosity in Indian astronomy and mathematics greatly aroused by the visitor, the caliph ordered two scholars, Ibrahim al-Fazari and Yaqub ibn Tariq, to translate the two critical works of Brahmagupta (Chapter 8), *Brahmasphutasiddhanta* and *Khandakhadyaka*. Through the resulting Arabic translations, known as *Sindhind* and *Arkand*, the knowledge of Indian numerals passed on to the Islamic world (Bose *et al.* 1989: 48–9, 134, 210–11). Similarly, the Persian astronomical tables, known as *Zig-I shahriyarr*, which were influenced by Indian astronomy, were translated into Arabic under the title of *Zijashshahriyar* (Bose *et al.* 1989: 134). The ninth-century scholar al-Khwarizmi learned Sanskrit and explained to his readers the Indian system of notation, and through his work the internationalisation of the Indian number system began. Another scholar from the same century, al-Kindi, wrote four books on Indian numerals.

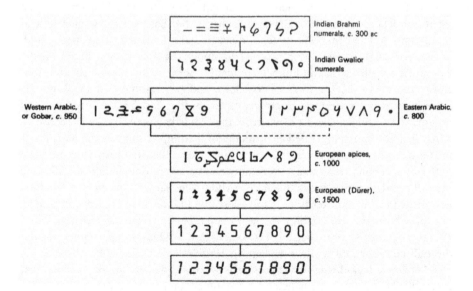

Figure 11.7 The Gwalior numerals

Indian medical methods and drugs were also in great demand in the Islamic world. A large number of Sanskrit medical, pharmacological and toxicological texts were translated into Arabic under the patronage of Khalid, the *vizier* of Al-Mansur. Khalid was the son of a chief priest of a Buddhist monastery in Balkh. Some of his family were killed when the Arabs captured Balkh; others, including Khalid, survived by converting to Islam. They were to be known as the Barmakis of Baghdad, who were fascinated by new ideas from India (Majumdar and Pusalker 1955: 450; Bose *et al.* 1989: 586–7). Indian medical knowledge was given a further boost under the caliph Harun al-Rashid (788–809), who ordered the translation of *Susruta Samhita* into Arabic. A great Arabic medical text of the late ninth and tenth centuries, *Kitab al-hawi*, translated into Latin as late as the thirteenth century and known as *Liber continens*, was written by al-Razi, or Rhazes (865–925), who embodied much Indian knowledge in that work.

The region of the world that was perhaps most influenced by Indian cultural ideas and practices was South East Asia. Many of the personal or place names in countries such as Thailand, Cambodia, Indonesia and Malaysia bear the hallmark of Sanskritic influence. The ideas drawn from ancient Hindu religious literature, such as the *Ramayana* and the *Mahabharata*, pervade much of the mythology and notions of sacred space held by the peoples of that region. The artistic forms and styles of dance, drama and puppetry have also been drawn from Indian antecedents. Similarly, no one can fail to recognise the impact of Hindu and Buddhist architecture on such iconic buildings as the Angkor Wat in Cambodia and Borobudur in Java. Historians have long argued over the reasons for Indian cultural influences, and three sets of reasons have been advanced. First, as early as the second or third century BCE, Indian mariners and traders were plying the Bay of Bengal and reaching out to varied settlements in the region. This mercantile connection carried on throughout the first millennium CE, and we also noted in Chapter 10 the very strong commercial interests that led to the war between the Cholas and the kingdom of *Sri Vijaya* in CE 1025. The mercantile connections would have facilitated the movement of people to and from India. Much would have been learned in India by the visiting dignitaries from South East Asian kingdoms. The influence of merchants, however, can be overstated, because merchants are essentially profit-makers, not cultural missionaries. Second, at a time when Indian nationalism was pitted against British colonial rule in the late nineteenth and early twentieth centuries, some Indian historians were prone to hark back to an imagined past, when the so-called 'Greater India' included South East Asia. The evidence of any permanent Indian territorial gains as a result of military campaigns in the region is distinctly lacking; even the Chola victory over *Sri Vijaya* did not lead to any colonisation as such. In any case, it is difficult to imagine such an extensive and embedded Indian cultural influence in the region as an outcome of Indian militarism. Third, and more credibly, there is the argument that the main carriers of cultural influences from India were the *brahman* priests and ritual specialists, along with the *kshatriya* administrators, who were invited by indigenous rulers who wished to legitimise themselves in the way Indian rulers used to (as noted in Chapters 9 and 10). The consultants from India brought with them concepts that were articulated in such texts as the various *Dharmashastras*, the *Arthashastra* and the architectural manuals of *Shilpashastra*. South East Asians certainly borrowed many elements of Indian culture, but they did so in a proactive manner rather than as passive recipients. Using their own originality and genius, they changed the Indian import sufficiently to make it a natural part of their landscape, environment and personality. This is the reason why Indian cultural imprints and forms that still exist there are not regarded by the populace as an alien cultural burden. They adhere to this particular heritage with pride because it has become an integral part of their native cultures.

STUDY GUIDE

Key issues

- Reasons for the decline of Buddhism.
- Differences in architectural styles of northern and southern Hindu temples.
- New genres and schools of Indian literature.
- Comparative styles of writing by Al-Biruni and Kalhana.
- The extent of Indian influence in South East Asia.

Suggested readings

Dimock *et al.* 1974: 212–38; Omvedt 2003: 149–85; Sivaramamurti 1977: 195–9, 211–31; Wink 1990: 303–58; Wink 1997: 79–110.

INTERNET SELECTION

1) Nalini Bhushan and Jay Garfield: 'Can Indian philosophy be written in English? A conversation with Daya Krishna'. www.smith.edu/philosophy/docs/garfield_in_english.pdf
2) William Dalrymple: 'A point of view: the sacred and sensuous in Indian art'. www.bbc.co.uk/news/magazine-26873149
3) Leslie C. Orr: 'Cholas, Pandyas and "imperial temple culture" in medieval Tamilnadu'. www.academia.edu/3776849/cholas_pandyas_and_imperial_temple_culture_in
4) K.T.S. Sarao: 'On the question of animosity of the Brahmans and persecution by Brahmanical kings leading to the decline of Buddhism in India'. www.chibs.edu.tw/ch_html/chbs/10/chbs1010.htm
5) UNESCO Courier (1974): 'A universal genius in Central Asia a thousand years ago: Al-Biruni'. http://unesdoc.org/images/0007/000748/074875eo.pdf

QUESTIONS FOR GROUP DISCUSSION

1) Why is Buddhism reviving in India once again?
2) Why have the Jews left India in the modern period, while the Christians have stayed on?
3) In what ways is a Hindu temple different from a Christian church or an Islamic mosque?
4) What meaning is meant to be conveyed by Hindu religious iconography?
5) For what reasons did Sanskrit lose its status as a language of communication in India?

Note

1 In the fourth century CE the merchant Thomas Cana emigrated from Syria, leading out some 400 families to establish the Kerala Nestorian church (p.279).

Select glossary of Indic terms

The following list is only a selection of Indic terms most frequently used in the book. All others have been explained within the text.

Aryan An Indo-European-speaking group of people who came to India soon after 2000 BC
atman Soul
Bhagavan God
Bodhisattava An incarnation of Buddha before his birth, symbolising compassion
brahman A member of the highest caste (priests and teachers)
chakravartin A strong, peaceful universal king
dana Gift
dharma Religious duty
Dravidian A group of four southern languages of India: Tamil, Kannada, Telugu and Malayalam
ghats The embankments of the River Ganges at Varanasi/Benares
Hindutva The ideology of Hindu religious nationalism
jana People
kshatriya A member of the warrior/bureaucratic caste (second in ritual ranking)
maha Great
mahajanapada A great kingdom
Mahayana The great vehicle; an important school of Buddhism
nadu A local self-governing peasant community unit in south India
nagara Town
nirvana Release from the cycle of rebirth
Pali The language in which the early Buddhist Canon was recorded
pandit A learned man
pradesh Province
Prakrit A name given to many non-standard vernacular languages, as distinct from the highly literary and refined language of Sanskrit
prasasti A royal eulogy
raga Indian musical mode or scale

raja	King (*maharaja*: great king)
rajdhani	Capital city
rasa	Essence, or flavour, as in drama or music
sangam	A literary festival; an academy of learning in the south Indian literary context
sangha	An assembly; a Buddhist monastic community
Sanskrit	One of the oldest of the Indo-European languages; a language of refined culture in ancient India
Shaivite	A follower of the god Shiva
Shastra	A text of learning
shudra	A member of the lowest caste (fourth in ritual ranking)
stupa	A Buddhist building housing the Buddha's relics
tirthankara	A founding teacher of the Jain faith
Vaishnavite	A follower of the god Vishnu
vaishya	A member of the trading caste (third in ritual ranking)
varna	Colour; used in the ritual ranking of castes
Veda	Truth, as expressed in the four *Vedas*

Select glossary of archaic Indic place names

Anga	Vedic state in Bengal-Bihar
Aryavarta	Indo-Gangetic plains of north India which the Aryans colonised
Asmaka	Vedic state in the Deccan
Avanti	Vedic state in ancient India
Barbaricum	Ancient port in Sind, near modern Karachi
Barygaza	Port of Broach in Gujarat
Chedi	Vedic state in central India
Dakshinapatha	Southern India
Drasadvati	Ancient river of the Indus basin, now the dried up Ghaggar-Hakra River
Gandhara	The town in the north-west, known to the Persians and the Greeks, and famous for Gandhara sculptures
Gauda	Vedic state in Bengal
Hiranyabahu	River Son
Indraprashtha	Delhi
Jambudvipa	The Indian subcontinent
Kalinga	Orissa
Kamarupa	Assam
Kamboja	Vedic state in north-west India
Kanauj	Kanyakubja in the Gangetic plain
Kashi	Benares/Varanasi
Kosala	Vedic state in the Gangetic valley
Kuru	Ancient Vedic state
Madhyadesha	Western Gangetic basin
Magadha	Area covered by modern Bihar
Mallas	A Vedic state in ancient India
Meluhha	The Indus region
Meru	A mythical mountain in the Himalayas
Muziris	Cochin
Panchala	An early Vedic state
Pataligram	Patna
Pataliputra	Patna

Pracya	Eastern India
Praticya	North-western India
Prayag	Allahabad
Purushapura	Peshawar
Sapta-Sindhava	Punjab
Sarasvati	Ancient river of the Indus basin, now the dried up Ghaggar-Hakra River
Saurasena	Vedic state in the Gangetic valley
Sindhu	River Indus
Sthanivishwara	Haryana state
Tamralipti	Ancient Bengali port
Tondaimandalam	Modern Tamil Nadu
Uttarapatha	Northern India
Vikramshila	Ancient site of Buddhist learning in Bihar
Vriji	A Vedic state in ancient India

Classification of ancient Indian texts by subject

The four Vedas (Chapter 4)

1 *Rig-Veda*
2 *Sama-Veda*
3 *Yajur-Veda*
4 *Atharva-Veda*

Other Vedic and post-Vedic religious literature (Chapters 4, 8)

5 Brahmanas (Aitreya, Jaiminiya, Taittiriya, Satapatha)
6 Aranyakas
7 Upanishads
8 Vedangas
9 Upavedas
10 Bhagvad Gita (part of the epic Mahabharata)
11 Puranas
12 Vaishnavite and Shaivite hymns

Dharmashastras and Dharmasutras (religio-legal works) (Chapter 7)

13 Manusmriti
14 Yajnavalkyasmriti
15 Naradasmriti
16 Parasarasmriti
17 Katyayanasmriti

Epics (Chapter 5)

18 Mahabharata
19 Ramayana

Buddhist texts (Chapters 5, 7)

20 Vinayapitaka
21 Suttapitaka
22 Abbidhammapitakas
23 Dipavamsa
24 Mahavagga
25 Mahavastu
26 Vaipulyasutra
27 Suddharmapundarika
28 Prajnaparamita
29 Mahabhashya
30 Jatakas
31 Milindapanha

Jain texts (Chapter 5)

32 Angas
33 Upangas
34 Chadasutra
35 Prakirnakas
36 Nandisutra
37 Anuyogadvara
38 Surya Prajnapti
39 Jambu Dwipa Prajnapti
40 Tamdula Veyaliya

Mathematical and astronomical texts (Chapters 4, 7, 8, 11)

41 Taittiriya Brahmana
42 Satapatha Brahmana
43 Jyotisha Vedanga
44 Sulvasutra
45 Romaka Siddhanta
46 Paulisa Siddhanta
47 Bakhshali Manuscript
48 Aryabhatiya
49 Brahmasphutasiddhanta
50 Khandakhadyaka
51 Gwalior numerals

Grammars and lexicons (Chapters 5, 7, 9)

52 Ashtadhyayi
53 Mahabhashya
54 Amarakosha

Sanskrit works of literature, arts and aesthetics (Chapters 6, 7, 8, 11)

55   Panchatantra
56   Natyashastra
57   Kama Sutra
58   Rudra-Rakshasa
59   Shakuntala
60   Ratnavali
61   Priyadarshika
62   Nagananda
63   Dhvanyaloka
64   Gita Govinda

Tamil literature (Chapters 7, 11)

65   Tolkppiyam
66   Patthuppattu
67   Ettuthokai
68   Padinenkilkanakku
69   Purananaru
70   Kurunthokai
71   Kural
72   Mattavilasa
73   Shilappadikaram
74   Tirukurral

Kannada literature (Chapter 11)

75   Kavirajamarga (Kannada)

Medical knowledge (Chapters 7, 11)

76   Ayur-Veda
77   Susruta Samhita
78   Charaka Samhita

History and biography (Chapters 7, 11)

79   Buddhacharita
80   Harsha-charita
81   Rajatarangini

Political economy (Chapters 6, 9, 10)

82 Arthashastra
83 Haritasmriti
84 Nitisara
85 Aparajitaprccha
86 Civakacintamani

Architecture (Chapters 3, 11)

87 Sthapathya Veda
88 Shilpashastra (Chapter 11)

Philosophy (Chapters 4, 11)

89 Upanishads
90 Brahmasutra
91 Brahmasutra Bhashya
92 Nyaya texts
93 Advaita Vedanta texts

Contemporary foreign accounts (Chapters 6, 9, 11)

94 Indica
95 Si-Yu-Ki
96 Kitab fi Tahqiqi ma li-l Hind

Select inscriptions (Chapters 6, 7, 8, 9, 10)

97   Major rock edicts of Ashoka
98   Minor rock edicts of Ashoka
99   Pillar edicts of Ashoka
100 Hathigumpha Inscription of Kharavela
101 Junagadh Rock Inscription of Rudradaman
102 The Pillar of Heliodorus Inscription
103 Allahabad Pillar Inscription of Samudragupta
104 Aihole Inscription of Pulakeshin II
105 Sasanam of Rajendra I
106 Ayyavole Guild Inscription

Bibliography

Agrawal, D.P. and Sood, R.K. (1982) 'Ecological Factors and the Harappan Civilization', in G. Possehl (ed.) *Harappan Civilization: A Contemporary Perspective*, Warminster: Aris & Phillips, at 223–31.

Alam, M. (2003) 'The Culture and Politics of Persian in Pre-Colonial Hindustan', in S. Pollock (ed.) (2003) *Literary Cultures in History: Reconstructions from South Asia*, Berkeley: University of California Press, at 131–98.

Ali, D. (1999) 'The Hindu World', in N. Smart (ed.) *Atlas of the World's Religions*, Oxford: Oxford University Press, at 34–53.

Ali, D. (2000) 'Royal Eulogy as World History: Re-thinking Copper-Plate Inscriptions in Cola World', in R. Inden, J. Walters and D. Ali (eds) *Querying the Medieval: Texts and the History of Practices in South Asia*, Oxford: Oxford University Press, at 165–229.

Ali, D. (2006a) 'Feudalism', in S. Wolpert (ed.) *Encyclopedia of India*, Vol. 2, New York: Thomson Gale, at 70–4.

Ali, D. (2006b) 'War, Servitude and the Imperial Household: A Study of Palace Women in the Chola Empire', in I. Chatterjee and R.M. Eaton (eds) *Slavery and South Asian History*, Bloomington: Indiana University Press, at 44–62.

Allchin, B. (1984) 'The Harappan Environment', in B.B. Lal and S.P. Gupta (eds) *Frontiers of the Indus Civilisation: Sir Mortimer Wheeler Commemoration Volume*, New Delhi: Indian Archaeological Society, at 445–54.

Allchin, B. and Allchin, R. (1982) *The Birth of Indian Civilization*, Cambridge: Cambridge University Press.

Allchin, F.R. (1961) 'Ideas of History in Indian Archaeological Writing: A Preliminary Study', in C.H. Philips (ed.) *Historians of India, Pakistan and Ceylon*, London: Oxford University Press, at 241–59.

Allchin, F.R. (1982) 'The Legacy of the Indus Civilization', in G. Possehl (ed.) *Harappan Civilization: A Contemporary Perspective*, Warminster: Aris & Phillips, at 325–33.

Allchin, F.R. (ed.) (1995) *The Archaeology of Early Historic South Asia: The Emergence of Cities and States*, Cambridge: Cambridge University Press.

Allen, C. (2002) *The Buddha and the Sahibs*, London: John Murray.

Allen, C. (2012) *Ashoka: The Search for India's Lost Emperor*, London: Little, Brown.

Altekar, A.S. (1959) *The Position of Women in Hindu Civilization*, Delhi: Motilal Banarsidass.

Ambedkar, B. (1989) *Writings and Speeches*, Vol. 5, Bombay: Education Department, Government of Maharashtra.

Associated Press (2006) 'Ancient Axe Casts Light on North–South Divide', *The Guardian*, 2 May 2006, 20.

Auboyer, J. (2002) *Daily Life in Ancient India, from 200 BC to 700 AD*, London: Phoenix Press.

Avari, B. (2013) *Islamic Civilization in South Asia: A History of Muslim Power and Presence in the Indian Subcontinent*, Abingdon: Routledge.

Bahn, P. (ed.) (1996) *The Cambridge Illustrated History of Archaeology*, Cambridge: Cambridge University Press.

Bala, M. (2004) 'Kalibangan: Its Periods and Antiquities', in D.K. Chakrabarti (ed.) *Indus Civilization Sites in India: New Discoveries*, Mumbai: Marg, at 34–43.

Ballantyne, T. (2002) *Orientalism and Race: Aryanism in the British Empire*, London: Palgrave.

Basham, A.L. (1954) *The Wonder that was India*, London: Sidgwick and Jackson.

Basham, A.L. (1964) *Studies in Indian History and Culture*, Calcutta: Sambodhi.

Basham, A.L. (ed.) (1975) *A Cultural History of India*, Oxford: Clarendon Press.

Beal, S. (trans.) (1884) *Si-Yu-Ki: Buddhist Records of the Western World*, 2 Vols, London: Trubner.

Begley, V. (1991) 'Ceramic Evidence for Pre-Periplus Trade on the Indian Coast', in V. Begley and R. de Puma (eds) *Rome and India*, Madison: University of Wisconsin Press, at 157–96.

Bhan, S. (2002) 'Aryanisation of the Indus Civilization', in K.N. Panikkar, T.J. Byres and U. Patnaik (eds) *The Making of History: Essays Presented to Irfan Habib*, London: Anthem Press, at 41–55.

Bhandarkar, D.R. (1925) *Asoka*, Calcutta: University of Calcutta Press.

Bhardwaj, S.M. (1973) *Hindu Places of Pilgrimage in India*, Berkeley: University of California Press.

de Blois, F. (1990) *Burzoy's Voyage to India and the Origin of the Book of Kalilah wa Dimnah*, London: Royal Asiatic Society.

Bose, D.M., Sen, S.N. and Subbarayappa, B.V. (1989) *A Concise History of Science in India*, New Delhi: Indian National Science Academy.

Bose, M. (ed.) (2000) *Faces of the Feminine in Ancient, Medieval and Modern India*, New York: Oxford University Press.

Bose, M. (2010) *Women in the Hindu Tradition: Rules, Roles and Exceptions*, London: Routledge.

Bosworth, A.B. (1995) *A Historical Commentary on Arrian's History of Alexander*, Vol. 2, Oxford: Oxford University Press.

Bosworth, A.B. (1996) *Alexander and the East: The Tragedy of Triumph*, Oxford: Clarendon Press.

Boyce, M. (1984) *Zoroastrianism*, Manchester: Manchester University Press.

Boyce, M. (2002a) 'The Parthians: Defenders of the Land and Faith', in P. Godrej and F.P. Mistree (eds) *A Zoroastrian Tapestry: Art, Religion and Culture*, Ahmedabad: Mapin, at 99–115.

Boyce, M. (2002b) 'Zoroastrianism in Iran after the Arab Conquest', in P. Godrej and F.P. Mistree (eds) *A Zoroastrian Tapestry: Art, Religion and Culture*, Ahmedabad: Mapin, at 229–45.

Boyce, M. (2002c) 'The Teachings of Zoroaster', in P. Godrej and F.P. Mistree (eds) *A Zoroastrian Tapestry: Art, Religion and Culture*, Ahmedabad: Mapin, at 19–27.

Bradnock, R. and Bradnock, R. (1998) *India Handbook*, Bath: Footprint Handbooks.

Breckenridge, C. and Veer, P. (eds) (1993) *Orientalism and the Post-Colonial Predicament: Perspectives on South Asia*, Philadelphia: University of Pennsylvania Press.

Briant, P. (1996) *Alexander the Great: The Heroic Ideal*, London: Thames and Hudson.

Bright, W. (ed.) (1992) *International Encyclopaedia of Linguistics*, Vol. 2, Oxford: Oxford University Press.

Brockington, J. (1984) *Righteous Rama: The Evolution of an Epic*, Oxford: Oxford University Press.

Brockington, J. (1998) *The Sanskrit Epics*, Leiden: Brill.

Brown, T.S. (1973) *The Greek Historians*, Lexington: D.C. Heath.

Cardona, G. (1976) *Panini: A Survey of Research*, The Hague: Mouton.

Casson, L. (1989) *The Periplus Maris Erythraei*, Princeton, NJ: Princeton University Press.

Casson, L. (1991) 'Ancient Naval Technology and the Route to India', in V. Begley and R. de Puma (eds) *Rome and India*, Madison: University of Wisconsin Press, at 8–11.

Chakrabarti, D.K. (1998) *The Archaeology of Ancient Indian Cities*, Delhi: Oxford University Press.

Chakrabarti, D.K. (1999) *India, An Archaeological History: Palaeolithic Beginnings to Early Historic Foundations*, New Delhi: Oxford University Press.

Chakrabarti, D.K. (ed.) (2004) *Indus Civilization Sites in India: New Discoveries*, Mumbai: Marg.

Champakalakshmi, R. (1995) 'State and Economy: South India *c*. AD 400–1300', in R. Thapar (ed.) *Recent Perspectives of Early Indian History*, Bombay: Popular Prakashan, at 266–308.

Champakalakshmi, R. (1996a) *Trade, Ideology and Urbanisation – South India 300 BC to AD 1300*, Oxford: Oxford University Press.

Champakalakshmi, R. (1996b) 'From Devotion and Dissent to Dominance: The Bhakti of the Tamil Alwars and Nayanars', in R. Champakalakshmi and S. Gopal (eds) *Tradition, Dissent and Ideology*, Oxford: Oxford University Press, at 135–63.

Champakalakshmi, R. (2001a) 'Reappraisal of a Brahmanic Institution: The Brahmadeya and its Ramifications in Early Medieval South India', in K. Hall (ed.) *Structure and Society in Early South India: Essays in Honour of Noboru Karashima*, New Delhi: Oxford University Press, at 59–84.

Champakalakshmi, R. (2001b) 'The Medieval South Indian Guilds: Their Role in Trade and Urbanisation', in R. Chakravarti (ed.) *Trade in Early India*, New Delhi: Oxford University Press, at 326–43.

Chattopadhyaya, B. (1994) *The Making of Early Medieval India*, Oxford: Oxford University Press.

Chattopadhyaya, B. (1995) 'State and Economy in North India: Fourth Century to Twelfth Century', in R. Thapar (ed.) *Recent Perspectives of Early Indian History*, Bombay: Popular Prakashan, at 309–46.

Chattopadhyaya, S. (1974) *Achaemenids and India*, Delhi: Munshiram Manoharlal.

Chaudhuri, N.C. (1974) *Scholar Extraordinary: The Life of Professor, the Right Hon. Friedrich Max Muller PC*, London: Chatto & Windus.

Claessen, H.J.M. and Skalnik, P. (eds) (1978) *The Early State*, The Hague: Mouton.

Clear, E.H. (2000) 'Hindu Philosophy', in *Concise Routledge Encyclopedia of Philosophy*, London: Routledge, at 353–4.

Cohen, R. (1978) 'State Origins: A Re-appraisal', in H.J.M. Claessen and P. Skalnik (eds) *The Early State*, The Hague: Mouton, at 31–75.

Colas, G. (2003) 'History of Vaisnava Traditions: An Esquisse', in G. Flood (ed.) *The Blackwell Companion to Hinduism*, Oxford: Blackwell, at 229–70.

Collins, R. (1991) *Early Medieval Europe 300–1000*, London: Macmillan.

Coningham, R. (2005) 'South Asia: From Early Villages to Buddhism', in C. Scarre (ed.) *The Human Past: World Prehistory and the Development of Human Societies*, London: Thames & Hudson, at 518–51.

Cook, J.M. (1983) *The Persian Empire*, London: J.M. Dent.

Cousins, L.S. (1997) 'Buddhism', in J.R. Hinnells (ed.) *A Handbook of Living Religions*, London: Blackwell, at 369–444.

Cowell, E.B. and Thomas, F.W. (n.d.) *The Harsa-Charita of Bana*, Delhi: Motilal Banarsidass.

Craven, R. (1997) *Indian Art*, London: Thames & Hudson.

Crystal, D. (1997) *The Cambridge Encyclopaedia of Language*, Cambridge: Cambridge University Press.

Cunningham, A. ([1872–73] 1979) 'Harappa', in G. Possehl (ed.) *Ancient Cities of the Indus*, New Delhi: Vikas, at 102–4.

Daheja, V. (1997) *Indian Art*, London: Phaidon.

Dales, G.F. ([1964] 1979) 'The Mythical Massacre of Mohenjo Daro', in G. Possehl (ed.) *Ancient Cities of the Indus*, New Delhi: Vikas, at 293–6.

Dales, G.F. ([1966] 1979) 'The Decline of the Harappans', in G. Possehl (ed.) *Ancient Cities of the Indus*, New Delhi: Vikas, at 307–12.

Dales, G.F. ([1968] 1979) 'Of Dice and Men', in G. Possehl (ed.) *Ancient Cities of the Indus*, New Delhi: Vikas, at 138–44.

Dange, S.S. (2002) 'Zoroastrianism and Hinduism: The RigVeda and the Avesta', in P. Godrej and F.P. Mistree (eds) *A Zoroastrian Tapestry: Art, Religion and Culture*, Ahmedabad: Mapin, at 185–91.

Dani, A.H. (1973) *Alberuni's Indica: A Record of the Cultural History of South Asia about AD 1030*, Islamabad: University of Islamabad Press.

Daniélou, A. (2003) *A Brief History of India*, K. Hurry (trans.), Vermont: Inner Traditions.

Date, G.T. (1929) *The Art of War in Ancient India*, Oxford: Oxford University Press.

Desai, D. (1975) *Erotic Sculpture of India: A Socio-Cultural Study*, New Delhi: Tata McGraw-Hill.

Devahuti, D. (1970) *Harsha: A Political Study*, Oxford: Oxford University Press.

Devasthali, G.V. (1955) 'Language and Literature: Sanskrit', in R.C. Majumdar and A.D. Pusalker (eds) *The Age of Imperial Kanauj*, Bombay: Bharatiya Vidya Bhavan, at 177–206.

Dhar, S. (1957) *Chanakya and Arthasastra*, Bangalore: Indian Institute of World Culture.

Diamond, J. (1998) *Guns, Germs and Steel: A Short History of Everybody for the Last 13,000 Years*, London: Vintage.

Dikshitar, V.R. (1993) *The Gupta Polity*, Delhi: Motilal Banarsidass.

Dimock, E.C., Gerow, E., Naim, C.M., Ramanujan, A.K., Roadarmel, G. and Van Buitenen, J.A.B. (eds) (1974) *The Literatures of India: An Introduction*, Chicago: University of Chicago Press.

Dolcini, D. and Freschi, F. (eds) (1999) *Tessitori and Rajasthan: Proceedings of the International Conference at Bikaner, 1996*, Udine: Societa Indologica.

Doniger, W. (2010) *The Hindus: An Alternative History*, London: Penguin.

Doniger, W. and Kakar, S. (2002) *Kamasutra*, Oxford: Oxford University Press.

Drekmeier, C. (1962) *Kingship and Community in Early India*, Stanford, CA: Stanford University Press.

Dunbar, G. (1943) *A History of India from the Earliest Times to the Present Day*, London: Nicholson & Watson.

Edgerton, F. (1965) *The Panchatantra*, London: Allen & Unwin.

Elst, K. (1999) 'Update on the Aryan Invasion Debate'. http://koenraadelst.bharatvani.org/books/ait/index.htm

Embree, A. (ed.) (1992) *Sources of Indian Tradition*, London: Penguin.

Erdosy, G. (ed.) (1995a) *The Indo-Aryans of Ancient South Asia: Language, Material Culture and Ethnicity*, Berlin: Walter de Gruyter.

Erdosy, G. (1995b) 'City States of North India and Pakistan at the Time of the Buddha', in F.R. Allchin (ed.) *The Archaeology of Early Historic South Asia: The Emergence of Cities and States*, Cambridge: Cambridge University Press, at 99–122.

Evans, K. (1997) *Epic Narratives in the Hoysala Temples*, Leiden: Brill.

Fagan, B. (1999) *World Prehistory: A Brief Introduction*, New York: Longman.

Fairservis, W., Jr (1971) *The Roots of Ancient India: The Archaeology of Early Indian Civilization*, London: Allen & Unwin.

Fischer, S.R. (2005) *A History of Writing*, London: Reaktion Books.

Flood, G. (1996) *An Introduction to Hinduism*, Cambridge: Cambridge University Press.

Flood, G. (ed.) (2003) *The Blackwell Companion to Hinduism*, Oxford: Blackwell.

Fort, A.O. (2000) 'Sankara', in *Concise Routledge Encyclopedia of Philosophy*, London: Routledge, at 792.

Francfort, H.P. (1984) 'The Harappan Settlement of Shortughai', in B.B. Lal and S.P. Gupta (eds) *Frontiers of the Indus Civilisation: Sir Mortimer Wheeler Commemoration Volume*, New Delhi: Indian Archaeological Society, at 301–10.

Frasch, T. (2006) 'Engineering Expansion: Technological Progress in the Early States of South and Southeast Asia', unpublished paper based on a research project on 'Irrigation, Labour and the State in Early India' at Manchester Metropolitan University, 2003–04.

Frawley, D. and Rajaram, N.S. (1995) *Vedic Aryans and the Origins of Civilization: A Literary and Scientific Perspective*, Quebec: World Heritage Press.

Frye, R.N. (1996) *The Heritage of Central Asia: From Antiquity to the Turkish Expansion*, Princeton, NJ: Marcus Weiner.

Gadd, C.J. and Smith, S. ([1924] 1979) 'The New Links between the Indian and Babylonian Civilizations', in G. Possehl (ed.) *Ancient Cities of the Indus*, New Delhi: Vikas, at 109–10.

Gajjar, I.N. (1971) *Ancient Indian Art and the West: A Study of Parallels, Continuity and Symbolism from Proto-Historic to Early Buddhist Times*, Bombay: D.B. Taraporevala.

Gamkrelidze, T.V. and Ivanov, V.V. (1990) 'The Early History of Indo-European Languages', *Scientific American*, March 1990, 82–90.

Ghani, M.A. (1941) *Pre-Mughal Persian in Hindustan*, Allahabad: Allahabad Law Journal Press.

Ghosh, A. (1982) 'Deurbanization of the Harappan Civilization', in G. Possehl (ed.) *Harappan Civilization: A Contemporary Perspective*, Warminster: Aris & Phillips, at 321–4.

Ghoshal, U.N. (1955) 'Political Theory, Administrative Organisation, Law and Legal Institutions', in R.C. Majumdar and A.D. Pusalker (eds) *The Age of Imperial Kanauj*, Bombay: Bharatiya Vidya Bhavan, at 231–55.

Goitein, S.D. (1973) *Letters of Medieval Jewish Traders*, Princeton, NJ: Princeton University Press.

Gottlob, M. (2003) *Historical Thinking in South Asia: A Handbook of Sources from Colonial Times to the Present*, Oxford: Oxford University Press.

Griffith, R.T.H. (1920) *The Hymns of the RigVeda*, 2 Vols, Benares: E.J. Lazarus.

Gupta, B. (1995) 'Shankara', in I.P. McGreal (ed.) *Great Thinkers of the Eastern World*, New York: HarperCollins, at 214–19.

Gurukkal, R. (1995) 'The Beginnings of the Historic Period: The Tamil South', in R. Thapar (ed.) *Recent Perspectives of Early Indian History*, Bombay: Popular Prakashan, at 237–65.

Hall, K. (2001a) 'Merchants, Rulers and Priests in an Early South Indian Sacred Centre: Cidambaram in the Age of the Colas', in K. Hall (ed.) *Structure and Society in Early South India: Essays in Honour of Noboru Karashima*, New Delhi: Oxford University Press, at 85–116.

Hall, K. (2001b) *Structure and Society in Early South India: Essays in Honour of Noboru Karashima*, New Delhi: Oxford University Press.

Havell, E.B. (1920) *A Handbook of Indian Art*, London: John Murray.

Hayes, R.P. (2000) 'Indian and Tibetan Philosophy', in *Concise Routledge Encyclopedia of Philosophy*, London: Routledge, at 387–91.

Heffening, W. (1993) 'Muta', in *The Encyclopaedia of Islam*, Vol. 7, Leiden: E.J. Brill, at 757–9.

Heitzman, J. (2001) 'Urbanisation and Political Economy in Early South India: Kancipuram during the Cola Period', in K. Hall (ed.) *Structure and Society in Early South India: Essays in Honour of Noboru Karashima*, New Delhi: Oxford University Press, at 117–56.

Herodotus (1972) *The Histories*, London: Penguin.

Heskel, D.L. (1984) 'Iran–Indus Valley Connections: A Revaluation', in B.B. Lal and S.P. Gupta (eds) *Frontiers of the Indus Civilisation: Sir Mortimer Wheeler Commemoration Volume*, New Delhi: Indian Archaeological Society, at 333–46.

Hinnells, J.R. (1985) *Persian Mythology*, London: Newnes.

Hinnells, J.R. (ed.) (1997) *A Handbook of Living Religions*, London: Blackwell.

Hinnells, J.R. and Sharpe, E. (1972) *Hinduism*, London: Oriel Press.

Inden, R. (1990) *Imagining India*, London: Hurst & Co.

Inden, R. (2006) *Text and Practice: Essays on South Asian History*, Oxford: Oxford University Press.

Isherwood, C. (ed.) (1952) *Vedanta for Modern Man*, London: Allen & Unwin.

Iyengar, K.R.S. (1955) 'Dravidian Languages and Literature', in R.C. Majumdar and A.D. Pusalker (eds) *The Age of Imperial Kanauj*, Bombay: Bharatiya Vidya Bhavan, at 219–30.

Jaggi, O.P. (1969) *History of Science and Technology in India*, Vol. 1: *Dawn of Indian Technology: Pre- and Proto-Historic Period*, Delhi: Atma Ram.

Jain, H.L. (1955) 'Apabrahmasha Language and Literature', in R.C. Majumdar and A.D. Pusalker (eds) *The Age of Imperial Kanauj*, Bombay: Bharatiya Vidya Bhavan, at 212–19.

Jaiswal, S. (1967) *The Origin and Development of Vaisnavism*, New Delhi: Munshiram Manoharlal.

Jamison, S. (1996) *Sacrificed Wife, Sacrificer's Wife: Women, Ritual and Hospitality in Ancient India*, Oxford: Oxford University Press.

Jamkhedkar, A. (2002) 'Parsi and Hindu Sacraments', in P. Godrej and F.P. Mistree (eds) *A Zoroastrian Tapestry: Art, Religion and Culture*, Ahmedabad: Mapin, at 193–7.

Jarrige, J.F. (1982) 'Excavations at Mehrgarh: Their Significance for Understanding the Background of the Harappan Civilization', in G. Possehl (ed.) *Harappan Civilization: A Contemporary Perspective*, Warminster: Aris & Phillips, at 79–84.

Jarrige, J.F and Meadow, R.H. (1980) 'The Antecedents of Civilization in the Indus Valley', *Scientific American*, Vol. 243, 102–10.

Jash, P. (1974) *History of Saivism*, Calcutta: Roy & Chaudhury.

Jha, D.N. (2004) *Early India: A Concise History*, New Delhi: Manohar.

Johnson, G. (1996) *Cultural Atlas of India*, New York: Facts on File.

de Jong, A. (2002) 'Zoroastrianism and the Greeks', in P. Godrej and F.P. Mistree (eds) *A Zoroastrian Tapestry: Art, Religion and Culture*, Ahmedabad: Mapin, at 65–81.

Joseph, G.G. (2003) *George Joseph: The Life and Times of a Kerala Christian Nationalist*, Hyderabad: Orient Longman.

Joseph, G.G. (2010) *The Crest of the Peacock: Non-European Roots of Mathematics* (3rd ed.) Princeton, NJ: Princeton University Press.

Jyotsna, M. (2000) *Distinctive Beads in Ancient India*, Oxford: Archaeopress.

Kachroo, V. (2000) *Ancient India*, New Delhi: Har-Anand.

Kak, S. (n.d.) 'Edmund Leach on Racism and Indology'. www.omilosmeleton.gr/english/skak.html.

Katre, S.M. (1987) *Astadhyayi of Panini*, Austin: University of Texas Press.

Keay, J. (2000) *India: A History*, London: HarperCollins.

Keay, J. (2001) *India Discovered: The Recovery of a Lost Civilization*, London: HarperCollins.

Keer, D. (1971) *Ambedkar: Life and Mission*, Bombay: Popular Prakashan.

Keith, A.B. (1928) *A History of Sanskrit Literature*, Oxford: Oxford University Press.

Kenoyer, J.M. (1998) *Ancient Cities of the Indus Valley Civilization*, Oxford: Oxford University Press.

Khan, F.A. (1964) *The Indus Valley and Early Iran*, Karachi: Pakistan Ministry of Education.

Khazanov, A.M. (1984) *Nomads and the Outside World*, Cambridge: Cambridge University Press.

Khazanov, A.M. and Wink, A. (eds) (2001) *Nomads in the Sedentary World*, London: Curzon Press.

Klein, R.G. (2005) 'Hominin Dispersals in the Old World', in C. Scarre (ed.) *The Human Past: World Prehistory and the Development of Human Societies*, London: Thames & Hudson, at 84–123.

Klostermaier, K. (1984) *Mythologies and Philosophies of Salvation in the Theistic Traditions of India*, Waterloo, Ontario: Wilfrid Laurier University Press.

Klostermaier, K. (1994) *A Survey of Hinduism*, Albany: State University of New York Press.

Knox, R. (1992) *Amaravati: Buddhist Sculpture from the Great Stupa*, London: British Museum Press.

Kochhar, R. (2000) *The Vedic People: Their History and Geography*, Hyderabad: Orient Longman.

Kondo, S. (2002) 'Feudal Social Formation in Indian History', in K.N. Panikkar, T.J. Byres and U. Patnaik (eds) *The Making of History: Essays Presented to Irfan Habib*, London: Anthem Press, at 56–77.

Kosambi, D.D. (1965) *The Culture and Civilisation of Ancient India in Historical Outline*, 2nd ed., London: Routledge & Kegan Paul.

Kosambi, D.D. (1975) *An Introduction to the Study of Indian History*, Bombay: Popular Prakashan.

Kotwal, F. and Mistree, K. (2002) 'Protecting the Physical World', in P. Godrej and F.P. Mistree (eds) *A Zoroastrian Tapestry: Art, Religion and Culture*, Ahmedabad: Mapin, at 337–65.

Kramrisch, S. (1959) 'Traditions of the Indian Craftsman', in M. Singer (ed.) *Traditional India: Structure and Change*, Philadelphia: American Folklore Society, at 18–24.

Krishna, K.R. and Morrison, K.D. (2009) 'History of South Indian Agriculture and Agroecosystems'. www.academia.edu/606254/History_of_South_Indian_Agriculture_and_Agroecosystems

Kriwaczek, P. (2002) *In Search of Zarathushtra*, London: Weidenfeld & Nicolson.

Kulke, H. and Rothermund, D. (1990) *A History of India*, London: Routledge & Kegan Paul.

Kumar, B. (1973) *The Early Kusanas*, New Delhi: Sterling.

Lal, B.B. and Gupta, S.P. (eds) (1984) *Frontiers of the Indus Civilisation: Sir Mortimer Wheeler Commemoration Volume*, New Delhi: Indian Archaeological Society.

Lal, D. (1988) *Hindu Equilibrium: Cultural Stability and Economic Stagnation*, Vol. 1, Oxford: Oxford University Press.

Lamberg-Karlovsky, C.C. ([1972] 1979) 'Trade Mechanisms in Indus–Mesopotamian Interrelations', in G. Possehl (ed.) *Ancient Cities of the Indus*, New Delhi: Vikas, at 130–7.

Leshnik, L. ([1968] 1979) 'The Harappan "Port" at Lothal: Another View', in G. Possehl (ed.) *Ancient Cities of the Indus*, New Delhi: Vikas, at 203–11.

Liu, X. (1994) *Ancient India and Ancient China: Trade and Religious Exchanges, AD 1–600*, Oxford: Oxford University Press.

Ludden, D. (1985) *Peasant History in South India*, Princeton, NJ: Princeton University Press.

Ludden, D. (1999) *An Agrarian History of South Asia: The New Cambridge History of India, Vol. IV.*, Cambridge: Cambridge University Press.

Ludden, D. (2002) *India and South Asia*, Oxford: Oneworld.

McCrindle, J.W. ([1901] 1971) *Ancient India as Described in Classical Literature*, Amsterdam: Philo Press.

Mackay, E. (1948) *Early Indus Civilization*, London: Luzac.

Maclean, D. (1989) *Religion and Society in Arab Sind*, Leiden: E.J. Brill.

McMahon, B. (2006) 'Long in the Tooth: Skeletons Reveal Secrets of 9000 year old Dentistry', *The Guardian*, 18 April 2006, 17.

McNeill, W. (1967) *A World History*, Oxford: Oxford University Press.

Maddison, A. (2003) *The World Economy: Historical Statistics*, Paris: OECD.

Mahalingam, T.V. (1969) *Kanchipuram in Early South Indian History*, London: Asia Publishing House.

Mainkar, V.B. (1984) 'Metrology in the Indus Civilization', in B.B. Lal and S.P. Gupta (eds) *Frontiers of the Indus Civilisation: Sir Mortimer Wheeler Commemoration Volume*, New Delhi: Indian Archaeological Society, at 141–51.

Maisels, C. (1999) *Early Civilizations of the Old World: The Formative Histories of Egypt, the Levant, Mesopotamia, India and China*, London: Routledge.

Maisels, C. (2010) *The Archaeology of Politics and Power: Where, When and Why the First States Formed*, Oxford: Oxbow Books.

Maity, S.K. (1957) *Economic Life of North India in the Gupta Period*, Calcutta: World Press.

Majumdar, R.C. (1961a) 'Ideas of History in Sanskrit Literature', in C.H. Philips (ed.) *Historians of India, Pakistan and Ceylon*, London: Oxford University Press, at 13–28.

Majumdar, R.C. (1961b) 'Nationalist Historians', in C.H. Philips (ed.) *Historians of India, Pakistan and Ceylon*, London: Oxford University Press, at 416–28.

Majumdar, R.C. (1977) *Ancient India*, Delhi: Motilal Banarsidass.

Majumdar, R.C. and Pusalker, A.D. (eds) (1954) *The Classical Age*, Bombay: Bharatiya Vidya Bhavan.

Majumdar, R.C. and Pusalker, A.D. (eds) (1955) *The Age of Imperial Kanauj*, Bombay: Bharatiya Vidya Bhavan.

Makdisi, G. (1981) *The Rise of Colleges: Institutions of Learning in Islam and the West*, Edinburgh: Edinburgh University Press.

Mallory, J.P. (1989) *In Search of the Indo-Europeans*, London: Thames & Hudson.

Marett, P. (1985) *Jainism Explained*, London: Jain Samaj.

Marr, J.R. (1975) 'The Early Dravidians', in A.L. Basham (ed.) *A Cultural History of India*, Oxford: Clarendon Press, at 30–7.

Marshall, J. ([1923–24] 1979) 'Harappa and Mohenjo Daro', in G. Possehl (ed.) *Ancient Cities of the Indus*, New Delhi: Vikas, at 181–6.

Marshall, J. ([1924] 1979) 'First Light on a Long-Forgotten Civilization', in G. Possehl (ed.) *Ancient Cities of the Indus*, New Delhi: Vikas, at 105–7.

Melling, D. (1993) 'Indian Philosophy before the Greeks', Nehru Lecture, delivered at Manchester Metropolitan University, 3 December 1993.

Menon, A.S. (1990) *Kerala History and its Makers*, Madras: S. Viswanathan.

Miller, B.S. (1977) *Love Song of the Dark Lord: Jayadeva's Gita Govinda*, New York: Columbia University Press.

Miller, J.I. (1969) *Spice Trade of the Roman Empire*, Oxford: Oxford University Press.

Mirza, H.K. (2002) 'Literary Treasures of the Zoroastrian Priests', in P. Godrej and F.P. Mistree (eds) *A Zoroastrian Tapestry: Art, Religion and Culture*, Ahmedabad: Mapin, at 164-83.

Mishra, M. (2004) *The Aryans and Vedic Culture*, Delhi: Shipra.

Mistree, K. (2002) 'Parsi Arrivals and Early Settlements in India', in P. Godrej and F.P. Mistree (eds) *A Zoroastrian Tapestry: Art, Religion and Culture*, Ahmedabad: Mapin, at 411–33.

Mittal, S. and Thursby, G. (2004) *The Hindu World*, London:Routledge.

Mookerji, R. (1928) *Asoka*, London: Macmillan.

Mukerjee, R. (1958) *A History of Indian Civilisation*, Vol. 1, Bombay: Hind Kitabs.

Mukherji, R. (1989) *Hindu Civilisation*, Bombay: Bharatiya Vidya Bhavan.

Mukhia, H. (1981) 'Was There Feudalism in Indian History?', *Journal of Peasant Studies*, Vol. 8, No. 3 (April 1981), 273–310.

Mukhia, H. (1985) 'Peasant Production and Medieval Indian Society', *Journal of Peasant Studies*, Vol. 12, Nos 2–3 (Jan–April 1985), 228–51.

Nagaraj, D.R. (2003) 'Critical Tensions in the History of Kannada Literary Culture', in S. Pollock (ed.) *Literary Cultures in History: Reconstructions from South Asia*, Berkeley: University of California Press, at 323–9.

Narain, A.K. (1957) *The Indo-Greeks*, Oxford: Oxford University Press.

Narain, A.K. (1974) 'Alexander and India', in E. Borza (ed.) *The Impact of Alexander the Great*, Hinsdale, IL: Dryden Press.

Narain, A.K. (1990) 'Indo-Europeans in Inner Asia', in D. Sinor (ed.) *The Cambridge History of Early Inner Asia*, Cambridge: Cambridge University Press, at 151–76.

Narasimhiah, B. (1981) 'Pre-Neolithic and Neolithic Cultures in Tamil Nadu', in M.S. Nagaraja Rao (ed.) *Madhu: Recent Researches in Indian Archaeology and Art History*, Delhi: Agam Kala Prakashan, at 19–22.

Nicholas, R.W. (2003) *Indian History: Ancient and Medieval*, New Delhi: Encyclopaedia Britannica.

Nicholson, L. (1993) *India Companion*, London: Vermilion.

ODNB (2004) *Oxford Dictionary of National Biography*, Vols 39, 45, 47 and 59, Oxford: Oxford University Press.

Omvedt, G. (2003) *Buddhism in India: Challenging Brahmanism and Caste*, New Delhi: Sage.

Oppenheim, A.L. ([1954] 1979) 'The Seafaring Merchants of Ur', in G. Possehl (ed.) *Ancient Cities of the Indus*, New Delhi: Vikas, at 155–63.

Orr, L.C. (2001) 'Women in the Temple, the Palace, and the Family: The Construction of Women's Identities in Pre-Colonial Tanilnadu', in K. Hall (ed.) *Structure and Society in Early South India: Essays in Honour of Noboru Karashima*, New Delhi: Oxford University Press, at 198–234.

Orton, N.P. (1991) 'Red Polished Ware in Gujarat: A Catalogue of Twelve Sites', in V. Begley and R. de Puma (eds) *Rome and India*, Madison: University of Wisconsin Press, at 46–81.

Osborne, R. (2006) *Civilization: A New History of the Western World*, London: Jonathan Cape.

Pal, R. (2008) *Women in Early Medieval North India*, Delhi: The Women Press.

Pande, B.M. (1982) 'History of Research on the Harappan Culture', in G. Possehl (ed.) *Harappan Civilization: A Contemporary Perspective*, Warminster: Aris & Phillips, at 395–403.

Pandit, L. (1996) 'Dhvani and the "Full Word": Suggestion and Signification from Abhinavagupta to Jacques Lacan', College Literature [West Chester University, Pennsylvania], February 1996. www.findarticles.com/p/articles/mi_qa3709/is_199602/ai_n8752166.

Parpola, A. (2006) 'Vedic Aryan India', in S. Wolpert (ed.) *Encyclopedia of India*, Vol. 4, New York: Thomson Gale, at 211–15.

Pathak, V.S. (1997) *Ancient Historians of India*, Gorakhpur: Purva Samsthana.

Patil, P. (2004) *Myths and Traditions in India: A Fusion of the Past and the Present*, New Delhi: BPI India.

Pereira, J. (1995) 'Badarayana', in I.P. McGreal (ed.) *Great Thinkers of the Eastern World*, New York: HarperCollins, at 170–4.

Pettitt, P. (2005) 'The Rise of Modern Humans', in C. Scarre (ed.) *The Human Past: World Prehistory and the Development of Human Societies*, London: Thames & Hudson, at 124–73.

Philips, C.H. (1961) 'James Mill, Mountstuart Elphinstone, and the History of India', in C.H. Philips (ed.) *Historians of India, Pakistan and Ceylon*, London: Oxford University Press, at 217–29.

Pieterse, J.N. (1995) *White on Black: Images of Africans and Blacks in Western Popular Culture*, New Haven: Yale University Press.

Pinney, C. (1990) 'Colonial Anthropology in the Laboratory of Mankind', in C. Bayly (ed.) *The Raj: India and the British 1600–1947*, London: National Portrait Gallery.

Poliakov, L. (1974) *The Aryan Myth: A History of Racist and Nationalist Ideas in Europe*, London: Heinemann.

Pollock, S. (ed.) (2003) *Literary Cultures in History: Reconstructions from South Asia*, Berkeley: University of California Press.

Ponting, C. (1991) *A Green History of the World*, London: Penguin.

Possehl, G. ([1976] 1979) 'Lothal: A Gateway Settlement of the Harappan Civilization', in G. Possehl (ed.) *Ancient Cities of the Indus*, New Delhi: Vikas, at 212–18.

Possehl, G. (ed.) (1982) *Harappan Civilization: A Contemporary Perspective*, Warminster: Aris & Phillips.

Possehl, G. (2002), *The Indus Civilization: A Contemporary Perspective*, New York and Oxford: Altamira Press.

Previte-Orton, C. (1971) *The Shorter Cambridge Medieval History*, Vol. 1, Cambridge: Cambridge University Press.

Prinja, N. (ed.) (1996) *Explaining Hindu Dharma: A Guide for Teachers*, Norwich: Religious and Moral Education Press.

Prinsep, J. (1858) *Essays on Indian Antiquities: Historic, Numismatic and Palaeographic*, Vol. 2, London: John Murray.

Raikes, R.L. ([1964] 1979) 'The End of the Ancient Cities of the Indus', in G. Possehl (ed.) *Ancient Cities of the Indus*, New Delhi: Vikas, at 297–306.

Ramesh, R. (2006) 'A Tale of Two Indias', *The Guardian G2*, 5 April 2006, 10–13.

Rao, S.R. ([1968] 1979) 'Contacts between Lothal and Susa', in G. Possehl (ed.) *Ancient Cities of the Indus*, New Delhi: Vikas, at 174–5.

Rapson, E.J. (ed.) (1922) *Cambridge History of India*, Vol. 1, Cambridge: Cambridge University Press.

Ratnagar, S. (1995) 'Archaeological Perspectives on Early Indian Societies', in R. Thapar (ed.) *Recent Perspectives of Early Indian History*, Bombay: Popular Prakashan, at 1–52.

Rawlinson, H.G. (1965) *India: A Short Cultural History*, London: Cresset Press.

Rawson, P. (1977) *Indian Asia*, London: Elsevier-Phaidon.

Ray, H. (1986) *Monastery and Guild: Commerce under the Satavahanas*, Oxford: Oxford University Press.

Ray, N., Chattopadhyaya, B.D., Chakravarti, R. and Mani, V.R. (eds) (2000) *A Sourcebook of Indian Civilization*, Hyderabad: Orient Longman.

Raychaudhuri, H. (1996) *Political History of Ancient India*, Delhi: Oxford University Press.

Renfrew, C. (1987) *Archaeology and Language: The Puzzle of Indo-European Origins*, London: Penguin.

Renfrew, C. and Bahn, P. (eds) (2000) *Archaeology: Theories, Methods and Practice*, London: Thames & Hudson.

de Riencourt, A. (1986) *The Soul of India*, London: Honeyglen.

Risso, P. (1995) *Merchants and Faith: Muslim Commerce and Culture in the Indian Ocean*, Boulder, CO: Westview Press.

Rocher, L. (1986) *The Puranas*, Wiesbaden: Otto Harrassowitz.

Rocher, L. (2003) 'The Dharmasastras', in G. Flood (ed.) *The Blackwell Companion to Hinduism*, Oxford: Blackwell, at 102–15.

Rocher, R. (1993) 'British Orientalism in the 18th Century: The Dialectics of Knowledge and Government', in C. Breckenridge and P. Veer (eds) *Orientalism and the Post-Colonial Predicament: Perspectives on South Asia*, Philadelphia: University of Pennsylvania Press, at 215–49.

Roebuck, V. (2000) *The Upanisads*, London: Penguin.

Rowland, B. (1977) *The Pelican History of Art*, London: Penguin.

Rypka, J. (1968) *History of Iranian Literature*, Dordrecht: D. Reidel.

Sachau, E. (1888) *Alberuni's India*, Vols 1 and 2, London: Trubner.

Saletore, R.N. (1973) *Early Indian Economic History*, London: Curzon Press.

Samaddar, J.N. (1922) *The Glories of Magadha*, Patna: Patna University Press.

Sankalia, H.D. (1972) *The University of Nalanda*, Delhi: Oriental.

Sarasvati, S. (1986) *A Critical Study of Brahmagupta and his Works*, Delhi: Govindram Haranand.

Sarkar, J.C. (1928) *Some Aspects of the Earliest Social History of India*, London: Oxford University Press.

Sastri, G. (1960) *A Concise History of Classical Sanskrit*, Oxford: Oxford University Press.

Sastri, K.N. (1957) *New Light on the Indus Civilization*, Vol. 1, Delhi: Atma Ram.

Sastri, K.N. (1965) *New Light on the Indus Civilization*, Vol. 2, Delhi: Atma Ram.

Sastri, N. (1977) *A History of South India*, Madras: Oxford University Press.

Satianathaier, R. (1957) 'The Cholas', in R.C. Majumdar and A.D. Pusalker (eds) *The Struggle for Empire*, Bombay: Bharatiya Vidya Bhavan, at 234–55.

Scarre, C. (ed.) (2005) *The Human Past: World Prehistory and the Development of Human Societies*, London: Thames & Hudson.

Schimmel, A. (1973), *Islamic Literatures of India*, Wiesbaden: Otto Harrassowitz.

Schwartzberg, J. (1992) *A Historical Atlas of South Asia*, Oxford: Oxford University Press.

Sen, A. (2005) *The Argumentative Indian: Writings on Indian History, Culture and Identity*, London: Allen Lane.

Sen, K.M. (1961) *Hinduism*, London: Penguin.

Sengupta, P. (1950) *Everyday Life in Ancient India*, Oxford: Oxford University Press.

Sengupta, R. (1993) *Ajanta and Ellora: Our World in Colour*, Hong Kong: The Guidebook Company.

Shamasastry, R. (trans.) (1923) *Arthasastra*, Mysore: Wesleyan Mission Press.

Sharma, J.P. (1968) *Republics in Ancient India*, Leiden: Brill.

Sharma, R.N. (1977) *Brahmins through the Ages*, Delhi: Ajanta.

Sharma, R.S. (1958) *Sudras in Ancient India*, Delhi: Motilal Banarsidass.

Sharma, R.S. (1959) *Aspects of Political Ideas and Institutions in Ancient India*, Delhi: Motilal Banarsidass.

Sharma, R.S. (1985) 'How Feudal was Indian Feudalism?', *Journal of Peasant Studies*, Vol. 12, Nos 2–3 (Jan–April 1985), 19–43.

Sharma, R.S. (2001) *Early Medieval Indian Society: A Study in Feudalisation*, Hyderabad: Orient Longman.

Shrimali, K.M. (2001) 'Medievalism Defined', in *Frontline* [magazine of the newspaper *Hindu*], 18 (June–July 2001).

Sidebotham, S.E. (1991) 'Ports of the Red Sea and Arabia–India Trade', in V. Begley and R. de Puma (eds) *Rome and India*, Madison: University of Wisconsin Press, at 12–38.

Siegel, L. (1978) *Sacred and Profane Dimensions of Love in Indian Traditions as Exemplified in the Gita Govinda*, Delhi: Oxford University Press.

Singh, G.P. (2003) *Ancient Indian Historiography: Sources and Interpretations*, New Delhi: D.K. Printworld.

Sircar, D.C. (1971) *Studies in the Geography of Ancient and Medieval India*, Delhi: Motilal Banarsidass.

Sivaramamurti, C. (1977) *The Art of India*, New York: Harry Abrams.

Smart, N. (ed.) (1999) *Atlas of the World's Religions*, Oxford: Oxford University Press.

Smith, V. (1924) *Early History of India, from 600 BC to the Muhammadan Conquest*, Oxford: Oxford University Press.

Smith, V. (1958) *The Oxford History of India*, 3rd ed., rev. P. Spear, Oxford: Oxford University Press.

Soundararajan, K.V. (1981) 'In Quest of Man: Anthropological Bias in Archaeology', in M.S. Nagaraja Rao (ed.) *Madhu: Recent Researches in Indian Archaeology and Art History*, Delhi: Agam Kala Prakashan, at 3–7.

Spellman, J.W. (1964) *Political Theory of Ancient India: A Study of Kingship from the Earliest Times to c. AD 300*, London: Oxford University Press.

Srivastava, K.M. (1984) 'The Myth of Aryan Invasion of Harappan Towns', in B.B. Lal and S.P. Gupta (eds) *Frontiers of the Indus Civilisation: Sir Mortimer Wheeler Commemoration Volume*, New Delhi: Indian Archaeological Society, at 437–43.

Stein, B. (1985) 'Politics, Peasants and the Deconstruction of Feudalism in Medieval India', *Journal of Peasant Studies*, Vol. 12, Nos 2–3 (Jan–April 1985), 228–51.

Stein, B. (1998) *A History of India*, Oxford: Blackwell.

Tarn, W.W. (1951) *The Greeks in Bactria and India*, Cambridge: Cambridge University Press.

Thapar, R. (1975) *The Past and Prejudice*, New Delhi: National Book Trust.

Thapar, R. (1993) *Interpreting Early India*, Oxford: Oxford University Press.

Thapar, R. (1995) 'The First Millennium BC in Northern India', in R. Thapar (ed.) *Recent Perspectives of Early Indian History*, Bombay: Popular Prakashan, at 80–141.

Thapar, R. (1998) *Asoka and the Decline of the Mauryas*, Oxford: Oxford University Press.

Thapar, R. (2002) *Early India: From the Origins to AD 1300*, London: Allen Lane.

Thapar, R. (2011) 'Historical Traditions in Early India: c. 1000 BC to c. AD 600', in A. Feldherr and G. Hardy (eds) *The Oxford History of Historical Writing*, Vol. 1, Oxford: Oxford University Press, at 553–76.

Time-Life Books (1994) *Ancient India: Land of Mystery*, Alexandria: Time-Life Books.

Tomber, R. (2000) 'Indo-Roman Trade: Ceramic Evidence from Egypt', *Antiquity*, 74 (285) (September 2000), 624–31.

Tomory, E. (1989) *A History of Fine Arts in India and the West*, Hyderabad: Orient Longman.

Toth, N. and Schick, K. (2005) 'African Origins', in C. Scarre (ed.) *The Human Past: World Prehistory and the Development of Human Societies*, London: Thames & Hudson, at 46–83.

Trautmann, T. (1981) *Dravidian Kinship*, Cambridge: Cambridge University Press.

Trautmann, T. (1997) *Aryans and British India*, Berkeley: University of California Press.

Tripathi, R. (1999) *History of Ancient India*, Delhi: Motilal Banarsidass.

van der Veer, P. (2001) *Imperial Encounters: Religion and Modernity in India and Britain*, Princeton, NJ: Princeton University Press.

Walker, B. (1968) *The Hindu World*, Vols 1 and 2, London: Allen & Unwin.

Warder, A.K. (2002) *Indian Buddhism*, Delhi: Motilal Banarsidass.

Watters, T. (1904) *On Yuan Chwang's Travels in India, 629–645 AD*, London: Royal Asiatic Society.

Wells, S. (2003) *The Journey of Man: A Genetic Odyssey*, New York: Random House.

Wheeler, M. ([1947] 1979) 'Harappan Chronology and the Rig Veda', in G. Possehl (ed.) *Ancient Cities of the Indus*, New Delhi: Vikas, at 289–92.

Wheeler, M. (1966) *Civilization of the Indus Valley and Beyond*, London: Thames & Hudson.

Wheeler, M. (1968) *The Indus Civilization*, London: Cambridge University Press.

Wickens, G.M. (1976) 'The Middle East as a World Centre of Science and Medicine', in R.M. Savory (ed.) *An Introduction to Islamic Civilization*, Cambridge: Cambridge University Press, at 111–19.

Williamson, F. (1999) *Marx and the Millennium: A Short Guide to the Universe*, Ceredigion: Owain Hammond.

Wink, A. (1990) *Al-Hind: The Making of the Indo-Islamic World*, Vol. 1: *Early Medieval India and the Expansion of Islam, 7th to 11th Centuries*, Leiden: Brill.

Wink, A. (1997) *Al-Hind: The Making of the Indo-Islamic World*, Vol. II: *The Slave Kings and the Islamic Conquest, 11th to 13th Centuries*, Leiden: Brill.

Witzel, M. (1995) 'RigVedic History: Poets, Chieftains and Polities', in G. Erdosy (ed.) *The Indo-Aryans of Ancient South Asia: Language, Material Culture and Ethnicity*, Berlin: Walter de Gruyter, at 307–52.

Witzel, M. (2005) 'Indocentrism: Autochthonous Visions of Ancient India', in E. Bryant and L. Patton (eds) *The Indo-Aryan Controversy: Evidence and Inference in Indian History*, London: Routledge, at 341–404.

Witzel, M. (2006) 'Languages and Scripts of India', in S. Wolpert (ed.) *Encyclopedia of India*, Vol. 3, New York: Thomson Gale, at 50–6.

Witzel, M. and Farmer, S. (2000) 'Horseplay in Harappa', *Frontline* [magazine of the newspaper *Hindu*], 20 (30 September–13 October 2000).

Wolpert, S. (ed.) (2006) *Encyclopedia of India*, 4 vols, New York: Thomson Gale.

Wright, R. (2010) *The Ancient Indus: Urbanism, Economy and Society*, Cambridge: Cambridge University Press.

Yano, M. (2003) 'Calendar, Astrology and Astronomy', in G. Flood (ed.) *The Blackwell Companion to Hinduism*, Oxford: Blackwell, at 376-92.

Yashaschandra, S. (2003) 'From Hemacandra to Hind Swaraj', in S. Pollock (ed.) *Literary Cultures in History: Reconstructions from South Asia*, Berkeley: University of California Press, at 567–611.

Yazdani, G. (1960) *The Early History of the Deccan*, Vol. 1, Hyderabad: Oxford University Press and Government of Andhra Pradesh.

Yu, Y.-S. (1990) 'The Hsiung-nu', in D. Sinor (ed.) *The Cambridge History of Early Inner Asia*, Cambridge: Cambridge University Press, at 118–49.

Zelinsky, A.N. (1970) 'Kushans and Mahayana', in B. Gafurov, M. Asimov and D. Chattopadhyaya (eds) *Kushan Studies in the USSR*, Calcutta: Indian Studies Past and Present, at 156–7.

Zevmal, E.V. (1970) 'Kaniska's Dates', in B. Gafurov, M. Asimov and D. Chattopadhyaya (eds) *Kushan Studies in the USSR*, Calcutta: Indian Studies Past and Present, at 152–5.

Index